THE EPIC GUIDE TO AGILE

MORE BUSINESS VALUE ON A
PREDICTABLE SCHEDULE WITH SCRUM

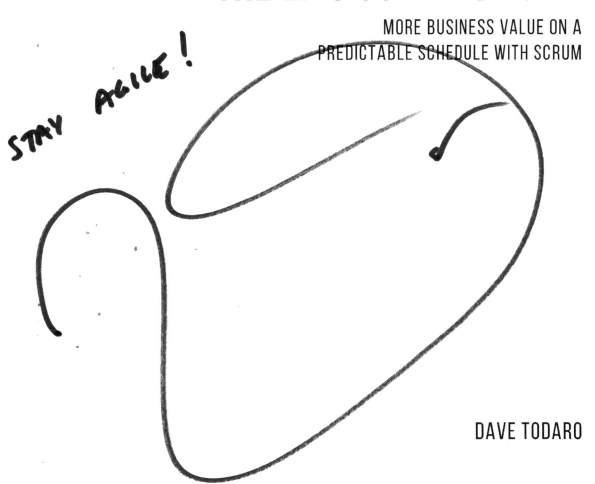

STAY AGILE !

DAVE TODARO

Published by:

R9 Publishing LLC
PO Box 232
North Hampton, NH 03862

Copy Editor: Noleen Arendse
Content Editor: Wayne Arendse
Proofreaders: Steven Codd, Diana Getman, Allison Grappone, Susannah Parnin Mitchell, Tom Schwendler
Marketing: Sara Janjigian Trifiro
Interior Design: Dave Todaro
Cover Design: Global Deziners

Paperback ISBN: 978-1-7330004-0-6

Digital ISBN: 978-1-7330004-1-3

Contents at a Glance

Preface xi

I. Understanding Scrum Fundamentals 1

  1   Introduction to High-Performance Teamwork... 3

  2   Scrum's 10 Guideposts 13

  3   The Product Backlog 19

  4   User Stories.. 29

  5   The Sprint 39

  6   Scrum Ceremonies... 49

  7   Scrum Roles... 67

  8   The Sprint Backlog 77

  9   The Product 87

II. Understanding Agile Software Construction 97

  10 Introduction to Agile Software Construction 99

  11 Creating a Shippable Increment Requires Team Test Environments 105

  12 Managing Source Code Properly Avoids Pain When "Life Happens" 119

  13 Automated Unit Testing: The Foundation of Code Quality 135

  14 Acceptance Testing: Making Sure Everything Works Together 151

  15 Agile Architecture and Technical Design... 161

III. Laying the Groundwork 181

  16 Here Be Dragons: Preparing for the Challenges You'll Face........................ 183

  17 Forming Your Pilot Scrum Team.. 199

  18 Your Team's Path to Excellence 219

  19 Creating the Initial Product Backlog.. 233

  20 Estimating the Size of the Product Backlog 247

  21 Creating an Initial Schedule Projection... 269

  22 Splitting User Stories for Increased Momentum.. 283

  23 Final Preparations Before Your First Sprint 303

IV. Building the Product 317

24   Determining Sprint Logistics 319

25   Planning the Sprint 333

26   Orchestrating the Daily Work of the Sprint 351

27   A "Zero Defects" Approach to Dealing with Bugs 377

28   Providing Transparency and Getting Feedback with the Sprint Review 405

29   Driving Continuous Improvement with the Sprint Retrospective 425

30   Confidently Releasing Your Product into Production 445

References 479

Index 491

Table of Contents

Preface xi

    Product Development Is About Business Value...xii

    Scrum Done Right Delivers Results xii

    Why I Wrote This Book xiii

    What You'll Get Out of This Book..xiv

    How This Book Is Organized..xiv

    Final Thoughts..xv

I. Understanding Scrum Fundamentals 1

1 Introduction to High-Performance Teamwork.................................. 3

    1.1 Creating Dream Teams...3

    1.2 Why Does Scrum Work? 4

    1.3 Is Scrum Just for Software Development? 6

    1.4 How Agile Differs from a Traditional Waterfall Approach 7

    1.5 Scrum Is for Any Complicated or Complex Project 10

2 Scrum's 10 Guideposts 13

    2.1 Three Roles 13

    2.2 Four Ceremonies 14

    2.3 Three Artifacts... 16

    2.4 This Is Too Simple. How Can It Possibly Work?................................. 16

3 The Product Backlog 19

    3.1 The Single Shared Source of Truth.. 20

    3.2 The Product Backlog Belongs to the Product Owner 22

    3.3 Requirements Evolve Over Time... 24

    3.4 Discussing the Backlog with the Team Is Important.......................... 24

    3.5 Tracking the Projected Schedule with a Release Burndown Chart 25

    3.6 Projecting a Range of Dates with the Version Report 26

4 User Stories..29

    4.1 A User Story Is a Descriptive Sentence 29

    4.2 Details Are Added Through Conversations 31

    4.3 What, Not How.. 32

    4.4 Each User Story Has a Size Estimate 33

    4.5 Additional Written Details Are OK 34

    4.6 Some Traditional Specifications Are OK, Too 36

5   The Sprint..**39**

5.1 Eliminating the Death March 40

5.2 The Imminent Deadline and the Power of Positive Stress 40

5.3 Everything Is Done During a Sprint 42

5.4 Benefits of the Sprint Approach 44

6   Scrum Ceremonies..**49**

6.1 Sprint Planning 50

6.2 Daily Scrum 54

6.3 Sprint Review 56

6.4 Retrospective 58

6.5 Other Optional Ceremonies 59

6.6 A Typical Ceremony Schedule 64

6.7 Aren't All These "Ceremonies" Wasting a Bunch of Time? 64

7   Scrum Roles...**67**

7.1 The Product Owner 68

7.2 The ScrumMaster 69

7.3 The Development Team 73

8   The Sprint Backlog...**77**

8.1 Visualizing the Work of the Sprint with a Sprint Task Board 78

8.2 Keeping Track of Who's Working on Each Subtask 80

8.3 Understanding How Much Time Is Left for Each Subtask 81

8.4 Tracking Sprint Progress with a Sprint Burndown Chart 81

8.5 My Company Requires Status Reports. Can We Do That? 83

9   The Product...**87**

9.1 The Product Is Built Iteratively and Incrementally 87

9.2 The Traditional Approach: Building 100% of Nothing 88

9.3 The Agile Approach: Building 100% of Something 90

9.4 The Definition of Done 91

9.5 Shippable vs Something You Would Ship 94

II.   Understanding Agile Software Construction...**97**

10   Introduction to Agile Software Construction.....................................**99**

10.1 What Is "Software Construction?" 100

10.2 Why Is Software Construction So Important in an Agile Context? .. 101

10.3 Why You Need to Know About This Technical "Stuff" 102

10.4 Agile Software Construction Concepts 103

11 Creating a Shippable Increment Requires Team Test Environments 105

11.1 Testing at the End Doesn't Work with Agile 106

11.2 Test Environments Eliminate "Works on My Machine!" 106

11.3 What the Scrum Team Needs for Test Environments 107

11.4 Providing Test Environments May Require Creative Thinking 111

11.5 The Scrum Team Needs to Control Their Test Environments 112

11.6 The Ability to Automatically Deploy Code Is Critical 113

11.7 Tools to Manage Team Test Environments 114

12 Managing Source Code Properly Avoids Pain When "Life Happens" 119

12.1 Version Control Allows Effective Collaboration 120

12.2 Branches Isolate Code to Manage the Unexpected 120

12.3 A Distributed Version Control System Makes Branching Easy 122

12.4 Reviewing Code Before Merging a Branch Increases Quality 122

12.5 Git Flow Provides a Strategy for Branch Management 124

12.6 Keys to Avoid Merge Hell and Code Review Bottlenecks 132

13 Automated Unit Testing: The Foundation of Code Quality 135

13.1 The Problem with Relying Solely on Integration Testing 136

13.2 Automated Unit Testing: Ensuring Code Works All the Time 138

13.3 Running Tests Automatically Avoids Human Error 139

13.4 Unit Tests Document Code for Future Programmers 141

13.5 Isolating Dependencies Makes Testing Easier 142

13.6 Test-Driven Development (TDD) Creates a Test-First Culture 144

13.7 Code Coverage Analysis Keeps Everyone Honest 145

13.8 Adding Unit Tests Keeps Bugs from Coming Back 146

13.9 Should We Use Integration Tests Instead of Unit Tests? 147

14 Acceptance Testing: Making Sure Everything Works Together 151

14.1 Scenarios Help Pre-Visualize a User Story to Avoid Disappointment 152

14.2 Given, When, Then: Making Tests Understandable to Everyone 154

14.3 Write Acceptance Tests Early During a Sprint to Reduce Risk 156

14.4 Perform Acceptance Testing in Every Environment 157

14.5 Create an Automated "Smoke Test" with Critical Scenarios 157

15 Agile Architecture and Technical Design 161

15.1 Architecture Doesn't Disappear with Agile: It Becomes "Emergent" 161

15.2 Avoiding YAGNI by Leveraging the "Last Responsible Moment" 167

15.3 Attaining Technical Excellence Without Telling Them How to Do It 171

15.4 Development Teams Need to Consider the Big Picture 173

15.5 An Experienced Technical Team Member Can Be a Big Plus 175

15.6 Creating a Technical Design for a Story Encourages Collaboration 176

15.7 Coding Standards Are a Critical Success Factor 177

15.8 Communities of Practice Encourage Innovation and Consistency 178

III. Laying the Groundwork 181

16 Here Be Dragons: Preparing for the Challenges You'll Face 183

16.1 How Your Organization Will Change 184

16.2 How Project Managers and the PMO Fit In 189

16.3 How to Start: Pilot Team or the "Big Bang" Approach? 192

16.4 Success Factors to Guide Your Agile Adoption 193

16.5 How Long Will It Take to Adopt Agile? 195

16.6 A Sample Agile Adoption Timeline 196

17 Forming Your Pilot Scrum Team 199

17.1 Select a Team You Think Can Be Successful 199

17.2 Select a Product Built Using Agile-Friendly Technology 201

17.3 Select Team Members Who Can Be Dedicated to the Pilot Team 202

17.4 Choosing the Product Owner 202

17.5 Choosing the ScrumMaster 205

17.6 Don't Have One Person Be Both Product Owner and ScrumMaster 207

17.7 Assembling the Development Team 209

17.8 Seat Your Co-Located Team Together 211

17.9 Distributed Teams and Multiple Time Zones 213

18 Your Team's Path to Excellence 219

18.1 Four Stages of Learning: The Conscious Competence Model 220

18.2 The Cognitive Apprenticeship Learning Method 221

18.3 Teaching the Fundamentals 222

18.4 Starting Your Team's Experiential Learning 227

18.5 Agile Coaches 229

18.6 What About Agile Certifications? 230

19 Creating the Initial Product Backlog 233

19.1 The Backlog Creation Process 233

19.2 Create a List of Roles to Understand Your Users Better 234

19.3 Brainstorm Features for Each User Role 236

19.4 Convert Roles and Features into User Stories 237

19.5 Group User Stories by Priority 238

19.6 Prioritize the Backlog by Business Value 240

19.7 Write Acceptance Criteria 243

20 Estimating the Size of the Product Backlog 247

20.1 The Power of Relative Size 248

20.2 Story Points: An Abstract Measurement of Size 251

20.3 Rapid Estimation with Planning Poker 253

20.4 Preparing to Estimate 256

20.5 Story Points Are Not About Time 260

20.6 The Planning Poker Process 261

20.7 How Long Should Estimating Take? 264

21 Creating an Initial Schedule Projection 269

21.1 The Chicken and Egg Problem: What's the Velocity? 269

21.2 Options to Predict the Team's Velocity 270

21.3 Breaking Down Stories into Subtasks to Estimate Velocity 271

21.4 Using the Cone of Uncertainty to Anticipate the Unknown 277

22 Splitting User Stories for Increased Momentum 283

22.1 Avoid "Traveling" Stories by Splitting Them 284

22.2 The Six-Way Model for Splitting User Stories 284

22.3 SPIDR: An Alternative Method for Splitting Stories 291

22.4 "There's No Way to Split This User Story" 295

22.5 Use INVEST to Ensure the Quality of Split Stories 296

22.6 Who Splits User Stories and When? 298

23 Final Preparations Before Your First Sprint 303

23.1 What You Should Have in Place Before Starting Your First Sprint 304

23.2 Complete Initial User Experience (UX) Design 305

23.3 Deploy Agile Tools 306

23.4 Define Scrum and Technical Standards 307

23.5 Configure Developer Workstations 309

23.6 Set Up Distributed Version Control 310

23.7 Create an Initial Code Framework: The "Walking Skeleton" 310

23.8 Configure Continuous Integration 311

23.9 Provision Team Test Environments 311

23.10 Establish Continuous Deployment 312

23.11 Research Production Deployment Considerations 312

23.12 Should We Use a "Sprint Zero?" 314

IV. Building the Product 317

24 Determining Sprint Logistics 319
24.1 Selecting the Best Sprint Duration...319
24.2 Picking the Best Day of the Week to Start a Sprint....................321
24.3 Scheduling the Sprint Planning Ceremony................................326
24.4 Preparing for the Sprint Planning Ceremony.............................328
24.5 A Sample Sprint Planning Agenda...330

25 Planning the Sprint...333
25.1 Setting the Stage for the Team..334
25.2 Estimating the Team's Capacity for the Sprint..........................334
25.3 Determining How Much Work Can Be Done and the Plan of Attack...........335
25.4 Decomposing a Task or Bug into Subtasks................................339
25.5 How Much of the Team's Capacity Should Be Planned?...........341
25.6 What If There Isn't Enough Time to Finish the Plan?................343
25.7 Scheduling Scrum Ceremonies for the Sprint...........................344
25.8 Finish Sprint Planning by Transitioning to Immediate Action.......348

26 Orchestrating the Daily Work of the Sprint.................................351
26.1 Using the Daily Scrum to Stay in Sync.......................................352
26.2 Tracking Progress Against the Plan with the Sprint Task Board.......355
26.3 Keeping the Sprint Task Board up to Date Every Day................360
26.4 Using the Sprint Burndown Chart to Stay on Track...................368
26.5 Summary of Best Practices...373

27 A "Zero Defects" Approach to Dealing with Bugs.........................377
27.1 Fix Bugs Before Writing New Code..377
27.2 How to Create a Zero-Defects Culture..379
27.3 Using a Standard Bug Format to Effectively Document Defects.......380
27.4 How Nasty Is It? Using Priority and Severity to Classify Bugs.......384
27.5 Handling Bugs Introduced during the Sprint.............................387
27.6 Newly-Discovered Bugs That Existed at the Start of the Sprint.......390
27.7 Dealing with a Customer Issue Caused by a Critical Bug..........392
27.8 Timeboxing the Bug-Fixing Effort...394
27.9 What to Do with Bugs That You Won't Fix...................................397
27.10 Handling Bugs That Can't Be Reproduced...............................398
27.11 What to Do with a Legacy Bug List Inherited by the Team.......400

28 Providing Transparency and Getting Feedback with the Sprint Review 405

28.1 Who Should Be Invited to the Sprint Review? 406

28.2 Selecting the Best Sprint Review Duration, Day, and Time 408

28.3 Preparing for the Sprint Review 411

28.4 Discussing What the Team Completed and the Sprint Goal 413

28.5 Demonstrating New Functionality in the Product Increment 415

28.6 Talking About What's Next on the Product Backlog 418

28.7 Discussing Average Velocity and the Projected Schedule 419

28.8 Tips for a Successful Sprint Review 419

28.9 A Sample Sprint Review Agenda 422

29 Driving Continuous Improvement with the Sprint Retrospective 425

29.1 Is This Really a Valuable Use of Time? 426

29.2 The Art of Self-Reflection: A Variety of Retrospective Formats 427

29.3 Leading Questions to Ask During the Retrospective 434

29.4 Leave Egos, Titles, and Experience at the Door 435

29.5 Don't Be Too Nice 436

29.6 How to Make Sure Change Happens 437

29.7 Common Problems and How to Address Them 438

30 Confidently Releasing Your Product into Production 445

30.1 A Tried-And-True Release Process 446

30.2 Test Environments Required to "Certify" the Release 448

30.3 The Five-Step Release Process in Detail 456

30.4 Triaging Bugs Discovered During the Release Sprint 467

30.5 Orchestrating the Work of the Release Sprint 470

30.6 But It's Not This Easy at My Company 471

30.7 Life After the Release Sprint 473

References 479

Index 491

Preface

An expert is a person who has found out by his own painful experience all the mistakes that one can make in a very narrow field.

- **Neils Bohr**, *Danish physicist.*

Years ago, I was in charge of developing a new product at my software company. After about 10 months of discussions, research, and focus groups, we had identified a new business problem to solve for our customers, and we decided to spin up a development team to get it built.

About a year and a half later, we were nearing the release of version 1.0. The only problem was we were running about six to seven months behind my original schedule estimate, and we had started pulling developers off other projects to drive it to done. Everyone was working crazy hours to get the thing out the door, and we were all ready to be finished.

As we neared the release, I sat down for a meeting with the CEO and the lead sales rep to give them a status update. From my perspective, I felt that although it was later than I originally thought, the project was a huge success. We had worked *really* hard, with everyone putting everything else second for months—including their families. I came into the meeting with a smile on my face.

That didn't last long.

As I sat down, I looked over to the CEO—who was also my business partner—and he said, "You've failed."

It didn't really sink in at first. Feeling my face start to get hot I said, "What the hell do you mean? We busted our asses to get this thing done and it's about a week away from shipping. Customers are psyched to get their hands on it."

"Yeah, but you're *seven months late!* We were planning on having money from that product in the bank. You've put us in a tough spot."

After more than a year and a half of putting all I had into this new product—at the expense of everything else in my life—I was exhausted. In hindsight, I was probably on the edge of a nervous breakdown.

The meeting quickly went downhill from there, evolving into a yelling match with plenty of finger-pointing, and ending with me storming out of the conference room and leaving the office for the day.

It was one of the worst days of my life.

Product Development Is About Business Value

My team and I had *finished the product*, which is a feat given that over half of IT projects fail (Florentine, 2016). Everyone agreed it was a great piece of software.

I had done a road tour to a handful of customers during the previous month and they were all excited to get their hands on what we had created. How could I have possibly *failed*?

Once I had time to reflect, I realized two things:

- Software development—unless in an academic or research context—isn't about technology, it's about delivering business value. In this case, that business value was in the form of a new product to drive higher revenue from our customers.

- Delivering business value doesn't matter if it's not on a *predictable schedule*. Otherwise, it's impossible for the business to create plans to maximize that value. "When will I get this revenue?" is a critical question to answer.

The problem wasn't the product—customers loved it. It was that I had spent too much time and money getting it done. The company needed to get business value faster than my team and I provided.

Even though I had started to use an agile Scrum framework a year or two before starting this product, I later realized that I didn't really know what I was doing. I was using the right terminology and having the right meetings, but I wasn't properly leveraging Scrum to ship the product on a schedule.

After a lot of soul-searching, I finally admitted to myself that I had, in fact, failed.

Scrum Done Right Delivers Results

My experience with that project—now close to ten years ago—was a pivotal moment in my life. A year or two later, I decided to sell my business interest to my partner and start a new company, which I called Ascendle.

I had one goal: leverage all my hard-won experience to provide world-class, "turnkey" agile development teams to enterprise clients.

These self-contained teams could be free to innovate at an unprecedented pace, leveraging the best of today's tools and technologies.

Everett Rogers, in his book *Diffusion of Innovations*, described *skunkworks* to mean "an especially enriched environment that is designed to help a small group of individuals escape usual organizational procedures, so that innovation is encouraged." (Rogers, 1995)

This is exactly what we provide—an on-demand skunkworks—and we deliver results daily at a blistering pace our clients have never experienced.

Why I Wrote This Book

Software development is *hard*. I've spent more than three quarters of my life figuring out how to make it easier. And I've finally arrived at a specific set of tools and techniques to deliver on that promise.

It's still a lot of work to ship a world-class product, but using the information in this book will make your life a hell of a lot more enjoyable.

Over the last 35+ years, I've made three key discoveries:

- Leveraging an adaptable and flexible framework such as Scrum is critical. No two organizations are the same, so prescriptive, one-size-fits-all "methodologies" don't work.

- Being *fanatical* about disciplined adherence to the rules—while constantly innovating within their boundaries—is a key success factor.

- Attempting to use agile techniques without the appropriate technical underpinnings is a recipe for failure.

I tried to find one book that included a complete "how-to" guide for both Scrum *and* the required technical tools and techniques. As I searched through my own library and browsed books on Amazon, I couldn't find one.

Most focus on the fundamental details of Scrum, including forming a team and running the day-to-day process. Other books have a narrow focus on a small portion of the process, such as testing or how to scale Scrum in larger organizations or include only lightweight technical details.

None that I found included the right level of detail about *both* the agile process *and* technology.

What You'll Get Out of This Book

This book is a comprehensive cheat sheet, saving you the years of heartache and frustration you'd experience if you were forced to learn everything through trial and error. It has all you need, from an overview of Scrum and why it works, to practical tips to create and guide your Scrum team to deliver at a world-class level.

Most important, it addresses the technical foundation required for success. It has explanations of software construction and the technical tools and techniques your team needs to deliver rock-solid software consistently and predictably.

However, it's not written for a technical audience. Everything is spelled out in plain English, so you'll be able to understand it even if you're not technical.

This book will empower you to work with your entire team—project managers, business analysts, software architects, developers, and testers alike—and understand what they need to do in order to achieve your company's business goals.

How This Book Is Organized

This book is organized into four parts.

- **Part I, Understanding Scrum Fundamentals** provides an introduction and high-level overview of the Scrum framework and its associated roles, ceremonies, and artifacts. If you are well-versed in agile techniques, you may recognize a lot of the content here, but I encourage you to read this part to refresh your memory of the building blocks of Scrum.

- **Part II, Understanding Agile Software Construction** introduces the fundamental technical concepts required to support the agile process. If you are non-technical, don't be intimidated; I wrote this section with you in mind. It's critical for everyone involved with agile to understand these foundational concepts.

- **Part III, Laying the Groundwork** outlines the steps required to set the stage for launching an agile process in your organization. From forming your first Scrum team to creating a concise vision and initial schedule estimate, the steps in this part will set your team up for success.

- **Part IV, Building the Product** walks you through the steps to launch and run iterations for the Scrum team. Starting with the all-important process of creating a plan for each sprint via the sprint planning ceremony, and including details about tackling day-to-day challenges, this is where vision turns into reality by producing a shippable product increment. This part ends by describing the process to smoothly get the product into production so you can put it into the hands of your end users.

Although each part builds upon those that come before it, feel free to jump around to different chapters of the book as you see fit.

Each part, chapter, and section is written in a fairly standalone fashion, so you can get details about the topics that interest you the most. At the end of each chapter you'll find a *Key Takeaways* section, summarizing its main points.

Final Thoughts

Agile transformed my life. Yelling matches with business stakeholders are a thing of the past, and our clients are amazed by how we leverage Scrum to deliver on a schedule while allowing them to retain full control over the priorities of the team.

I'm excited to share my hard-won experience with you, so you can experience the same skunkworks-driven results that delight our clients each and every day.

Thank you for reading and enjoy your journey!

Dave Todaro
North Hampton, New Hampshire
Spring, 2019

If you have questions, see any errors, or would like to provide suggestions for new books or a second edition of this book, I'd love to hear from you!

The best way to contact me is via LinkedIn: http://bit.ly/davetodarolinkedin

For bonus materials and to receive updates about new editions of this book, sign up at https://www.davetodarobooks.com

---

Part I
Understanding Scrum Fundamentals

The business we're in is more sociological than technological, more dependent on workers' abilities to communicate with each other than their abilities to communicate with machines.

- **Tom DeMarco**, *Peopleware: Productive Projects and Teams*

Chapter 1
Introduction to High-Performance Teamwork

Never confuse movement with action.

- Ernest Hemingway

Have you ever been frustrated by the work of your software development team? Do you sometimes feel like they aren't working on the most important things? Or they can never give you an accurate estimate of how long it will take? Or they're not communicating very well?

Do you feel like the quality of their work could be better? Do they demonstrate ownership and accountability? Does it seem like they could be happier?

You're not alone. Almost everyone I've talked to about software development in the past 35 years has had at least some level of frustration. I've certainly experienced everything outlined above with my own software teams prior to really learning how to "do agile right."

1.1 Creating Dream Teams

Some people have the good fortune to stumble upon high-performing "dream teams." They hire perfect people, assemble them into teams, and enjoy the astounding results they produce with little to no training or management.

The team members "gel" almost immediately and exceed all expectations. Their communication skills make it seem like they can read the minds of product managers, executives, and each other. They somehow magically produce software applications that everyone loves. They also frequently review their process and consistently improve it to deliver even better results. They are a *machine*.

Although it's possible, what I outlined above seldom happens in the real world. Some team members will be great communicators. Others will have amazing technical skills. Some will always stay focused and get things done. But seldom will everyone on the team have the discipline to do all the right things—at the right time—every day. Very rarely will a high-performing team materialize by chance.

It seems like it should be pretty simple. As a business leader I want the following from my development team:

- Have them work on what delivers the highest value to the business.

- Get an accurate schedule forecast I can rely on.

- See them take ownership and be accountable.

- Get a high-quality product that users love.

To achieve the above, we need a way to help teams become…teams. We need a way to ensure they are always working on producing what's most important to the company and its customers. We need to help them learn how to understand business goals, effectively communicate with each other, and coordinate their work in a way that drives the best results.

We also need a way to predict how long it will take to complete their work, and ensure they consistently produce the same high-quality results. Finally, we need a way for them to improve over time so they can keep getting better at what they do.

We need a *system* to ensure that groups of individuals employ the same proven practices which allow the "dream teams" to produce their amazing results. The system must be simple and flexible. It must empower business leaders to drive priorities and help teams produce results consistently, reliably, and predictably. In short, we need a system that facilitates and creates high-performance teamwork.

Scrum is such a system.

A lightweight framework consisting of three roles, four meetings, and three artifacts, Scrum is a flexible and adaptable tool that allows a group of individuals to become a high-performance team.

Scrum provides a way for business leaders to drive priorities and have a development team produce results consistently, reliably, and predictably—which to me is the definition of "high-performance teamwork."

1.2 Why Does Scrum Work?

Scrum is what I call a *social engineering framework*. By imposing a small set of rules, it allows a group of normal individuals to do the right things, at the right time, to produce extraordinary results.

Work is completed in fixed-duration production cycles called "sprints," sometimes also called "iterations." This time period—most commonly two weeks, but ranging from one week to a calendar month—turns the traditional long-term deadline on its head and forces the Scrum team to produce results *now*. This imminent deadline creates a heightened sense of awareness that drives the team's focus and effort.

Leonard Bernstein—a composer and one of the most successful musicians in American history—once said, "To achieve great things, two things are needed: a plan, and not quite enough time." (Classic FM, n.d.) This is exactly what Scrum provides, with its imminent deadline at the end of each sprint.

Scrum Forces a Team to Make a Plan

At the beginning of each sprint, the Scrum team works together to create a plan, breaking down items into individual subtasks. Each subtask represents a discrete step required to complete the work.

This forces them to think strategically about what they need to do, leading to increased productivity during the sprint because they can keep their heads down and focus on completing the work.

Scrum Doesn't Give a Team Quite Enough Time

Each fixed-duration sprint helps prevent the development team from working on anything that's not critical to driving things to "done" as quickly as possible.

This helps avoid time-consuming but low-value activities, and also helps avoid over-building the product—so-called "gold plating."

Scrum Forces a Team to Communicate

Many technical people are not natural communicators, and most companies don't know how to create a framework that drives effective collaboration. Scrum solves this by creating an environment that requires communication on a regular basis.

From a 15-minute daily team meeting to coordinate their work, to an emphasis on personal interaction over comprehensive written specifications, Scrum gets team members communicating much more than they might without such a framework.

Scrum Forces a Team to Be Held Accountable

When I talk to business leaders and ask them what they want most, I typically hear, "I'd like my team to have more ownership and accountability." Scrum delivers on this promise by empowering the team to decide on what they will commit to completing, and putting them in front of business stakeholders at the end of the sprint to report on their results.

Everyone knows the "higher-ups" will be reviewing the results of their work and holding them accountable, which results in a strong feeling of ownership and a, "We really need to get this done" attitude.

1.3 Is Scrum Just for Software Development?

Scrum was created in the early 1990s by Jeff Sutherland and Ken Schwaber, to help organizations struggling with complex software development projects. According to them, Scrum is, "A framework within which people can address complex adaptive problems, while productively and creatively delivering products of the highest possible value." (Schwaber & Sutherland, 2017)

Scrum is especially helpful for managing projects that have the following characteristics (Lenfle & Loch, 2010):

- *Emergent requirements.* There is a general vision or direction, but the detailed goals of the project are not 100 percent known and are at least partially emergent. That is, they become clearer during the course of the project.

- *Capabilities don't necessarily exist.* How exactly the project will be completed is not known at the beginning, and some research and invention will be required along the way.

- *Unforeseeable uncertainty.* There are risks and other "gotchas" that will come up during the project that can't be anticipated at the start of the project.

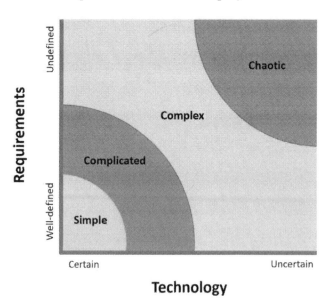

Scrum is a good fit for complicated and complex projects. (Schwaber & Beedle, 2001)

Scrum isn't for every project. If you're building a new office building using traditional construction techniques, you probably don't need this type of adaptive framework.

However, if you have requirements that are likely to evolve over the course of the project, and at least some technical unknowns about how exactly the work will be completed, Scrum will likely make your life a heck of a lot easier.

Software development projects are a particularly good fit for Scrum. This is one reason it continues to become more popular as software development continues to grow at a rapid pace. As Marc Andreessen would say, "In short, software is eating the world." (Andreessen, 2011)

Although Scrum has its origins in software development, it's been used to successfully manage many types of projects. From software and hardware to autonomous vehicles, schools, and marketing, Scrum has been used to manage a variety of complex work projects. (Schwaber & Sutherland, 2017)

In short, Scrum is a good fit for *complicated* or *complex* projects. The diagram illustrates these types of projects, defined by a degree of uncertainty about requirements and a degree of uncertainty about technology—or how exactly the project will get done.

1.4 How Agile Differs from a Traditional Waterfall Approach

A few years ago, I was approached by the CEO of a small software company in Massachusetts which specialized in a vertical market software application for the construction industry. After five years of building their software application, the technical co-founder and sole programmer had decided to leave the company, and they were in a bind.

The product he had built was working fairly well, but it was a traditional client-server application that required installation on-site at each of their customer locations. Plus, it included a custom mobile application based on legacy, outdated hardware.

Maintaining all those on-site systems and finicky mobile devices was becoming a hassle. Plus, the product had some fundamental design flaws, and was buggy and slow.

Their strategy for the future involved moving the application to the cloud and utilizing contemporary Android-based industrial mobile devices. That would eliminate the on-site deployment hassles, allow the use of more modern mobile hardware, and would give them an opportunity to take a "clean-sheet approach" to build a fresh, new replacement product.

I stepped in as a temporary "virtual" Chief Technology Officer and helped stabilize the current product while assembling a development team to build the new product. The company didn't have much money, so the team was tiny, with just two half-time developers and a tester working about ten hours a week.

Because time was very limited, using an agile approach was critical. We prioritized ruthlessly and drove new features to "done" each sprint, with demonstrations to company stakeholders every two weeks.

We released version 1.0 two months ahead of schedule when they deemed some of the features on the list could wait until after the initial version.

To put this in perspective, we had replaced a product that took *five years* to build in *less than seven months*, with the same resources—one full-time equivalent developer—and we *shipped two months early*. This was in stark contrast to my past experience outlined in the Preface.

This was possible *only* because we used an agile approach as opposed to a waterfall approach.

The Waterfall Approach

A plan for a traditional waterfall-based software development project often looks something like this at the beginning:

- Perform customer research: 3 mo.

- Write thorough requirements specification: 3 mo.

- Create detailed technical design: 2 mo.

- Implement technical framework: 3 mo.

- Build product functionality: 6 mo.

- Perform user acceptance testing and fix bugs: 3 mo.

- Deploy to production: 1 mo.

Total: 21 months

There are two big problems with this type of plan:

- By the time the team reaches the alpha and beta testing stage, there's really no way to know how long it will take to fix all the things that were broken along the way.

- When the team reaches the two-year mark—assuming it didn't grow to three years—what customers wanted at the beginning of the project is no longer what they need. Business conditions have changed.

Most 21-month waterfall software projects do not get done in 21 months, and they seldom meet the needs of users in the way everyone envisioned up front.

The Agile Approach

In contrast, a typical agile-based approach to build the same product might look something like this:

- Perform customer research: 1 mo.

- Write user stories: 2 wks.

- Create detailed technical design: (during each sprint)

- Implement technical framework: (during each sprint)

- Build product functionality: every two-week sprint; reaching "minimum viable product" state after 10 sprints, or 20 weeks.

- Perform user acceptance testing and fix bugs: (during each sprint)

- Deploy to production: 2 wks.

Total: less than 7 months

Just to be clear, I am in fact saying that by using Scrum, the agile approach shaves approximately *14 months* off the schedule.

How Agile Accelerates Delivery

How was it possible for the agile approach to remove over a year from the waterfall schedule?

There were a few reasons.

First, the team built a *fraction of the functionality* that they would have otherwise. They built only enough of the product to be "viable." That is, they completed enough functionality that a potential customer looked at it and said, "I can use that." In agile, we call this the "minimum viable product" and it's a key reason why using this approach leads to shorter development timeframes.

Second, they did technical design, built out the framework, built the functionality, tested and fixed bugs, *all during each two-week sprint*.

This provided two benefits:

- They spent no time building any technical framework that wasn't absolutely needed to support the features being built.

- They were forced to build the simplest thing that could possibly work. They had no time to get distracted by things that were more "fancy" than what was required.

Finally, instead of writing a requirements specification with hundreds of pages that no one would ever read, the requirements *emerged* throughout the process.

Later, I'll talk about how Scrum embeds the perspective of business stakeholders right into the team. This allows on-the-fly changes to requirements as necessary; especially when a requirement turns out to be too difficult to implement within the two-week deadline that otherwise would have been overlooked when the deadline was months or years away.

By getting the software into the hands of users more quickly, they'll give you feedback about what additional functionality they need. This avoids building features that sound like a great idea to the development team but will never be used by most users.

1.5 Scrum Is for Any Complicated or Complex Project

Many of the techniques, tips, and tools in this book can be applied to non-software projects, even though my examples and the technical portion of this book are focused on designing and building software.

If you have a complicated or complex project on your hands, I encourage you to experiment with Scrum techniques. I've seen non-software teams add just a daily meeting to their process and experience a significant improvement in their ability to get things done.

Scrum is very flexible and lightweight and has been used on a variety of projects in numerous industries—even to build a new jet fighter (Furuhjelm, et al., 2017). I'm sure you can adapt the techniques in this book to your specific challenge.

Key Takeaways

- Although you can get lucky, most teams don't naturally reach a state of high performance on their own. Scrum ensures teams do the right things to produce the highest business value in the shortest amount of time.

- Scrum is a social engineering framework to get teams to deliver amazing results to the business, including forcing them to make a plan, not giving them quite enough time, ensuring they communicate effectively, and driving empowerment and accountability.

- Scrum shortens timeframes by forcing all work to be done during each fixed-length production cycle, called a sprint. This ensures the only work that's completed is driving the highest business priorities. At the end of each sprint, the product is in a usable state, including all completed functionality to date. At any time, business leaders can decide to ship with fewer features than originally outlined, even if it's months earlier than planned.

- Although Scrum was created for software development, it can be used for work that has uncertainty about requirements and uncertainty about how exactly the work will be completed—so-called *complicated* or *complex* projects.

Chapter 2
Scrum's 10 Guideposts

Everything should be made as simple as possible, but not simpler.

- Albert Einstein

One of the reasons I love Scrum is because it's *simple*. Three roles, four ceremonies, three artifacts. Within these 10 guideposts, you have free reign to decide exactly how to do the work.

By design, Scrum is super lightweight and incomplete. It acknowledges that no two teams will have exactly the same needs. Instead of attempting to create a rigid methodology, Scrum instead provides a framework within which you evolve your own customized process.

This book provides you with lots of ideas based on what I've learned over the last 35-plus years, but what I've outlined is by no means the only way you can get things done. I fully expect you to take what works for you and abandon the rest.

This chapter dives into the fundamentals of Scrum, providing a foundation of knowledge for you to leverage as you read through the rest of this book. Later, I delve deeper into the details and how to apply these fundamentals in the real world.

2.1 Three Roles

Instead of talking about job titles, Scrum identifies *roles*, with each having specific responsibilities.

Titles within the Scrum team are discouraged because a key part of the process is ensuring team members avoid, "That's not my job." Team members do whatever they're capable of, which helps speed the process.

The **Product Owner** is responsible for the overall vision of the application being built. They are responsible for what the development team will work on, and in what order. I like to call the product owner the "embedded business representative" on the team, as they are responsible for distilling the views of all the various business stakeholders and carrying that into the Scrum team.

The **ScrumMaster** is responsible for the process. I like to call them the "embedded Scrum coach" on the team. They help everyone understand and adhere to the fundamental Scrum concepts I outline in this chapter. They also protect the team from outside influences to avoid distractions, and they help the team resolve impediments to their progress. Finally, they help the team reflect on how well the process is running and help facilitate improvements.

Sometimes I jokingly call the ScrumMaster the "mom" of the team—male or female, it doesn't matter—as their job is to protect and nurture the team to the greatest extent they can.

The **Development Team** is a group of individuals who collectively possess all the required skills to complete the work. For a software project, this may include skills such as coding, testing, architecture, databases, user experience, visual design, etc.

This group—typically comprised of "seven plus or minus two" individuals—does all the work on the product. The product owner and ScrumMaster are not included in this number unless they are performing work to get the product done, in which case they are also part of the development team.

Note that even though this is termed "development team," it is used to represent any group of individuals performing the work of a Scrum team, regardless of the type of work being done.

2.2 Four Ceremonies

Instead of calling them "meetings," in Scrum we call get-togethers of team members "ceremonies" or "events." I prefer ceremonies, so that's the terminology I've used in this book.

Each of the ceremonies below is timeboxed. That is, they must be completed in the time defined by the timebox, or less whenever possible. This avoids losing productivity by spending too much time in group discussions, while at the same time ensuring the right amount of group planning and communication actually happens.

Sprint Planning happens at the beginning of each sprint, and is comprised of what I call "micro-planning." The development team, with help from the product owner and ScrumMaster, starts with the most important item and creates a plan to get the work done by breaking down the item into subtasks, each with a time estimate in hours. This ceremony is timeboxed to no more than four hours for teams with two-week sprints, and eight hours for month-long sprints.

The **Daily Scrum**, sometimes called the daily standup, ensures all members of the development team are communicating on a regular basis. Timeboxed to 15 minutes, this ceremony occurs at the same time and place each work day during the sprint.

The exact format is up to the development team, but a typical structure is to have each member of the development team answer the following three questions:

1. What did you get done since the last daily scrum?

2. What do you commit to getting done before the next daily scrum?

3. What impediments are standing in our way of completing the work in the sprint?

The product owner and ScrumMaster only participate if they are also a member of the development team.

The **Sprint Review** occurs at the end of each sprint and is a way to provide insight and transparency to business stakeholders. The Scrum team discusses the work of the sprint and their results. It typically includes a demonstration of the product, including any new functionality completed during the sprint and driven to a "shippable" level of quality. Finally, the Scrum team usually discusses what's coming up next on the product backlog.

Although it often includes a demonstration, this ceremony is designed to be a two-way interactive conversation between the Scrum team and the business stakeholders.

This ceremony is timeboxed to two hours for a two-week sprint and four hours for a month-long sprint.

The **Retrospective** is a way for the Scrum team to discuss how things went during the sprint and determine changes to improve their process. Because Scrum is just a series of guideposts, it's critical that each team adjusts what's inside those guideposts to what works best for them.

This ceremony typically follows the sprint review and often marks the end of the sprint.

Formats vary but one approach is to have the team discuss the following three questions:

1. What went well?

2. What could be improved?

3. What experiments should we try next sprint to improve?

This ceremony is timeboxed to a maximum of an hour and a half for two-week sprints and three hours for month-long sprints.

2.3 Three Artifacts

Keeping within Scrum's theme of extreme simplicity, there are only three artifacts that you need to manage in order to effectively utilize the framework.

The **Product Backlog** is a single shared source of truth as it pertains to the vision for the product. The product backlog represents the entire scope of the product to be produced by the team, typically broken up into releases or versions. For example, the Scrum team may be working toward version 2.3 of their product.

Included on the product backlog is all the work the team needs to do. This includes:

- *User stories,* which represent new functionality to be built.

- *Bugs* that were discovered in user stories that were previously thought to be "done."

- *Tasks* that provide value to the development team but not direct value to business stakeholders. Some Scrum teams call these *chores* but I call them *tasks,* to align with the terminology used in Jira, the most popular agile management tool.

The product owner prioritizes the product backlog by business value, and the development team works from the top down, completing as many product backlog items as possible during each sprint.

The **Sprint Backlog** is a set of product backlog items the development team has committed to driving to "done" during the current sprint, as well as a plan to get the work done, in the form of subtasks for each product backlog item.

The **Product** is the end result and is used to describe the output of the team, regardless of the type of work being done. For software, the product is the application being built. The Scrum framework dictates that the product must be at a "shippable" level of quality at the conclusion of each sprint.

This artifact is sometimes referred to as the "shippable product increment," as each sprint builds onto the state of the product at the end of the prior sprint, adding the product backlog items completed during the current sprint.

2.4 This Is Too Simple. How Can It Possibly Work?

When I explain these fundamental concepts to project managers unfamiliar with Scrum, I usually encounter a fair bit of skepticism. They can't believe that something that's so simple can be used to manage the types of complex projects they're used to.

"Where's the rest?" they may wonder, accustomed to a variety of charts, graphs, tables, documents and reports from their traditional project management training.

I think the answer is threefold.

First, Scrum puts a heavy reliance on interpersonal interaction, as opposed to comprehensive written specifications. My feeling is that most traditional project artifacts are designed to accommodate a lack of human communication. Specifications are detailed to such a degree that they'd hold up in a courtroom, all because they're designed to ensure no amount of misinterpretation, months or years later when the developers implement them.

Second, Scrum forces everyone needed to produce the product to work side-by-side throughout its production. Unlike waterfall, there is no "tossing it over the fence" from one group of specialists to another—for example from business analysts to technical architects, to user experience designers, to coders, to testers.

Finally, business interests are connected into the team through the role of the product owner. Because the business is represented the whole time, throughout every day, decisions can be made on the spot as questions come up.

The founders of agile software development summarized their principles succinctly in the Agile Manifesto: (Beck, et al., 2001a)

Individuals and interactions over processes and tools
Working software over comprehensive documentation
Customer collaboration over contract negotiation
Responding to change over following a plan

That is, while there is value in the items on the right, we value the items on the left more.

I realize that in some environments—for example, development of life sciences and medical software—there are additional documentation needs. There is nothing wrong with adding additional documentation as necessary, for your unique combination of business problem, team, and technology. However, Scrum essentially says, "Start small. Start with the simplest thing that could possibly work. Add additional things only if you really need to."

This approach has proven to result in better products produced in less time, that better meet market needs. This is in stark contrast to traditional software development approaches which seldom "start small."

Key Takeaways

- Scrum includes three roles: the **product owner**, who is in charge of the vision and is the embedded business representative on the team; the **ScrumMaster**, who is in charge of the process and is the embedded Scrum coach on the team; and the **development team**, comprised of five to nine individuals who collectively can do all the required work to produce the product.

- Instead of "meetings," which have a bad reputation, Scrum uses four "ceremonies" for the team to coordinate their work. These include **sprint planning**, during which a plan is created for getting the work done during the current sprint; the **daily scrum**, where development team members coordinate their work for the day; the **sprint review**, which is an interactive discussion with stakeholders about the state of the product; and a **retrospective**, where the team improves their process.

- There are three artifacts in Scrum. They include the **product backlog**, which is a prioritized "wish list" representing the wants and needs of users and other stakeholders; the **sprint backlog** which includes a selection of product backlog items plus a breakdown of the work required to get them done; and the **product**, which is the result of the team's work and must be in a potentially shippable state at the end of each sprint.

- Scrum is much simpler by design than traditional project management approaches. It works by supporting the key concepts from the Agile Manifesto, including individuals and interactions over processes and tools, working software over comprehensive documentation, customer collaboration over contract negotiation, and responding to change over following a plan.

- Scrum ensures the work of the development team is always aligned with business needs, by connecting stakeholder priorities directly into the team through the role of the product owner, and the use of the product backlog.

Chapter 3
The Product Backlog

The bottom line is, when people are crystal clear about the most important priorities of the organization and team they work with, and prioritize their work around those top priorities, not only are they many times more productive, they discover they have the time they need to have a whole life.

*- **Stephen Covey**, author of The 7 Habits of Highly Effective People.*

Many software teams fail to produce the right functionality to drive the priorities of the business. After months or even years of work, they'll show the finished product to stakeholders only to hear, "That's not what I wanted."

The team coded against the specification and they felt pretty good about how well the product functionality matched what's in the document. Confused by their reaction, the team may ask for an explanation and stakeholders respond, "Things changed since that spec was written" or "I was thinking it would work differently."

The problem is threefold with traditional waterfall software development:

- Features are seldom force-ranked by business value, so teams spend too much time on functionality that produces little return on investment.

- Too much time goes by between the spec being written and the stakeholders seeing working, shippable software. By the time they provide feedback, it's too late to make substantial changes.

- There isn't enough interaction between business visionaries and the development team to keep them informed about changing priorities along the way.

Use of the product backlog in Scrum solves these problems by providing a shared vision used by business stakeholders and the team throughout the development of the product. Interaction between the product owner and the development team happens throughout every day. This ensures the needs of the business are directly connected to the ongoing development work throughout the entire process.

Finally—and probably the most important—the product owner places the most valuable stories at the top of the backlog. This ensures high value-generating items are completed first and are delivered sooner rather than later. This prevents less important items stealing development time from other, more profitable user stories.

3.1 The Single Shared Source of Truth

The product backlog provides a shared "source of truth" as it pertains to the vision for the product. It allows both the business stakeholders and development team to always understand the vision for the product.

It's essentially a whole-product wish list, owned by the business, and ordered by business value.

The backlog contains everything the team needs to do in order to complete the product in a way that matches the vision of the product owner.

Types of Items on the Product Backlog

The backlog contains three different types of items: user stories, tasks, and bugs.

Different types of items on the product backlog.

- *User stories* are lightweight requirements that represent new functionality that delivers value to business stakeholders; including end users. For example, "As a Shopper, I want to check out, so I can get my products shipped to me."

- *Tasks* represent items the development team would like to do, that provide direct value to the team and indirect value to business stakeholders. For example, "Update developer workstations to the latest version of coding tools."

- *Bugs* are defects that made it into the product when it was deemed shippable in a prior sprint—bugs that made it through the development team's testing process undetected. For example, "Search results are incorrect if I enter two words separated by a space."

The Order of the Product Backlog

When a new product backlog is first created, it will likely only contain user stories. An example product backlog for a fictitious e-commerce web application is shown below.

1. As a Shopper, I want to check out, so I can get my products shipped to me

2. As a Shopper, I want to review my cart, so I can make adjustments prior to checkout

3. As a Shopper, I want to view a list of products, so I can select some to purchase

4. As a Shopper, I want to log in, so I can manage my account

5. As a Shopper, I want to review my orders, so I can see what I've purchased in the past

6. As an Administrator, I want to modify the list of products, so I can adjust our offerings over time

7. As a Fulfillment Specialist, I want to print a picking report, so I can prepare products to ship

8. As a Fulfillment Specialist, I want to print packing labels, so I can ship packages

9. As a Finance Employee, I want to view analytics about orders and revenue, so I can see how we're tracking against our goals

10. As a Shopper, I want a gift registry, so I can share what I want with friends and family

At first glance, the order in which I've put the stories in my example may be a little confusing. You may wonder how a user can check out if they can't browse the list of products yet.

In this case, the company understands that their checkout experience is the most critical part of the application. By working on checkout first, they can ensure that they spend the most amount of time "living with" the feature, as the rest of the product is built around it.

Many teams start with building the login screen. They figure, "The first thing the user will do is log in." But how much time does a user spend on logging in to your application, and just how risky is it that you'll get it wrong?

Tasks and Bugs on the Product Backlog

Once the Scrum team is up and running, the development team will likely ask for some tasks to be added. For example, there may be an upgrade to one of their development tools that was recently released, and they'd like to upgrade the developer workstations. They might ask the product owner to add, "Update developer workstations to latest version of coding tools."

By managing this type of work on the product backlog, it provides visibility to the product owner and allows him to properly prioritize it. If the sales team is waiting on a handful of features to demonstrate to a billion-dollar customer in a few weeks, the product owner can work with the development team and ask, "Can this wait a few weeks?" Without this level of visibility and control over priorities, the development team could have gone off and spent a few days on the upgrade, instead of completing the critical features.

Once the first shippable product increment is produced, there will inevitably be a bug or two discovered during each sprint missed by the development team during their testing of the product in an earlier sprint. For example, a bug might be added along the lines of, "Incorrect message shown when removing an item from the cart if the item was the last one in the cart."

3.2 The Product Backlog Belongs to the Product Owner

With traditional software development, many teams take liberty with written specifications and decide independently to add some "neat" or "cool" enhancements—what I call "four-letter word" features.

They have the best intentions, and most teams make a valiant effort to attempt to support what they believe are the priorities of the business. But they seldom succeed. They don't have the perspective of the business to make the right decisions. They simply don't have the context of what stakeholders need from the product.

One of the things I love about Scrum is that we *shove* the business right into the Scrum team, in the form of the product owner. The product owner is the business representative, embedding the collective intelligence and vision of all stakeholders directly into the team.

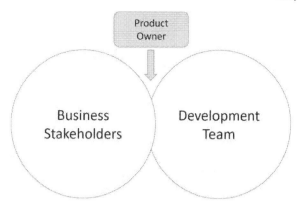

The product owner is the only one who has the perspective of both the business and ongoing development of the product.

The product owner is responsible for understanding the business drivers related to the product. Because she is the only one who has the perspective of both the business as well as the ongoing development of the product, she is the only one permitted to decide what's on the product backlog, and in what priority order.

The product owner is the only person in the entire company who has the perspective of both the needs of business stakeholders and an intimate understanding of what's happening day-to-day on the development team. Therefore, she is the only one who is actually *qualified* to own the product backlog.

No one else in the company—not even the CEO—can overrule the decisions of the product owner.

Of course, this means there is quite a bit of pressure on her to make decisions that result in the team delivering the highest possible business value, but she won't be able to please everyone all the time.

Certainly, the opinions of the CEO and other powerful figures in the company are going to heavily influence her decision-making process, but her decisions about the product backlog are final.

3.3 Requirements Evolve Over Time

The comprehensive software specifications that are common with waterfall projects assume that requirements can be nailed down at the beginning and remain largely unchanged.

However, when we try this approach we discover three things:

- When the software is built, and it's placed in the hands of actual end users, changes will be requested when they discover that it doesn't quite work as well as it seemed "on paper." Since this happens at the end, it's too late to make significant functionality updates.

- Certain parts of the software application will be more difficult to build than originally anticipated, so it takes a lot longer to complete the product when the team has little flexibility in changing the specified behavior along the way.

- During the time the product is being built, business conditions change. New markets or specific customers are targeted, resulting in a change of the vision and, by extension, the required functionality.

Scrum acknowledges the high-risk nature of software development and instead of attempting to lock things down for long spans of time, it says, "Let's embrace change." The product backlog is in a constant state of evolution. The only requirement to "lock down" a portion of the product is for the scope of work in the very next sprint, ranging from one week to a calendar month.

3.4 Discussing the Backlog with the Team Is Important

Most development team members don't spend as much time reading project documentation as we'd like. To combat human nature, instead of assuming the team will read the documentation, we talk about the product vision instead.

The process of refining the product backlog—sometimes also called grooming the backlog—happens throughout the development of the product. Most Scrum teams get together one or two times during each sprint to talk about what's coming up next on the product backlog.

This has the following benefits:

- The product owner can explain the vision for each upcoming story, often discussing the background of the story and how it provides value.

- The team can ask questions to get more details, increasing their understanding of what the product owner has in mind.

- Because the team will be on the same page, the planning process at the beginning of the next sprint will go much more smoothly and take less time.

- If there is anything confusing about upcoming stories or open questions from the development team, the product owner has some time to get things straightened out before the next sprint planning ceremony.

Collectively, this discussion does what I call "programming the team's collective subconscious." It gets everyone thinking about what's coming up next and, in the back of their minds, they'll start thinking about how they might build it during the next sprint.

3.5 Tracking the Projected Schedule with a Release Burndown Chart

Although the product backlog typically represents all the envisioned work on the product far into the future, the focus of most Scrum teams and their stakeholders is on a more short-term goal, often measured in terms of months as opposed to years. This short-term goal is defined by the product owner, and is aligned with the needs of stakeholders and the organization.

This goal is represented by a subset of the product backlog, starting at the top and including everything the product owner believes should be the next milestone for development of the product. This group of product backlog items is called a *release*, and allows tracking progress toward the goal and forecasting a timeframe to reach it.

The release burndown chart helps everyone understand how much time is left to complete the release, based on how fast the team is moving and how much work is left.

The amount of work remaining is driven by a size estimate, measured in *story points*, which I'll talk about in the next chapter. The speed of the team is determined by how many story points they have completed during prior sprints, which is called *velocity*. Typically, an average velocity of the last three sprints is used for the release burndown.

For example, if there are 20 story points remaining to be completed for the release, and the team's average velocity for the last three sprints is 7 story points per sprint, the release burndown calculates that the team has 3 sprints left.

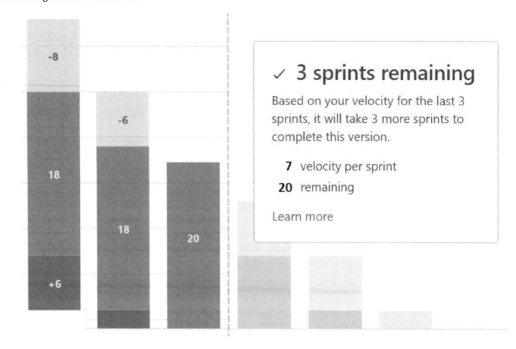

The release burndown chart uses the average velocity of the team to project the number of sprints to complete the release, based on the amount of remaining work. This report, generated by Jira, shows the velocity of the team, as well as any increase in scope added during each sprint.

If you multiply this by your sprint length—for example, 2 weeks—that gives you a projected timeframe. In this case, it's 3 sprints times 2 weeks per sprint, or 6 weeks.

Because the velocity of the team can change over time, this is only an estimate, so be careful about making promises about a hard date based on this information.

3.6 Projecting a Range of Dates with the Version Report

Other types of charts and reports can be used to track progress with the current release. For example, Jira includes a version report, which uses the same information as the release burndown—the velocity of the team and the amount of work remaining—but shows the information in a slightly different way.

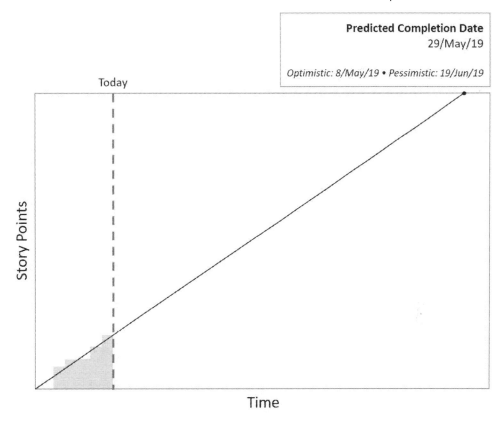

The version report is an alternative way to visualize how long it will take to complete the current release.

One nice feature of the version report is it shows a completion date *range*, recognizing that this is an inexact science. Included is a predicted date based on the team's current average velocity, as well as an optimistic and pessimistic date based on a plus or minus 10% range of velocity.

This considers the possibility that the team's velocity to date may go up or down a bit from now until the completion of the release.

The release burndown, version report, and other tools are extremely valuable to the product owner and business stakeholders, as they allow them to see what happens if they add or remove scope to or from the current release.

As I talked about in an earlier chapter, one of our clients was able to ship months earlier than originally planned by trimming down the number of user stories in the release of their product. We were able to do this by leveraging these reports as we worked together to adjust scope and immediately see the effect on the date.

We did this in *real time*. We moved some low-priority user stories to the next release, then we looked at the predicted, optimistic, and pessimistic dates on the version report. If the pessimistic date was after the date we wanted, we pushed off some more stories. We repeated this process until we were satisfied with the date.

Key Takeaways

- The product backlog allows stakeholders to drive the work of the Scrum team by directly connecting business priorities into the team. It represents a single shared source of truth representing the vision for the product.

- The product backlog includes **user stories**, which represent new functionality; **bugs**, which represent software defects; and what I call **tasks**, which represent the work the development team would like to do to move faster but provides no direct value to stakeholders.

- The backlog is force-ranked by business value, so the most important work is always done first. This prevents less important items stealing development time from other, more profitable user stories.

- The Scrum team routinely discusses the product backlog, so everyone is familiar with the vision for the product.

- The short-term goal of the Scrum team is represented by a subset of the product backlog, which is termed a *release*.

- The release burndown chart lets the Scrum team and stakeholders understand how much time is left to complete the current release, by using the velocity of the team and the amount of work remaining. This gives a lot of power to the product owner and stakeholders by immediately seeing the effect of any scope changes on the projected release date.

Chapter 4
User Stories

The single biggest problem in communication is the illusion that it has taken place.

- **George Bernard Shaw**, *Irish playwright and novelist, winner of the Nobel Prize in Literature.*

Much of the frustration I've seen on software teams over the years can be boiled down to one problem: communication. Whether it's a misunderstanding about what needs to be built or how a feature should work, time is lost and tempers can run high due to poor communication.

This problem is especially important to address with agile projects, with their focus on rapid delivery and adapting to change. Although with agile there aren't verbose written specifications, there still needs to be a way to ensure proper communication takes place.

User stories provide the basis of communication in Scrum and are the foundation of shared understanding. They facilitate the direct connection between the business and the development team, to ensure that what gets built delivers the highest business value in the shortest time.

User stories are part of an agile approach that helps shift the focus from *writing* about requirements to *talking about them*. User stories include a written sentence that summarizes the desired functionality in the product and—more importantly—a series of conversations about the desired functionality. (Cohn, n.d.)

4.1 A User Story Is a Descriptive Sentence

The key to any user story is the sentence, which is a brief phrase that describes a desired capability of the product from the perspective of a specific type of end user.

The type of end user is typically specified in the form of a role—what some may also call a persona or actor.

Here's an example user story for a fictitious e-commerce web application:

As a Shopper, I want to check out, so I can get my products shipped to me

This story is written using the following format:

As a [role], I want [capability], so I [benefit]

Where:

- *Role* explains the type of user who is interested in the capability. For example, if we were building an accounting application, a role might be *Bookkeeper* or *CFO*. As I'll talk about in Section 19.2, a role can also represent another software system, for example if your product will support electronic interaction via an API.

- *Capability* is a description of the desired functionality. This could be: *reconcile bank accounts* or *print a paper check*.

- *Benefit* is a description of the value delivered once the functionality is in the application. It helps answer the question, "Why does this type of end user care about this feature?"

Some Scrum teams include just the first and second parts for their stories—As a [role], I want [capability]. But this third part is often a helpful reminder about what's in the product backlog—the *why* behind each user story.

It may sometimes make sense to omit the benefit if it's obvious why someone would want the feature. However, I find it's helpful to always include the third part of the sentence, to ensure everyone is on the same page and they understand the "so what" behind each story.

This provides value not only to the product owner and business stakeholders—as a reminder of why the story is important—but also to the development team so they can understand what drives the desire for a story.

The development team may have creative ideas about exactly how to implement a user story. Helping them understand the underlying motivation can provide them with additional context to help them complete the story more quickly and leverage their collective insight and experience.

Here are some complete examples of user stories you might have for a financial application:

- As a Bookkeeper, I want to reconcile bank accounts, so I can make sure the bank balance in the application is accurate

- As an Accounts Payable Specialist, I want to print paper checks, so I can pay bills for vendors that don't accept electronic payment

- As a Chief Financial Officer, I want to view a financial dashboard, so I can monitor financial metrics

4.2 Details Are Added Through Conversations

When initially writing user stories, the sentence is typically enough to start a conversation with stakeholders and within the Scrum team, which is the primary goal of this technique.

As I said at the beginning of the chapter, *talking about requirements* is the goal, as opposed to creating comprehensive written specifications. This helps support the Agile Manifesto principle of *working software* over *comprehensive documentation*, which I discussed in Chapter 2.

However, once the conversations begin, it's helpful to make some notes about the details that come out of those discussions. These serve as a high-level reminder to the team about the fine-grained details of each story, so they don't have to keep everything in their heads.

This is *not* falling back into old habits by writing pages of information about each user story. Instead, a few notes—I recommend shooting for 5 to 15 bullet points—are added to the story to capture details.

There are different ways to manage these notes. I prefer the use of *acceptance criteria*, which is a list of conditions that need to be met to consider the user story "done."

I like to call the list of acceptance criteria the "product owner's checklist." That is, they document the answer if the product owner was asked, "What are the key things you want to see when you use the application to determine whether this story satisfied your vision?"

This is important because before a story can be called "done," the product owner must review and accept the work of the development team. The acceptance criteria, at that point, can be used as a high-level checklist for the product owner, along with any acceptance tests the team has chosen to write.

Here's an example story and its acceptance criteria:

As an Accounts Payable Specialist, I want to print paper checks, so I can pay bills for vendors that don't accept electronic payment

- I can set the starting number for checks.

- The number is automatically incremented each time I print a check.

- I can override the automatically-assigned number when I print a check.

- I can manually enter a check, to record a paper check I wrote by hand.

- I can customize the layout of printed checks.

- I can print checks for more than one checking account.

There are only a few acceptance criteria in the above example, but compared to just the sentence, the level of clarity has been dramatically increased. The team can now gain a much better understanding of what the product owner is thinking for this functionality.

You'll notice I started the acceptance criteria with "I can…" I like to use this convention because it helps put the team in the shoes of the end user. This helps the team think about what acceptance criteria are required and helps ensure everyone is always thinking about delivering value to the user.

Notice that *The number is automatically incremented each time I print a check* doesn't use the "I can…" format because it's something the application should do behind the scenes, as opposed to a capability it provides directly to the user.

4.3 What, Not How

Notice that the acceptance criteria in the previous section are fairly vague. There is no description of how the user interface might look, for example. And there isn't any description of how, exactly, the end user will customize the layout of checks.

Talking about the *what*, but not the *how* is by design, and provides a few benefits:

It gives the development team more latitude to come up with solutions. One of the development team members might have worked on another team a few months ago, and they built something that might be reusable in our product. We want them to have enough wiggle room to leverage their creativity and experience, which often results in faster development.

What that other team built for their product may not exactly match the product owner's vision, but since the user story is focused on the end result—and not how to achieve it—there's a higher likelihood the developer's experience can be used as-is.

It helps defer the details. The team can discuss the story at a high level, and start to think through it, without the user experience (UX) design. This is especially helpful to avoid progress being held up while waiting for the UX team to perform their initial usability research and product visioning.

It keeps the user story lightweight. Keeping the details at a high level helps avoid the urge to write pages of specifications about each story. However, there's enough detail captured to give the development team a good idea of the scope of the story and generate additional discussion as necessary as the functionality is built.

4.4 Each User Story Has a Size Estimate

One of the challenges business leaders face when working with development teams is determining how long it will take to add a specific feature to the product. If the feature is quick to implement and provides a decent amount of value to end users, it's likely to be prioritized higher on the backlog. However, if the feature will take a lot of work and provides only a small amount of value, it's likely to be deferred until later, or sometimes never built at all.

All too often business leaders will walk up to one of the developers and say, "Hey, Cyndi, how long do you think this will take?" Being put on the spot, Cyndi has only a few moments to think about the feature and replies, "Hmm. Probably a day or so."

The business leader smiles and says, "Thanks." Then he proceeds to promise the feature to a customer with a specific timeline. Chaos ensues when it ends up taking much longer than Cyndi anticipated.

What Cyndi isn't thinking about is all the various implications of implementing that feature, including properly testing it, finding and fixing any bugs, and discussions that may need to happen to ensure it's implemented properly. The other problem is *she might not be the one implementing it*, and another developer might take much longer.

Size, Not Time

Experience has shown this type of ad-hoc estimating is highly inaccurate.

First, it's based on the opinion of one individual, which doesn't consider the dramatic variation from developer to developer in the amount of time it will take to complete a particular feature. Second, one person is unlikely to think about everything involved in implementing that feature.

Instead of using time, I recommend an agile estimating technique of determining the *size* of each user story. The size of the story is related to other stories. This allows understanding that some stories are larger, which will take more effort, and some smaller, which will take less effort.

Techniques for Specifying Size

There are different ways to specify a size of a user story. One technique used by some Scrum teams is using t-shirt sizes—extra-small, small, medium, large, extra-large, etc. This is an OK approach, but I don't like it because you can't easily add the sizes from multiple stories. What's the sum of a small, two larges, and an extra-large?

Instead, I prefer using *story points*, which is a scale that allows assigning a number-based size to each story. 0.5, 1, 2, 3, 5, 8, etc. The big benefit of this approach is you can add the story points together. $1 + 3 + 5 + 5 = 14$.

This allows the use of simple math to determine the size of the remaining work for the next version of the product and—based on how many points the team can complete during each sprint on average—how much time is left.

The Development Team Determines the Size Estimate

An agile estimating technique called *Planning Poker* is used to facilitate a group discussion about each user story and generate a collective opinion from all members of the development team about its size. This avoids the problem of asking just one person to come up with an estimate, and results in a more accurate size for each story.

I get into much more detail about story points and agile estimating techniques later in this book.

4.5 Additional Written Details Are OK

As I've worked with teams over the years, I've seen them want to capture additional details in the user stories. There is nothing wrong with this. The detail in the user stories should be kept succinct, but not so abbreviated that the team gets slowed down.

The agile concept of always trying to find "the simplest thing that could possibly work" applies here, so you want to start with lightweight details. But don't kill yourself by saying, "We're not really supposed to be writing a lot of stuff down," if that comes at the expense of better communication.

How do you know when to add additional details? The simple answer is, "When the development team needs them." When discussing a story and there's any level of confusion, talk it through then capture the important points in the story.

Below are some examples of additional details I've found can be helpful to capture. Keep in mind that you don't need *all* of these details for *every* story, so use them selectively.

Background

When the product owner describes a story to the rest of the Scrum team, he will often talk a little bit about the origins of the story—the background of why the story is needed. Sometimes it's helpful to write a sentence or two to capture this background, describing what led to including the story in the product backlog. This can be especially important for stories that seem like they are at a higher level of priority than they deserve.

Here's an example:

Background: When we released version 1.0, we thought this feature would be used only intermittently, and we implemented a very basic version. We found that some of our largest customers are using this feature almost every day, so this story includes enhancements they've requested.

Notes

This is a general catch-all for any information that might be helpful, but isn't captured in the acceptance criteria.

Example:

Notes: We're still waiting on some feedback from a handful of top customers for some of the fine-grained details about this story. We should make sure we have that feedback before this story is added to a sprint.

Technical Notes

When discussing a story with the development team, they will often talk a bit about how they might implement it. Although extensive discussion related to every detail should be deferred until the story is in a sprint, sometimes it's helpful to capture some technical details when the information is fresh in the team's head.

Example:

Technical Notes: Alex has used the following spell-checking library in some other products. We should consider it when we work on this story:

https://www.npmjs.com/package/azure-cognitiveservices-spellcheck

Estimating Assumptions

When the development team estimates the size of stories, they will often make some assumptions. It's helpful to make a note about these assumptions because if they change, the story will need to be re-estimated.

Example:

Estimating Assumptions: We will use an open-source component and will not build the spell-checking engine from scratch.

A Complete Example

If the team decided they needed *all* the optional information I've described above, a complete example might look like the following:

As a Bookkeeper, I want to reconcile bank accounts, so I can make sure the bank balance in the application is accurate

Background: Customers need to make sure their banking transactions in the application match what's in their bank account, so they can ensure the bank balance in the app matches reality.

Acceptance Criteria:

- I can import transactions from my bank.

- I can see matching transactions based on dollar amount.

- I can create a new transaction on the fly if it's not in the system yet.

- I can create a new vendor on the fly if it's not in the system yet.

- I can create rules that will automatically classify recurring transactions.

Notes:

Jane Smith from our customer ACME Inc. said she'd love to show us an example of how she does this by hand today using Excel.

Technical Notes:

Natalie has used this package on a prior project:

- https://www.nuget.org/packages/Mocoding.Ofx/

Estimating Assumptions:

- Transactions will be imported from a file.

- We'll be able to find a pre-built component, so we don't have to write this from scratch.

- Up to two import formats. If more formats are required, we should re-estimate.

4.6 Some Traditional Specifications Are OK, Too

When I work with new teams that are used to working with extensive written documentation, they sometimes ask, "Are we *allowed* to use any other types of specifications?" The answer is absolutely "Yes!"

The idea behind this lightweight user story-based approach to software specifications is not to *prevent* you and your team from utilizing documentation that's helpful, it's to avoid doing *more than what's necessary.*

Many traditional software specifications include a multi-part document template for each feature. With agile what we're saying is, "Let's not assume we need to complete this entire 14-part template for *every* feature. Let's just add what we need."

This lets teams move more quickly because they have less baggage. But there's no rule in Scrum that says, "Don't you dare create a flowchart!"

The simple fact is, some stories are more complex than others and can use more written details to ensure proper communication and shared understanding. As is the case with the additional written details I described in the previous section, the key way to decide whether to produce additional materials for each story is only if the development team needs them.

Examples

Some examples of supporting materials you might utilize are:

- User interface wireframes, showing the layout of screens in the application.

- User interface mockups or comps, showing the exact visual look of screens, including colors and other visual design elements.

- A business domain model, showing real-world concepts and the relationships between them.

- Spreadsheets, modeling calculations in the application.

- Flowcharts, showing various paths through the story.

- Technical reference documents, such as specifications for a third-party API.

- Written standards, such as company or legal documents or regulations that include compliance standards to which certain stories must adhere to.

- Other charts, diagrams, pictures of whiteboard brainstorming, and anything else the development team finds useful to facilitate accurate and clear communication.

Add Additional Details as Late as Possible

When you do add supporting materials based on the needs of the development team, add them as late as possible.

Because priorities are always changing on an agile team, if you invest a lot of time creating supporting materials for a user story, you may find next week that same story has been moved to the bottom of the product backlog.

Ideally, create supporting materials in the *same sprint as the work to code and test the user story*. Completing them the sprint before is the second-best.

Avoid creating supporting materials months before the story will enter a sprint.

Key Takeaways

- User stories are part of an agile approach that helps shift the focus from *writing* about requirements to *talking about them*.

- A user story is a descriptive sentence. For example, *As a Shopper, I want to check out, so I can get my products shipped to me*, which follows the conventional format of *As a [role], I want [capability], so I [benefit]*.

- Additional details are captured using acceptance criteria, which is a high-level checklist for the product owner, to ensure key points about each story are recorded as a reminder to the Scrum team about conversations they've had about the story.

- User stories describe *what* is desired but not *how* to build it. This provides flexibility for the development team to come up with creative solutions.

- User stories have size estimates, expressed in story points, which allows everyone to understand the level of effort the development team estimates will be required to complete the story and drive it to a shippable state. This technique eliminates a focus on ad-hoc time estimates, which are highly inaccurate.

- It's OK to include additional notes and written details to clarify a user story, and even add some traditional requirements specifications. The key is to spend time writing down additional details only when needed to provide clear communication for the development team. Creating pages of documentation for every single user story is not necessary.

Chapter 5
The Sprint

How does a project get to be a year late? One day at a time.

*- **Fred Brooks**, The Mythical Man-Month*

When a deadline is 6 months, 12 months or a year and a half away, it's difficult for a development team to feel a sense of urgency. But this is exactly what happens with traditional waterfall-based projects.

Decisions are made along the way in the context of feeling like there's plenty of time, and teams don't realize it's too late until close to the end. At that point, they often look back and think, "I wish we had known we'd be this late. We would have done things differently."

In addition, by doing some of the riskiest work last—driving the product to a shippable level of quality and deploying it into production—the waterfall process introduces a huge amount of uncertainty into the completion timeline.

Project managers do their best to estimate the schedule, but software development timelines are notoriously difficult to predict, especially when product features aren't driven to "done" along the way.

Another issue with traditional waterfall development is the sequential nature of the work. Specifications are written, technical designs created, and technical infrastructure built. Coding of features begins and finally, there's user acceptance testing. At that point, a bunch of bugs are inevitably discovered and take what seems like forever to fix. This is no surprise since the time to fix bugs is also difficult to estimate. Bugs can take minutes, hours, or even days to fix.

These problems combine into missed deadlines and an increasing amount of pressure. This often results in "death march" projects", where the team is expected to work insane hours to get the product done. The all-too-common outcome is team members sprucing up their resume for a quick exit following the release.

To address the unpredictable nature of software development, Scrum uses a sprint—a short, fixed-duration production cycle—to timebox the work required to complete a set of shippable functionality.

5.1 Eliminating the Death March

Death march projects are typically caused by a variety of factors, including company politics, over-optimism about what can get done in a certain amount of time, intense competition, changing market conditions, and unexpected or unplanned crises. (Yourdon, 1997)

To combat these all-too-real challenges faced by every software team, Scrum compresses the deadline to an extreme degree, reducing it to a sprint lasting one week to a calendar month. Everything required to build a small part of the product is completed during this timeframe, including technical design, coding, testing, bug fixing, and acceptance by the product owner.

Using this technique dramatically reduces risk because everyone knows exactly where the product stands, simply by looking at working functionality at the end of each sprint. In addition, everyone knows exactly how long it's taken to get the product to that point, and this information can be used to predict how much longer it will take to complete the remaining work.

This is important because for any software development effort, there is a unique combination of team members, technology, and business problem to solve. Seldom will all three of those be identical to past work, so there is no baseline level of productivity that can be used from past projects. Empirical evidence, in the form of a specific team's pace of progress, is required to predict the future.

Finally, the use of sprints dramatically increases the company's flexibility to release. Since the product is always kept in a shippable state, business stakeholders can choose to release at any time they use the product and realize, "This can help drive our business goals *right now*. We don't need to wait for more functionality to be added."

This is in stark contrast to traditional software development, which results in the product being shippable only at the very end—the date of which is extremely difficult to predict—and providing little flexibility to reduce scope and ship immediately.

5.2 The Imminent Deadline and the Power of Positive Stress

"I'm stressed out" is typically an indication of an unhealthy state of mind, and one that leads to lower levels of productivity. This state, typically due to *distress*, can result in burnout, physical symptoms, counterproductive behaviors, and withdrawal behaviors. However, its counterpart, *eustress*, can result in feelings of wellbeing, commitment, performance, and engagement. (Hargrove, et al., 2015)

The Scrum sprint routinely produces a feeling of eustress among the development team members, leading to a happier and more productive team.

Scrum includes a handful of rules that combine to produce this emotion—and its related high level of productivity—sprint after sprint:

The development team selects the scope to be completed. Starting at the top of the product backlog, the development team decides how much work they take on. No one is permitted to tell them, "You must complete these five stories this sprint." The decision is 100% in the hands of the team, whether it's three stories or six. This results in a high degree of ownership among the development team members.

The product must be in a shippable state at the end of the sprint. Everything required to get the product to a level of quality that it could be put into an end user's hands must be completed by the end of the sprint. This is called the "shippable product increment" in Scrum or just "product increment." This prevents wasted work, as the only work that is done is directly related to producing the highest possible business value. There's no time to work on anything unrelated to driving toward that goal.

The development team decides how to complete the work. If you want to know how to make an assembly line work more efficiently, you ask the assembly line workers. Scrum leverages the same concept: those with the most information about the problem—the development team—are empowered to decide exactly *how* to complete the work during the sprint. This avoids bottlenecks by team members waiting for approval for every minor technical decision, and drives innovation by providing more flexibility for creative solutions.

No scope changes are permitted during the sprint. Once the sprint begins, no scope changes can be made by the product owner, the development team, or anyone else. This provides a "safe place" for team members to put their heads down and get the work done, without fear of the rug being yanked out from under them, and eliminates distractions.

The product owner isn't allowed to say, "Hey, things have changed, and now I need you guys to stop working on this stuff and work on this other thing." He must wait until the start of the next sprint, at which point he can present the development team with a different set of priorities.

The end date of the sprint cannot be changed. The value of an imminent deadline evaporates if it's not real. When the Scrum team begins a two-week sprint, it must end at the two-week mark. I call this "pencils down time." The team can decide along the way that they would like to experiment with a different sprint length for an upcoming sprint, but once the current sprint begins, its duration is fixed.

When everyone follows these simple rules, amazing things happen. Development team members are empowered to own their work and have the freedom to get creative. They collaborate and solve problems side-by-side. There's no time to get distracted by things that aren't related to driving their committed-to stories to "done," and the imminent deadline looms over everyone's head.

These factors all combine to produce an almost continuous feeling of positive stress—eustress—and the team produces consistent, high-quality results sprint after sprint.

Because the development team decides what to commit to each sprint, there may be a few late nights here and there, but a "death march" is impossible. Scrum teams can produce at a high level of throughput, in a sustainable fashion, forever.

5.3 Everything Is Done During a Sprint

Only when a story is added to a sprint, does the work begin to turn it into shippable functionality. Before that point, the Scrum team will spend some time talking about a user story, but no heads-down work commences until the development team has committed to bringing it into a sprint.

Once a story is in a sprint, work begins in earnest, including technical design, coding, testing, and acceptance by the product owner.

For those new to Scrum, this seems impossible. "How can we do all of that within the timeframe of one two-week sprint? It usually takes us six weeks or even a few months to do all of that!" The secret is to work on one small part of the product at a time—the scope defined by a handful of user stories.

Because the scope is small, every step in the process takes a lot less time. This allows driving that small part of the product completely to "done," producing a shippable product increment by the end of every sprint.

I realize this seems like a tall order, and many development teams will need to up their game to make it happen. But by using the techniques I outline in this book, it's not only possible but absolutely required to realize the benefits of an agile approach.

Waterfall: One Thing at a Time

With waterfall projects, work is performed in phases, with a focus across the entire scope of the product during each phase.

For example, requirements specifications are written for the entire application, then the technical design is completed. Next, coding begins, typically by building out the architectural framework for the entire product.

Feature coding is completed, then quality assurance, and finally user acceptance testing. At that point, once all the bugs are fixed, the product is deployed.

As I outlined earlier in this chapter, this introduces a high degree of risk due to the unpredictable nature of software development. We've learned a valuable lesson over the years of attempting to apply waterfall to software projects: it's only once user-facing functionality is completed and ready for use that we know how long it's *really* going to take. Until that step is completed, the timeline is largely a guess.

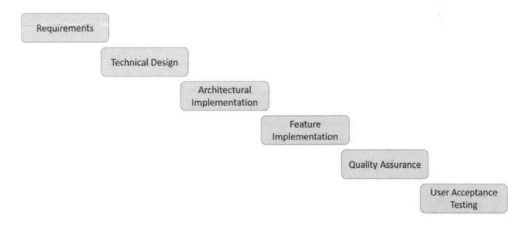

Waterfall largely involves doing one thing at a time for the entire product.

With waterfall, that means it will be months or even years until anyone knows how long it will take. The only time you have a predictable schedule is the day you ship.

Scrum: A Little Bit of Everything All the Time

Scrum, on the other hand, focuses on driving new features to "done" on an almost continuous basis.

During a two-week sprint, the development team may take on three or four stories. This means the entire process typically executed within waterfall over months or years is compressed to *two or three days*.

Instead of doing one thing at a time, Scrum teams do a little bit of everything all the time.

Except for lightweight "requirements" in the form of user stories, all of the work is completed during a sprint.

5.4 Benefits of the Sprint Approach

Reducing the production lifecycle from months or years down to a matter of weeks is dramatically different from the traditional approach.

I won't lie to you—making this transition is not an overnight thing, and it's not easy. It requires dramatically raising the bar with respect to your team's ability to execute at a very high level.

To reach this level of competence takes training, coaching, practice, and discipline—for both the agile process and raising the bar on your software engineering techniques—but the payoff is well worth the investment.

In this section, I outline just a few of the benefits of this approach.

Ability to Respond to Changing Business Conditions

When the product is driven to a shippable level of quality every sprint—one week to a calendar month—business leaders have a lot more power. They can decide to re-prioritize features in the product backlog to get them done more quickly. They can also decide to ship the product sooner than expected, whether it's to a select group of key customers or the entire user base.

This is simply impossible with a waterfall approach. Because a little bit of the product is being built at all times, but no part of the product is driven to "done," a waterfall project simply can't turn on a dime.

If there's a budget cut in the middle of the project, for example, there is nothing to show for all the time, effort, energy, and money that's been spent, because nothing can be put into the hands of end users.

Right-Sizing the Time Investment

Because all the work within each sprint is focused on delivering the stories that the development team has taken on, and nothing else, there is no time wasted working on things that later turn out to be unimportant.

Because the product owner has prioritized ruthlessly—and pushed off anything that's not important right now—there is a guarantee that the team is always working on the highest-value functionality.

Early Discovery of Technical Challenges

Many traditionally-managed software projects suffer from unfortunate surprises at the worst possible moment—the end. When the release date is weeks away and the development team is attempting to deploy the product to a "clean" environment for the first time, issues can come up that weren't encountered earlier.

Because the product must always be shippable according to the rules of Scrum, the development team is charged with doing everything they need to verify it will, in fact, work once deployed. This typically involves integration with external systems, deploying to test environments that are a lightweight version of the eventual production environment, and creating "release" builds of the code. This all happens during *every* sprint.

This approach ensures that surprises are discovered early in the process and eliminated. The result is at the critical time leading up to the release to production, those surprises have been addressed long in the past and won't come up and bite the team at the worst possible moment.

Knowing What It Actually Takes to Get to "Done"

Writing some code is only the first of many steps to drive a new product feature to a shippable state. Testing, bug fixing, and user acceptance—which come very late in a waterfall project—typically uncover unexpected work that the team didn't anticipate.

When the development team is forced to "make it *really* work," and the product owner is reviewing what they produced and ensuring it will satisfy the needs of users, there is no, "We'll take care of that later." Later is *right now*, and everyone is forced to buckle down and put all the finishing touches on the work.

This has a side benefit of avoiding a backlog of "stuff we'll take care of later." Because the "ship date" for the work in the current sprint is days or weeks away, there is no "later" to fall back on.

Predicting How Long It Will Take

Using the story points estimate for each user story that I described in Chapter 4, the speed of the team can be expressed in terms of the total number of points they complete during each sprint, which is called "velocity." Over the course of a few sprints, an average of that number can be calculated and used to predict how long it will take to complete the balance of the story points remaining in the current version of the product they're working to finish.

Once a development team has been working on the product for a few sprints, and assuming they're following the rules of driving the product to a shippable state at the end of each sprint, their velocity can be tracked and used to predict the completion timeframe for the full product release.

For example, a team might establish a velocity of 21 story points per sprint. If the remaining user stories in Version 2.3 total 128 story points, that means the team has approximately 6 sprints remaining to complete the work for the release.

I talk in detail about agile estimating techniques later in this book, but the key takeaway is that by using the sprint-based approach, schedule projections move from being based on wishful thinking to being based on *evidence*. (Spolsky, 2007)

This results in a schedule forecast that's accurate to within plus or minus 10 percent after four sprints have been completed—for two-week sprints this is after only eight weeks of development, which is virtually unheard of—and provides a *huge* amount of insight for everyone involved.

Part of the power of this approach is providing flexibility for the product owner to make changes to the product backlog—for example, adding or removing user stories from a release—and seeing exactly what the impact is on the schedule.

Key Takeaways

- A traditional waterfall approach results in software being driven to a shippable state only at the end—so throughout the project there is a high degree of uncertainty about the schedule. Scrum addresses this by accelerating the riskiest work to be done very early, and forcing the team to always keep the product at a usable level of quality.

- Scrum uses sprints—fixed-duration production cycles—of one week to a calendar month. All work must be completed during each sprint for a small set of functionality—including technical design, coding, testing, bug fixing and user acceptance by the product owner.

- The output from a sprint is a shippable product increment—including all the work the team has completed to date—which is at a level of quality that it could be put into the hands of an end user.

- This approach forces the development team to focus tightly on what needs to be done and introduces positive stress by creating an imminent deadline. The result is a dramatic reduction in wasted effort, since there's no time to work on anything that's not driving the highest business value.

- The scope of a sprint cannot be changed by the product owner. This produces a high level of momentum for the team since they know the plan is locked down for the duration of the sprint.

- The schedule can be forecast to within plus or minus 10% once about four sprints have been completed. This provides an understanding of how long it will take to complete the current release based on the team's velocity, expressed as the average story points per sprint of completed stories.

- Product backlog items that are not in the current sprint can be modified at any time by the product owner, including changing the order of user stories. This provides the business with the ability to react to changing business conditions at any time without interrupting the work of the current sprint.

Chapter 6
Scrum Ceremonies

The more technologically advanced our society becomes, the more we need to go back to the basic fundamentals of human communication.

- **Angela Ahrendts**, *Senior Vice President of Retail at Apple.*

For teams to produce amazing results, they need to ensure they are all in sync. Seldom does a group of individuals coordinate their work in a way that produces the best output without extensive communication.

The Agile Manifesto tells us that *individuals and interactions* are more important than *process and tools*. That's not to say that process and tools are unimportant—I'm a big fan of both. What it means is one of the keys to success with agile is focusing on the *people* involved and *getting them to talk to each other*.

It's easy to fall into the trap of assuming the "system" will handle communicating for us.

After learning that Alex had just spent two days figuring out a problem she had solved a week ago, Sofia asked, "I put that in the system. Didn't you see my note?"

He didn't.

Instead, if they had *talked* about what they were both working on, Alex would have two days of his life back. Either Alex would have learned from Sofia that she had solved the problem before he started working on it, or Sofia would have learned that Alex was digging into the problem and could have stopped him.

The problem is, many individuals don't know how to communicate the right way to effectively work as a cohesive group. This can be especially difficult since many people favor electronic over verbal communication.

Scrum solves this problem by including a handful of ceremonies—so named to set them apart from "meetings," their often-time-wasting cousins—that are specifically designed to get team members communicating about the right things at the right time.

To the greatest extent possible, everyone on the team participates in every ceremony, and they are all conducted verbally. This is done either face-to-face with co-located teams, or electronically for distributed teams using a tool such as GoToMeeting, WebEx, Zoom, or Skype.

This chapter contains a high-level overview of each ceremony. I'll get into much more detail in later chapters.

6.1 Sprint Planning

The sprint planning ceremony occurs at the beginning of each sprint, and allows the development team to accomplish three key things:

- Decide on how much work they can take on, given the availability of each team member during the duration of the sprint.

- Create a detailed plan for how they will complete as many product backlog items as possible by breaking them down into individual subtasks, each with a time estimate.

- Select a sprint goal, which acts as an overall vision for what they want to accomplish during the sprint.

By working as a group to create an execution plan for the sprint, the entire development team understands the overall strategy of how work will be completed. This allows them to focus on tactical execution once they complete the sprint planning meeting and get started with the work. As the saying goes, *plan your work and work your plan.*

An even bigger benefit of this process is the sense of ownership the team gains. Sitting down as a group and thinking through, "How will we do this?" is dramatically different from a traditional project manager telling everyone, "Here's what I want you to do. Oh, and by the way, you have to get all this done in the next three days."

Sprint planning lays the groundwork for the sprint and is one of the keys to success.

Determining Gross Capacity

Another important part of sprint planning is the development team determining how much work they can take on, given their availability during the sprint.

The team does this by first identifying the number of hours each team member can dedicate to working on the sprint during the calendar timeframe of the sprint. For example, if the team is running two-week sprints, everyone looks at their calendar for the next two weeks.

They'll each think about how much time they can dedicate to this particular sprint as part of the Scrum team. This includes time attending Scrum ceremonies as well as "heads-down" time working on the product itself. This total number of hours should omit any time related to their other responsibilities outside of the Scrum team.

This may include upcoming all-hands company meetings, other meetings unrelated to this Scrum team such as departmental meetings or one-on-ones, time off, holidays, and time spent on housekeeping work such as email, etc.

The available hours for everyone are added up and the total number of hours is the *gross capacity* for the development team to work on the product.

Determining Net Capacity

Scrum requires some "care and feeding" for it to work. Sprint planning, daily scrums, the sprint review, and retrospective will take time and should be subtracted from the gross capacity.

These are all critically important, and part of "working on the product," but it isn't time spent heads-down on completing work outlined on the sprint task board.

Your team may also choose to introduce optional ceremonies such as what I'll outline in Section 6.5. Time for these should be subtracted as well.

Once you take the gross capacity and subtract the various Scrum ceremonies, you end up with *net capacity*.

This is the capacity you'll use to determine how much time can be spent working on the subtasks the team will create during the sprint planning process.

Micro-planning

All of us, because we're humans, procrastinate. We wait until the last possible moment to get things done, and typically get stressed out because we waited just a *bit* too long. Part of the secret of Scrum's social engineering rules is its ability to combat our natural human behaviors that get in the way of high productivity.

By breaking each product backlog item into subtasks, team members are set up to create daily commitments for themselves by volunteering for one or more subtasks each day, that they promise to complete by the next business day. This builds in a personal deadline, which has been shown to combat procrastination more effectively than if there was only the end-of-sprint deadline for the team as a whole. (Gafni & Geri, 2010)

As the team goes through the process, they keep track of how many hours of work they've identified and compare it to their net capacity, ensuring they don't take on more work than they can reasonably complete during the sprint.

The output of this planning process is the sprint backlog. This is comprised of the product backlog items the development team believes they can get done and an execution plan, captured by a set of subtasks for each item.

Sprint Goal

Sometimes things don't work out exactly as planned, and though no scope changes are allowed during the sprint, things might come up that require a change of plans to deliver as much business value as possible during the sprint. A sprint goal can help keep the Scrum team focused on a big-picture outcome and provides an opportunity to be flexible when necessary if the plan doesn't work out exactly as the team thought it would.

For example, the development team might be working on adding tax calculations to the shopping cart and realize that the tax rules in California are more complex than they thought, and they won't have enough time to get them completely working.

Because they selected a sprint goal of "Get tax calculations working in the shopping cart," they negotiate with the product owner and say, "How about we get the tax calculations working for everywhere *except* California? That's still in the spirit of the sprint goal, though we realize you'll need to add a new story to the backlog to handle California taxes, and it's not quite what you hoped you'd have at the end of this sprint."

The product owner thinks about it and realizes she'd much rather have the development team focus on getting the fundamentals of tax calculations working and agrees to back off on the original vision for the user story which was to get the calculations working for all the states.

In this case, the sprint goal helped prevent the team getting tied up in knots and distracted from producing as much business value as possible. They remained focused on the goal, got the basic tax calculations working, and the next sprint they will put their heads down and focus on California.

Sprint Planning Summary

Timing: Beginning of the sprint.

Attendees: Product owner, ScrumMaster, development team.

Timebox:

- 1-week sprints: 2 hours maximum

- 2-week sprints: 4 hours

- 3-week sprints: 6 hours

- 4 weeks or a calendar month: 8 hours

Agenda:

1. The development team determines the total time that they can dedicate to this sprint during the calendar duration of the sprint. They omit time for personal time off, holidays, company events, and anything else that will distract them from working on the product. This "capacity" of the team to work on the sprint is expressed in hours.

2. The product owner summarizes the first product backlog item for the development team to refresh their memory.

3. The development team breaks the product backlog item down into the subtasks required to complete the work and drive it to a shippable state and estimate the total hours required for each subtask. The product owner answers any questions as they come up.

4. The development team reviews the total hours estimated for all subtasks identified so far and compares it to the total hours available determined in step 1.

5. The development team repeats steps 2 through 4 until they feel comfortable that the total hours they've estimated can be completed within their capacity.

6. The development team selects a sprint goal based on the product backlog items that fit into the sprint. For example, "Add tax calculations to the shopping cart" or "Implement a basic gift registry."

7. If the project management tool being used requires that the sprint is "started," the ScrumMaster completes the steps to start the sprint.

8. Facilitated by the ScrumMaster, each team member volunteers for a subtask or two that they'll work on between the end of sprint planning and the first daily scrum.

Desired Outcome:

- The sprint backlog has been created with the product backlog items broken down into subtasks, each with an hour estimate.

- A sprint goal has been determined and written down.

- Any steps to start the sprint in the project management tool being used have been completed.

- Each development team member has volunteered for the first subtask they'll focus on completing prior to the next daily scrum.

Notes:

For new teams, I recommend they plan to only 50% of their capacity since it's likely they will dramatically under-estimate what it *really* takes to get to "done" when they are learning Scrum.

It's typically better to under-estimate and be faced with adding more work to the sprint if things go well, than to over-estimate what can be done and be faced with a crisis toward the end of the sprint when they realize they're in trouble.

As the team gains more experience, they can increase this percentage, though they should still leave some wiggle room, perhaps planning to 75% to 80% of their capacity.

6.2 Daily Scrum

The *daily scrum*, also known as the *daily standup*, is a time for the development team to get on the same page about the state of the sprint. It's a critical ceremony in that it keeps the work of the development team coordinated and helps avoid other unnecessary meetings.

It also helps the development team members be accountable to each other. Finally, it helps to keep a heightened sense of awareness among the team members that progress needs to be made every day.

The daily scrum occurs once every working day at a time and place determined by the team. Each development team member provides an update using the following format:

1. *What you did.* What did you do since the last daily scrum to help meet the commitment of the development team? For example, what subtask or subtasks did you complete?

2. *What you'll do.* What will you do between now and the next daily scrum to help meet the commitment? For example, what subtask or subtasks will you take on?

3. *Impediments.* What impediments are getting in the way of us making progress toward meeting the sprint goal? For example, what is blocking your work? Or what do you anticipate will cause the team to stop making progress in the next day?

Only development team members may participate in the daily scrum. The product owner and ScrumMaster do not participate unless they are also members of the development team.

Other individuals may attend, but they are not allowed to speak. The ScrumMaster is responsible for enforcing this rule.

This update is timeboxed to 15 minutes. If a team member is not able to attend the daily scrum, they should provide their update to the ScrumMaster for sharing with the development team during the ceremony.

At the end of the ceremony, it's helpful to review the sprint burndown chart which shows the development team's progress toward completing the work in the sprint.

The ScrumMaster is responsible for making sure the development team conducts the daily scrum.

Note that the purpose of the development team members providing their update is not to "give a status report to the ScrumMaster." This is part of the social engineering framework that Scrum provides—the discussion is for the benefit of the development team and provides an opportunity to make *commitments to each other* when team members promise to get something done by the next daily scrum.

Daily Scrum Summary

Timing: Every working day, ideally at the same time every day.

Attendees: Product owner, ScrumMaster, development team.

Timebox: 15 minutes

Agenda:

1. Each development team member provides an update, answering the following questions: What have you gotten done since the last daily scrum? What are you committing to getting done before the next daily scrum? What impediments are in the way?

2. The items requiring additional discussion are captured.

3. The sprint burndown chart is reviewed.

Desired Outcome:

- The team members understand the status of the work of the sprint.

- Every development team member has made a commitment to the other team members about how they'll do their part to drive the sprint forward, typically by volunteering for one or more subtasks they'll complete before the next daily scrum.

- The impediments have been identified and someone has volunteered to remove them. This is often the ScrumMaster, whose role includes protecting the development team and removing impediments.

6.3 Sprint Review

One of the challenges with traditional software development is a lack of understanding of how much progress is really being made. One of the reasons for this problem is not driving things to done like we do with Scrum. The other reason is a disconnect between the work of the development team and business stakeholders.

With Scrum, this problem is addressed through the sprint review. Taking place at the end of each sprint, it's a time for the entire Scrum team to connect with stakeholders, demonstrate the completed work, and have an interactive conversation about how things are going.

Sometimes things are going great, and other times the team may have run into a few issues. Regardless, this open and honest communication between the Scrum team and stakeholders lets everyone get on the same page and leads to a strong feeling of, "We're all in this together."

I've found this also establishes a high amount of trust. Too often, because business leaders have little insight into what it really takes to get a product built, they don't trust what they don't understand. This drives a wedge between business leaders and the development team. In contrast, the sprint review provides total transparency about what happened during the sprint. This, coupled with the delivery of *fully-functional and stable* software, very quickly closes the gap and brings the business and developers closer together.

In addition to discussing how things went during the sprint and the demonstration of new functionality, the sprint review is also a time to talk about what's coming up next on the product backlog. This not only allows stakeholders to understand what the development team is going to focus on during the next sprint, it also allows them to provide additional input about changing business conditions and new opportunities.

"Hey, we probably haven't talked about this, but I got off a call yesterday with one of our customers. They're ready to spend an additional $2.5 million with us once we have such and such functionality in the product." This kind of input helps the product owner immediately adjust the product backlog to maximize the return on investment of the development team's work.

In this case, guess which functionality she'll push to the top of the backlog? Whatever is needed to get that $2.5 million more quickly!

The sprint review provides an opportunity for the stakeholders to inspect the work of the development team. The product owner invites the relevant stakeholders to attend. This ceremony provides an opportunity for collaboration between the Scrum team and the stakeholders.

Note that stories that are not "done" should not be demonstrated, as this would lead to a mischaracterization of the actual status of progress.

Sprint Review Summary

Timing: At the end of each sprint.

Attendees: Product owner, ScrumMaster, development team, and key stakeholders invited by the product owner.

Timebox: The maximum times are listed below, but I recommend experimenting with about half of what's shown. This makes it easier to get the ceremony scheduled. The last thing you want to do is risk key stakeholders not being able to attend because they can't set aside enough time in their schedule.

- 1-week sprints: 1 hour maximum

- 2-week sprints: 2 hours

- 3-week sprints: 3 hours

- 4 weeks or a calendar month: 4 hours

Agenda:

1. Discussion about what product backlog items the development team committed to completing at the start of the sprint, and the sprint goal.

2. Discussion about whether everything was completed and, if not, why?

3. Discussion about what went well during the sprint, and what problems were encountered.

4. A demonstration of the stories that were driven to "done" by the development team.

5. A review of what is coming next on the product backlog, including feedback from the stakeholders about anything they see that's missing or any factors that may drive the priority order.

6. The projected completion timeline.

Desired Outcome:

- The stakeholders understand the status of the development of the product.

- The Scrum team has heard the feedback from the stakeholders.

- Anything that may impact the product backlog has been discussed—especially anything that may affect the product backlog items that may make it into the next sprint.

6.4 Retrospective

Because every development team has a different challenge, Scrum is by design very lightweight and incomplete. Instead of providing prescriptive details for absolutely everything a team needs to do, it provides guideposts and a framework. That means it's up to each Scrum team to fine-tune their process, so it works best for their situation.

The retrospective, held at the end of every sprint, is dedicated to this process improvement. Though improving the process can happen at any time—and certainly great ideas don't have to wait until after the end of the sprint—the retrospective ensures that the Scrum team dedicates time to this important part of Scrum.

Specific formats of the retrospective vary but most include a discussion about:

- What went well during the sprint.

- What could be improved.

- A plan of action to experiment with the identified improvements.

Because this ceremony repeats every sprint, it helps drive one of the fundamental goals of Scrum: continuous improvement.

Retrospective Summary

Timing: At some point after the sprint review, but prior to the next sprint planning ceremony. I recommend teams have the retrospective immediately following the sprint review when things are fresh in their heads about how things went during the sprint.

Attendees: Product owner, ScrumMaster, development team.

Timebox: I've listed the maximum durations below, but don't feel like you need to fill up the time if it's not valuable. Some teams will spend only 30 minutes for a sprint duration of 2 weeks once they get used to the process.

- 1-week sprints: 45 minutes maximum

- 2-week sprints: 1 ½ hours

- 3-week sprints: 2 to 2 ½ hours

- 4 weeks or a calendar month: 3 hours

Agenda:

1. Discussion about how things went during the sprint: What went well? What could have gone better?

2. Discussion of ideas on how to improve the process and experiments to try during the upcoming sprint.

Desired Outcome:

- The team has a shared understanding of how the sprint went.

- One or more things to try during the upcoming sprint have been identified.

6.5 Other Optional Ceremonies

In addition to the Scrum ceremonies I outlined above, there are also "unofficial" ceremonies that many Scrum teams have utilized to make their process even more effective.

Parking Lot

During each daily scrum, things will come up that require additional discussion. To keep things moving along and to stay within the 15-minute timebox, it's important that these items are captured.

It's often natural to wrap up the daily scrum, then talk through the discussion items while the Scrum team is all together. But the problem is, most issues don't require the *entire* Scrum team.

To solve this problem, many teams use a parking lot, which is an additional 15-minute timeboxed discussion that takes place immediately following the daily scrum. The ScrumMaster typically would say, "OK, let's move to the parking lot. Here are the items I've captured. Who needs to be here?"

At that point, anyone who doesn't need to be involved in the discussion can leave and start getting some work done. Those who are needed can remain to participate in the parking lot.

There are times where it makes sense for the entire Scrum team to participate, but there are times when you'll want to avoid, "I don't really need to be here for this, but I'm too polite to stand up and leave." The parking lot approach gives everyone explicit permission to get the heck out of there if they're not needed.

This is *not* permission to allow all your daily scrums to run to 30 minutes. The parking lot is used selectively and only as required to keep things moving along and, to repeat a key point, it includes *only* those Scrum team members who are necessary.

Parking Lot Summary

Timing: Immediately following the daily scrum.

Attendees: Any Scrum team members required to discuss and resolve items that came up during the daily scrum.

Timebox: 15 minutes

Agenda:

1. Discuss each item captured during the daily scrum.

2. If some items require more people than others, they are discussed first, then unnecessary attendees leave when moving to the next item.

3. If a resolution to one or more items can't be determined during the timebox, those Scrum team members necessary to resolve the items agree on a time to get together to get them addressed.

Desired Outcome:

- Issues that came up during the daily scrum are resolved.

- Follow-on meetings are scheduled for items that can't be resolved during the 15-minute timebox.

Backlog Refinement

One of the keys to making the sprint planning process go smoothly is ensuring the development team is familiar with the top of the product backlog, and it's prepared for the sprint planning process.

Although the product backlog is intended to be refined on an almost continuous basis—and the product owner should absolutely feel free to make changes any time business conditions change—most Scrum teams find that setting aside time for a ceremony focused on refining the product backlog pays off.

The backlog refinement ceremony is typically held once per sprint, or sometimes twice per sprint, especially when a team is just starting to work on a product.

The product owner talks through the first few items on the product backlog, answers questions and adds additional details at the request of the development team. If user stories near the top of the backlog are too large to fit into a sprint, they are split into smaller stories. Any stories without story point estimates are typically estimated by the team during refinement.

Another benefit of backlog refinement is providing the product owner an opportunity to get any outstanding questions answered prior to sprint planning.

Although this ceremony is optional, keeping the backlog up to date is a key part of Scrum. If you choose not to utilize a backlog refinement ceremony, you will need to find some other way to ensure the backlog is kept in good shape.

Backlog Refinement Summary

Timing: At the discretion of the Scrum team. I recommend about three to four days before the end of the sprint. If it's too close to the end of the sprint, the team may be tempted to skip it, because they're focused on getting everything done.

Also, the product owner may not have enough time to address any questions prior to the next sprint planning. However, if it's too early in the sprint, the product backlog may not reflect all the latest updates from the product owner due to changing business conditions.

Attendees: Product owner, ScrumMaster, and as many development team members as possible.

Timebox:

- No more than 10% of the development team's capacity for the sprint.

- I find that one or two backlog refinement ceremonies of 2 hours each is about right for a two-week sprint.

Agenda:

1. The Scrum team discusses the items at the top of the product backlog.

2. Stories that are too big to fit into a sprint are split into smaller stories.

3. Story point estimates are determined for un-estimated stories.

4. Additional details are added to stories as necessary.

5. The product owner keeps track of open questions to resolve prior to sprint planning.

Desired Outcome:

- Team members understand the upcoming product backlog items likely to make it into the next sprint, including any details necessary for them to complete the sprint planning process.

- Stories at the top of the backlog are small enough to fit into a sprint.

- Un-estimated stories have story point estimates assigned.

- The product owner has a list of open questions.

Notes:

The team should avoid getting into detailed implementation discussions. A good rule of thumb is to shoot no more than a 5- to 15-minute discussion of each user story.

Backlog Estimating

It's important for user stories to have story point estimates, both to drive the schedule forecast as well as provide insight for the product owner as to how much effort will be required to complete each story.

Part of the backlog refinement ceremony is estimating any un-pointed stories, but sometimes there isn't enough time, or some members of the development team were unable to make it to the ceremony.

Another situation that may come up is the product owner may want to have an estimate for a new story he just added to the product backlog, to help determine where he force-ranks it in the list.

Backlog Estimating Summary

Timing: At the discretion of the Scrum team. I recommend immediately following a daily scrum two or three days before the end of the sprint.

Attendees: Product owner, ScrumMaster, development team.

Timebox: 30 to 60 minutes maximum.

Agenda:

1. The product owner discusses the first user story that doesn't have a story point estimate.

2. The team uses the Planning Poker process to determine a story point estimate.

3. The process is repeated for any additional un-estimated stories.

Desired Outcome: Un-estimated stories have story point estimates assigned.

Notes:

A good rule of thumb is to shoot for no more than 5 to 15 minutes for each user story.

Backlog Prioritization

Most product owners don't independently have enough information to properly prioritize the product backlog. To determine the relative business value and opportunities that may arise by prioritizing certain user stories above others, the product owner needs to understand the perspective of a variety of stakeholders, from end users to the customer support department to the sales team.

Most of the time, product owners will solicit input from various stakeholders throughout each sprint and use that information to prioritize the backlog appropriately. Other times they may decide to schedule a specific meeting with stakeholders.

Backlog Prioritization Summary

Timing: From time to time throughout the sprint, ideally finalizing priorities prior to backlog refinement to ensure the focus of that ceremony is on the right items, and definitely prior to the next sprint planning ceremony.

Attendees: Product owner, ScrumMaster, and any relevant stakeholders from whom the product owner would like input and feedback.

Timebox: As needed.

Agenda:

1. Product owner discusses the priorities with the stakeholders.

2. Prioritization of the backlog is adjusted based on the input.

Desired Outcome:

The product backlog is in the appropriate order prior to sprint planning.

6.6 A Typical Ceremony Schedule

Putting it all together, this is what a typical schedule of ceremonies might look like for a two-week sprint:

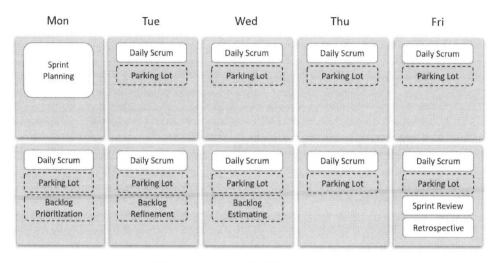

A typical Scrum ceremony schedule for a two-week sprint.

6.7 Aren't All These "Ceremonies" Wasting a Bunch of Time?

When I talk to members of a company's management team and begin to discuss the various Scrum ceremonies, they often make the comment, "This seems like a lot of time in meetings. Are all of these really necessary?"

I can understand the concern. On one hand I tell them how fast their development team is going to be able to move once they're up to speed, then I make it sound like they're going to spend a bunch of time sitting around chatting.

The short answer is no, these ceremonies aren't a waste of time. They're what's required to ensure the Scrum team members communicate enough to all be on the same page and pushing in the same direction. Scrum ceremonies are *part of doing the work*.

Let me briefly touch on why each ceremony is required:

Sprint Planning. Without this ceremony, the team would have no direction, no plan, and no sense of ownership and empowerment. Everyone would be working on their own thing, regardless of its actual level of importance. No strategy would be employed to allow the team to leverage everyone's contribution in the most effective way.

Daily Scrum. Without close coordination of everyone's work, things quickly go sideways. A "re-sync" of the team's collective efforts once a day ensures everything is on track and helps avoid unnecessary meetings. This keeps the level of focus high and drives a sense of urgency that prevents distractions from eroding the team's productivity.

Sprint Review. Without a regular check-in and update provided to stakeholders, lack of transparency would quickly turn into a lack of trust and lack of accountability. A lack of a real, imminent deadline would allow team members to slip into complacency and slow production. And finally, the Scrum team wouldn't have insight about changing business conditions that stakeholders can provide.

Retrospective. Scrum is not a cookie-cutter methodology that can be adapted as-is. It needs to be molded and adjusted to maximize its effectiveness. Without this ceremony, there would be no time set aside for the development team to look in the mirror and ask the question, "How can we do this better?"

In short, without setting aside time for these ceremonies, the Scrum team would waste much *more* time because of their lack of a plan, lack of coordination, lack of accountability, and lack of continuous improvement.

There are also benefits from the personal interaction these ceremonies provide, including building up relations and networks within and for the project team, building trust, tracking project progress and giving energy and motivation to the Scrum team. (Pries-Heje & Pries-Heje, 2011)

The optional ceremonies I've included in this chapter have provided a lot of benefit to the Scrum teams that I've worked with. However, they don't need to be adopted by every team.

I encourage teams to experiment with them and see if they help with delivering the highest business value in the shortest amount of time. If so, they can keep doing them. If not, they're easy to abandon.

Key Takeaways

- There are four core Scrum ceremonies: sprint planning, the daily scrum, the sprint review, and the retrospective.

- Sprint planning ensures the development team creates a plan for the upcoming sprint, so everyone is on the same page about how to drive the sprint goal to done.

- The daily scrum allows the development team to synchronize their work and identify any impediments that threaten accomplishing the sprint goal.

- The sprint review provides transparency to the stakeholders about the status of the product and allows them to have an interactive discussion with the Scrum team.

- Because Scrum is lightweight and incomplete by design, the retrospective provides a time for the Scrum team to inspect and adapt their process, which supports continuous improvement.

- Additional "unofficial" optional ceremonies can be used to help the Scrum team better accomplish their sprint goal and keep things moving along.

- Optional ceremonies include a parking lot for discussing items that come up during the daily scrum, backlog refinement to prepare the backlog for sprint planning, backlog estimating to assign points to new user stories, and backlog prioritization to provide a time for the product owner to interact with the stakeholders to ensure the backlog is ordered appropriately.

- Although at first glance it may appear that the Scrum team spends a lot of time in ceremonies, each has a specific purpose and saves time due to ensuring the proper level of communication and eliminating unnecessary meetings.

Chapter 7
Scrum Roles

I am a member of a team, and I rely on the team, I defer to it and sacrifice for it, because the team, not the individual, is the ultimate champion.

*- **Mia Hamm**, professional soccer player, two-time Olympic gold medalist, and two-time FIFA Women's World Cup Champion.*

In soccer, a team needs forwards, midfielders, defenders, and a goalkeeper. Although each team member has their strengths—and their position plays to those strengths—the real job of every team member is to *do whatever is necessary to win.*

If a forward has an opportunity to stop a scoring drive by the opposing team, they'll stop the drive. They won't step aside and say, "That's not my job."

Scrum takes the same approach. There are specialists on a Scrum team—front-end programmers, back-end programmers, user experience architects, visual designers, testers, database experts, etc.—but everyone is focused on doing whatever they are capable of in order to achieve the sprint goal.

Sometimes this means a developer might help test, a database expert might proofread end-user documentation, and the ScrumMaster might help the product owner manage the product backlog.

Even though the job of each Scrum team member is to do whatever is necessary to achieve the sprint goal, Scrum uses *roles* to describe key areas of responsibility. By focusing on roles and not titles, there is an emphasis on the responsibilities that help drive Scrum, rather than individual technical specialties.

The result of this approach is achieving two critical business goals: empowerment and accountability for the development team. By eliminating the need to tell everyone what to do, creativity and productivity are dramatically increased. This is in stark contrast to traditional project management techniques that rely on close oversight and top-down distribution of daily tasks to team members.

To make this magic happen, there are three roles in Scrum that collectively facilitate the process: product owner, ScrumMaster, and development team.

7.1 The Product Owner

As I've talked about throughout this book, one of the big challenges of traditional software development is the inherent disconnect between the needs of the business and the activities of the development team. The inventors of Scrum witnessed this problem first-hand in the large enterprise projects they worked on and decided to fix it. Their solution was to do what I call, "embedding the business into the team."

This is accomplished through the product owner role. By placing a product owner into a Scrum team and empowering them to decide what the development team will build and in what order, the business can guide the work. Sometimes the product owner is likened to a race car driver, steering the development team in the right direction to take advantage of business opportunities and deliver the most value.

The product owner is sometimes likened to a race car driver, steering the development team in the right direction.

The product owner owns the return on investment (ROI) of the development team. This results in the product owner seeking out all available information about what will drive the highest value for the business, and ensuring that information drives the priority order of the development team's work. What work provides value to the business will vary widely, but in the context of a for-profit business it typically means whatever will drive the highest profit.

The product owner is the *overall vision holder* for the product produced by the development team. The product owner decides what work is to be done, in what order, and the criteria against which the development team's work is measured to determine whether the work is acceptable. This information is contained in the product backlog.

The product owner is the *only* individual in the organization empowered with ownership of the product backlog. Others in the organization may provide input to the product owner, but she is the only one who can make decisions about the contents and priority of the backlog, and everyone in the organization must respect her decisions.

The product owner is not allowed to tell the team *how to do the work*. Only the development team can decide how the work is to be completed to the product owner's satisfaction.

This avoids what many developers have experienced over the years, which is a non-technical manager trying to tell them how to do their job.

One variation of this is the non-technical manager going to the whiteboard and explaining how to design the database. If the developers ignore the suggestions and do what they know is right, they risk the manager's wrath. If they instead implement the manager's suggestions and later encounter problems, that can cost time to fix. It's a no-win situation.

Scrum solves the problem by expressly forbidding this scenario.

Product owner responsibilities include the following:

- Create and maintain product backlog items. Others on the Scrum team can help with this, but the product owner is ultimately responsible for everything on the product backlog.

- Prioritize the product backlog to maximize the business value produced by the development team.

- Ensure product backlog items are clear, and answer questions as necessary to ensure everyone on the Scrum team understands them.

- Work closely with the development team to adjust product backlog items as necessary to maximize value as the product is built. For example, adjusting acceptance criteria to make a user story easier and faster to build if the development team encounters problems.

- Review and accept or reject the work of the development team.

7.2 The ScrumMaster

Lots of companies are eager to jump on the agile bandwagon. They get three days of training for their developers then turn them loose, expecting serious improvement.

For a short time, things might seem like they're going better. Daily scrums are happening. More code is being written. Stuff is being tested earlier than before. There's a lot of activity and things seem to be on the right path.

But then things start to go downhill. The daily scrums start to happen a few times a week. Time doing sprint planning is reduced, then eliminated altogether when developers say, "We don't have time to plan. We need to get more work done!"

All too often it's the beginning of the end. The company abandons Scrum altogether, things quickly go back to the way they were, and the result is a determination that "agile doesn't work."

The problem is because Scrum is so simple, most people underestimate what it really takes to become proficient.

Swinging a tennis racquet is simple too, but it's not easy to get good enough to win a tournament. I can't just take one lesson and expect to become a champion. I need continued practice, as well as continued coaching. I need someone to look at how I'm hitting the ball and help me make minor corrections. Then I need to practice those changes until they become automatic.

Scrum requires the same thing. Continued training, coaching, and mentoring are required to get team members to follow the guidelines and do the right things at the right times. They need to plan at the beginning of the sprint, they need to have a daily scrum, and they need to remain focused on the sprint goal and avoid getting distracted.

They also need to understand Scrum fundamentals and hear reminders about why the various moving parts of the process are important. Finally, they need to talk about the process and improve it over time.

Scrum solves this problem by embedding a Scrum coach right into the team, in the form of the ScrumMaster.

The ScrumMaster is the *owner of the process* and has the responsibility to ensure the development team members and product owner adhere to fundamental Scrum concepts, along with additional best practices that the development team has adopted over time as they've improved their process.

Extending our race car analogy, if the product owner is the race car driver, then the ScrumMaster is the mechanic, ensuring the car is always firing on all cylinders and moving as fast as possible.

The ScrumMaster is like a mechanic, ensuring the race car is always in top shape.

The ScrumMaster is responsible for helping the team identify impediments to progress and to the greatest extent possible, takes responsibility for ensuring impediments are resolved as quickly and efficiently as possible.

They may not have the ability to resolve impediments themselves, but they'll locate and manage the appropriate resources to ensure issues are resolved quickly.

Finally, the ScrumMaster ensures the team discusses how well the process is working to produce the highest business value in the shortest amount of time and identifies potential improvements. The ScrumMaster ensures the team actively experiments with their ideas and is responsible for adopting any successful experiments into the team's standard process.

Although the entire Scrum team should work together to adopt process changes that improve throughput, because the ScrumMaster is the owner of the process, he has the final say if there is disagreement. For example, if the Scrum team is debating between trying one-week versus two-week sprints and can't come to a decision, the ScrumMaster is empowered to say, "We're going to try two-week sprints for the next two sprints and see how it goes."

The ScrumMaster provides value to the product owner, the development team, and the organization. (Schwaber & Sutherland, 2017)

ScrumMaster responsibilities in service to the product owner:

- Ensure that the vision of the product owner—including goals, scope, and the context of the product—are understood by everyone on the Scrum team.

- Help the product owner with the product backlog, experimenting with new ideas for managing it effectively.

- Educate the Scrum team about why it's important that product backlog items are clear and concise.

- Help the product owner and development team understand the estimating and release planning process utilizing user stories, story point estimates, and velocity.

- Ensure the product owner knows how to prioritize the product backlog to maximize value.

- Assist the product owner and development team with understanding how user stories, bugs, and tasks are utilized on the product backlog.

- Facilitate Scrum ceremonies.

ScrumMaster responsibilities in service to the development team:

- Help the development team understand the Scrum framework and ensure they are working within its guideposts.

- Coach the development team on how to become self-organized and cross-functional.

- Ensure effective communication between the product owner and the development team.

- Remove impediments to the development team's progress.

- Facilitate Scrum ceremonies and ensure each development team member is engaged and participating during each ceremony.

- Protect the development team from outside distractions and an overly aggressive product owner.

- Ensure the development team continually innovates and improves the process.

ScrumMaster responsibilities in service to the organization:

- Help the organization in its Scrum adoption.

- Support Scrum implementations within the organization.

- Help those outside the Scrum team understand Scrum and how it benefits the business.

- Facilitate change that increases the productivity of the Scrum team.

- Work with other ScrumMasters to increase the effectiveness of Scrum throughout the organization.

- Help those not on the Scrum team understand which interactions with the team are helpful and those that are getting in the way of progress and help them change these behaviors to maximize value produced by the Scrum team.

7.3 The Development Team

In some companies, developers are viewed as a commodity.

Others will do the hard work of figuring out what to build, then the developers will be instructed about what needs to be done. Much like assembly line workers, they will simply put together some lines of code and produce the working product. Seems pretty easy. Their contribution isn't that important, is it?

I think this type of thinking squanders a valuable resource. The brainpower of some of the smartest people in the company is often under-utilized by traditional project management techniques, which focus on daily tasks rather than business results.

As I've discussed, Scrum turns this on its head, by empowering the development team with ownership and responsibility. Instead of telling them *how* to do the work we instead tell them what *outcomes* we want, then we say, "You figure out the rest."

This is one of the most valuable aspects of Scrum because it taps a resource—the collective brainpower of the development team—in a way that is seldom seen without this framework. Individual developers suddenly become first-class members of not only the development team, but the Scrum team as a whole.

Work goes from being "us" business analysts and project managers and "those" developers, to "us as a Scrum team."

Defining the Development Team

The group of individuals who create the product is called the development team. To drive a sense of teamwork, titles for each team member are downplayed in Scrum. The "job" of each member of the Scrum team is to do whatever they can each day to drive the work of the sprint to done and achieve the sprint goal.

If the product owner and/or ScrumMaster also works on the product in addition to their work in their Scrum role, they are considered to also be a member of the development team.

To round out the race car analogy, if the product owner is the driver, and the ScrumMaster is the mechanic, then the development team is the car itself.

If the product owner is the driver, and the ScrumMaster is the mechanic,
then the development team is the race car.

The Development Team Is Cross-Functional

The development team includes individuals collectively possessing the required skill sets to complete the work of each sprint. Although team members will possess certain special skills, to the greatest extent possible they do whatever they can to complete the work of the sprint, regardless of what that work may be.

This doesn't mean that testers will be asked to brush up on their programming skills and write production code or developers will be going to class to learn how to become visual designers. However, it may mean that developers may do some testing, or a front-end developer might do a peer review of a back-end developer's code.

This not only avoids silos—"Maria is out sick and she's the only one who knows how this code works"—but it increases the flexibility of the team as each team member learns more about each other's area of specialty over time. This is important because if the Scrum team is made up of only highly-specialized individuals who can only do one narrow type of work, it can hurt the team's productivity. (Brede Moe, et al., 2008)

Development Team Size

In addition to ensuring the development team is cross-functional—possessing the required skills to produce the product—it's also important that the team is the right size.

Too small, and the team won't collectively have enough skills to complete the work and make substantial progress.

Too large, and the ability to effectively communicate will become much more difficult. (DeMarco & Lister, 2013) Another side-effect of a development team that's too large is everyone not working as hard, typically called "social loafing." This concept describes team members not putting in as much effort because they assume others on the team will pick up the slack. (Latane, et al., 1979; Alnuaimi, et al., 2010)

The ideal team size is one that strikes a balance between these two extremes. The typical "best size" recommendation is between three and nine individuals. (Schwaber & Sutherland, 2017)

Jeff Bezos, founder of Amazon.com, uses a "two-pizza" rule for any team within the company. That is, the team should be able to be fed with no more than two pizzas. (Cohn, 2010b)

My guidance for maximum effectiveness is "seven plus or minus two." This is everyone on the development team, including the ScrumMaster if they will be doing the work of the sprint. It doesn't include the product owner.

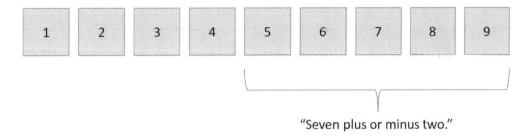

"Seven plus or minus two."

My recommendation for Scrum development team size is five to nine, applying the rule "seven plus or minus two."

This is based on research that shows humans can hold about seven plus or minus two objects in their working memory. Extending this to team design, this can lead to an ability to get to know team members better—and create a better group dynamic—if the size is aligned with this characteristic of how our minds work. (Miller, 1956)

Development team characteristics include:

- The team is self-organizing. That is, they decide *how* to do the work. No one, including the product owner and ScrumMaster, is permitted to tell the development team how to transform the product backlog into working, shippable software.

- The team is cross-functional, collectively possessing all the necessary skills to create the product.

- No titles are used for members of the development team, regardless of the skills possessed by each team member.

- Though individual team members may have specialized skills and a type of work they typically focus on, the development team as a whole is accountable for completing the work of each sprint.

- The development team decides how much of the product backlog they commit to completing during each sprint. No one outside the development team, including the product owner and ScrumMaster, can tell them, "You must complete the following product backlog items this sprint."

Key Takeaways

- The product owner permits the wants and desires of the business to be connected directly to the development team, steering them to work on the highest-value work.

- The ScrumMaster is the embedded Scrum coach on the Scrum team, ensuring team members understand and adhere to Scrum fundamentals.

- The development team is cross-functional, possessing all the necessary skills to produce a working, shippable product.

- The ideal size of the development team is three to nine individuals, and my recommendation is a slightly narrower range of "seven plus or minus two." Fewer than three results in not enough breadth of skill sets and more than nine leads to loss of productivity due to the amount of communication that's necessary and "social loafing," which results in lower individual productivity.

- No one outside the development team can decide how to do the work to produce a shippable increment, nor decide how much of the product backlog to commit to completing during each sprint.

- Using a race car analogy, the product owner is the driver, the ScrumMaster is the mechanic, and the development team is the car itself.

Chapter 8
The Sprint Backlog

All you need is the plan, the road map, and the courage to press on to your destination.

- **Earl Nightingale**, *radio speaker and author of The Strangest Secret, termed "…one of the great motivational books of all time."*

Where the rubber meets the road in Scrum is the day-to-day work of the sprint. For the sprint to be successful, everyone needs to know what they can work on each day to drive toward completing the sprint goal. Given the short duration of each sprint, it's critically important to avoid any wasted time because one or more team members are unfamiliar with the plan.

The sprint backlog documents the plan and allows day-by-day management of the work by the development team. It's a tool useful to *everyone* on the team and is at the heart of what allows the team to be self-managed.

During sprint planning, the team breaks down a handful of product backlog items into subtasks, each representing about a day or less worth of work. This "micro-planning" process results in the sprint backlog, which is the collection of those product backlog items and their related subtasks.

The sprint backlog includes:

- The product backlog items the development team believes they can complete during the sprint.

- For each product backlog item, a list of subtasks required to get it to "done." Ideally, each subtask could be completed in one day or less.

- For each subtask, an hour estimate of how long the development team thinks it will take to complete it.

As work is completed, team members update the remaining time on each subtask once or twice a day, which allows them to always understand how much work is left to be done to achieve the sprint goal.

8.1 Visualizing the Work of the Sprint with a Sprint Task Board

Although the sprint backlog can be managed in different ways—a document, spreadsheet, wiki page, or even on paper—most Scrum teams find the use of a *sprint task board* the most effective way to manage and visualize the sprint backlog.

A sprint task board facilitates collaboration through a graphical representation of the stories and their associated subtasks.

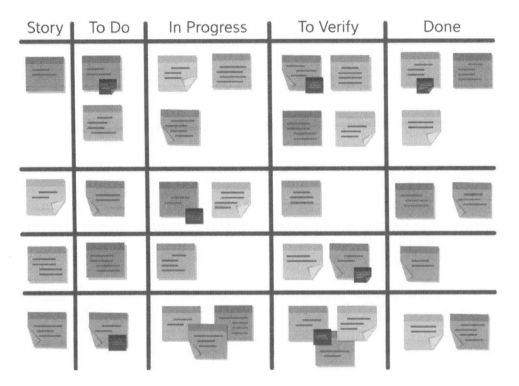

A sprint task board can be used to visualize the product backlog items and subtasks that make up the sprint backlog.

This prevents the plan from residing only in the heads of the team members. It's out there for the entire team to see and understand, and it's easy to find what to work on next. This allows the team to focus on strategic thinking during sprint planning, and heads-down tactical execution during the sprint.

The sprint task board typically has a row for each product backlog item and columns to represent different states for each subtask. As work is completed, subtasks move left to right from column to column. Once every subtask is in the "done" column, the item is done.

The columns include:

- *To Do,* which includes subtasks that have not yet been started.

- *In Progress,* which includes subtasks where some work has been started.

- *To Verify,* which includes subtasks that have been completed and are awaiting verification by another development team member.

- *Done,* which includes subtasks which do not require any remaining work.

Some teams omit the To Verify column, but I've found this column helpful to make it clear that, "This work is done, but it hasn't been checked yet." It helps development team members remember that everything should be cross-checked by another team member before it's considered done.

Some teams will skip the To Verify column for some types of subtasks. For example, our teams typically will include a variety of coding subtasks but also include a separate "Code Review" subtask. They will move the coding subtasks directly from In Progress to Done, knowing that the code will all be reviewed when they get to the Code Review subtask.

A low-tech sprint task board can be created using a whiteboard or piece of paper on the wall and sticky notes, such as the one shown below.

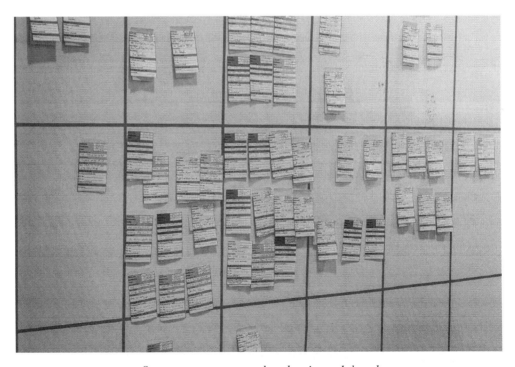

Some teams use a paper-based sprint task board.

Many teams, especially those that are distributed, find that a cloud-based tool is more effective for managing the sprint task board than a paper-based system.

Even for teams working side-by-side, a cloud-driven approach has benefits such as handling situations when a team member is traveling or working from home, the ability to support email notifications, and automatic generation of the sprint burndown chart, which I talk about later in this chapter.

Our teams use Jira, which is the leading agile project management tool, at least as of the time of this writing. A sprint task board in Jira is shown below.

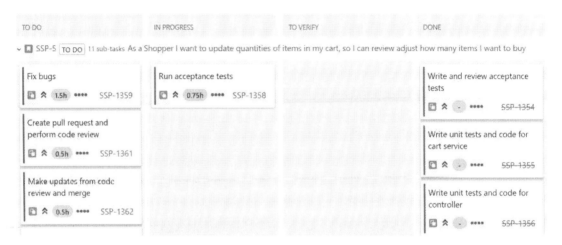

A sprint task board in Jira, a popular cloud-based agile project management tool.

8.2 Keeping Track of Who's Working on Each Subtask

When someone on the team volunteers for a subtask, they put their name on it so everyone on the team knows who owns the subtask. Typically, team members volunteer only for the work they'll either complete or make progress on prior to the next daily scrum.

Some teams fall into the trap of putting a name on every subtask in the sprint, resulting in a lack of flexibility. If Alex gets sick and he has his name on a bunch of subtasks, other team members who could help might be hesitant to grab one of those subtasks that Alex has claimed. I recommend avoiding this by sticking to the rule of adding names to represent only work for the day.

8.3 Understanding How Much Time Is Left for Each Subtask

Each subtask includes an estimate of the remaining hours required to drive it to done, including any time required in the To Verify column. As work progresses on a subtask, the remaining time estimate is updated by the development team based on their current estimate.

For example, if a developer spent 2 hours on a subtask in the morning and thinks he has 3 hours left to wrap it up after lunch, he'll update the remaining time to 3 hours before he heads out of the office. This keeps everyone up to date with the remaining work and drives the sprint burndown chart, providing a visual way for the team to track sprint progress.

Note that the remaining time may not be exactly in line with the team's original estimate. For example, Sara has spent some time working on a subtask. The original estimate was 4 hours and she spent 3 hours working on it, so she may feel like she should set the remaining time to 1 hour when she leaves for the day.

The problem is when she dug in she discovered it was harder than anyone thought, so she thinks there's still 3 hours of work left. Since it's much more important to know what's *really* left for work, she should set the remaining time to 3 hours, not 1 hour.

All that matters is the current estimate is as accurate as possible, based on the *current* understanding of the remaining work. This is often different from what was thought during sprint planning before everyone rolled up their sleeves and started the detailed work.

8.4 Tracking Sprint Progress with a Sprint Burndown Chart

Because the work of the sprint is broken down into subtasks, and each subtask has an estimate of how many hours are remaining, it's easy to sum them up and find out how much time is left. By comparing how fast the development team is completing the work—or "burning it down"—to how much time is left in the sprint, you can get a pretty good idea of whether things are on track.

Although this can easily be done in a spreadsheet using only numbers, a visual representation is easier to understand. A *sprint burndown chart* provides a graphical representation of the progress of the sprint by plotting the remaining hours of work over the calendar time of the sprint.

The sprint burndown chart can be generated by a tool, such as Jira, or created in a software application such as Microsoft Excel. The development team reviews the sprint burndown chart on a regular basis to monitor their progress.

The chart shown below is from Jira, for one of our current Ascendle client projects. The chart shows the remaining hours in red (1), and a "guideline" shown in gray (2) which shows where the team should be if they were burning down the same number of hours each day.

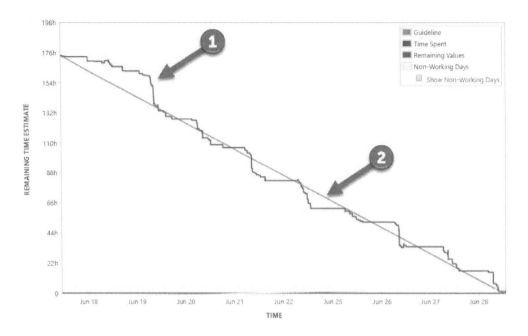

The sprint burndown chart shows a graphical representation of the sum of all subtask hours remaining in the sprint over time, with a history of the remaining hours (1) and a guideline showing the ideal burndown rate (2).

The status of the sprint can be immediately understood by looking at the current hours remaining as compared to the guideline.

If the remaining hours are **tracking with the line**, that means the sprint is on track and the development team is on their way to successfully delivering on their commitment to the product owner.

If the remaining hours are **below the line**, the development team is ahead of the game and if things continue along the way they've been going, they may finish early. In that case, they may be able to pull in additional work toward the end of the sprint.

If the remaining hours are **above the line**, the development team is behind and needs to make a course correction to get back on track. Our teams know if they're half-way through the sprint and above the line, they need to make a change—working smarter, staying a little late, or even pitching in over the weekend—or the sprint's success is in jeopardy.

The sprint burndown chart is the "health meter" of the sprint and I recommend teams closely monitor it and review it at the end of each daily scrum.

8.5 My Company Requires Status Reports. Can We Do That?

I often get a question along the lines of, "I'm required to create a weekly status report for management. I'm not sure that's going to magically go away. Is that allowed with Scrum?"

Scrum is all about the *simplest thing that could possibly work* and strips away anything and everything that's not absolutely necessary. After being used on thousands of projects over the years, every ounce of extra complexity has been beaten out, and what remains is what's fundamentally necessary to succeed. However, that doesn't mean the use of Scrum in your organization restricts you from conforming to standard company policies.

Status reports are often a necessary evil, especially in larger organizations. On most teams, these types of reports are often created by the ScrumMaster. Standardized reports can also be created by someone else in the project management office (PMO), to help shield the Scrum team from the report-creation process and boost their productivity. (Cohn, 2010b)

Your Reports May Become Redundant

What I often see is due to the increased transparency Scrum provides, especially in the form of producing a shippable increment each sprint along with a reliable schedule forecast, many reports become redundant. This is typically due to the reports being created to attempt to provide transparency to a waterfall approach, which is difficult due to not driving the product to a shippable state until the end.

Once you gain experience with Scrum within your organization, you may find opportunities to reduce or eliminate reporting requirement. This is a good topic for your sprint retrospective. Question whether reports are redundant now that there is more transparency and be careful to avoid falling into the trap of, "But this is how we've always done it."

Remember to be sensitive to management's perspective on Scrum. They may fear a loss of control, so if you immediately propose dropping all existing reporting requirements after your first sprint, there may be skepticism. (Mahnic & Zabkar, 2012)

This is where the ScrumMaster on the team can help. They can talk with those requesting the reports from the team and understand more about whether they can be replaced due to the increased transparency provided by the Scrum framework. Sometimes simply inviting those requesting the reports to sprint reviews will completely address their need for information.

In most cases, I've seen management quickly realize they're getting more than they ever did in the past and are quick to agree to remove any redundant reports.

Other Documentation Requirements

There are other types of requirements that may need to be dealt with during the sprint based upon your particular environment.

These may include compliance-related documentation for highly regulated industries such as healthcare or life sciences, tracking time to permit capitalization of development costs, and more.

You may want to consider including items such as these in your definition of done, to ensure the team considers them and adds appropriate subtasks to the sprint backlog to track the required work for each product backlog item.

Remember that "shippable" might include this kind of required documentation if the product can't go out the door without it. The related work to produce these documents may slip through the cracks if the team doesn't track it using subtasks.

As always, the product owner should work with stakeholders and the Scrum team to ensure all documentation requirements are, in fact, real. One of the best ways of boosting the throughput of the team is to eliminate work that's unnecessary.

Key Takeaways

- The sprint backlog is the collection of product backlog items the development team believes it can complete during the current sprint, and related subtasks that represent a breakdown of the plan to get the work done.

- Each subtask has an hour estimate of how much time is remaining to complete the work it represents. The development team updates the remaining hours at least once or twice a day, so the team always knows how much work remains.

- When a development team member volunteers for a subtask, they put their name on it. Most teams find it effective to volunteer only for subtasks that can be done in the next day, to permit the most flexibility for team members to work on any part of the sprint work.

- The sprint burndown chart provides a visual representation of the work to be completed. It can be generated using a spreadsheet or using an agile project management tool such as Jira.

- Scrum focuses on the simplest thing that could possibly work, and therefore is very lightweight. That doesn't prevent managing additional information required by your company, such as status reports, time tracking for capitalizing costs, and compliance-required documentation in highly regulated industries.

- Since Scrum provides much more transparency than waterfall projects, especially in the form of a demonstration of a shippable product increment at the end of each one-week to calendar-month sprint, many reports you're using today may become redundant. Take time at each retrospective and talk about whether any reporting requirements can be eliminated to save time, while still ensuring compliance with company or legal requirements.

Chapter 9
The Product

Build something 100 people love, not something 1 million people kind of like.

- **Brian Chesky**, *cofounder of Airbnb.*

One thing I love about agile is it focuses on the *process* of creating a product, but not at the *expense* of the product.

The product is always a first-class citizen. All the planning and day-to-day effort of each sprint is driven toward one single outcome—the production of a shippable product increment.

The team is a servant to the product.

Without a strong focus on the product, teams can slip into a routine of working hard, but slowly drifting away from aligning their efforts with what's in the best interest of the business and the end user. Instead, they start focusing on what's exciting to *them*.

This threatens the number one goal of the team: produce the highest business value in the shortest amount of time in a consistent and predictable manner. Scrum's continuous focus on creating incremental value at the end of each sprint eliminates this problem.

9.1 The Product Is Built Iteratively and Incrementally

Traditional waterfall development often has a very broad focus, across the entire software application. From requirements documents to technical specifications, there is consideration and detailed treatment for every aspect of the application from the start to well into the future. The application is often built in layers, and not driven to a state where it could be put into real users' hands until late in the process.

In contrast, agile shifts the focus from broad to deep. Although there is an appreciation for the overall vision, there is a razor-sharp focus on "thin slices"—small portions of the product that can be driven to a usable state—to deliver something usable as quickly as possible. The Scrum development team builds only a small part of the most important functionality during each sprint, and everything else waits until later.

Then they repeat the same process during the next sprint, which is again focused on creating a shippable product increment.

Collectively this gives us the "iterative and incremental" approach that is at the heart of the agile process.

For example, if a team was building a new social media app, they would start with "the simplest thing that could possibly work." They might decide that means starting with simply creating a post within the app, viewable by anyone who installs it.

Is that something the product owner would deploy to the app store? No. But it would be usable and would allow everyone to try out the most important feature of any social app—the ability to create and consume a message. They would also gain a solid understanding of what it really takes to drive some portion of the application to a "usable" state, including all related testing, bug fixing, and other adjustments.

This approach allows a Scrum team to start producing value very quickly—as early as their very first sprint. This supports transparency, since everyone knows exactly how much progress has been made toward the complete product vision by simply looking at what is "done." It also supports empiricism, by providing the ability for people to use and provide feedback about how well the product works. This avoids months or even years of work only to hear from users, "That's not what we wanted."

The "product" in Scrum—also called the "increment" or "potentially shippable product increment"—is the result of the Scrum team's work from all the completed sprints to date.

At the end of each sprint it must be in a usable state. That is, if the product owner decides to deploy it to production after the conclusion of any sprint, the development team wouldn't panic and say, "Um. We can't do that. We need to fix a bunch of things before it's *really* usable."

9.2 The Traditional Approach: Building 100% of Nothing

I'm sometimes asked to speak to a company because a waterfall software project has been chugging along for months or even years, and there is no end in sight. Everyone knows how long it's taken and how much it's cost the company to date, but no one knows when it will be done. The answer from the development team is, "It's coming along and we're making great progress!" But deadlines keep getting missed and the schedule is a pipe dream.

When they ask me how far along I think they are, I take a hard look at what they've been doing, and I'm not surprised when I see they haven't driven any part of the product to "done" yet. They've written a lot of code, and done some testing and bug fixing, but no one can sit down and use the product without explanations along the lines of, "Oh don't click there,

there's nothing there yet." Or, "There are still some problems with the calculations, so those numbers aren't right yet."

Due to this approach, there's no way to give the product to a customer, because none of it is done. It's like a bedroom renovation that's still missing a couple of sheets of drywall, is half-painted, part of the floor has been installed, and there are wires sticking out of the wall. "It's almost done" is not the same as "I can live here."

Because there is no part of the product that is ready for someone to use unsupervised by an excuse-maker, they are dismayed when I say, "You're zero percent complete."

I always say this with a smile on my face, so they don't get *too* upset. But I'm trying to make a point and get their attention because they are in *serious* trouble.

I explain that there is absolutely no way to accurately predict how much longer the product will take to complete because nothing has been driven to "done" yet.

Then I draw a diagram like this on the whiteboard:

Because traditional software development focuses on building a small part of the entire application, but finishing nothing until the end, there is no way to accurately predict how long it will take to complete because nothing has been driven to "done."

Using a waterfall approach involves building individual components of the product that will eventually come together to form the entire product. First, the data layer might be coded. Then some business logic might be layered on top of it. Then perhaps the user interface. Finally, everything is tied together, and testing begins, only to find out that there are fundamental issues.

The diagram illustrates this problem. Work has been done on a little bit of every aspect of the product, but no part of the product is really done. Because testing comes at the end, nothing is driven to 100% until the conclusion of the process.

9.3 The Agile Approach: Building 100% of Something

In contrast, the agile approach is to build just a little bit of the product, but *drive it to completion* by the end of each sprint.

That is, the team focuses on just a small bit of product functionality—a handful of user stories—and that part of the product is truly "done" by the end of the sprint. All coding, testing, fixing bugs, and acceptance by the product owner is 100% complete and there are no open issues.

In contrast to the waterfall approach of building a little bit of everything, but driving nothing to done until the end, the Scrum approach looks something like this:

The Scrum approach is to work on only what's in the current sprint, and drive that to a fully-tested, shippable state. The process repeats each sprint to build out more functionality, but what's in the product is always 100% complete and shippable.

There are three major benefits to this approach.

First, **everyone knows how much time it took** to drive a portion of the product to "done," in contrast to the traditional approach where you don't really know until the day you ship.

Because you know how fast you're moving and how far you have to go—the total story points in the remaining user stories—you can create a pretty accurate schedule forecast.

Second, **no time is spent on any work that's not the highest priority**. This means priorities for work not in the current sprint can change at any time, and no work will be thrown away.

Finally, **the company gains a huge amount of flexibility in their schedule**, simply by reducing scope. For example, a release that was estimated to take 8 months can be reduced to 6 months simply by moving stories to the next release. Because the product owner prioritized the highest business value stories to be built first, you're guaranteed that what gets pushed off is of lesser value.

"Shipping two months early" becomes easy with Scrum. Simply defer enough low-value stories to the next release to get the timeframe you want.

You might say, "Um. Yeah, Dave. Reducing scope is nothing new. I can do that today."

You'd be right, you can definitely reduce scope. But there are three major benefits when you're reducing scope *and* using an agile approach:

- You *don't lose money.* With a waterfall project, you'd have to rip out a bunch of code that was written in anticipation of features that have now been shelved. With Scrum, no code is written that's not necessary to support the current functionality being built.

- You *know how much scope to defer.* Because you have a schedule forecast based on empirical evidence and not wishful thinking, you can determine exactly how many user stories you need to push off.

- You *still get the highest amount of value.* Since the highest-value stories are always built first with Scrum, those you defer will be of lesser value.

The big takeaway here is that driving the product to "done" early and often grants you *power.*

You have the power to make changes. You have the power to put the product into someone's hands whenever you want. And, you have the power to ship when you want.

9.4 The Definition of Done

An important part of Scrum working is making sure everyone knows what "done" actually means. This is critical because if the product owner assumes that "done" means all testing has been completed and all bugs have been fixed—a reasonable expectation if the product is to be in a shippable state—but the development team assumes testing and fixing will come later, that can cause a big problem.

A solid definition of done is a critical success factor for Scrum teams. That is, teams with a more well-defined and strict definition of done are typically more successful than those that have no definition of done, or one that's less well-defined. (Green, 2011)

The definition of done applies to the completion of a product backlog item—for example, a user story or a bug fix—and collectively the product increment as a whole. That is, at the end of the sprint, all new product backlog items that are considered "done" are expected to meet the definition of done.

Example Definition of Done

The definition of done varies, but might look something like the following:

- All code that has logic or calculations is covered by automated unit tests, and all unit tests are passing.

- For bug fixes, a unit test has been written that fails when the bug is present and passes after the bug has been fixed.

- All new code has been peer reviewed and any suggested adjustments have been made.

- All acceptance criteria are satisfied.

- New stories have been tested manually using a written test plan based on the story's acceptance criteria.

- All bugs have been fixed.[1]

- Code for stories that meet this definition of done has been integrated with all other code completed to date, and that code is what is used by the product owner for their review.

- All functionality meets documented performance standards.

- No code is in the product that doesn't meet this definition of done.

- The product owner has reviewed the functionality for new stories, any requested adjustments have been made by the development team, and the product owner has accepted the story.

- Any pertinent end-user documentation has been written, reviewed, and accepted by the product owner.

---

[1] Some teams adjust this slightly, for example permitting a product owner to not fix minor bugs that are very time-consuming to address and that she decides are unlikely for users to encounter. Or, deferring fixing bugs introduced in prior sprints until the next sprint, to avoid distracting the team during the current sprint.

It may seem like a lot of work is involved to drive any story to "done," if it needs to satisfy all these criteria. And that's the point. Scrum essentially accelerates the entire software development lifecycle to happen multiple times per sprint, once for each product backlog item.

Benefits of a Good Definition of Done

The benefits of a solid definition of done are both understanding what it takes to get new functionality to the right level of quality and knowing that everything completed to date is ready and doesn't need more work.

Another key benefit of a good definition of done is preventing last-minute delays. There's nothing worse than starting the process of deploying to production and someone realizing, "Oh shoot. I just remembered we didn't do X." By sitting down and thinking through what would truly make everyone feel good about the product being usable, those types of "I forgot" issues tend to go away.

What Makes a Good Definition of Done?

The overall themes of most good definitions of done are twofold:

- *Quality*. For example, notice how many items I listed above that are designed to detect and eliminate bugs.

- *Completeness*. For example, my list included a reminder that end-user documentation needs to be kept up to date.

I encourage you to sit down with your Scrum team and key stakeholders to discuss what "done" means to them. What checklist items would make everyone comfortable that the product is always in a usable state?

Capture what you come up with in your definition of done.

"Done" and Sprint Reviews

The most successful teams employ a best practice of only demonstrating stories at sprint reviews that meet the definition of done, to ensure everyone understands how much of the product is *really* shippable.

Those stories that don't satisfy *all* the criteria of the definition of done are not demonstrated and are returned to the product backlog.

9.5 Shippable vs Something You Would Ship

Many teams I've worked with get confused when I talk about making the product "shippable." They say, "Dave, if we only build the ability to create a post in our social media app, but anyone who installs the app can see all posts created by everyone, can we really *ship* that? That wouldn't make any sense."

I then reply, "Don't confuse *shippable* with *something you would ship*."

Shippable is a statement of quality. It means, "We're comfortable that what has been built to date is at a level of quality that someone can use it, and we won't have egg on our face because it doesn't work correctly."

It also means that the development team hasn't built a portion of a feature that's not actually usable. For example, they haven't slipped into old habits and built the data layer and business layer for a new feature, but no user interface yet. I often say, "You can't ship a layer." It has to be *usable* from the perspective of your target users."

Something you would ship is instead a decision that says, "We've completed enough functionality that someone can use it and get at least some value from it."

A common term used to describe something that you would want to ship is the *minimum viable product* or MVP. This is the smallest amount of functionality that delivers value to some portion of your user base.

In *The Lean Startup*, Eric Ries describes the minimum viable product as one that helps, "…start the process of learning as quickly as possible." (Ries, 2011)

This idea—building something small and learning about how users react—acknowledges that you don't *truly* understand what users want until they see working software. (Lacey, 2012) The MVP approach allows you to get the product in front of users as quickly and as inexpensively as possible.

There are variations on this theme, such as *minimum usable product* or even *minimum lovable product*.

The key point is although you might not decide to deploy the product to end users at the end of a sprint, everything that is completed to date could theoretically be put in the hands of a user.

Key Takeaways

- The product—also called the increment, shippable increment, or shippable product increment—is the collection of all the work to date by the Scrum team from all prior sprints.

- In contrast to traditional software development, the focus in Scrum is on building 100% of a small portion of functionality and driving it to a usable state at the end of each sprint.

- Driving the product to done each sprint grants you *power*, by allowing you to truly understand how long it will take to complete the current version, as well as shorten the schedule by deferring lower-value user stories.

- A definition of done is a critical tool to ensure everyone knows what "done" means. Its main areas of focus are on quality and completeness, which avoids last-minute delays by ensuring everything required has been completed.

- Shippable is a statement of quality, whereas something you would ship is a statement of completing enough of the product that at least some portion of the user base can use it every day and get at least some value.

- Minimum viable product, or MVP, is a term often used to describe the smallest amount of functionality that can deliver value to end users. Another way to think about this is, "What's the minimum feature set that we'd need to have in order for someone to buy our product?"

Part II

Understanding Agile Software Construction

It is not the beauty of a building you should look at; it's the construction of the foundation that will stand the test of time.

- **David Allan Coe**, *American singer and songwriter.*

Chapter 10
Introduction to Agile Software Construction

Quality is not an act, it is a habit.

- ***Aristotle***

So far in this book I've talked a lot about Scrum, which I've called a *social engineering framework*. I've told you that people are the most important part of the equation, and the members of the Scrum team communicating and working together effectively is the key byproduct of adopting this approach.

What I've also talked about is a pretty radical way to develop software, as compared to traditional waterfall development. Instead of long, drawn-out phases of requirements, design, coding, testing, and acceptance, I've explained how Scrum crams everything into a very short amount of time—a sprint lasting one week to a calendar month.

You've taken it on faith that this is, in fact, possible—that you can successfully streamline software engineering processes that historically have taken months or years and compress them into a matter of weeks or even days. But I haven't told you exactly *how* to accomplish this feat.

Scrum doesn't include any guidance on software engineering techniques. Instead, it says that teams are "self-organizing and cross-functional" and they "choose how to best accomplish their work, rather than being directed by others outside the team." (Schwaber & Sutherland, 2017)

I love this concept—keeping those with the most knowledge about building the product in charge of how to get it done. But I've found that in practice, most development teams don't know enough about contemporary software engineering techniques to successfully do what's being asked: deliver high-quality software in a very short amount of time.

This isn't to say they don't know what they're doing. Many software engineers are well-read about the latest software development techniques and are likely pushing the organization to utilize more contemporary practices. For example, designing more flexible architectures, adding more test automation, and automating the process of deploying code.

But what I've found as I've worked with mid-sized and Fortune 500 companies is although they are typically on the right track, there hasn't been a compelling reason to focus on consistent adoption of these techniques. The result is when it comes time to adopt Scrum and speed things up, there is a focus on learning the process, but not enough emphasis on tuning up the technical discipline to support rapid development.

It's not for lack of desire on the part of the developers, but more lack of appreciation—particularly by the rest of the organization—of just how important certain software construction techniques are to the success of the Scrum team.

This chapter and those that follow in this part of the book are my answer to that problem. I describe the software construction practices I've seen help teams deliver the most consistent and successful results, day after day and sprint after sprint.

My goal is to help you understand not only what these concepts are and how they fit into the development process, but also why they are so critical to your team's success.

10.1 What Is "Software Construction?"

The chapters leading up to this one have focused on the Scrum framework, describing how the needs of the business are connected directly into the Scrum team, how the details of what needs to be built are managed, how the team is designed, and how they communicate.

What I didn't talk about is what happens between the point the product owner writes a story and discusses it with the development team, and the point where that story is completed and ready for end users.

Everything between these two points is software construction, which is what's required to turn the product owner's vision into a shippable product.

"Software construction" is everything needed to turn the vision of the product owner into a shippable product increment.

"Construction" typically means "the act of building something." It's the hands-on work of turning vision into reality.

In the context of software development, construction is mostly about writing and debugging code, but also includes managing development and testing environments, technical design, unit testing, integration testing, test automation, and other activities. (McConnell, 2004)

10.2 Why Is Software Construction So Important in an Agile Context?

With waterfall projects, all the steps in the construction process happen, but they tend to get a higher or lower level of focus depending on the current phase of the project. For example, if coding is just starting, there may not yet be much time spent thinking about how to deploy the product into a separate, clean environment to permit quality assurance testing. And it's unlikely the team is thinking through what it will take to deploy it to a production environment at that early stage.

In contrast, with Scrum there's one big reason you can't "wait until later" to figure these things out—the product must be potentially shippable at the end of each sprint. That is, newly-completed stories are bug-free and no new bugs have been introduced into functionality completed in prior sprints.

An additional challenge is that "shippable" means if the product owner decides that enough stories have been completed to provide value to users, and he wants to release it, the development team can't say, "Oh. I didn't realize 'shippable' meant it should be ready to be deployed to production. It will take us *months* to get the production environment ready." That would defeat the whole concept of a "potentially shippable product increment" being produced each sprint.

Though not part of "official" Scrum, I also recommend this rule: the product must be deployable into production within the timeframe of one sprint or less. Many teams call this a "release sprint," since the goal is to release the shippable product increment. It includes the process required to deploy and verify the product in the production environment.

To put this into perspective, if you use two-week sprints, *everything* required to finalize the product and get it into production needs to happen within two weeks.

A release sprint might also include some final integration testing that is too time-consuming to complete every single sprint, though this shouldn't be viewed as permission to "cheat" on the standard of making sure the product is at a shippable level of quality at the end of each sprint. (Cohn, 2010b)

What this means in practice is as the Scrum team gets up to speed and prepares to start their first sprint, they need to be thinking about how to get the product properly tested each sprint and how to quickly and easily deploy it into production. I'll talk more about this later in Part III, *Laying the Groundwork*.

This puts a lot of pressure on not only the development team, but also many other parts of the organization. For example, DevOps groups that are used to the slower pace of waterfall projects need to learn how to adapt to the needs of Scrum development teams and help them get their ducks in a row much earlier.

Some of the world's leading companies have gotten so good at agile and its related software construction techniques that they have reached the pinnacle of "rapid development." Etsy deploys code 50 times per day into production, Netflix deploys code thousands of times per day, and Amazon deploys every 11.7 *seconds*. (Miranda, 2014; Null, 2015) Those numbers are a few years old, so they may be even more impressive today.

Do you need to be able to deploy your code to production hundreds or thousands of times per day? Perhaps not. But I bet your development teams can learn some lessons from these industry leaders, who are using most if not all the software construction techniques I describe in this book.

I call the process of writing code and the related design and testing work *agile software construction*. This type of construction has the characteristic of needing to dramatically accelerate all the technical "stuff" that waterfall teams have the luxury of figuring out over the course of months or years.

10.3 Why You Need to Know About This Technical "Stuff"

This book is focused on how to use agile techniques to help you deliver better results faster by using the Scrum framework. The target audience includes those charged with rolling out Scrum in their organization and facilitating the fundamentals of the process, and they are not always highly technical.

If this is the case, why am I including a bunch of technical concepts?

What I've found is that it's helpful for *everyone* on the Scrum team to know—at least at a high level—how the software construction process works. This raises the level of empowerment on the team by making everyone aware of what's happening under the covers and putting the daily work of the developers in context. This ensures everyone is capable of effectively driving toward completion of the sprint goal.

For example, one of the concepts I'll be talking about in Chapter 12 is managing source code for a new user story. I'll talk about a way to keep the not-yet-tested code separate from the shippable code completed in prior sprints. If I want to test that new story, it's important for me to understand this concept so I know where to find the right code to use. Otherwise, I may get confused and slow down progress.

10.4 Agile Software Construction Concepts

In the rest of the chapters in this part of the book, I'll be talking about a variety of concepts to allow you to accomplish the following:

- *Get solid code written,* by creating a clear technical design and the use of peer code reviews.

- *Empower any Scrum team member to test quickly and easily,* through the use of lightweight "team test" environments and a "product owner" environment that can be used to accept or reject the work of the development team.

- *Keep the product shippable,* through the use of automated unit tests and test-driven development, as well as keeping new code isolated until it's ready to be incorporated into the product increment.

- *Adapt to change,* by using refactoring techniques to evolve code over time as new functionality is added.

Key Takeaways

- Software construction is everything that goes into moving from the product owner's vision as represented by the product backlog to a shippable product increment. This includes not only coding, but also technical infrastructure such as development and testing environments, automated unit testing, and integration testing.

- Because Scrum requires the product to be shippable at all times, things that typically can "wait until later" with waterfall projects need to be accelerated and figured out at the very beginning of a Scrum team's work on the product. For example, the process of deploying the product into a clean environment for testing purposes is critical to allow the team to test code and for review and acceptance by the product owner. I call this *agile software construction.*

- Though many development teams are pushing for adoption of high-productivity software construction concepts such as test-driven development and automated deployment, moving to Scrum brings a much higher level of importance to utilizing these techniques.

- Many teams use a "release sprint" to complete the process of getting the shippable product increment into production when the product owner determines it's ready for use. This should take no longer than one sprint.

- Even though agile software construction concepts are technical in nature, it's important for everyone on the Scrum team to understand the moving parts, to empower them to fully contribute to completing the work of each sprint.

Chapter 11

Creating a Shippable Increment Requires Team Test Environments

No one knows the cost of a defective product—don't tell me you do. You know the cost of replacing it, but not the cost of a dissatisfied customer.

*- **W. Edwards Deming**, American engineer whose ideas formed the foundation of the Toyota Production System and which launched the Total Quality Management movement.*

A Fortune 100 company had been attempting to make their teams successful with the Scrum framework when they asked me for some help. As we were getting started, I asked the leader of the group how things were going, and he said, "We're having trouble with quality."

I asked for more details and he explained, "Our teams are writing code during one sprint, handing it off to the QA team the next sprint, and fixing bugs the third sprint.

"We are having a hard time getting a lot done, because most of every sprint is just spent fixing bugs, and that takes a lot of time, especially since it's been over a month since they wrote the code. They haven't been able to produce the predictable schedule I was promised when we started this whole thing."

I smiled as I asked, "Have you considered having the development team do their own testing in the same sprint in which they're writing new code?"

He looked at me and said, "I don't think that's possible. They don't have access to the testing environments. Only the QA team does." He looked down at the table and thought for a moment, then looked up. "Can you help us?"

That was the beginning of what's become a great relationship. I've helped the Scrum team and—more importantly—the management team understand that creating a "potentially shippable product increment" at the end of each sprint does, in fact, mean it needs to be at a *shippable* level of quality—*every* sprint.

They fell into a trap I see many teams experience. First, they glossed over the whole "potentially shippable increment at the end of each sprint" thing. Second, they didn't sit down and think through how they'd empower the team to test.

I see this pattern over and over, and it's not usually something that can be solved overnight. This chapter talks about what I feel is the most important success factor for making Scrum work in your organization: providing your Scrum team with the environments they need to test their own code throughout every sprint; to empower them to truly create a shippable product increment at the end of each sprint.

11.1 Testing at the End Doesn't Work with Agile

Dr. Winston W. Royce wrote a landmark paper in 1970, which many point to as the origin of the waterfall concept. But even then, Dr. Royce acknowledged a major limitation to this approach. He believed in the sequential process he described but he said, "…the implementation described…is risky and invites failure."

He went on to say that since it's only at the end of the development cycle that the software is "experienced" as opposed to "analyzed," that if the software doesn't work as expected, "…invariably a major redesign is required." He points out that, "In effect, the development process has returned to its origin and one can expect up to a 100-percent overrun in schedule and/or costs." (Royce, 1970)

That doesn't sound like a lot of fun, but it's what we see over and over again with waterfall.

As you've read in previous chapters, Scrum combats this directly by driving the product to a potentially shippable state at the end of every sprint. If this standard is not met, the team quickly runs into the same issues pointed out by Dr. Royce all those years ago and introduces the risk of re-work. This slows the team down and increases time and cost.

However, some companies don't recognize the importance of adhering strictly to this standard. They keep their separate quality assurance department and the development team "hands it over the fence" at the end of each sprint, and the QA folks take it from there.

To realize the benefits of Scrum, there needs to be a shake-up with the organization's approach to testing, and it needs to be accelerated to occur within each sprint.

11.2 Test Environments Eliminate "Works on My Machine!"

Your first reaction to the idea of the development testing during the sprint might be, "That's not a big deal. We can still keep our QA team separated and we'll just have developers test on their own computers during the sprint."

Some teams take this approach. Some time after the sprint ends, the code—which was deemed rock-solid by the developers—is deployed by the QA team into a test environment. Much to the dismay of everyone involved, it doesn't work.

This is a classic case of, "It works on my machine! You guys need to figure out what the problem is on your end." This is typically the result of the mistaken assumption that if the code runs properly on a programmer's computer, it will run properly in a production environment.

Developers often have special tools installed on their computers and unknowingly introduce dependencies upon those tools. Once the code is moved to a "clean" computer that doesn't have those tools, the product breaks. All too often, the first time the product is run on a clean computer is a few weeks before the scheduled release date.

To solve this problem, the Scrum team needs their own "clean" environments, less like programmer workstations, and more like the environment that will eventually be used when the product goes live in production.

By using a test environment that's similar to what the production environment will look like, your team will accelerate the discovery of issues caused by differences between the developer machines and the test environment. This avoids "works on my machine" problems from happening too late in development. (Duvall, et al., 2007)

Note that you do *not* need the performance of a production-class environment. Team test environments can be very lightweight. The important thing is that they are configured in a way that's similar to what will be used in production. For example, if the application will be deployed to a cloud-based configuration, create a cloud-based setup for your test environments.

But this server doesn't need to have the same horsepower, redundancy, and scalability of your eventual production environment. The *simplest thing that could possibly work* principle is definitely applicable here, so keep it simple.

11.3 What the Scrum Team Needs for Test Environments

Many companies already use test environments. Common environments include QA, Staging, and Production. But what I've seen at most companies is these are used at some point *after* the conclusion of each sprint. The problem I see time and time again is there's no easy way for the Scrum team to ensure their code works *before* the end of the sprint.

The solution is simple: give teams their own environments. In this section, I outline a way to address this challenge, and later in this chapter I talk about ways to create these environments quickly, simply, and inexpensively.

Three Types of Environments

Over the years I've experimented with a variety of test environment strategies with my teams and have found that if they have three types, they can do the testing they need throughout each sprint.

This ensures they can drive the product to "done" before it reaches other downstream environments, increasing the quality of the product, the speed of development, and the accuracy of the schedule.

They include:

Programmer workstations, which allow individual software developers to write and run their own code.

Team test environments, to empower the team to deploy and test code for new stories being completed during the sprint. I recommend two of these to enable deploying code for two different stories—one in each environment—to permit testing them both simultaneously.

The product owner acceptance environment, which allows the product owner to test and accept or reject new stories in a fully integrated fashion.

Three types of environments empower the team to perform required testing throughout each sprint.

Programmer Workstations

Each programmer on the team needs their own computer to write and run their code. It's probably obvious that a programmer needs a computer, but what sometimes slips through the cracks is the developer's ability to *run the product*.

The technical requirements vary, but often there needs to be a way for the developer to have a local database and in many cases other related components. In some cases, it may not be feasible for the developer to run everything locally—though that is the ideal situation—and may instead need to tie into a shared environment.

For example, if the product depends upon a third-party web service, the developer may need to connect to a "sandbox" version of that service.[2] That developer will need to know how to access that web service and likely will need some sort of credentials to establish the connection.

The key point is the development team needs to figure out what they require, and management needs to support them. For example, someone from another department might need to provide the appropriate access to some of the components they require to run the product.

Team Test Environments

Because Scrum focuses on doing a little bit of everything all the time, that means testing should start shortly after coding begins for each user story. This helps identify any bugs quickly so they can get resolved right away.

As I talked about in the last section, the risk of testing on programmers' computers is the software may work fine in that type of environment, but not in a "clean" environment.

What I call "team test" environments provide this type of clean configuration. I use the term "team test" to differentiate them from "QA" environments, which can mean different things in different companies. Plus, "team test" makes it clear they're for the team's use.

When a user story's code is ready for testing, the code for that story is deployed to a clean team test environment and testing is performed there.

To prevent fighting over one team test environment, I recommend having two. This permits testing two stories simultaneously, while keeping the code for each story separate from the main product code until it's fully tested. The code for one story can be deployed to the first environment, and the code for another story can be deployed to the second. Testing can then be performed on both.

This helps teams be more flexible, since it's often not feasible to have everyone working on one user story at a time without getting in each other's way.

---

[2] A sandbox is a special version of a service that behaves exactly like the real thing but doesn't process live data. For example, a sandbox environment for a payment processing service would allow the application to process transactions, but they wouldn't be charged to a real credit card. This approach ensures the application will in fact work when tied into the live version of the service.

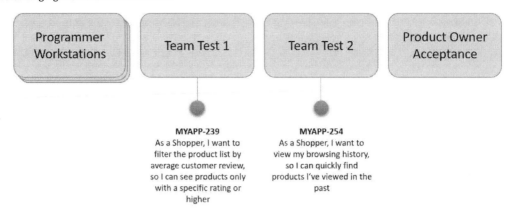

Two team test environments permit testing two different user stories simultaneously.

Once any discovered bugs have been fixed, the code can be re-deployed to the appropriate team test environment and re-tested.

Once a user story is complete and has been handed off to the product owner for his acceptance, one of the team test environments can be used for the next story to be completed.

Product Owner Environment

Before any story can be considered "done," the product owner needs to review and accept it. Over the years, our teams have found the most effective way to do this is to ensure the product owner reviews user stories in a fully integrated fashion. That is, the code for the user story should be tested alongside all other code completed to date.

The product owner environment always has the latest integrated code. Before handing off a story to the product owner, the development team completes their testing and bug fixing, performs a code review, and merges the code with the rest of the completed code to date. That code is then deployed to the product owner's environment and he does his testing there.

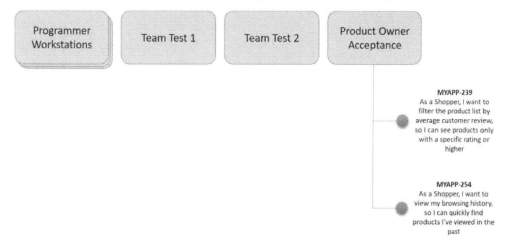

When a user story is ready for the product owner's review, its code is integrated with the rest of the completed stories to date and deployed to the product owner's environment.

If the product owner finds any issues, the development team fixes it in the integrated codebase, and re-deploys it to the product owner's environment.

Note that when things are working effectively, the product owner shouldn't find any major issues during their review. The development team should have fully tested and "certified," so to speak, that the user story is fully shippable and free of bugs.

11.4 Providing Test Environments May Require Creative Thinking

One major problem I've seen at larger companies is the development team's lack of control over their test environments. This is typically for a good reason—most environments created and maintained to date are customer-facing and need to have strict controls over things such as security and operating system updates. They also often have complex configurations of multiple, clustered servers to handle high workloads.

One thing to keep in mind is the environments required by the team are not of the same variety of those containing sensitive data, so you should be careful not to hold the team back by requiring their environments meet the same standard of centralized control.

In the worst case, I sat down with some of the leaders at a company I was helping with their agile adoption. I explained to them the required environments the Scrum team would need for testing. "That's going to be a problem," they said. "We have outsourced IT and it usually takes about six months to provision a new environment." Given the team was scheduled to start in a couple of weeks, this was a major issue.

The managers negotiated with their higher-ups and through some creativity, they were able to provision some Amazon cloud-hosted computing resources.

This illustrates the type of shift required when moving to an agile approach. It requires a change in most areas of the company. In this case, the company needed to adjust their mindset from "we're at the mercy of our outsourced IT company" to "we need to figure this out, and quickly." Otherwise, they wouldn't have been able to properly support Scrum teams in the organization.

One point I'd like to make here is the team test environments I'm talking about in this chapter are *not* customer-facing. They should never have any "real" data or tie into "real" systems. That is, they should only use fake test data and tie into sandbox and other types of test environments.

They also don't need the same level of computing resources required for production use. In most cases, a very light amount of computing horsepower can be utilized, because the primary purpose of the environments is for functional testing. Performance testing is also important, and a specific environment might be required for that, but the day-to-day testing by the Scrum team can be done in simple environments.

11.5 The Scrum Team Needs to Control Their Test Environments

A couple of years ago I was helping a new Scrum team at a large company with the process of provisioning their test environments, to prepare for starting their sprints in a few weeks. The team requested environments from the DevOps group, which soon got them ready and handed them over to the team.

The DevOps group told them, "We've locked everything down, so you can't screw them up. If you need any changes, come see us." This sounded good at first—someone else would be responsible for maintaining the environments!

As the team got into their first sprint, they quickly learned they didn't have the access they needed to get their code running correctly. They went back to DevOps and found out new priorities had come up and were told, "We'll enter a ticket and we should be able to get to it in about three weeks."

That didn't help, since the team was part of the way through their two-week sprint. After a lot of begging and promises of bringing in some coffee and donuts the next day, one of the DevOps guys stayed late and got them up and running. It worked out in the end, but it was a little stressful for a few days when the team thought they were dead in the water.

The Scrum development team really needs *full* control over their environments. As far as "messing things up," this is part of the responsibility of ownership. DevOps can certainly provide guidelines to help the team understand any specific company policies to which they need to adhere. But other than that, give them free reign.

If the team does run into trouble and needs help or has questions that they can't answer, they can typically find someone within the organization to resolve the problem. In my experience this seldom happens, because the collective experience of the development team members is usually enough to deal with things like installing software components and configuring security within the environment.

This concept is a key part of empowering the team—let them own their test environments and trust that they'll do the right thing.

11.6 The Ability to Automatically Deploy Code Is Critical

Many, *many* years ago, at my software startup, our product was deployed on 3 ½ inch floppy disks. Twelve of them. That meant to install our product you needed to sit by your computer and wait for it to prompt you to, "Please insert disk 8." It took forever.

The good news is those days are long behind us. The bad news is many teams don't do much better. They aren't using floppy disks, but they do have a multi-step manual process to deploy the product into an environment.

This results in a very time-consuming process to get code for a new story onto a test environment and, human nature being what it is, will typically result in the team resorting to just testing on programmer workstations. They quickly go back to "Works on my machine!" and encounter bugs very late in the process, typically during final testing before deploying to production.

The good news is today there are many tools that support *continuous deployment*. This is a fancy way of saying, "I can have the latest code configured and ready for use without any human interaction." Click a button and the code is automatically deployed in minutes to a specific environment.

The "continuous" part comes into play because you can connect the source code repository directly to a test environment. When a developer makes a code change—for example, to fix a bug—a re-deployment is kicked off automatically and the environment has the latest updates in a few minutes.

If your team is not familiar with this type of technology, I strongly recommend they spend some time learning about it. There is an up-front investment to get continuous deployment configured, but it's done *once*, then it "just works." It's a huge time-saver, especially since teams need to deploy each story multiple times to more than one environment. An automated process saves a *lot* of time.

11.7 Tools to Manage Team Test Environments

Years ago, at my old company, we had to purchase physical servers to create our team test environments. Later came virtualization, which allowed us to create separate virtual servers on one piece of hardware.

Fast-forward to today, and our teams don't deal with hardware at all. Every one of our test environments is managed in the cloud, in Microsoft Azure. What used to take weeks—from ordering the hardware, to configuring it with the required software—now takes about 15 minutes per environment.

A new Scrum team can spin up the two test environments and the product owner environment in less than an hour. Our total cost for the environments required by a typical development team ranges from about $150 to $300 per month, depending upon the specific resources that are required.

It's a beautiful thing.

Cloud-hosted Testing Environments

Although testing can be performed on in-house servers, I strongly recommend you consider cloud-hosted resources. Amazon and Microsoft are the market leaders with Amazon Web Services (AWS) and Microsoft Azure.

Leveraging the cloud offloads the heavy lifting to vendors who have spent billions on building and managing their hardware and software infrastructures, to make life easier for those of us who just want to deploy and run our products.

We've used this approach at Ascendle from the beginning, and our teams can spin up a new test environment in a matter of minutes—as compared to days, weeks or even months at many other companies. Another benefit is these environments are available to every team member, even though they're distributed across seven time zones.

Since most of our development utilizes Microsoft technology, Azure is the best fit for us, but both platforms are extremely capable and cost-effective.

There are two typical approaches when leveraging the cloud:

Infrastructure as a service (IaaS). This is very similar to the old way I used to manage our test environments. You create virtual servers on the cloud platform, and you manage everything within them. The cloud vendor handles the underlying hardware, storage, and networking.

For example, you create a Windows or Linux server, install the software you need, and keep it up to date with the latest service packs and updates, and configure it any way you want. This gives you the most control, but also increases the time you need to spend on its care and feeding.

Platform as a service (PaaS). In this case, you utilize just the specific services you need. For example, you can provision and pay for just a web server, or just a database. The platform vendor—Amazon or Microsoft, for example—manages everything else under the covers for you. The underlying server and operating system are always kept up to date, and you pay based on how much horsepower you need.

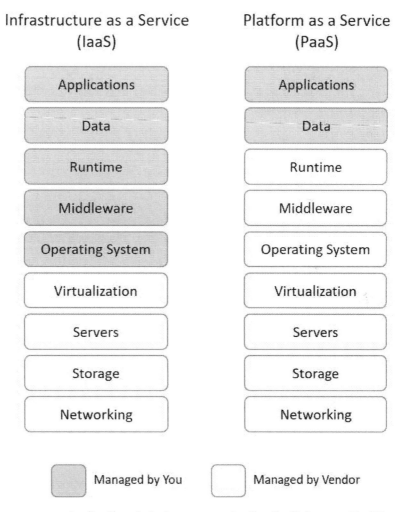

Infrastructure as a service (IaaS) and platform as a service (PaaS) offerings provide different ways of leveraging the cloud.

Recommended Approach

Most teams have found the PaaS approach to be both the most flexible and cost-effective. This is the approach we use and is what allows us to create our environments so quickly and at such a low cost.

This approach can also be used to deploy code to *containers*, which are fully-isolated computing environments that have come into widespread use in recent years. A container is like a virtual server, but much more lightweight and flexible.

Technologies such as Docker allow you to create, manage, and monitor containers. They are also portable. For example, a Docker container can be run on Linux or Windows and deployed to AWS or Microsoft Azure.

Development teams have found the cloud offers benefits such as the following: (Gao, et al., 2011)

- Dramatically reduce capital and licensing expenditures, by as much as 50% to 75%.

- Reduce operating and labor costs by as much as 30% to 50% by automating deployment and testing resource and provisioning.

- Shorten development and testing setup time from weeks to minutes.

- Improve product quality and reduce detected defects by as much as 15% to 30%.

- Help accelerate cloud computing initiatives.

Another benefit to cloud-hosted test environments is it's easy to empower teams to create and manage them. As I mentioned earlier in this chapter, it's critical that the development team has full control over their test environments.

Continuous Deployment Tools

Once you have your test environments set up, it's important for the development team to be able to deploy their code quickly. Continuous deployment tools allow the team to connect an environment directly to the source code management system. This type of tool monitors the source code repository for changes and automatically deploys them within minutes.

There are a variety of tools that you can use, including:

- *Jenkins*, a tool that can build and deploy your software in a variety of ways.

- *Bamboo*, which is similar to Jenkins, allowing you to automate the build and deploy process.

- *Bitbucket Pipelines*, which can automatically build and deploy your code to a cloud infrastructure. Pipelines is especially useful for deploying to Docker containers.

- *AWS CodeDeploy*, which supports building and deploying code to virtual servers.

- *Azure Continuous Deployment*, which allows automatically building and deploying code to an Azure App Service—essentially a web server—for your cloud application.

Our teams use Bitbucket Pipelines for our microservices-based projects, and Azure Continuous Deployment for other projects.

Key Takeaways

- "Testing at the end," which is common with a waterfall-based approach, isn't compatible with an agile approach. Because the product must be potentially shippable at the end of each sprint, the development team must perform their own testing of new stories and fix every bug they created during the sprint.

- If the Scrum development team doesn't have testing environments, they'll resort to testing on developer workstations. This introduces a major risk, since it can cause "Works on my machine!" That is, it works fine on the developer's computer but not on a "clean" server environment.

- In addition to the programmers' computers, I recommend two "team test" environments, used for testing each user story before it's deemed ready for review by the product owner. I also recommend a "product owner" environment, used by the product owner to test each story once its code has been integrated with the rest of the code completed to date.

- Many organizations are built around "testing at the end," and may need to get creative when provisioning test environments for their Scrum team. If it takes six months to provision an environment, company leadership may need to get involved to push things forward more quickly.

- It's critical that the development team has control over their environments. They can't run off to DevOps every time they need to make an adjustment to test their latest code— they'll never be able to move quickly enough to get their testing done before the end of the sprint.

- I strongly recommend leveraging a virtual cloud infrastructure to create and maintain test environments for the Scrum team. Today's market leaders are Amazon Web Services (AWS) and Microsoft Azure.

- Automatic deployment of code is a critical success factor. In many cases, code needs to be updated on the test environments multiple times per day. A manual process will be too slow and again, the team will face a barrier to getting to "done" during the sprint.

- There are a variety of *continuous deployment* tools, that automate the process of building and deploying code to test environments. Both Amazon and Microsoft have their own tools included with their cloud platform, and there are other third-party tools as well.

Chapter 12

Managing Source Code Properly Avoids Pain When "Life Happens"

Life is what happens to us while we are making other plans.

- **Allen Saunders**, *American writer, journalist, and cartoonist.*

Much of this book so far has focused on a fairly small timeframe—the duration of one or a handful of sprints, and the lifetime of the current release being driven to a point where it can go out the door and into the hands of users.

I've taken a fairly optimistic, "sunny day" approach to discussing the ins and outs of Scrum. I haven't discussed things such as how, exactly, you get the shippable product increment fully deployed into production.

I also haven't talked about how to deal with things that can go wrong, often at the most inopportune time.

These could include:

- The last user story in the sprint doesn't get to "done" by the end of a sprint.

- A weak developer writes code that is almost impossible to understand, and no one knows about it until months or years later when the next developer starts to enhance that area of the product.

- A severe bug is discovered in production, and it needs to be fixed *right now*, but the coding for the current sprint has begun and there are two user stories that are half-finished.

- The development team starts coding a user story, things go sideways, and the product owner decides to abandon the story and possibly return to it later.

In this chapter, I walk you through ways to anticipate and address each of these problems. I'll introduce you to a source code management strategy that ensures you have the maximum amount of flexibility, while keeping the product in a shippable state.

I'll also explain how this strategy provides a specific point in the process for a code review, to ensure there are no unpleasant surprises hiding in your product's source code.

12.1 Version Control Allows Effective Collaboration

When I was a kid, my sixth-grade teacher introduced me to programming. I immediately fell in love and started writing my own programs—text-based adventure games—and shared them with my classmates. That was 1984, and it was pretty novel to have a computer in the classroom. All the kids were enamored with what this new machine could do.

When I wrote a program, I started with some ideas on paper, then moved to the computer and wrote the source code. I saved the code on my computer, then copied it to a floppy disk to bring to school—did I mention this was a long time ago?

Today, it's rare for source code to live on just one computer, and we're well beyond using a floppy disk to move code around. To produce today's software, we work in teams; we need to share and manage source code, and we need to deploy it.

To effectively collaborate on code, developers need to keep track of the changes they make, and it's helpful to be able to see a history of those changes across each version of each source code file.

Version control—also called *source control* or *revision control*—addresses these issues by providing centralized storage of source code and tools that allow developers to collaborate and see a history of the changes each person has made over time

A software tool that facilitates version control is called a *version control system*. Popular version control systems include Team Foundation Version Control, Subversion, and Git. (Stack Overflow, 2018)

12.2 Branches Isolate Code to Manage the Unexpected

One of the main benefits of a version control system is the ability to manage changes by various developers over time. It's immensely helpful for each programmer to understand what changes others have made to the code. This helps keep them in sync and ensures they're working together in the most effective manner.

Contemporary version control systems allow *branching*, which permits a programmer to make what's effectively a virtual copy of the master source code of the product, to which they can make changes. These changes are isolated from the main product code.

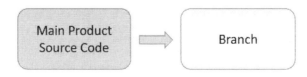

Branching allows making changes to code in isolation, protecting the main product code.

The benefit of this approach is all the changes made to the branch are completely isolated from the main codebase.

Later, they can *merge* that branch back into the main code base.

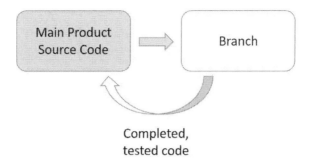

Only after changes in the branch have been tested and are working properly are they merged back into the main product code.

If something goes wrong in the branch and it's not working properly, there's no impact to the main product code because the developers will wait until everything is correct before merging it back in.

This technique works very nicely with an agile approach. A branch can be created for each user story, all the code for the story can be written and tested, bugs can be fixed, and code can be reviewed—all before it's merged back into the main product code.

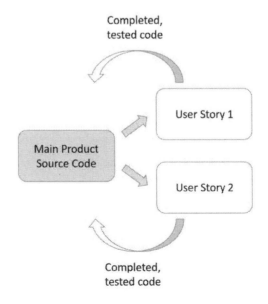

A branch can be used for each user story, allowing its code to be isolated until it's ready to go.

12.3 A Distributed Version Control System Makes Branching Easy

Traditional version control systems such as Team Foundation Version Control and Subversion support the concept of branching, but the way they handle it is very heavyweight and tends to be slow. This is because branching typically involves creating a complete, separate copy of all the source code for the entire product on the centralized server and this isn't nimble enough to be leveraged effectively by an agile team. (Chacon & Straub, 2014)

In contrast, a *distributed version control system* uses a different technique to manage files, based on each programmer workstation having a complete copy of all the source code—hence the term "distributed." This permits a much more lightweight branching technique, making creating a branch virtually instantaneous.

Although this may sound like it could increase complexity with a bunch of copies of all the code floating around the team, in practice it dramatically simplifies day-to-day coding work. Each developer can make changes and commit them to their local source code repository. Once they have a good batch of code written, working, and all the unit tests are passing, they can push those changes to the centralized source code repository so others on the team can access it.

This approach fits in well with the typical developer workflow, which is very individualized and "chunky." That is, there are specific times when a batch of code is working together properly, interspersed with periods of incompleteness as the programmer works on each building block piece-by-piece.

To empower your development team with the best tools, I highly recommend a distributed version control system. This will allow your developers to create and manage a branch for each user story. Since I recommend at least three to four stories per two-week sprint, branches will be created and merged, at most, every few days.

The most popular distributed version control system is Git. (Stack Overflow, 2018) Git is available for both Mac and Windows programmer workstations and is supported on centralized storage systems such as GitHub, Bitbucket, Team Foundation Server, and Azure DevOps.

12.4 Reviewing Code Before Merging a Branch Increases Quality

As I've written this book and handed off chapters to my editors, they never cease to find minor mistakes that got past me, even though I carefully read what I wrote before sending it to them. I'm convinced everything is right when I send it, but I always get back edits due to a missing word or two.

There is psychology behind this: someone reading my words for the first time will find errors that my brain simply skips over since I was the source of the writing. (Stockton, 2014)

The same psychology that makes it very hard to find our own typos can cause software bugs. When a programmer is writing code, they're focused on the big-picture logic of what's going on, and they don't always catch the minor details.

To combat this problem, *code reviews*, sometimes called *code inspections,* are used to detect these kinds of errors. Just like proofreading a chapter of this book, code reviews involve a human read-through of the code. This results in "aha" moments for the reviewer, discovering issues the programmer overlooked. Believe it or not, without running any code, this technique can effectively detect bugs.

If this technique is not used, for example when code reviews are performed only occasionally or on a small part of the code, quality can be significantly lower—with as much as twice the likelihood of introducing bugs. (McIntosh, et al., 2014; Bavota & Russo, 2015)

In contrast, when code reviews are done regularly and on a majority of the code base, there are fewer bugs. Plus, they can also lead to a higher-quality technical design. (Morales, et al., 2015)

Using branches to isolate code provides a natural opportunity to perform the code review— just before it's merged into the main product source code.

There are various ways to do this, but a *pull request* is most common. The name originates from open-source projects, where various programmers would make their own enhancements then send a request to the owner of the project to "pull" their changes in, hence the name pull request. (Johnson, 2013)

The benefit of using a pull request is it collects all the incremental changes made in the branch in one spot, and they can all be reviewed together. Tools such as Bitbucket allow reviewers to add comments to the pull request as a whole, individual files that have been modified, or even specific lines of code.

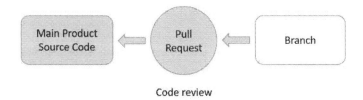

Code review

A pull request provides a spot for all the changes made to a branch to be reviewed before those changes make it into the product code.

If the reviewer thinks everything looks good, she can merge the code from the branch into the main product code. If changes need to be made, a developer—often the one who wrote the code, but this is not always the case if they're not available—makes the updates and either merges the code or submits it for another peer review, depending upon the extent of the changes.

12.5 Git Flow Provides a Strategy for Branch Management

Using branches with a distributed version control system such as Git will get your development team a long way toward being highly effective, giving them flexibility to manage code and always keep the main product code in a shippable state.

This will keep your team organized from sprint to sprint, but I've found it's helpful to think ahead a little bit and adopt a version control strategy that will handle both the initial development of the product and the other various development lifecycle events.

Lifecycle events include:

- Writing, testing, and fixing code for a new user story.

- Fixing a bug and re-testing it.

- Performing a code review.

- "Freezing" the code when it's ready for release, to permit final testing and bug fixing during a release sprint.

- Creating a releasable version of the code, for example to represent Version 2.3.

- Allowing for hotfixes—critical bug fixes that need to be surgically applied to the released code, that can't wait until the next version is deployed to production.

There are several different models for managing source code branches in an agile environment. One of the most popular was created by Vincent Driessen in 2010, and has been coined *Git Flow*, sometimes written *GitFlow*. (Driessen, 2010)

Git Flow provides a strategy to address all the lifecycle events I outlined above, and at its heart is keeping code isolated in a way that allows a high degree of control over the state of the code. Git Flow is particularly suited for products that have some sort of release cadence, what I've called a "release" or "version" throughout this book. (Atlassian, n.d.)

This provides a lot of flexibility for the Scrum team, keeps the product shippable at all times, and permits work to continue on the next release even as the current release is being prepared for deployment.

The "Master" Branch

In Git, the "Master" branch is the default branch. (Chacon & Straub, 2014) If you don't implement any sort of branching strategy such as Git Flow, all code changes would go into this single branch.

With Git Flow, instead of being used for day-to-day code changes, the Master branch is used to contain only code that has been fully-tested and has been—or is about to be—deployed to production.

The Master branch contains code that has been or is about to be deployed to the production environment.

One benefit of this approach is if your team uses a continuous deployment technology to get code into production, they could connect the production environment directly to the Master branch, which would automatically deploy any code changes.

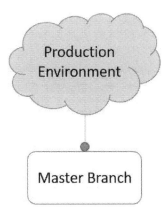

Since the Master branch contains only code "certified" to go into production, it can be directly connected to the production environment using continuous delivery technology.

Since the only time a change is made to the Master branch is when a new batch of code has been fully "certified" to go into production, this ensures that the production environment is only updated with production-ready code.

I'll talk later in this section about how releasable code gets into the Master branch.

The "Develop" Branch

The "Develop" branch contains code that is destined for the next release but hasn't been released yet.

Therefore, **the Develop branch contains the code for the potentially shippable product increment**.

The code is at a shippable level of quality but has not yet been shipped.

Once the product owner determines the code is ready to be deployed, final testing is performed, the code is merged to the Master branch, and the production environment is updated.

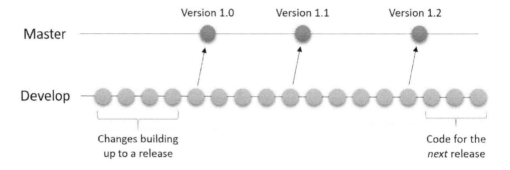

The Master branch contains the release code, and the Develop branch contains the potentially shippable product increment—the code for the next *release.*

I talked about the product owner environment in Chapter 11, which is where the product owner does their testing and accepts or rejects the work of the team. The Develop branch contains the code that's deployed to the product owner environment.

The Develop branch code is what's deployed to the product owner acceptance environment.

Feature Branches

A *feature branch*—sometimes called a *topic branch*, is used for active development. A feature branch is created by taking the current code in the Develop branch and copying it—which is called "merging" in Git-speak—to a new branch.

Feature branches are created from the Develop branch and are used for coding a new story or fixing a bug.

In his blog post explaining Git Flow, Vincent Driessen talks about a feature branch having a lifetime of an entire feature, even if that feature takes multiple sprints to complete. However, as I'll discuss in Section 12.6, I propose feature branches have a short lifetime—a few days at most.

To accomplish this, I suggest using a feature branch to represent the work of one product backlog item—user story or bug fix—in your sprint.

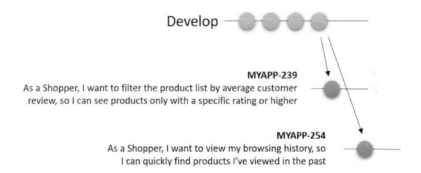

Feature branches are used for the work of a user story or bug fix.

When a user story or bug fix has been fully tested and verified by the development team, it's merged into the Develop branch for review by the product owner.

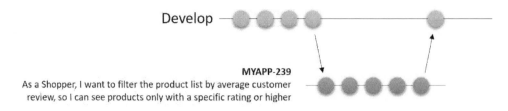

MYAPP-239
As a Shopper, I want to filter the product list by average customer review, so I can see products only with a specific rating or higher

When fully tested by the development team, a feature branch is merged to Develop for product owner acceptance.

To permit the development team to test, feature branches are deployed to the team test environments I talked about in the last chapter.

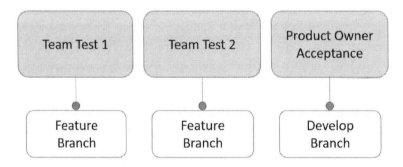

Feature branches are used to deploy code to team test environments, permitting testing of individual user stories or bug fixes before being merged into the Develop branch.

Release Branches

Once the product owner decides that the shippable increment is ready to be put into users' hands, it's helpful to "freeze" the source code. This prevents additional changes that might distract from the process of making sure the code completed to date is solid and ready to go.

The problem with traditional "code freezes" is no one can work on anything for the *next* release while final testing is occurring for the *current* release.

Git Flow addresses this by using a *release branch*. When the product owner says, "We're ready," the code currently in the Develop branch is merged to a new branch for the release, for example "Version 1.1."

When the shippable increment is ready for release, code is merged from the Develop branch to a new release branch.

This frees up the Develop branch for continued work toward the next release, in this case Version 1.2.

The release branch is used to perform final testing and make last-minute adjustments and bug fixes prior to deployment to production.

When the release is deemed ready, the release branch code is merged into the Master branch and is deployed to the production environment.

The release branch is also merged to the Develop branch, so it will receive all the last-minute fixes and adjustments made during the finalization of the current release so these changes won't be left out of the next release.

The release branch is deleted once it's been merged with both Master and Develop.

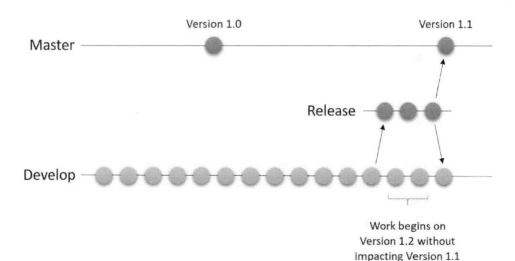

When ready for release, the release branch is merged to Master, which is then deployed to production. It's also merged to Develop, to ensure any last-minute changes aren't lost with the next release.

Hotfix Branches

Although we'd love it if we were perfect and no bugs ever made it into production, in the real world this seldom happens. There's always something that sneaks by all the testing and gets into users' hands.

Many times, bug fixes can wait until the next release. They can be added to the product backlog, fixed during a sprint, and deployed when the next version goes into production. Sometimes, however, a bug is so critical that it simply can't wait. To address this, you create a *hotfix*.

A hotfix is what I call a "surgical" micro-release, containing only code to fix a specific bug and its related unit tests, to ensure it never comes back.

The code in the Develop branch can't be used for this purpose, because it has code that's underway for the next release. It would be too risky to have any of that code included in the hotfix because it would increase your exposure—you want the smallest amount of code required to fix the bug, to keep the testing process simple and ensure you don't introduce *another* bug.

To address this, a hotfix branch is created by merging from the Master branch to a new branch, for example *MYAPP-321 Cart Calculation Error*.

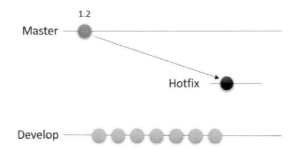

A hotfix branch allows you to create a "surgical" fix. It's created from Master, so it has only the current released code and none of the in-progress code to date in Develop.

The bug is fixed and retested in the hotfix branch, and the version number is updated, for example Version 1.2.1. Once it's deemed ready for release, it's merged back into the Master branch and deployed to production. It's also merged into the Develop branch to ensure the bug fix isn't lost in the next release.

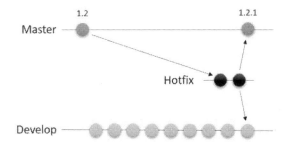

Once the hotfix is ready to go, the hotfix branch is merged to Master as well as Develop.

Once merged to Master and Develop, the hotfix branch is deleted.

Putting It All Together

This strategy of using two long-lived branches—Master and Develop—and several short-lived branches—feature branches, release branches, and hotfix branches—addresses every lifecycle event you'll face during both initial development of your product as well as ongoing enhancements over its lifetime.

A big-picture view of the Git Flow process is shown below.

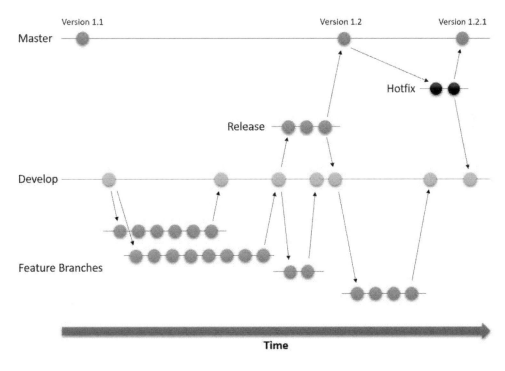

The big picture of the Git Flow process.

12.6 Keys to Avoid Merge Hell and Code Review Bottlenecks

If you Google "Git Flow," you'll find a variety of blog posts criticizing this strategy and proposing alternatives. Deciding which branch management strategy to use can turn into a bit of a religious debate, often descending into an emotionally-charged, drag-out fight.

I've carefully studied a variety of other branch management techniques and although they all have their merits, I haven't found one that fits quite as nicely with release-based product development as Git Flow.

We've been using Git Flow across a variety of projects for close to six years and have never encountered any major problems. Our secret? Short-lived branches.

Merge Hell Is Caused by Long-lived Branches

If you dig more deeply into the Internet posts criticizing Git Flow, you'll find that at the heart of the arguments is the concept of *long-lived branches*.

A long-lived branch is one that hangs around for a long time and includes many different changes. The challenge with long-lived branches occurs when a developer wants to merge the branch back into the main product code —back into the Develop branch when using Git Flow. Because other changes may have been merged into the Develop branch over the course of time, there may be *merge conflicts*.

A merge conflict is when the same code has been modified in two different branches, and there is a conflict introduced when there's an attempt to merge them.

Git essentially says, "I don't know what to do here." This requires manual intervention, with one or more developers reviewing the conflicts line-by-line and determining what code should be kept. This can be tedious and in worst-case scenarios, can introduce subtle bugs if developers are not careful.

This is lovingly termed *merge hell* by developers.

Solving Merge Hell with Short-lived Branches

I completely agree with the detractors: Git Flow falls apart if branches are allowed to live for a long time. I define this as more than about one to three days.

The technique we've used to ensure branches have a short lifetime is tying them to the product backlog items in the sprint. If you follow my recommendation of including at least three to four user stories in a two-week sprint, by definition each of those stories needs to be wrapped up in a few days at most if they're all going to get done.

Part of closing out a product backlog item is merging the feature branch into the Develop branch and deleting the feature branch, as I described in the last section. This approach reduces the exposure to other changes and although merge conflicts can still happen, they are typically small. This approach avoids merge hell.

Rapid Code Reviews Avoid Bottlenecks

Another criticism of Git Flow is that it requires code to be reviewed before it can be merged. This is, of course, optional—technically code can be merged at any time with or without a code review.

I view this criticism as actually highlighting one of the *strengths* of Git Flow: there is a specific checkpoint—the point where the code is about to be merged—where the team knows code reviews must happen.

Disciplined teams understand the benefits of code reviews that I outlined in Section 12.4 and are careful not to skip them in the interest of rushing to get done. However, some teams do get caught in a trap of allowing only one person on the development team to review the code—often the senior developer or architect on the team.

Although I like to ensure the architect on our Ascendle teams reviews critical code, particularly at the beginning of the project, our teams are careful to not let that slow them down. Any developer can perform a code review, though I do encourage that they don't review their *own* code. A second set of eyes is important.

Rotating the code reviews between developers, with the architect or senior developer keeping an eye on the code overall, not only avoids one development team member becoming a bottleneck, it helps to cross-pollinate knowledge about the entire codebase among all the developers.

One thing to watch out for is if certain developers never seem to find any issues with the code they review. They may need a second set of eyes to make sure they are in fact carefully reviewing the code, and you may consider a checklist of things to look for during a code review, which should be created by the development team based on your company's coding standards.

Don't have written coding standards? This is a great reason to create them.

Key Takeaways

- A version control system is a software tool that allows management of source code files, including tracking the history of changes made over time. This empowers the development team to allow better management of their source code, as well as providing a backup copy.

- Because the product must always be potentially shippable, it's important to prevent incomplete and untested code from polluting the main code repository. Branches allow isolation of in-progress code until it's stable and usable.

- A distributed version control system makes branching much easier than traditional centralized version control systems. Git is the most popular version control system, and it is a distributed system.

- Code reviews are a manual, human peer review of code, and can dramatically reduce bugs. Pull requests provide a spot to review all the changes in a branch before they're merged into the main product code.

- Git Flow is a branching strategy to address common software lifecycle events such as writing new code, preparing a new release, and addressing critical production bugs via hotfixes.

- Two keys to effectively using Git Flow are short-lived branches—no more than one to three days—and frequent code reviews. This avoids "merge hell"—widespread conflicts when code from a long-living branch is merged.

- All programmers should review each other's code, with the senior developer or architect on the team keeping an eye on overall software quality. This avoids a bottleneck that can be caused if the architect was required to review every line of code.

Chapter 13

Automated Unit Testing: The Foundation of Code Quality

The first rule of any technology used in a business is that automation applied to an efficient operation will magnify the efficiency. The second is that automation applied to an inefficient operation will magnify the inefficiency.

- **Bill Gates**

Years ago, I was driving the development of a new product at our software company. We had spent years using a manual testing approach for our products, and each new release took weeks of effort and involved almost everyone in the company. Inevitably, once the product went out the door, the support lines would light up with calls about bugs we missed.

Attempting to solve this problem, we experimented with automating some tests on a few more recent products, and it seemed to help shorten the release timeframe.

With the new product we were about to start, I decided we were going to go all-out with test automation. I discussed it with the development team and there were two approaches proposed. The first was automating testing at the code level—called *unit testing*. The other was to automate testing of the entire product end-to-end, called *integration testing*.

In hindsight, I didn't take the time to fully understand the implications of each option. I made a quick decision to proceed with the second option, automating testing of the full product, without any unit testing.

That was a mistake.

Although it helped increase our quality, automated integration testing was a huge pain. Every time a single test ran, the database needed to be reset back to a known state, which resulted in the tests taking *hours* to run as the product grew larger. Plus, sometimes the database didn't reset properly, resulting in erroneous test results. This meant the entire test suite needed to be run again.

Each time we made a change to add a new feature, the tests needed to be adjusted. They were highly unstable, and we had a lot of "boy who cried wolf" situations—tests that would fail when run automatically but would work just fine when run by hand.

The final problem was that tests couldn't be used until an entire feature was fully coded. There was no way to test each building block along the way.

When I started Ascendle, I made the decision to rectify that mistake and set a standard that automated unit testing would be the foundation of our quality strategy. We'd automate some integration tests—which I talk about more in the next chapter—but only for a small part of each product we built. We wouldn't try to test every variation of functionality through integration tests.

Now, close to 6 years later, I can conclusively say the strategy has worked. The products we produce for our clients today are dramatically more stable than any product my teams have built in the last 30 years.

Our development teams know the product is always potentially shippable, and comprehensive unit tests provide a safety net. As they make changes, they can run the tests and in a matter of seconds know that the entire product still works properly.

This approach of using unit tests as our foundation of quality, and adding focused but limited integration test automation, has dramatically increased the speed of development compared to my teams all those years ago. It allows us to deliver business value to our clients at a blistering pace, and ensures the product works correctly throughout the entire development process.

Most of our clients have never seen anything like it.

13.1 The Problem with Relying Solely on Integration Testing

I've discussed why "testing at the end" won't work with agile; it prevents you from knowing that the product is usable at the end of each sprint. But, what about applying traditional end-to-end testing—often a combination of manual and automated techniques—to the agile process?

Early on in a project, this approach works well. As each user story is completed, it's manually tested, and perhaps some automation is added to permit a computer to reproduce the same testing steps, such as clicking here, entering text there, and verifying a result over here.

The work of producing new code and performing thorough testing fits into the sprint nicely, and may look something like this:

Early on, both coding new user stories and testing everything completed to date fits into the sprint.

The problem is that as the number of completed user stories grows, manual testing becomes time-consuming and comprehensive interface-driven test automation often takes too long.

Creating the automated test scripts is tedious, the time to execute them continues to grow, they tend to break as new features are added, and there is a lot of time involved in maintaining the required testing environments. (Osherove, 2014)

As the product grows, the time required to perform new manual testing, create new automated integration tests, and maintain the existing unstable automated tests increases.

As the product grows, more and more time is spent each sprint on manual testing and creating and maintaining unstable automated integration tests.

Pretty quickly the amount of work adds up, and the time required to test both the newly-coded stories in the current sprint *and* everything else that's been finished in prior sprints is more than what's available in a sprint.

As the product grows, an integration-based test strategy reaches the tipping point—it can't all be completed within the sprint.

Soon some corners are cut. Parts of the product stop being tested. Problems in the test scripts are left unaddressed. The team starts talking about writing code in one sprint and testing in the next. Now they're back to Scrummerfall, and they've lost the benefits of an agile approach.

As a result, quality starts to go down but in a way that's particularly troubling: you don't know where the problems are. A bunch of small, ticking time bombs start to creep into the code, but you don't know where until an end user starts to find issues after the product ships.

13.2 Automated Unit Testing: Ensuring Code Works All the Time

Testing from the user's perspective—whether manually, in an automated fashion, or both—is great. But it's not an effective way to ensure *every* part of the product is always working flawlessly.

To completely test every possible scenario that can be encountered within the software would take an inordinate amount of time to do manually, and the time and effort to create, maintain, and run comprehensive automated scripts often increases dramatically as the product grows.

To address this problem, *automated unit testing*—also described simply as *unit testing*—involves a different approach. Instead of testing from the user's perspective, unit testing involves testing at the code level.

How Unit Testing Works

Unit tests exercise a very small part of the software in a variety of ways and validate that it works as expected.

As a simple example, let's assume you're building a basic calculator app. You just wrote the code to add two numbers together, and you want to make sure it works. You put the code into a function named *Add.*

You think a bit about how you'd make sure your code works, and decide to write a unit test that checks that 1 + 2 equals 3. Every time that unit test is executed, it will call your Add function, provide 1 and 2 as parameters, and verify that 3 is returned as the result.

In code, you'd write a unit test along the lines of: Add_OnePlusTwo_ReturnsThree. This clearly tells anyone who's reading the unit test: a) what code is being tested—in this case, the Add function, b) what scenario is being tested, and c) the expected result. This lets other developers read your tests and understand exactly what's going on, without having to read all the test code. (Osherove, 2014)

You then think some more and come up with other tests:

- 2 + 0 = 2 (Add_TwoPlusZero_ReturnsTwo)

- 2 + (-1) = 1 (Add_TwoPlusMinusOne_ReturnsOne)

- (-1) + (-1) = (-2) (Add_MinusOnePlusMinusOne_ReturnsMinusTwo)

That looks pretty good to you, but then you realize you need to test some non-integer scenarios as well:

- 2 + 0.5 = 2.5 (Add_TwoPlusZeroPointFive_ReturnsTwoPointFive)

- 2 – 0.5 = 1.5 (Add_TwoMinusZeroPointFive_ReturnsOnePointFive)

I'm sure you could come up with many more scenarios, but hopefully these illustrate the concept.

Using this technique of thinking through scenarios, then using concrete examples to test those scenarios, results in your code being executed in a variety of ways and verifying that it does, in fact, work as you expect.

As the product continues to grow, unit tests are written for each individual piece. Extending the calculator example, you'll have tests for *Divide, Subtract, Multiply, Square Root*, etc.

13.3 Running Tests Automatically Avoids Human Error

As the product grows, so does the suite of unit tests that exercise every part of each feature. Running unit tests as often as possible ensures the product always remains at a high level of quality because you know everything is still working.

There is one drawback to this approach: it assumes every developer is executing the unit tests frequently enough to quickly detect a bug that's been introduced into the code. It also assumes they are not only running unit tests on *their* code, but code written by *all other developers*. This ensures everyone's code works correctly when put together. You want to know quickly if Jack's code broke some code that Sofia wrote.

This is critical, as the cost of fixing a bug dramatically increases over time. It can cost as much as 10 to 25 times more to fix a bug if it makes it to an end user than it does if detected and fixed during the sprint where the work is being done. (McConnell, 2004)

As we all know, we humans tend to be a bit undisciplined. Simply asking the developers to, "Remember to run unit tests frequently!" won't cut it. Inevitably someone will forget, and Murphy's Law tells us *that* will be the moment a nasty bug is introduced.

To combat this problem, you can add some additional automation to your unit testing solution. *Continuous integration* addresses this challenge by continually monitoring the central source code repository for changes and automatically running all the unit tests after each change.

This means the *entire* product is tested *multiple times per day*, ensuring it's always kept at a shippable level of quality.

How Continuous Integration Works

Any time a change is made, the continuous integration tool retrieves all the code, compiles it, and runs all the unit tests. This ensures everything works properly when the work from everyone on the team is put together, hence the *integration* part of the tool's name.

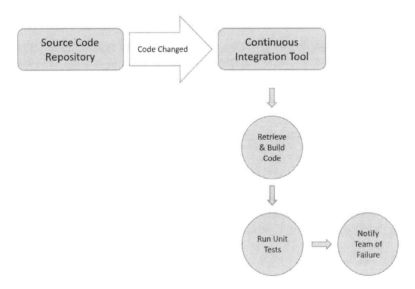

A continuous integration tool monitors the source code repository for changes, automatically builds the product, runs all the unit tests, and notifies the development team of any test failures.

If all the unit tests pass, the tool quietly records the results and its job is done.

The real power comes when there is a failure. The tool will detect the failure, and immediately notify the team.

Depending on how it's configured, this could include an email to the developer who was the last to commit any changes to the source code repository, a notification posted to the team's chat room, and more.

Addressing a Unit Test Failure

The Scrum team should consider any unit test failure to be a serious problem. Any failed test means the product is no longer in a shippable state.

On our teams, the rule is that any unit test failure is a "drop everything and fix it" event. Someone on the development team volunteers to fix the cause of the failing test—often the developer who committed the problem code—and they focus on nothing else until all unit tests are again passing.

13.4 Unit Tests Document Code for Future Programmers

One complaint about agile development is that it de-emphasizes technical documentation. Some technical leaders find this concept unsettling. They are concerned about the ability of future programmers to understand and maintain the product.

This is a valid concern, as more than half the cost of a software product is *after* version 1.0 goes out the door, as it's modified and enhanced over time. (McConnell, 2004)

But the Agile Manifesto tells us we should be focused on *working software* over *comprehensive documentation*. How do we rationalize these two competing concepts?

Enter unit tests. Because they fully exercise every aspect of the system based on a series of concrete scenarios, they form a complete set of technical documentation of, "What the code does." Not only that, but each test presents a working example of exactly how to use each small part of the product code. (Grenning, 2011)

With a solid unit testing approach, you get the best of both worlds. You not only have a comprehensive strategy to ensure product quality, you also get full technical "as-built" documentation of the entire system that's always up to date. Everyone wins.

13.5 Isolating Dependencies Makes Testing Easier

One of the challenges of integration testing is that all the components of the software system are required for tests to function. This may include a database server, the file system, or external systems such as third-party web services.

It could even be other parts of the product itself. For example, when building the front end, I need the back-end server code to be written and working before I can run the product. In larger companies, there may sometimes be dependencies between teams. Unit tests address this dependency problem. (LaToza, et al., 2006)

One of the key benefits of unit testing is the ability to *isolate* the code being tested. This allows a unit test to exercise code that saves data to a database, for example, without the database actually being called. The isolation framework intercepts the call to the database, records what happened, and the unit test code can verify its proper behavior.

This same technique is used to isolate the code being tested from other types of dependencies I mentioned above, including web services, the file system, and other parts of the product.

This provides several benefits: (Mackinnon, et al., 2000)

- A programmer can write code and fully test it without relying on dependencies. This saves time by empowering the programmer to move forward without having to wait for other product code to be done, or without having to worry about configuring a database or external web service connection.

- It isolates the code to ensure that if a bug is discovered it is related to that specific code, and not due to a failure in some other part of the product or in an external dependency.

- It makes the tests run very quickly because slower resources such as a database or cloud-based web services are never involved. This makes it more likely for each programmer to run the unit tests frequently, which ensures that his new code works properly and checks that he hasn't broken any other previously-written code.

How Dependency Isolation Works

Let's say we have code that's supposed to retrieve a record from the database. Because I don't want to mess around with a database to test my code, I use an isolation framework to simulate it.

This prevents me from having to worry about configuring a real database server, loading it up with test data, adjusting the test data for each scenario, etc.

Suppose I need to load a contact from the database and display it in the user interface (UI). Since it's an architectural best practice to not have the presentation layer talk directly to the database, I write some business layer code to retrieve the contact and provide it to the UI.

It needs to handle two scenarios, based on what the database tells it:

- If the contact is found, take the data from the database and return it to the presentation layer, so it can be displayed in the UI.

- If the contact is not found, return a different result, telling the presentation layer it can't be found. That way the UI can tell the user something like, "The contact was not found. It may have been deleted by another user."

To verify these two scenarios, I'll write two business layer unit tests along the lines of the following:

- GetContact_ContactExists_ReturnsContact

- GetContact_ContactDoesNotExist_ReturnsNotFound

In each unit test, I'll configure the simulated database to match the scenario.

For the first test I'm going to tell my fake database, "When ID 1234 is requested, return a fake contact named Bill Jones."

In the unit test I'll write code that says, "Try asking for contact with ID 1234." The code runs, the fake database returns the fake contact, and then I check to make sure my code behaves as expected—in this case, returning Bill Jones back to whoever is calling it.

The presentation layer would usually call this code, but in this case the unit test is calling it.

For the next test I'll tell the fake database, "When 1234 is asked for, pretend it doesn't exist."

Now when the unit test calls the code with ID 1234, the fake database says, "I can't find that." In my unit test I check to make sure the business layer code returns, "Not found," as opposed to returning a contact.

So, in this case, I'm testing the following desired behavior of my product code:

- When the database gives you a contact for a particular ID, return that contact info.

- When the database doesn't have that contact, return a code that says it wasn't found

The isolation framework makes it easy for me to simulate two different scenarios, all without having to install and configure a real database server. Plus, because all this code is running in computer memory, as opposed to talking to a real database, it's very fast.

13.6 Test-Driven Development (TDD) Creates a Test-First Culture

What I've described so far might generate some questions. For example:

- Who writes these unit tests?

- When are they written?

- How do we make sure programmers remember to write them?

To address these challenges, *test-driven development* incorporates a workflow that guarantees unit tests are written to cover all the functionality in the product. By writing each unit test *before* writing code, test-driven development makes it impossible to have any code exist that's not covered by a unit test.

The process works like this:

1. A developer writes a unit test for a scenario he is going to handle next. At this time, since the code doesn't yet exist, the unit test will fail.

2. The developer writes the *smallest* amount of code that will make the unit test pass.

3. The developer enhances the code as necessary to make it more robust.

This three-step process is often referred to as "red-green-refactor," since at first the unit test will fail ("red"), then a small amount of code is written just to make the test pass ("green"), and finally the code is enhanced to an appropriate level of robustness ("refactor"). (Beck, 2003)

This approach has benefits well beyond simply ensuring unit tests get written, including the following: (Maximilien & Williams, 2003)

- It ensures unit tests will, in fact, fail if the code is not working correctly.

- It helps enhance the design of the product because the developer is thinking first about the desired behavior and where that behavior should be located in the code, then about the code itself.

- It forces the developer to make sure the code works *before* committing it to the central code repository.

- It facilitates a deeper understanding during peer code reviews. By reading the tests, the reviewer understands what the code *should* do, which helps them discover any errors as they look at the code.

Test-driven development takes some getting used to. When I first learned the technique, it took me about a week before it started coming more naturally to me. Once I was up to speed, however, I found test-driven development allowed me to slow down a little bit and *think*, which in the end sped up development, because I'd make fewer mistakes.

And, of course, I had a nice shiny set of unit tests that I was confident completely covered all the functionality I had coded.

I encourage your development team to experiment with test-driven development. There is an initial learning curve, but it is well worth the time due to the benefits once they get used to the technique.

You'll drive a culture of having developers "self-certify" their code before it's ever tested by someone else on the team, and you'll never again hear, "Oh shoot, I forgot the unit tests."

13.7 Code Coverage Analysis Keeps Everyone Honest

No one is perfect, including your development team members. Sometimes code is written or changed without writing or enhancing unit tests first. And sometimes that code ends up not being covered by unit tests.

By "covered" I mean "this code has been executed by one or more unit tests."

If some code is never executed by a unit test, this testing approach quickly loses its effectiveness because some portion of the product will not be exercised by the continuous integration tool. This increases the probability of introducing subtle, difficult-to-detect bugs into the application.

To address this problem, *code coverage* tools allow developers to run unit tests, then see what product code has been executed and—more importantly—what code has *not* been executed.

The developer can then write one or more additional unit tests to ensure the code is properly covered.

When to Check Code Coverage

I've found that the best approach is to incorporate checking code coverage into each user story. This ensures the appropriate unit tests have been written before the development team calls the story "done."

Once the unit tests and code are written and passing, a member of the development team will get the latest code for the story and run a code coverage tool to identify any un-covered code. Someone on the team will then add any missing unit tests.

It's often easiest if the developer who wrote the code adds the missing tests, but not if it would slow down overall progress on the current sprint. For example, if that person is out for the day.

To ensure this happens on our teams, we've added code coverage to our definition of done and include a subtask during sprint planning to check code coverage and address any issues.

What Percent of the Product Code Should be Covered by Unit Tests?

There are tools that can automatically monitor the code coverage in your application and detect any holes. One thing to be careful about is ensuring you don't get too hung up on the percentage of code that's covered by unit tests. It's more important that the *right* code is covered.

Some code is so simple that it's likely not worth the time to write unit tests for it. Our rule is that code must have corresponding unit tests if it contains a) if/then or some other branching type of logic, b) calls to other code in another part of the application, or c) calculations. Simple code doesn't need to be covered.

This puts the focus on making sure risky code is covered instead of attaining an arbitrary goal of 100% code coverage.

Creating an artificially high code coverage goal can also have a nasty side-effect: developers might focus more on meeting that number by writing tests that *run* the code but don't effectively *test* the code. (Staats, et al., 2012)

I saw this first-hand at one of our clients a few years ago. They had contracted out development of a new product and after about a year of delays and bug-ridden features, they had a few senior developers put the code under the microscope.

What they discovered was code coverage was 100%, but *the unit tests were all written incorrectly*. The tests executed the product code but didn't verify that *any* of the behavior was correct. In other words, the outsourced development team achieved perfect code coverage, but none of the unit tests would ever detect a bug.

Be careful about chasing an arbitrary code-coverage number.

13.8 Adding Unit Tests Keeps Bugs from Coming Back

Developers try to identify possible bugs in every line of code they write, and if they use an approach such as test-driven development, it's highly likely they'll get it mostly right. But it seems like users always find a way to break your product, no matter what you do to prevent it.

As I talked about at the beginning of this chapter, you should see dramatically higher quality by adopting a unit testing strategy similar to what I've outlined. To give you an idea of how radical a change you'll see, using my old approach of integration testing without unit testing, we'd see anywhere from 20 to 30 bugs when we released a new version of a product after about 3 months of development.

Today, we see about *two or three* bugs in our products after a similar amount of development.

Others find the same thing when utilizing unit tests—they discover significantly fewer bugs in production. (Osherove, 2014)

Some bugs *do* make it through the gauntlet of testing. The important thing to do before fixing a bug is to *write a failing unit test first*.

Writing a failing unit test before fixing the bug ensures two things:

- The bug will, in fact, be detected by the unit test. If you write the test after fixing the bug, you don't know if it will fail if the bug is present.

- It guarantees a unit test will be written, to ensure the bug never returns. There's nothing quite as frustrating as a bug coming back in six months that you already fixed.

Sometimes bugs can't be detected by unit tests but, in my experience, those are typically low-risk bugs. For example, the color of something on the screen is slightly off or the layout is mis-aligned by a few pixels.

Important bugs—those that frustrate your users—can almost always be detected by a unit test.

13.9 Should We Use Integration Tests Instead of Unit Tests?

First, let me say that using *any* type of structured testing strategy is better than *no* testing strategy. As I'll talk about in the next chapter, I'm a firm believer in the value of integration testing, just not relying on that strategy for testing the *entire* product. It's simply too difficult and time-consuming to attempt to cover every possible business workflow with this technique. (Liu, 2018)

I've found that attempting to test *everything* with integration tests delays the discovery of bugs because so much time is spent trying to achieve full coverage.

What I've learned in the last 35 years is if I had to pick one, I'd choose automated unit tests over automated integration tests. If I had the ability to pick two, I'd focus on unit tests to cover all the nitty-gritty variations in my code and rely on automated integration tests to ensure the major moving parts are always working when everything is put together.

Adopting unit testing can be a tough pill to swallow for organizations that don't have experience with it. Coding will, in fact, take longer—as much as twice as long when including the time to write unit tests in addition to product code. However, testing and fixing bugs will take less time, and there will be fewer bugs that make it into production. This results in the overall time from start to finish being less than if you don't utilize unit tests. (Osherove, 2014; LaToza, et al., 2006)

Don't forget, unit testing is not just about discovering bugs early. It's also about driving a more clean, maintainable, and simpler design, and speeding development by isolating dependencies. (Janzen & Saiedian, 2008) It also ensures your code is testable at the click of a button, and it leads to faster identification of the root cause of bugs as compared to integration tests. (Osherove, 2014)

I encourage you to experiment and see what works best. Just keep in mind that it's very difficult to "go back later" to add unit tests if they're not incorporated right from the start.

A quality strategy that includes both integration tests and unit tests is great. But abandoning unit testing is a mistake in my opinion.

Key Takeaways

- A testing strategy focused solely on manual testing or automated integration testing is typically not efficient enough to complete testing of the entire product every sprint, particularly as the product grows.

- Unit tests exercise the code of a product at the individual building block level, ensuring every piece of logic in the entire application works properly.

- Continuous integration is a technique of using a tool to monitor changes to the central source code repository. When a change is detected, the continuous integration tool retrieves the code, compiles it, and runs all the unit tests. Any test failures are immediately reported to the development team.

- Any test failure should result in the development team stopping work until the issue is resolved, since it means the product has become non-shippable.

- A side benefit of unit tests is they form a complete set of technical documentation for how the code works.

- Unit tests allow isolating dependencies, such as the database, web services, the file system, and other parts of the product. This speeds up development since programmers can write and test code quickly and easily, and makes unit tests run as fast as possible because they don't utilize slow resources.

- Test-driven development focuses on writing a unit test first, then writing the code to make the test pass. Finally, the code is refactored to make it more robust and maintainable. This "red-green-refactor" approach results in cleaner technical designs, simpler code, and ensures unit tests are written for all code.

- Code coverage analysis tools allow you to identify application code that is not exercised by unit tests. Avoiding artificial metrics such as requiring 100% code coverage will prevent problems such as programmers writing tests to attain higher code coverage instead of properly testing the product. Focusing on making sure the *right* code is being tested, as opposed to meeting an arbitrary percentage, will produce better results.

- When a bug is discovered, adding a failing unit test before fixing it will ensure the test will properly detect the bug and will ensure the bug never comes back again.

- Any testing strategy is better than none. However, if I had to pick one, I would choose unit testing over integration testing. Adopting both is better, but abandoning unit testing for an integration-only testing approach comes with serious drawbacks.

Chapter 14

Acceptance Testing: Making Sure Everything Works Together

More than the act of testing, the act of designing tests is one of the best bug preventers known.

*- **Boris Beizer**, American software engineer, author, and testing expert.*

One of the big challenges of product development is ensuring the development team builds the *right product*—one that matches what was envisioned at the start and meets end-user needs. The product owner role in Scrum is charged with being the vision-holder of the team, but it's often difficult to ensure everyone knows the specifics of that vision.

The unit testing strategy I described in the last chapter focuses on each individual building block of the product, ensuring specific code delivers the correct result. This bottom-up approach encourages thinking carefully about how each line of code is written, and continually ensures it delivers the desired outcome.

The limitation of unit testing is it doesn't test the behavior of the product when all the individual building blocks are combined and start talking to both each other and external systems such as cloud-hosted web services. That is, unit tests don't test the *integrated* product.

It makes sense that before the product is deemed ready for users, you'd want to kick the tires to make sure everything works. But how should you approach this in the most effective way, to find bugs in the shortest amount of time?

This applies to not only bugs, but also mismatches between vision and reality. The product owner saying, "That's not what I wanted" can be frustrating for everyone when the entire team spent hours talking through every detail, only to realize later that there was a misunderstanding.

This can be especially disheartening to development team members after they've spent a *lot* of time getting every detail just right.

Acceptance tests provide a structured way to think through how the product should behave once the code for a user story has been completed. They accomplish this by documenting a variety of scenarios and expected outcomes.

They not only form a strategy for how you'll test the product, but also provide a vision for each completed user story. This helps everyone ensure they're on the same page about what is to be built.

14.1 Scenarios Help Pre-Visualize a User Story to Avoid Disappointment

One of the challenges on any team is communication. Scrum addresses this by encouraging constant discussions among team members, with lightweight reminders of those conversations captured in the form of user story acceptance criteria and other related notes.

The product owner is responsible for the vision of the product, but sometimes it can be difficult to think through exactly how new functionality will work before it's built. This can make it challenging to convey the vision to the development team.

Acceptance criteria, by design, are lightweight. They capture only the high points of the product owner's vision, with details filled in through a series of conversations with the team. But even with the work of writing and refining acceptance criteria and talking through user stories, there can still be gaps between what's in the product owner's head and what the team produces.

Because of this, the product owner will often see a completed, tested user story and—even though it's working as she described—say, "Hmm. That's not quite what I had in mind."

Since the development team finished that user story in just a few days within their two-week sprint, the problem was identified quickly. This is light-years better than the waterfall pattern of finding out months down the road that there's an issue, but this can still lead to waste. Any time the development team spends on re-work due to poor communication is flushing money down the toilet.

However, this is still not the way it's supposed to work. The product owner should look at a completed user story and say, "Yes! That looks like what I was thinking."

Scenarios to Visualize Product Behavior

Acceptance tests provide a bridge between the lightweight acceptance criteria in a user story and finished, tested functionality. By outlining concrete scenarios, acceptance tests allow the product owner to "pre-visualize" the behavior of the user story before code is written.

By reading the scenarios she can say, "Yes, that's what I want." Or, if it's not quite right, she can say, "I was thinking it would work a little differently." At that point, changes are easy—

it's simply a matter of adjusting a few words. This is much different than re-writing and re-testing code.

Once the acceptance tests for a user story look right to the product owner, the development team can use those scenarios to understand exactly what they're building. Once coded, they can also be used to verify the product behaves as it should.

Finally, because acceptance tests outline the behavior of every user story, they provide a comprehensive as-built product specification—for free.

An Acceptance Test Example

Let's say we have a user story for a new spell-checker feature in our word processing app. It might be written something like this:

As an Author, I want an indication of misspelled words, so I can prevent spelling errors in my document.

One of our acceptance criteria details a simple implementation of spell-checking—a wavy red line under each misspelled word:

I can see misspelled words indicated by a wavy red line under each word.

As the QA engineer on the team, you volunteer to write a test strategy for this story. How would you document it?

One way would be to write a test along the lines of the following:

Type a word that's spelled incorrectly and make sure a red line shows up underneath it.

This *might* work just fine, but there are some drawbacks:

- It might not be tested the same way each time, since it's up to the individual to determine what word is typed in.

- It's difficult to visualize the exact steps a user would perform to get this behavior.

- It's not clear when, exactly, the wavy line should appear. Should it show up when I type the first letter? After I stop typing for a few seconds? When I press the space bar?

It might add clarity to write the test using a concrete, specific example, and use a little bit more of a description to ensure it's interpreted properly.

With this in mind, you might write something like this:

Scenario: Indicate Misspelled Word

Given I am viewing a new document

When I type helol

   And I press the space bar

Then I should see a wavy red line under helol

Now someone reading this can picture *exactly* what's expected to happen when the user mistypes the word *hello*. They understand not only what the user needs to do to see the behavior, but they also know what should happen and when.

14.2 Given, When, Then: Making Tests Understandable to Everyone

You'll notice three keywords in the example above: *given, when,* and *then.* These words provide the foundation for writing a *scenario.*

The use of a scenario allows visualizing the behavior and gets everyone on the same page as to, "What *exactly* should this do?"

The collection of acceptance test scenarios for a user story extends its acceptance criteria into a fully developed narrative of the desired behavior. Some call this "specification by example," which underscores its value by not only outlining a test plan, but also providing up-front guidance for implementing the user story. (Fowler, 2013)

This approach encourages closer collaboration among everyone on the Scrum team, provides a "contract" of sorts between the product owner and developers to better ensure the right behavior is produced, and decreases the likelihood of introducing bugs. (Agile Alliance, n.d.)

This style of structuring each acceptance test scenario is often utilized as part of a technique called behavior-driven development (BDD) and has the following parts: (North, 2007)

- *Given* some initial context (the givens).

- *When* an event occurs.

- *Then* ensure some expected outcomes.

Here's another, more detailed example, documenting a test scenario for a login page:

Scenario: Password Left Blank

Given I am viewing the login page

  And there is a user account in the system with "john@acme.com" as the email

When I enter "john@acme.com" for the email

  And I click Login

Then I should still be on the login page

  And I should see a message, "Password is required"

  And the password box should be red

Notice a few things about this example:

It includes a description of the scenario being tested. This makes it easy for readers to understand which scenario is being addressed and provides a reminder that each acceptance test scenario should focus on only one thing.

Writing, "Password Left Blank and User Has Been Locked Out" would make it obvious the scenario should be split into two—one for the blank password and one for the locked-out user.

It's written in plain, non-technical language. This makes it easy to understand for everyone, including the product owner and other business stakeholders, as well as others on the Scrum team who may be non-technical.

It uses a concrete scenario. Including specific information, such as an email address, ensures the vision outlined by the acceptance test is clear to everyone who reads it. It also makes the test easy to repeat, as anyone who performs it will do so in the same manner, limiting variations in the result based on the use of different information.

It's based on observable behavior. Because the test is written from the end-user's perspective, everything that's described is based on observable behavior. This helps avoid acceptance tests becoming too technical, which can confuse non-technical readers.

A technical description such as, "The system sets the blankPassword flag in the Login object" isn't something the user will see because it's part of the underlying implementation, and therefore it's clear that this type of detail should be omitted from the scenario.

14.3 Write Acceptance Tests Early During a Sprint to Reduce Risk

Developers often find that when they sit down to write code and read through a user story's acceptance criteria, they discover some holes. "What happens if the user does *this*?" or "Did you think about *that*?"

The last thing you want is for a developer to be ready to crank out code and instead they're dead in the water due to being confused and needing some questions answered.

Writing Acceptance Tests Early Surfaces Problems Early

A great way to address this risk is to ensure acceptance tests are written early during each sprint. Because the team member writing the acceptance tests needs to come up with concrete scenarios, they're forced to think in much the same way as the developer, focused on exactly how the functionality will work.

The result is they'll often identify the types of questions the developer would ask, just much earlier in the sprint.

I've seen this work extraordinarily well. The team member who is writing the tests—often the QA engineer on the team—will pull the product owner aside and pepper her with questions. The clarifications about how exactly things should work are captured in the acceptance tests so everyone can see the outcome of those discussions.

Once the acceptance tests are written, developers can read through them to get a concrete picture of the code they're about to write.

On the first day of the sprint, acceptance tests for the first user story might not be done yet, so I wouldn't recommend the programmers wait. But once they're written and reviewed, I encourage programmers to ensure their mental picture of the functionality they're creating matches the details in the related acceptance tests.

Sometimes Things Change

Sometimes discussions with the product owner result in subtle changes to the desired behavior of the user story. These should be reviewed with the development team, perhaps at the next daily scrum.

As long as the development team agrees that the adjustments are minor and don't fundamentally change the nature of the user story, small updates might be made to the user story's acceptance criteria.

If the product owner instead dreamed up some new enhancements that go beyond what the development team signed up for when they took on the story for this sprint, they should be captured as a new user story on the product backlog. This avoids breaking the rule that no scope changes are allowed once a sprint begins.

The Product Owner Should Review Acceptance Tests

Because acceptance tests expand the vision of each user story's acceptance criteria, it's important for the product owner to have an opportunity to review them.

If the acceptance criteria are misinterpreted and acceptance test scenarios are written that don't match the product owner's vision, the Scrum team needs to know that as quickly as possible to avoid writing and testing the wrong code.

14.4 Perform Acceptance Testing in Every Environment

Acceptance tests form the foundation of validating product behavior in the team test environments I discussed in Chapter 11. They can also be used as a guide for the product owner during their review of completed functionality in their acceptance environment.

The product owner should be able to trust that the development team has run through all the scenarios, so they often just select a handful to run themselves as a cross check.

Remember, the environments should be as "real" as possible. For example, if your product talks to a third-party payment processing service, every environment should talk to that service.

On developer workstations and team test environments they can talk to a "fake" or "sandbox" environment, so you don't have to worry about processing real credit cards. But be careful to call the product "shippable" if it's never been tested in the context in which it will be used when deployed.

The less "real" the configuration is when testing at each stage in the process, the higher the risk that things won't work later, such as during a release sprint.

Discovering for the first time that the customer can't purchase the products in their cart just days before the product is to go into production introduces a serious amount of stress. It can not only cause you to lose years off your life, but it can also be a career-limiting move. Trust me, I've been there.

14.5 Create an Automated "Smoke Test" with Critical Scenarios

In the last chapter, I came down pretty hard on the idea of using automated integration tests as the foundation of your quality strategy, instead recommending automated unit tests.

Attempting to test *everything* in the product with automated integration tests is extremely difficult, time-consuming, and expensive.

However, automating a *subset* of integration tests can be extremely helpful. By limiting the scope of tests that you automate, you limit your exposure to the challenges of creating and maintaining them.

Selecting a subset of the most important acceptance tests can form a *smoke test*, exercising the critical workflows of the application to ensure all the moving parts are still in working order.

The term "smoke test" comes from hardware testing. When you plug in the device and turn it on, do you see any smoke? If so, you know you have a serious problem!

One of the biggest benefits of the smoke test is it identifies critical integration problems, which can be costly to address if allowed to simmer in the product for too long. (McConnell, 1996)

Selecting Acceptance Tests for Your Smoke Test

When determining which acceptance tests to include in your smoke test, I find it helpful to think about how you'd prioritize your testing to ensure the product is fundamentally working.

A technique I use when coaching Scrum teams is to get them thinking about what they'd focus on if they only had four hours to manually test the product, to make sure it's working before deploying a new release to their entire user base.

This helps focus on the 80/20 rule. That is, what's the 20% of product functionality that represents 80% of the risk?

For example, if your team is building an e-commerce application, you might focus on automating tests that cover the key workflow of browsing the product catalog, adding products to the cart, and checking out.

In contrast, you probably don't need to try automating the calculation of sales tax for every possible state. That's something better handled by unit tests.

When to Run the Automated Smoke Test

Automated unit tests are run multiple times every day, by both developers and the continuous integration tool. Every time code is changed, all the tests are executed, and any failures are immediately dealt with

This strategy works well because unit tests run so quickly—the entire process of building the product and running thousands of tests can typically be completed in a few minutes.

Integration tests are slower to run, so it may not be realistic to run them as often as your automated unit tests. However, I encourage you to not wait *too* long to run them. I think the sweet spot is to create a scheduled build and smoke test each night. That way, your maximum exposure to an issue is 24 hours.

If you can execute the automated smoke test more frequently without running into any issues, go for it! Discovering bugs as fast as possible is always a good thing.

Remember that any time a bug is found, the development team should determine if they can write a unit test that would have detected it. Any bug that can be discovered within minutes during a developer's or continuous integration unit test run will save your team time and speed up your development.

Key Takeaways

- Although unit tests form the foundation of your quality strategy, they don't test all parts of the product working together, and they don't verify the behavior of the product as experienced by the end user.

- Scenarios help everyone visualize the desired behavior of the product before code is written. It's much easier to adjust acceptance test scenarios than code that's been written, tested, and reviewed.

- Writing acceptance tests enhance a user story's acceptance criteria by creating expanding versions of them in the form of concrete user scenarios.

- Acceptance tests are written using a "given-when-then" approach, which provides them with a consistent and easy-to-understand structure.

- Writing acceptance tests early in the sprint can identify confusing or incomplete acceptance criteria. This allows them to be addressed before impacting developer productivity.

- Acceptance tests can be used in any environment, from developer workstations all the way through to production.

- Because acceptance tests are validating the behavior of each user story, it's important for every test environment to be as realistic as possible, including accessing "sandbox" versions of third-party systems such as a cloud-based payment processor.

- Creating automated integration tests from a subset of acceptance test scenarios forms a "smoke test" that can be used to validate key product functionality.

Chapter 15
Agile Architecture and Technical Design

The heart and soul of the company is creativity and innovation.

- **Bob Iger,** *Chief Executive Officer of Disney.*

When I speak to technical leaders, I explain that one of the fundamental changes they'll need to make is to stop telling their development teams how to do the technical work.

This is usually met with a few uneasy glances around the table and eventually one of them will ask, "Then how do we prevent them from screwing up?"

This is one of the fundamental challenges of moving to an agile way of thinking and working. Many technical managers are used to providing close oversight and specific direction to the development team to at least some degree, not trusting that they'll know how to do the right thing at the right time to deliver the expected results.

When faced with the concept of the development team being left to their own devices, images of the Wild West come to mind, with every developer charging off in a different direction and "doing whatever they want."

In short, if developers have technical freedom, most technical leaders assume chaos will ensue.

In a healthy agile organization, this fear is unfounded. Technical leaders effectively leverage their years of experience to provide help and advice, while empowering development teams to come up with creative solutions and drive the "how" of building the product.

This shift can be a challenge and take some getting used to, but it's an important one to address. Failure to make this kind of cultural change is one of the leading threats to successfully adopting agile. (VersionOne, 2018).

15.1 Architecture Doesn't Disappear with Agile: It Becomes "Emergent"

Some development teams come from a company culture of creating comprehensive architecture strategies and technical designs for *everything* as part of their waterfall process. When they move to agile, they swing all the way in the other direction and do *no* architecture work or technical design at all.

The result is often a lack of critical thinking about the technical moving parts as the product comes together. Things start going sideways when the development team is six weeks in and they realize they've created a mess and need to rewrite most of what they have.

This is sometimes called "accidental architecture," and can get in the way of the team's ability to develop user stories and evolve the product over time. (Waterman, et al., 2015)

This can have an even worse side-effect: technical leaders can point to this as an example of why "agile doesn't work," and they may push for returning to their top-down approach of dictating all the technical decisions.

Moving to an agile approach doesn't mean abandoning architecture and detailed technical design. It's still critical to think through how the various parts of the application will come together, while ensuring the design can be extended over time as more user stories are added. This balances the needs of the business today while creating a foundation that's sustainable for many years to come. (Madison, 2010)

The only difference is the technical design work happens during the sprint in which the code will be written. This is part of "doing a little bit of everything all the time," which is an important part of Scrum.

As a result, architecture becomes *emergent*.

The Nature of Agile Development Forces Comprehensive Architectural Thinking

One of the objections I've heard to adopting agile development is there won't be enough comprehensive thinking up front about the product's architecture. There is a fear that code will be hacked together in a way that's not extensible and maintainable, and major rework will be required.

I would argue that the nature of agile development limits technical risk because the development team not only has to *think about* the technical design during each sprint, they also need to *make it work*.

With a waterfall approach, there's a lot of early technical design work, but many weeks or months can go by without writing any code for many parts of the application. The technical design might look great on paper, but when it comes time to connect the UI to the back end that was coded over the last five months, the team might discover things don't work quite the way they expected.

With an agile approach, the development team is forced to make *everything* work. The front-end and back-end code is completed in the same sprint—often on the same day—so technical issues become immediately apparent.

Plus, they also need to figure out how to deploy the product to a clean environment and prove that it will actually work once in production.

On our teams, we deploy the product to a *demo* environment. Although it doesn't have the same horsepower and redundancy as the production environment, it otherwise mimics its characteristics. In this way, the development team has designed, built, tested, and deployed the entire product to a production-like environment. And all in the first sprint.

The result? Any problems or issues are identified and addressed *now*, because the technical design was forced to be proven in practice, not solely "on paper."

Some Up-Front Decisions Are Required

Although agile avoids "big design up front," that doesn't mean that *no* early decisions are required. There are several fundamental choices that need to be made, typically before one line of code is written. (Vincent, 2016)

These are typically the types of decisions that are difficult to change later, since they form the foundation of the product's underlying technology.

This allows creating what some term a *walking skeleton*, providing a minimal framework upon which product code can be added for each user story. (Abrahamsson, et al., 2010)

It's important to spend time thinking through the implications of these decisions and how they'll impact not only the development team, but also the rest of the organization.

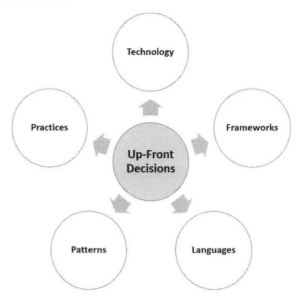

Agile's goal of avoiding "big design up front" doesn't mean "no up-front work."
Some early decisions are required.

Types of up-front decisions include:

- *Technology and frameworks.* What back-end server technologies will be used? ASP.NET? Node.js? What about the technique for generating web pages? Server-side technologies or a JavaScript-based single-page application technology? Angular or React? Which unit testing framework will be used? What continuous integration technology?

- *Languages.* C#? Java? JavaScript? TypeScript? You can't really write code for six weeks then re-write it all in a different language.

- *Patterns.* What fundamental design patterns will be used? For example, how will business logic be separated from data access logic? How will the development team ensure flexibility in the design without over-engineering it?

- *Practices.* How will source code be managed? How will testing environments be created? How will code be deployed? How will the team address build failures or failing unit tests?

We have a fundamental strategy that we use for all our client product development work for cloud applications. This strategy has evolved over the last 19 years of my experience with development using the Microsoft .NET platform, and continues to evolve as each Ascendle development team innovates and improves upon it.

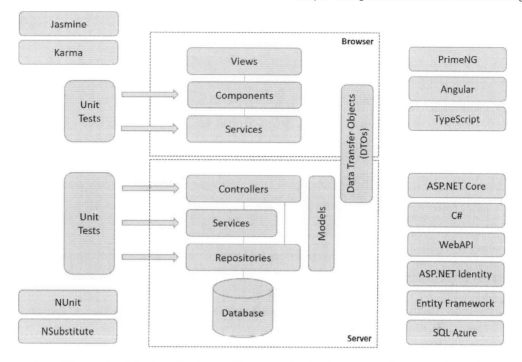

Ascendle's standard cloud application architecture and technology strategy documents the up-front decisions we've made to guide our client product development work.

This strategy allows each Ascendle development team to start with a reference architecture "cheat sheet," giving them a proven approach they can adopt as-is or modify as they see fit.

Your team will need to make similar decisions.

A Template Can Help Your Development Team Save Time

To save time, we've created a template based on our standard strategy, which serves as the starting point for new client projects. Within a few hours, a development team can have the basic building blocks of a new product up and running, including framework code, a full set of unit tests, continuous integration, testing environments, and automated deployment.

Having a baseline starting point takes care of all the boilerplate work, so they can more quickly focus on what's unique about the product they're about to build. They can then make adjustments to satisfy the unique needs of their product.

In our experience, this saves about *six to eight weeks* of time that would otherwise be spent making technical decisions, then building and testing framework code that has nothing to do with solving a client-specific business problem.

One thing I'd like to highlight here is we're not violating the Scrum rule that says the development team decides how to build the product. This framework isn't imposed on them. Instead, it's offered as a way to shortcut their work. Each development team is expected to make their own decisions about how they'll adapt it.

Since the template was created by the Ascendle development teams that came before them, it's highly likely they'll look at it and say, "This is fantastic. We don't want to build all this stuff if we can get it for free!"

On the other hand, they may say, "Unfortunately we can't use some pieces for this particular product, because it has different technical needs."

In the end, it's up to them.

Limiting Risk by Limiting Invention

Those of us who have been at this awhile realize that one of the keys to developing software quickly is to reduce *invention*. It's much faster and easier to leverage a solution that already exists than it is to invent something from scratch.

As one of my engineering professors liked to say, "Good engineers copy, great engineers steal." His somewhat tongue-in-cheek point was that to the highest degree possible, leverage the proven work of others instead of creating it yourself.

Most companies have a limited appetite for bleeding-edge development work, since the development team needs to figure out how to deliver business value quickly. This may not apply in a pure research and development (R&D) environment, but most of us need to produce results *yesterday*. Development teams can limit time and risk by leveraging existing resources.

In software, you can accelerate up-front decisions and limit risk in a few different ways:

Leverage pre-built components. Whether it's a feature of the development platform you're using, a popular open-source project, or a commercially purchased add-in, it's almost always faster and easier if you don't have to build it yourself.

Utilize existing company patterns and frameworks. It's likely that other development teams have figured out many of the problems the current development team will face. As they start in on the up-front decision-making process, it's important to understand what work they may be able to leverage. This is what we've done with our Ascendle template.

This is a great place for technical leaders to get involved and, as I'll talk about later in this chapter, a way for communities of practice to help spread the word about the work everyone has done and what reusable frameworks and architectures are available.

Ask the software community. It's likely that someone else out there has run into the same issue. Searching an online community for answers—such as the popular Stack Overflow—or posting your own questions, can shortcut problem-solving.

Tap outside expertise. Consulting firms and other companies abound with "been there, done that" knowledge. Whether it's support from a vendor—for example Microsoft if you're developing on their platform, or another independent firm—expert advice can save a lot of time.

Utilize internal knowledge and experience. Most likely you have your own "been there, done that" knowledge inside the company, in the form of the collective experience of senior technical personnel. Having your development team engage with them for help is an important strategy to speed things up and limit technical risk.

This last point—leveraging internal knowledge—is at the heart of an effective combination of traditional top-down direction and the kind of bottom-up innovation that agile provides.

15.2 Avoiding YAGNI by Leveraging the "Last Responsible Moment"

Before I discovered agile, I spent years of my life writing a bunch of code I didn't end up using. "I'm sure once we add feature X, we'll definitely need this fancy stuff." That never seemed to be the case. I wish I could have all that time back.

I was very focused on building products the traditional waterfall way—layer by layer.

First, we designed the database, then the code that loaded and saved data, then the business logic, and finally, the user interface in the presentation layer.

It looked something like this:

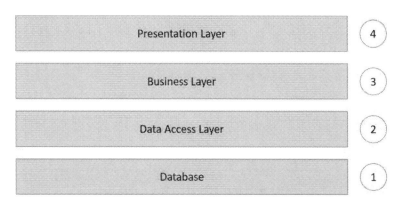

A waterfall approach focuses on building products layer by layer.

The problem was we didn't know what code we *really* needed, because we weren't focused on writing as little as possible to make one small part of the product work.

You've read a lot about this concept in this book—starting with the simplest thing that can possibly work and focusing on one feature at a time.

Instead of layers, the focus with agile is on building thin, vertical slices, with a little bit of code in every layer.

It looks like this:

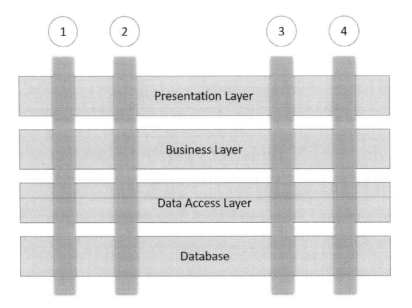

The agile approach is to build thin, vertical slices, which results in adding just the code that's absolutely necessary to get a user story working.

Only the code that's needed for the *current user story* is added, and nothing else.

One of my favorite terms in agile is *YAGNI*, which stands for, "You ain't gonna need it." This speaks to the developers' tendency to write code they *think* they'll need as opposed to just the code that's *actually required right now*.

I've seen time and time again that when code is added in anticipation—as opposed to satisfying a known need—it's usually never used or needs to be heavily reworked when it's needed.

This exemplifies why making technical decisions at the *last responsible moment*—a term coined from lean manufacturing—is so important. It means making as few technical decisions as you can get away with, because decisions made too early in a project are very risky. Those decisions lead to code never being used, or thrown away and re-written. (Atwood, 2006; Poppendieck & Poppendieck, 2003)

Focus on writing only the code that's needed now, in a thin vertical slice for the current user story, and you'll avoid YAGNI.

Think Long-Term, Act Short-Term, to Prevent Painting Yourself into a Corner

When I talk to technical leaders about the last responsible moment, they will often ask, "Won't this result in a crappy technical design? If you're just thinking about the current user story, how will the team produce a clean, extensible architecture?"

Scrum development teams avoid painting themselves into a corner by anticipating the needs of—but not writing code for—future user stories.

It's a great question, and a real concern. The development team shouldn't get to their third sprint and say, "Well, everything we've built to date needs to be thrown away since now we need to make the product do *this*."

What I tell teams is they should *think long-term*, so they can see a path for how the code they're writing today can be extended to support stories lower on the backlog. However, they should only *act short-term*, not writing any of that future code yet, to avoid the problems I outlined at the beginning of this section.

Because the development team is always heavily involved with talking through the entire product backlog, they understand where the product is headed. They can think about what's coming down the road and make sure what they're coding today won't paint themselves into a corner.

But that's different from *writing code they don't need yet*.

For example, the development team may know that the plan is to translate the user interface into a different language at some point because they see a user story about it way down in the product backlog. When they make technical decisions about how they'll build the UI, they should ask, "Will this approach support localization for language once we get to that?"

They're not going to *implement* any language translation, but they should be comfortable that when that user story comes up months or even years down the road, they won't have to say to the product owner, "We need to throw away the entire UI and re-write it from scratch."

The key point is when the development team comes to a fork in the road and needs to make a decision, they should choose a path informed by what they know is coming.

This is another reason why it's so critical that the entire Scrum team frequently talks through the product backlog and the overall vision for the product. It will empower them to make the best technical decisions for the long term.

Refactoring Is a Way to Incrementally Enhance and Simplify Code

Some development teams get tied up in knots with analysis paralysis, trying to figure out a way to write code today that they won't have to adjust when they get to future user stories. The usual result is they spend too much time trying to make things perfect and end up with code that's too fancy.

Then they're back to YAGNI.

It's expected that code will need to be adjusted over time as the product evolves. This is called *refactoring* and it's not a bad word.

Refactoring is not "throwing a bunch of working code away and rewriting it from scratch." It's enhancing and simplifying the existing implementation to support the functionality for new user stories, while increasing maintainability and limiting risk along the way. (Fowler, 1999)

In summary, the development team should focus on the present, avoid painting themselves into a corner, and be comfortable that they'll end up making small modifications to their code over time as development moves forward.

15.3 Attaining Technical Excellence Without Telling Them How to Do It

It is possible to both honor the agile philosophy of telling the development team *what*, not *how*, while ensuring that they are highly effective, and not charging off in a technical direction that doesn't support the company's goals.

The key change for technical leaders is to go from being a *manager* of the developers, to becoming an *advisor* to the developers. That is, to become a "servant leader," supporting and guiding the development team.

The easiest way I've found to teach this is by introducing minor language adjustments for anyone interacting with the development team.

Instead of, "Do it this way," technical leaders can try these alternatives:

- "You might want to consider…"

- "You might want to think about…"

- "We've solved that problem before and you can find more information by…"

- "We've established a standard approach for that and it's documented here…"

- "We need to adhere to a legal or regulatory standard, and you can find out more by…"

- "Did you think through how this technical decision will affect…"

- "I can help you figure that out if you'd like…"

- "Jack Thompson knows a lot about that, so you may want to talk to him…"

Notice the use of the word "you" throughout the above examples. This tells the development team loud and clear, "I'm here to help, but *you* are retaining ownership."

It's About Ownership

It may seem like I'm splitting hairs with this advice. Why does it matter if a technical leader says, "You might want to consider" as opposed to, "Please do it like this"?

There's one *huge* reason, and that's one of *ownership*.

I'm a pretty technical guy, and I've been doing this software thing for a *long* time. Because I have so much experience, and I want to help the development team avoid pitfalls I've faced in the past, I often want to give them advice.

I might have the urge to say to them, "Hey, I've thought a lot about this, and I've come up with a technical solution for you that will avoid all kinds of problems. Here it is. Please implement it and show it to me when you're done."

I might then pat myself on the back, knowing I helped them dodge a bullet and feeling like I still "have what it takes" to contribute my technical know-how.

However, there are a few problems with this approach:

- *I can no longer hold the team accountable.* If the team adopts my idea and it doesn't work out, I can't say to the team, "Well, that's a bummer. What are you going to do fix it?" They'd likely look around at each other and think, "What the hell is this guy talking about? It was *his* dumb idea that got us into trouble in the first place!" This is a major empowerment failure.

- *I didn't have all the facts.* The development team members are talking all day every day about the business problems they're trying to solve and the technical approaches they might use to address them. Unless I'm *on the team* and present for *every* conversation, I don't have enough information to make a fully-informed decision. It's highly unlikely I'll come up with the best solution without the comprehensive knowledge the developers possess.

- *I'm stifling innovation.* If I come up with the answers and dictate them to the team, I'm sending a message: "I'm going to do the thinking around here." The best-case scenario is I'll be pulled into the critical path of the team's work to support my idea and come up with more. The worst-case scenario is the development team members will restrict their own creativity and just assume, "Someone else will do the thinking. I'll just show up and do what I'm told."

The approach I suggest keeps the level of accountability high, while preserving the ability of the technical leaders to ensure developers have what they need in terms of support to drive their success.

Too often, I work with executives who complain that their company's development teams don't take enough ownership, while at the same time they want their technical managers to tell developers exactly how to do everything.

You can't have your cake and eat it too.

Pick one: development team empowerment and accountability, or top-down direction. I suggest you'll get dramatically better results from the former.

15.4 Development Teams Need to Consider the Big Picture

A problem I sometimes see with development teams is they don't want *any* constraints on their work. They want to flex their muscles and say, "Scrum means no one can tell us what to do," and charge off into implementing esoteric solutions just for the sake of doing something different.

Technically, the development team can, in fact, do whatever they want. Scrum guidance spells it out quite clearly: no one can tell the development team *how* to transform product backlog items into shippable functionality. (Schwaber & Sutherland, 2017)

But the development team is also responsible for ensuring they make the *right* technical decisions, for both the product they're building and the company as a whole.

It's Not Just About the Development Team

Many technical decisions have far-reaching implications, and the development team is responsible not only for the short-term effect of their choices, but the long-term as well.

For example, a development team might decide, "We're using Java for this product. We've always wanted to use Java and now's our chance!"

The problem is, for the last 10 years all the products at the company have been built with Microsoft .NET. In this case, selecting Java means introducing a technology that may be difficult for the company to deal with.

Customer support reps may not know how to troubleshoot problems. Technical leaders can't leverage their vast experience with .NET to provide insight and advice, and the development team won't be able to re-use any code that was developed for other products over the years.

When it comes time to deploy the product, an entirely new DevOps pipeline will probably be required since the current tools and techniques are all designed around the needs of .NET.

All these factors need to be considered when the development team makes technical decisions, and this is a great place for technical leaders to help them think through how their ideas will affect the company.

A Cautionary Tale

In one extreme example, a senior developer at one of our clients selected a technology called Couchbase to store the data for a new product. The problem was, all the other applications at the company were built using Microsoft SQL Server.

Was Couchbase better? It might have had a handful of advantages, but that wasn't the right question. The better question to ask would have been, "Can the technology we already know be used to successfully support the business requirements for this application?"

I'm all for pushing the envelope and leveraging the latest and greatest technology, but the big picture needs to be considered.

It turned out the product never really required the features of Couchbase and would have worked just fine using the somewhat "boring," time-tested SQL Server.

The developer left the company shortly after completing the initial version of the product, and the organization struggled for *years* to support it.

As it turned out, no one else in the company knew the first thing about Couchbase.

Instead of "No" Say "Tell me more"

Because no one is allowed to tell the development team how to turn user stories into potentially shippable functionality, technical leaders can't say to them, "You can't build it like that."

Of course, if they see that the development team is violating some legal or regulatory requirement, they may want to help them stay out of trouble by pointing that out!

However, if the team wants to do something that violates a company standard or long-held convention, I encourage technical leaders to listen carefully to their argument as to why they want to do what they're thinking.

Maybe the status quo needs to be challenged and the company standard needs to be changed. Technical leaders should say, "Tell me more about what you're thinking," as opposed to just saying, "No."

An Example

I faced this exact scenario myself several years ago. Our standard development approach for web applications at Ascendle utilized a server-side technology to generate web pages the user sees in their browser. Over time, web development had shifted from this approach to building "single-page applications," with more code running within the browser. This technology produces faster and more dynamic web applications.

One of our development teams met with me and said, "We want to use this new approach." My knee-jerk reaction was, "That's not our standard," but I suppressed that response and instead said, "Tell me more."

I asked a lot of questions, ensuring the team had thought through things such as how they'd write unit tests, whether our continuous integration tool supported this technology, and implications for automated deployment.

I also asked about community support. Were other people using this technology? Was it mature enough that they'd be comfortable using it in production? Is it likely that other developers we hire in the future to maintain this application will be familiar with it?

As it turns out, the technology they wanted to use—AngularJS, now called just "Angular"—was one of the most popular single-page application frameworks. They were able to confidently answer all my questions and make me feel confident about their decision.

I was the primary technical stakeholder—as the CEO of the company, the buck stops with me—but I didn't tell the development team, "No" or say, "I want you to use *this* technology."

If they were struggling to answer the questions I was throwing at them, I might have suggested they look around for an alternative that would have been less of a challenge for them. After all, *they* were the ones who had to build out the development and test environments, continuous integration tooling, and automated deployment.

Throughout these discussions, I was very careful to ensure that I didn't take on any ownership for their decision. They'd have to live with it.

As it turned out, it was a great move. We've since updated our standards to document both the "old way" and the "new way." I suspect that most new products we build will use the single-page application approach.

15.5 An Experienced Technical Team Member Can Be a Big Plus

A technique we use is including a senior software engineer or software architect on each development team.

Since there is no hierarchy on a Scrum team, this person is not the "boss of the developers." However, because of their degree of experience, they're often looked to by the other developers as a key resource for architectural guidance, troubleshooting help, and mentoring.

It's seldom that you can have a development team full of only the most experienced programmers. Utilizing this strategy helps to bring the technical capability of the collective team higher than if it was comprised solely of junior developers.

This strategy also helps drive the overall architecture strategy of the company. Senior developers typically have experience across multiple products, and often have a long history with the company's technology. They can also participate in an architecture community of practice to discuss high-level technical strategy with others at the company and bring that intelligence into the development team.

We rely on the architect to help get new products off on the right foot, ensuring a clean and extensible architecture, and mentoring the other developers on the team.

The architect or senior developer always needs to be vigilant to not allow any kind of "command and control" attitude to emerge. Everyone is equal on the development team, and everyone needs to drive the agile principles of collective code ownership and self-organizing, cross-functional teamwork. (Kajko-Mattsson, et al., 2010)

15.6 Creating a Technical Design for a Story Encourages Collaboration

Moving to agile doesn't mean that all of a sudden technical design is unimportant. Nowhere in Scrum literature does it say, "Make sure you stop doing all of that design stuff you've been doing with your waterfall process."

Technical design is still critical. But to realize the full benefit of Scrum, it needs to be done as late as possible, creating a technical design for user stories in the same sprint in which they're coded and tested. (Cohn, 2006a)

This approach gives you maximum flexibility since you don't risk a "micro-waterfall" approach of designing in one sprint and coding in the next, only to find out that user stories were de-prioritized and the designs are no longer needed.

The Implementation Strategy

What we've found works well is for the development team to create an *implementation strategy*. This is a lightweight document, typically in the team's wiki, that outlines the big picture of how the user story will be implemented.

Once someone on the team writes it, the rest of the developers get together to review and discuss it. This is a great way to foster technical discussion at a high level—before diving into the code—and encourage collaboration.

This is also a way for the senior technical team member to utilize their knowledge. They can create the implementation strategy and work through it with the team, making adjustments based on the group's feedback.

It can also work the other way. A junior developer can create the implementation strategy and more senior team members can ask leading questions to ensure they addressed everything.

Keep Technical Design Lightweight

Although technical design is important, during a sprint isn't the time to create a 15-page document for each story, to be reviewed by four committees.

On our development teams, we typically spend a maximum of one hour writing an implementation strategy, and a maximum of one hour for the developers to get together and discuss it.

Implementation strategies are just a high-level outline answering the question, "What's our technical plan?"

Each implementation strategy typically includes details about what parts of the code will be modified, what new code will be added and where, and how each section of code will be responsible for implementing a part of the user story's behavior.

A strategy often includes a list of unit test scenarios that will exercise the new code, especially if the user story is particularly tricky or intricate.

There should be enough detail for the developers to understand the high-level vision of how the code will be constructed, see that it will all work well together, and understand how they'll test it.

It doesn't take a lot of time, but this single part of our process has likely saved our teams weeks of work, simply by ensuring they get on the same page before writing code.

Sometimes technical documentation gets a bad rap in agile, but it's important to remember that it supports both *communicating* information as well as *remembering* perspectives and decisions. (Coplien & Bjørnvig, 2010)

We typically don't go back and update implementation strategies if the plan changes once coding begins, but it's sometimes helpful to be able to see what our original thinking was.

This is another example of *plan your work and work your plan*, just at a lower level than is discussed during sprint planning.

15.7 Coding Standards Are a Critical Success Factor

Many companies have written coding standards, but some development teams I talk to do not have a consistent culture of ensuring they're applied.

In some cases, it's because the development team doesn't even know coding standards exist, and in other cases, they're so out of date that no one pays attention to them.

Consistent code is important because it allows team members to collaborate more easily, because any code they look at is familiar to all of them. If each developer wrote code in a different style, time would be wasted by every other developer trying to figure out what they did.

I call this the "one hand" rule. That is, all the code should look like it was written by one developer.

This is especially important with agile. Since the approach is iterative and incremental, code will be touched over and over again as it's enhanced over time for each new user story.

Consistency also helps ensure there's quick and easy reuse of code because it's written in a style already familiar to the development team.

If your company doesn't yet have coding standards, I encourage you to work with your developers to help create them. Not only will this drive awareness higher, it will also drive buy-in since *they're* the ones generating standards they can all agree on.

If you do have coding standards that are seldom used, it's time to dust them off and work with the developers to spruce them up.

By getting coding standards in place and utilized, you'll be addressing one of the key technical factors that drive development team success. (Tanner & von Willingh, 2014; VersionOne, 2018)

Automating Coding Standards Adherence Can Be a Big Plus

There are tools that allow your development team to automate checking for adherence to coding standards. This technology, called *static code analysis*, automatically scans code as part of the continuous integration build and detects any violations of the rules.

When an issue is detected, a warning is generated, and the development team is notified so they can fix the problem.

In an unhealthy environment, this can feel a bit like "big brother" is watching. But if you get your developers to contribute to the coding standards through communities of practice, it's *their* standards to which they're adhering.

15.8 Communities of Practice Encourage Innovation and Consistency

Sometimes team members need encouragement to get together and talk about their ideas and drive innovation. Facilitating communities of practice can be a great way to do this.

A community of practice is a group of like-minded individuals coming together and talking about a specific topic. This can include groups focused on roles such as product owners or ScrumMasters, as well as technical communities of practice around topics such as front-end development, back-end development, specific programming tools, and architecture.

Technical communities of practice can include both team members and technical leaders and can be a great way to create a low-pressure, casual atmosphere to kick around new ideas. Benefits include not only knowledge sharing but driving innovation and buy-in.

From the perspective of developers, the technical direction moves from "their ideas" to "everyone's ideas," and helps everyone feel like they're contributing. (Eckert, 2006)

Key Takeaways

- Architecture doesn't disappear with agile, it becomes *emergent*. That is, it's developed as the product is built, not all up front.

- Even though agile abolishes "big design up front," some up-front decisions are required. These include technology, frameworks, languages, patterns, and practices.

- Leveraging the *last responsible moment* to make technical decisions as late as possible limits risk by ensuring the most amount of information is available, based on how the product has evolved to date.

- Thinking long-term and acting short-term allows developers to ensure a solid, extensible technical design, while avoiding YAGNI ("You ain't gonna need it"). This refers to the developers' tendency to add code they anticipate will be needed later, but in reality gets ripped out down the road when they have more context about what's *actually* required.

- When adopting agile, technical leaders need to ensure they empower their development teams to decide how to deliver the shippable product increment each sprint.

- Development teams can't charge off and do whatever they want; they need to keep the big picture in mind. They need to consider internal company knowledge and technical expertise, and the downstream effects of their work such as the company's ability to support the product once deployed.

- Some small shifts in language can go a long way. Instead of, "You should do it like this," simply saying, "You may want to think about…" ensures the experience of technical leaders can be leveraged, while making it clear the development team retains ownership over deciding how to build the product.

- If they don't empower the development team, technical leaders run the risk of stifling innovation, and not being able to hold the team accountable for results.

- Technology leaders can help development teams avoid pitfalls by asking leading questions. These help developers think through the implications of their technical decisions, which helps them avoid some of the problems that more experienced technical leaders have endured.

- Technical implementation strategies can be used to foster collaboration among development team members. Technical communities of practice are groups of team members focused on a particular technology or area of expertise. These can be used to foster bottom-up innovation throughout the company and help generate a feeling of inclusiveness among technical team members.

Part III
Laying the Groundwork

Luck is a matter of preparation meeting opportunity.

*- **Seneca**, Roman philosopher (4 B.C. – A.D. 65).*

Chapter 16

Here Be Dragons: Preparing for the Challenges You'll Face

We have met the enemy and he is us.

- **Walt Kelly,** *American animator and cartoonist, best known for the comic strip Pogo.*

As the legend goes, ancient mapmakers had limited geographic knowledge and much of the world was uncharted. They weren't really sure what lay beyond, so they included illustrations of creatures such as serpents, dragons, and more.

Supposedly, these maps included the inscription: *Hic sunt dracones*—Latin for "Here be dragons."

As it turns out, this legend was largely unsupported by fact. (Meyer, 2013) However, the concept is applicable here: you're entering uncharted territory, and unknown dangers lie beyond.

Agile failures aren't typically due to a mismatch between the process and the demands of software development. They're usually because of a botched rollout, where the organization becomes its own worst enemy.

Stories abound of unsuccessful attempts to adopt agile. "Agile doesn't work" is the typical result. Or, "We kind of do agile, but we don't really follow the rules." And there are other companies where upper leadership believes agile is going great, but a quick chat with any team member results in an eye roll and an explanation about how dysfunctional things really are.

The goal of this chapter is to help set you up for success as you embark on your agile journey, from strategies to get started to how you can be a critical part of Scrum's adoption throughout your entire organization.

Trust me, this thing works—better than anything I've seen. But you'll need to do some work to ensure you don't mess it up.

16.1 How Your Organization Will Change

Most organizations today know how to develop products that deliver business value. Otherwise, they wouldn't be profitable. However, many leaders are frustrated with the pace of product development and the frequent mismatch between what customers want and what the team built. They'd also love to get a more predictable schedule.

This is why agile has gained so much popularity in recent years—it delivers on these wants and desires.

Many of the leaders I've worked with thought that adopting agile would be limited to training their development teams how to do the process. Then results would magically appear.

What many don't understand—especially those in management—is agile isn't just a new set of tools and techniques to help keep track of the moving parts of developing a product. It's an entirely new way of thinking and working. It affects *everyone* directly or indirectly involved with product development. At most companies, this is the whole organization.

Going from training a small, somewhat isolated part of the company to realizing the *entire organization* may be affected, is an eye-opening revelation for most people.

Although a move to agile could impact everyone in the organization, there are four main areas that typically have the most involvement: product management, project management, software development, and upper leadership.

Product Management

The product managers I've worked with are some of the smartest, most creative, and driven individuals I've ever met.

They're also often the most frustrated.

The product group is typically responsible for figuring out what customers want and designing solutions to address their needs. They patiently produce hundreds of pages of specifications, diagrams, flowcharts, UI mockups, and explanations and hand them over to the development team. They have stars in their eyes, dreaming about how wonderful the product is going to be.

After months or sometimes years, they start to get some functionality that's "ready for final testing," and within about 10 minutes they usually find two things:

- Lots of bugs.

- Stuff that doesn't look anything like what they envisioned.

They can't imagine why they spent so much time, effort, and energy to produce specs that apparently no one read. And they don't understand why programmers can't write code that actually works.

There's typically a dramatic disconnect between what the product group wanted and what the development team built, due to a fundamental lack of communication.

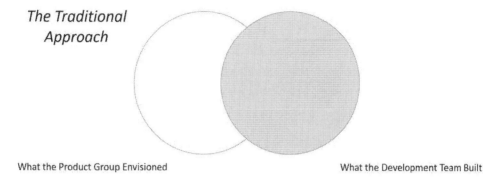

The Traditional Approach

What the Product Group Envisioned   What the Development Team Built

Most product teams are very disconnected from the development teams trying to realize their vision.

Agile solves this by directly connecting the product group into the development team, via the product owner role, as I talked about in Chapter 3.

For the first time there is a real-time conduit from the vision created by the product group into the work of the development team, allowing them to work side-by-side throughout every day to drive the product in the right direction.

With this new model, what the team builds matches what the product managers wanted, and everyone is happy. The result? The product management group can effectively do their job: manage the product to deliver the most business value possible.

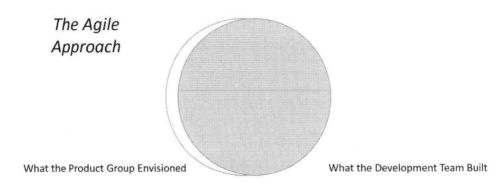

The Agile Approach

What the Product Group Envisioned   What the Development Team Built

Agile joins product management and development at the hip, ensuring the right product is built. Due to the nature of agile, there will always be "game time" adjustments as the product is built, leading to some difference between the original vision and the end result.

Project Management

Project managers are usually super detail oriented, process driven, and focused on excellence. They often act as a buffer between product management and development, helping keep all the balls in the air.

I've seen many of them become frustrated when they attempt to apply their plan-driven expertise to software development, only to find the results aren't on par with their level of experience and professionalism.

They may think, "Why isn't this working? I'm doing everything right."

It's not their fault. They've been trained in a method that's simply incompatible with the nature of software development. Managing the construction of a building, bridge, or underwater tunnel is suited for traditional project management. Software is not.

When faced with the prospect of moving to agile, they may be concerned about their future. Since their training is all centered around the technique that's about to be jettisoned by the company, they may wonder where they fit in.

The good news is their fundamental skills—facilitating a structured process and managing the social implications of getting a team effectively working together—are all completely transferrable to Scrum.

Although I'll talk more about project managers and the project management office (PMO) in the next section, the bottom line is that this group is critical to both the initial adoption of agile and its ongoing success over time.

Far from being marginalized by the adoption of Scrum as they may initially fear, project managers typically discover that they're playing an even more critical role in the organization's success once agile is adopted.

Software Development

The technical folks usually feel like they're the smartest people in the company. I was a software developer once. I'll admit it—I had a certain air of superiority.

One reason for this is the rest of the company typically doesn't really understand exactly how everything works, so the engineers, architects, and testers feel special.

Before the agile transition, the software development group may assume that nothing is really wrong, and they're doing their job well. It's not *their* fault that the product group can't communicate things clearly. And if they deviate from the specs, it's for a good reason—they came up with a better idea.

They usually get really frustrated when they've worked their butts off only to discover they allowed bugs to slip in, and it turns out that they didn't build what was wanted.

And they are typically as frustrated as the rest of the company when they never seem to be able to provide an accurate schedule estimate.

As agile is rolled out at the organization, most developers react well. They're excited to be trusted to make technical decisions, and they appreciate having access to the product owner throughout each day.

They get clear direction on priorities and have access to ask questions about how things should work. They get rapid feedback as to whether they're building the right thing, and they have positive pressure to increase their discipline, which often means they finally get to learn and implement the contemporary software practices they've been dreaming about.

They can finally leverage their creativity and technical know-how to produce stuff that *works* and *delights the product group*. They are equipped with techniques to finally create an accurate schedule, and they know that management won't ask them to produce six months of work in a third of the time.

In short, they are happy because they can focus on their craft within a safe structure of trust coupled with having others worry about figuring out what to build.

Upper Leadership

The big-picture folks at the top of the organization are pushing their strategic initiatives and need the results driven by product management, project management, and development.

They're often frustrated by the inability of these groups to reliably work together to make things happen as quickly as they want.

They likely have experimented with all kinds of ideas, from pushing harder, to offering incentives, to even begging and pleading to, "Just figure out how to fix this."

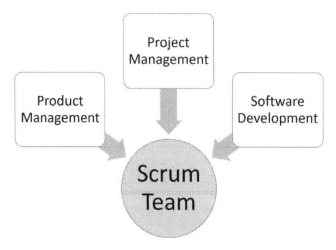

When Scrum is rolled out, team members from product management, project management, and software development are integrated into cohesive Scrum teams, allowing them to work side-by-side to deliver results.

A member of upper leadership may sometimes be the one who decides to roll out agile, based on their experience, what they've heard from their peers, or read in business books and magazines. They'll typically ask the project management group to take the lead.

Once Scrum has been rolled out, upper leadership starts seeing results they've only dreamed of in the past. They can pivot their strategy based on changing business conditions, and product management, project management, and development—now joined at the hip via their Scrum teams—can quickly respond.

They have insight into how fast the teams can move, and they finally have a predictable schedule that is accurate.

I've seen upper leadership become the biggest champions of agile within the organization, once it's working.

As I'll talk about later in this chapter, one thing you'll want to focus on is getting them excited *before* they start seeing results, to help the organization through the inevitable rough patches as it learns how to leverage Scrum to deliver the business outcomes they so desperately need.

16.2 How Project Managers and the PMO Fit In

I do a lot of public speaking, and I've talked to thousands of project management professionals (PMPs) about agile and Scrum. One question always comes up: "Where do we fit in?"

They fear they'll be marginalized, or worse—the PMO will be disbanded and they'll be laid off.

The news for project managers and PMOs couldn't be better. Key success factors for adopting agile in the organization are right in their wheelhouse:

- *Discipline.* If Scrum teams don't stick to the fundamentals, they'll spin their wheels and won't see the expected results. Project managers are trained to respect process and the required discipline to follow it.

- *Education and training.* One of the critical things your team members need is education about agile concepts and coaching along the way. The PMO is perfectly poised to be the change agent within the organization, guiding it through the agile journey.

- *Process improvement.* One of the key principles of Scrum is that it's not a one-size-fits-all methodology. Instead it's a framework designed to be adapted, so each organization can make it their own. Project managers can facilitate team members driving continuous improvement.

- *Process standardization.* Though this book is mainly focused on the fundamentals required to make one Scrum team successful, in most organizations there will be many teams. One of the top tips for scaling agile within the company is consistent practices and processes across teams, and the PMO can act as a central hub for sharing information. (VersionOne, 2018)

Possible Scrum Roles for Project Managers

After I make it clear that project managers absolutely have an important role, the next question is, "So what Scrum role is best for me?"

I think there are two roles that are a natural fit: ScrumMaster or product owner.

For those who love the behind-the-scenes machinery of managing details and facilitating communication, the ScrumMaster role is likely the best fit. As I talked about in Chapter 7, this role is focused on making sure the team follows all the rules of Scrum, innovates within that framework, and helps the team improve the process.

They also help facilitate the moving parts day by day, and ensure the team is always as effective as possible. For project managers of the "rule-follower" variety, the ScrumMaster role is likely for them.

The product owner role is more visible than the ScrumMaster, so it would be a fit for someone who would like to be the face of the team. I like to call this the "lead singer" role.

This role—which also requires someone who is detail-oriented—involves talking to stakeholders, interpreting their needs, and turning them into user stories. This is a fit for someone who would love working through the details to build new functionality with the development team.

Since the product owner is responsible for the return on investment (ROI) of the team, they can ensure they are always working on what's most valuable. A project manger's training will help them determine whether it's worth the team's time if they start spinning their wheels on lower-value user stories, for example.

This type of person might not be interested in the finer points of the process. They probably thrive when they have someone to help them with the nitty-gritty details.

They would be at their best when coupled with a strong ScrumMaster, and together they are a powerful duo.

Shifting from Directing the Work to Facilitating the Work

Many project managers are trained to direct the activities of a team. They determine which tasks are necessary, assign them to team members, and follow up to make sure things are staying on track.

That doesn't work with Scrum.

To be successful on a Scrum team, project managers need to make a shift to a model of the development team determining the breakdown of the work and *volunteering* each day for what they'll focus on. I'll talk more about how this works in Chapter 26.

This approach drives the ownership and accountability of the team, and personally I find it eliminates a lot of stress. Instead of trying to figure out how to give everyone something to do, the ScrumMaster can just say to the team, "Let's make sure you guys figure out what the plan is for today."

How the PMO Can Support Agile Adoption

The PMO can be at the heart of a successful agile adoption. They can help in any of the following ways: (Cohn, 2010b)

Launch the transition. The PMO is often the best part of the organization to take the lead on the agile adoption process. Because moving to agile is a company-wide endeavor, it makes sense that one group within the company would own it.

The PMO can develop the training program, either themselves or by evaluating and selecting outside vendors. They can also have their project managers participate in the training, to build internal knowledge and create an in-house agile coaching group.

Manage expectations. Communication is always helpful, and it's especially important when the entire organization is making a fundamental shift in how they work. The PMO can help educate executives and other company leaders about what's going on and why, keeping them comfortable that things are moving in the right direction.

This is especially important at the beginning, when the process is still in its formative stage and there aren't too many visible results quite yet.

Help with compliance. With agile comes development teams empowered to make technical decisions. The problem can be that many are making these types of decisions for the first time, and may not have all the information they need. They need to know details about standards such as ISO 9001, Sarbanes-Oxley, HIPAA, etc. The PMO can help teams be aware of which standards apply to them, so they can ensure they implement compliant solutions.

Facilitate communities of practice. It's important that there is cross-pollination of ideas throughout the organization, and ensuring like-minded or like-skilled team members get together on a regular basis is a great task for the PMO to take on. They can help get communities of practice formed and ensure they keep meeting regularly, even when things get busy.

Spread best practices. As individual teams adjust the process to improve it, it's important for those innovations to be spread through the company. Although they need to be careful about mandates, best practices that all or most agree are a good idea need to be shared, so the entire organization can improve at a rapid rate. The PMO can facilitate the required communication.

To help support this concept, I love the idea of ScrumMasters being part of the PMO.

Since the role of the ScrumMaster is to "own the process," this approach provides a great way for the PMO to spread consistency throughout the organization and ensure the innovations being developed by each Scrum team are being leveraged by everyone.

Avoiding duplicate work. Since the PMO has a high-level view across multiple Scrum teams, they can keep an eye out for those that are attempting to solve a problem that's already been addressed. A lot of the organization's time and money can be saved when someone in the PMO says, "Hey, guys, I think team X has already figured that out. You might want to talk to them to see if you can use what they've done."

16.3 How to Start: Pilot Team or the "Big Bang" Approach?

Once your company has decided to take the plunge and move to agile, your next question might be about the best way to roll it out. Should you use a pilot team or the "big bang?"

- *Pilot team.* This involves selecting one group of individuals and forming them into a Scrum team. That team then receives training and with the help of one or more agile coaches, creates a product backlog. They then start executing sprints.

- *Big bang.* In this case, the *entire company* adopts agile simultaneously. Everyone is immediately on a Scrum team, and everyone starts executing the process at the same time.

The Pilot Team Approach

I prefer the pilot team approach, because I think the big bang approach is too risky.

One important thing to remember is there are three things going on simultaneously as you move to agile:

- Scrum team members are learning the fundamentals.

- The company is learning what it means to be agile.

- Everyone is figuring out how to best adapt Scrum to work within your company's unique environment.

What I've found is it's much easier to deal with these challenges in the context of one Scrum team.

Once the first team is up and running, each additional team can leverage their work. They also provide a reference for other teams to observe and model.

I'll talk more in the next chapter about how to select members of your pilot Scrum team.

The Big Bang Approach

Big bang can be done. Salesforce.com took this approach for their move to agile, and they pulled it off. (Fry & Greene, 2007)

Before you decide to take this approach, I would consider some of its drawbacks:

It's going to cost more. Scrum teams need focused attention from a coach in order to succeed. A Scrum team that can succeed without someone to guide them along during at least their first few sprints is very rare. A good rule of thumb is each coach can handle roughly one to three teams, depending on how much those teams "get it" and how fast they come up to speed. Larger companies will need a *lot* of coaches to pull this off.

It's going to cause more immediate, widespread disruption to the company. With this approach, the entire company is going to be impacted *immediately*. This can lead to a lot of short-term pain. It will also likely halt progress on every bit of software development in the company, as it will take some time for teams to shift from how they work today to an agile approach.

Everyone is trying to figure out the same thing. One of the strengths of Scrum is that it's incomplete, which allows organizations to determine, "How it works *here*." It takes a bit of time to figure out how the process should work in each company, yours included. The big bang approach means that *everyone* is trying to figure it out at the same time.

There is a higher risk of failure. If you tell your entire company, "We're doing this brand-new thing, and doing it *right now*," that can be extremely jarring. Change is hard, and people need time to get their arms around what's going on. One of the biggest risks of failure is you're unlikely to get a second chance; if things don't go quite right and the entire organization is disillusioned, you might be dead in the water.

In contrast, if you make some mistakes with the pilot team, adjustments can be made to address the issues before rolling it out to the rest of the organization. (Cohn, 2010a)

16.4 Success Factors to Guide Your Agile Adoption

After Salesforce.com made their agile transition, their rollout team sat back and reflected on their experience. Two of their team members wrote a journal article describing what they went through and summarized the lessons they learned. (Fry & Greene, 2007)

Though they took the big bang approach, their key takeaways are applicable to anyone transitioning to agile. These points contain solid advice and certainly align with what I've seen during the agile rollout process.

Have executive commitment to the change. There were several times when there was resistance from a variety of teams. Because the executive team was unified and committed, they were able to push back on the teams to ensure the company stayed the course and remained on track.

Create a dedicated rollout team to facilitate the change. Salesforce.com created a dedicated, fully-empowered agile rollout team, comprised of individuals from every area of the company. They themselves used the new approach to manage their work and coordinated the effort across the entire organization.

Focus on principles over mechanics. One of the challenges the rollout team faced was helping everyone understand why they were moving to an agile process. Providing a core set of principles allowed teams to make day-to-day decisions about adjusting their process, while remaining aligned with core principles. The values they used were communication, empowered teams, continuous improvement, and delivering customer value early.

Focus early on automation and continuous integration. Although Salesforce.com already had automation in place, they needed to make substantial efficiency improvements to the automated build system. These enhancements permitted more frequent check-in/build/test runs and were critical to support the required short development cycles.

Provide radical transparency. The rollout team discovered that transparency in everything they did was critical to their success. They over-communicated vision, information, guidance, and plans to everyone in the organization. This permitted them to adapt on a daily basis to ensure they reached their goal.

Leverage external agile training and coaching. Salesforce.com sent approximately 25% of their R&D organization to professional training. They also hired external agile coaches who brought two key contributions. The first was the ability to leverage lessons learned from other organizations transitioning to agile. The second was because they were external to the organization, some people were more comfortable receiving constructive advice from their outside experts.

Don't Underestimate the Importance of Upper Leadership Support

It seems like every other week I hear about another company who failed to successfully adopt agile. Their intentions were pure; they embraced the idea, hired a coaching firm, and ramped things up. But some time later, no one was very excited.

In many cases the story I hear is, "We didn't get the right amount of support from above." This is a common occurrence. Managers and team members are trying to implement a massive change within the organization, and upper leadership provides only lukewarm support and expects immediate results.

This is a recipe for failure. Members of upper leadership need to listen to those on the frontlines of implementing the agile transformation and provide their unwavering support to help drive the types of changes that are necessary. From aggressively dealing with naysayers who are polluting the process to removing impediments to speeding technical change, those in charge *must* grease the skids for agile to properly take hold.

16.5 How Long Will It Take to Adopt Agile?

As much as I'd love to tell you that once you make the decision to adopt agile, it will happen overnight, that would be overly optimistic. The bottom line is there are some things that take a bit of time, regardless of how many resources you throw at it.

There are several sequential tasks that are involved in getting a team up to speed and can't be divided and executed in parallel. As Fred Brooks put it, "The bearing of a child takes nine months, no matter how many women are assigned." (Brooks, 1995)

It takes time to educate management about the process, select a pilot team, identify the right time for them to pause their current development work, and schedule training.

You can only stick team members in a classroom so many hours a day, and it may not be possible for them to *completely* ignore other responsibilities. It will take some time to create and estimate their product backlog, and get their technical infrastructure updated to support more rapid development.

Finally, they'll start executing and learn on the job as they experience the process for the first time. It will take them at least a few sprints to get the hang of it and produce results.

The rest of the company needs some time to come up to speed with what the pilot team is doing, ask questions, and get used to the process. This model will be new to them, too.

Once the pilot team is up and running, additional teams can be ramped up more quickly, but getting that first group successful takes some time.

What I tell business leaders is, "Suspend disbelief for 13 to 16 weeks." That's about the amount of time I've seen it take, on average, for a new team to gain momentum and start producing visible outcomes.

Some teams will be faster, and some slower. But there should be some positive results that can be produced in that timeframe.

Support from the Top Is Critical

The "suspend disbelief" part comes from the fact that it will be a little messy at first. People will be stressed out because they don't immediately understand how it all works and they'll get impatient.

Others will be complaining to their managers that, "This is stupid." They'll likely point out that they're not getting anything done, and at least with the old way they'd be making some progress.

This is why it's so important that there is strong support from the top. Employees need to be heard, but then they need to be given encouragement from optimistic higher-ups that, "I know this will work. Let's just give it a bit more time. I know this is hard but please stick with it."

16.6 A Sample Agile Adoption Timeline

This may all sound great, but it can be difficult to visualize exactly how it will work.

The diagram below shows the typical adoption timeline I've used with a variety of companies. The actual duration may vary depending upon how aggressive the company can ramp up resources to dedicate to the effort.

This plan has a strong focus on the pilot team early on, with additional teams added once that team is well underway and there's been enough time to understand how Scrum is best adapted.

Additional Scrum teams can be added faster or slower depending upon available agile coaching resources and the ability for the PMO to manage the pace of change.

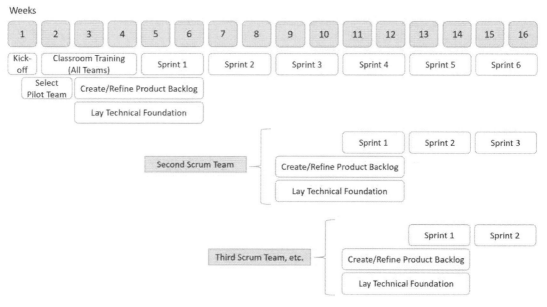

A typical agile adoption timeline. It's important for the pilot team to work independently ahead of rolling out Scrum to additional teams, to allow the company to adjust to an agile approach.

You'll notice quite a bit of time for each Scrum team to lay the technical foundation. Although the pilot team often faces the most work to implement infrastructure such as continuous integration, I've found that this is one of the largest up-front challenges for every team.

There's time involved with deploying the technical components each team needs, plus time for the development team to come up to speed with new tools and technical workflows during their first sprint.

Key Takeaways

- Moving to agile isn't limited to your technical personnel. The entire company is affected by this new way of thinking and working.

- The groups in the company that are typically affected most significantly are product management, project management, software development, and upper leadership.

- Project managers often fear they'll be marginalized when moving to agile, but in reality they can play a critical role in the company's adoption.

- Project managers are a good fit for either the ScrumMaster or product owner role. ScrumMaster is ideal for those who tend to be rule followers and thrive on the behind-the-scenes details. Product owner is a good fit for those who like to be the face of the team and enjoy working with both business stakeholders and developers.

- The project management office (PMO) serves a critical role, leading the agile adoption process and ensuring the right communication happens among everyone in the organization.

- The PMO can help encourage innovation and spread new ideas from within each Scrum team to all the other teams. This helps the entire organization innovate much more rapidly than if there were islands of knowledge locked up within each team.

- Key success factors include executive sponsorship, extreme transparency, focusing on core values, and an early focus on automation and continuous integration.

- Organizations can move to agile by starting with one pilot team or the "big bang" approach, moving all teams simultaneously to the new process. I believe the lowest-risk approach is starting with a pilot team, then rolling out additional teams once that team has settled in to the process.

- I typically recommend leaders to, "Suspend disbelief for 13 to 16 weeks," which is the average time it takes for a new team and the rest of the company to get used to this new way of thinking and working and producing visible results.

Chapter 17
Forming Your Pilot Scrum Team

When you form a team, why do you try to form a team? Because teamwork builds trust and trust builds speed.

*- **Russel Honoré**, Commander of Joint Task Force Katrina, responsible for coordinating military relief efforts for Hurricane Katrina.*

At this point you understand the fundamentals, you've read about some of the challenges you may face, and now it's time for the next step: selecting your pilot team.

The initial team will be the trailblazers. They'll be the first to transform their way of thinking and working as they adapt to this new model.

Since Scrum is incomplete, it's up to them to fill in the blanks and determine how agile will look at your company. No one knows that quite yet—everyone will be discovering what works best as they go through the process and experiment along the way. The pilot team will be the innovators.

You'll want to put some careful thought into the makeup of this Scrum team. They need to be the right group of individuals, with the right set of skills, and the right personality traits. If you select a bunch of people at random and shove them together, they may not succeed and that could result in a setback on your company's path to becoming agile.

Although this chapter is focused on your first Scrum team, I suggest keeping the advice it contains in mind as you form additional Scrum teams. This will help ensure you are giving each of your teams the greatest chance to be successful.

17.1 Select a Team You Think Can Be Successful

As I talked about in the last chapter, you're embarking on a challenging journey and there's nothing wrong with stacking the deck in your favor. The entire company will be looking at the pilot Scrum team to see what happens.

The skeptics will be thinking, "This will never work." The last thing you want to do is prove them right.

That said, you don't want to create a pilot team full of all the top superstars in the company. That could backfire, resulting in a feeling of, "Of course *they* can make this process work. They're the smartest and most capable people in the company! I doubt others will be able to be as successful."

I do suggest you pick superstars for three roles: product owner, ScrumMaster, and the senior developer or architect.

In my experience, strong people in these positions can help ensure success. Although they're not the boss, they will become the spiritual leaders for the Scrum team in three key areas: vision, process, and technology.

They'll come up to speed more quickly with the process and "get it" without much of a challenge. They'll be able to adjust to the inevitable changes along the way and charge full-speed ahead. The rest of the team will feed off this and keep a positive can-do attitude.

Avoid Junior Programmers

On the other end of the spectrum, I'd avoid including very junior programmers on the pilot development team. It's OK to have a mix of mid-level to upper-level people, but rank beginners will drag the team down and make it difficult for them to move quickly.

The entire team will be challenged as they learn Scrum, so you don't want to add the extra stress of dealing with developers who aren't yet fully proficient with programming.

To be clear, this limitation is specific to the pilot team, as part of stacking the deck in your favor to ensure their success. As you add more Scrum teams, having a mix of developer experience is a great way to help junior programmers become mid-level programmers, and mid-level to become senior.

Include a Skeptic

It makes sense to include someone on the team who is at least a little bit skeptical. You may not want someone who is so anti-agile that they'll be a constant pain, but someone who has a bit of an, "I'm not sure about this but I'll play along" attitude can be helpful.

Once that person starts getting a taste of success, they often become one of the biggest proponents of agile within your organization. Others in the company, knowing that person was skeptical going in, can come away with a feeling of, "If *she* is on board, there must be something to this."

Remember that you are introducing real, deep change, and fear within the organization will be pervasive. Your challenge is more emotional than procedural. Demonstrating success in a believable way is an important part of getting those who come after the pilot team on board.

Find Team Members Trusted by the Business

In some companies, there is animosity between certain members of the product team or management, and technical team members. For whatever reason, they have a poor working relationship. They may not trust each other, or simply may not get along.

Avoid including these folks on the pilot team. Similar to including junior programmers, your goal is to avoid introducing any extra challenges or distractions. A constant political battle due to personality conflicts isn't going to help.

17.2 Select a Product Built Using Agile-Friendly Technology

The theme of this book is combining a solid agile process with supporting technical discipline to produce the best results. Some technologies are better suited for techniques such as automated unit testing, continuous integration, and deployment to a variety of test environments. Others are not.

Biasing your selection toward a product that utilizes more agile-friendly technologies will help avoid adding technical hurdles.

Think about a product in your company built using commercial software development technology such as Microsoft .NET or Java. Both have rich tooling support for unit testing, continuous integration, source code control, and automated deployment to isolated test environments.

If the product is a web application and it uses a front-end framework, select one that's using Angular or React if possible, the two most popular. These both support unit testing and continuous integration.

Sticking to popular technologies will help your development team since they will be able to find answers to their inevitable challenges via training, consultants, or community websites such as StackOverflow.com. More obscure technologies will slow things down due to it being difficult to find answers to technical problems.

Although Scrum can be used for teams utilizing technologies such as Salesforce.com, or those building websites with a content management system (CMS), applying all the technical practices I describe in this book will be more challenging.

Salesforce.com supports unit testing and multiple "sandbox" test environments, but it doesn't work quite as seamlessly as .NET or Java. CMSs typically include the ability to write code, but much of the work on a website is not compatible with traditional source code management techniques and multiple test environments.

We've successfully used Scrum for client projects using Salesforce.com and CMS-based websites. The most complex website had over 15,000 pages. The agile approach got the team producing much better than they had been with their waterfall approach, but technical limitations made the process less smooth.

Teams in your company using these technologies can come along later, once the pilot team has demonstrated success.

17.3 Select Team Members Who Can Be Dedicated to the Pilot Team

One mistake I see companies make with their pilot team members is thinking they can work on anything else while they're coming up to speed.

It *might* be possible a few months down the road to have *some* be a member of more than one Scrum team, once they are well-versed in the process and things are humming along. For example, I find that ScrumMasters can be a member of two or three teams, and occasionally a product owner or architect/lead developer can be a member of two teams.

Programmers should be dedicated to only one team if possible. It's extremely difficult to keep all the technical ideas for more than one product in the heads of your technical people. Plus, interruptions and context-switching can take a toll on developers feeling productive. (Meyer, et al., 2014)

Each day, everyone aims to move the product forward at a very rapid rate—typically much faster than they are used to. This takes a lot of focused effort from each member.

Add into the equation that they'll be simultaneously learning how to work in this new way, and they won't have time for anything else.

I've met project managers who are trying to juggle as many as *15 projects*. That is absolutely not possible with this new model.

When you choose the members of your pilot team, make sure that you can get every other project off their plate and moved to someone else. You'll help set them up for success when they can focus on one thing.

17.4 Choosing the Product Owner

Though there is no hierarchy within a Scrum team, and no "boss," in my experience the product owner can make or break a team. A good product owner won't guarantee success, but a bad product owner will almost always doom your Scrum team to failure.

Though the product owner is not in charge, they are the visionary on the team, and since they are determining the direction in which everyone is moving, solid leadership qualities are important. Select a weak person or a bad fit, and the team will suffer.

It's also a challenging role. They will work with a variety of stakeholders, who seldom all want the same thing. They must distill all their wishes, needs, and desires into one single product backlog, and they alone select the priority order they believe will best deliver business value.

Someone is going to have a problem with the product owner's decisions, almost all the time. They will be challenged, and they need to be able to defend their thinking, even under pressure. They will often need to stand up to overbearing stakeholders who are trying to overrule them.

By the way, this is where support from the top comes into play. The manager of whoever is leaning on the product owner needs to say, "Back off. It's his decision, and his alone."

Traits of a Good Product Owner

The traits you're looking for in a product owner are:

Decisive. It's important for a product owner to consider all the inputs, but then make a decision and stand by it.

Personable. The product owner needs to be able to get along with just about everyone, inside and outside the team, even in the face of inevitable stress.

Calm. Because of the challenges of this role, it's important to have someone with a calm demeanor. I'm all for someone who is passionate—that's certainly my personality when I've been a product owner—but you want someone who won't fly off the handle and get into yelling matches.

This is especially important when the product owner is interacting with the development team. Few technical people—who tend to be at least a bit introverted—react well to brash individuals.

Detail-oriented. Building software is about the details, and it's up to the product owner to ensure those details are worked out with the development team when they ask, "When the user does this, then does that, and then does this other thing, what should happen?" Being able to think through things at a fine-grained level is a key success factor.

A little bit technical. It's helpful for the product owner to be at least a *little* bit technical. This helps them interact with the development team and grasp the technical challenges they face, so they can think about how to adjust their vision to keep things moving.

You don't want a product owner who is *too* technical. For example, I wouldn't select someone who is currently a developer. That may lead to them trying to tell the team *how* to do it as opposed to *what* to build—a no-no in Scrum. If they were a programmer in the past, that's fine, but I don't think a product owner should be able to sit down to write code. That will get too messy.

A good public speaker. Part of the sprint review process is instilling faith in the stakeholders who are attending. This is especially important as you're just getting going with agile, since they will likely be skeptical. A product owner who can stand in front of the room and talk through what the development team produced during the sprint, showing off what they were able to accomplish, and how it matches up with what the stakeholders asked for, goes a long way toward winning over the skeptics.

Sources of Good Product Owners

You likely already have some people in your company who would make great product owners. Here are some traditional job titles you can consider, as long as they possess the traits I listed above:

Product managers. Living and breathing the vision and details is what product managers do all day long. They're already part of the product group, which is the best part of the organization to "own" the product owners. They deal with interpreting user needs and the demands of stakeholders and are used to managing the details. They typically have extensive experience working with developers to help them understand the vision.

Project managers. Those with the right personality traits can make great product owners. Project managers are detail oriented and are typically well-versed in how software products get built. One challenge for a project manager who is used to directing the daily work of a team, is backing off from that tendency when they adopt the role of product owner. Instead, they should focus on laying out the vision and allowing the development team to figure out how to do it, with the ScrumMaster helping them through the process.

User experience architects. This is one of my favorite sources for product owners. Their entire professional career has been focused on some of the most challenging demands a product owner will face. They've talked with countless users and stakeholders about what they want a product to do. They've needed to then take those requirements and visualize exactly how it will work. And they've had to deal with myriad details.

Finally, they've had to explain their concepts to developers as well as defend the rationale behind their choices. If you have a strong user experience person who is interested in a new way to leverage their skills, consider them for a product owner role.

Business analysts. Like user experience architects, business analysts are used to dissecting the needs of users and creating details to be passed along to the development team. Given the right set of personality traits, a business analyst can make a great product owner.

17.5 Choosing the ScrumMaster

The ScrumMaster keeps everyone in line. They are a combination of the ultimate rule-follower and the ultimate rule-breaker. They ensure everyone stays within the boundaries of Scrum, while constantly saying, "Let's try something different," if it seems like a change may enhance the team's throughput.

They are an embedded Scrum coach within the team, helping everyone understand the fundamentals and evolving the process as they go.

This drives innovation within Scrum's 10 guideposts, ensuring the best process emerges given the unique context of the Scrum team, their product, and the technology they're using.

I like to call the ScrumMaster the "mom" on the team. They keep an eye on all the moving parts, and gently nudge things along. They may nag at times, to keep everyone accountable. "Anna, you've been saying for three days that you'll have that done 'tomorrow.' Do you need help?"

They also protect the team from outside influences, such as when someone from another team or department bugs the team members. "Noah, I notice you keep asking the developers on our team to work on things that aren't related to our product. Can you tell me more about that?"

Having others in the company siphon away time and attention from the development team interferes with their ability to get things done.

Finally, the ScrumMaster ensures the team remains clear of impediments. If one comes up, they're like a pit bull, latching on and ensuring it's resolved as quickly as possible, so the team can keep moving.

Steve Maguire, in his book *Debugging the Development Process*, uses an analogy of a house being moved across town. Not the contents of the house, but the *entire house*, lifted off its foundation. For that to happen smoothly, someone needs to be looking ahead, arranging to have power lines taken down and removing other obstacles that would block the progress of the truck as it slowly drives through town in the middle of the night. (Maguire, 1994)

I like to think of the ScrumMaster as that person who is out in front of the team, "taking down the wires." They're not taking them down themselves, but they are ensuring the right people are helping to remove those blockers, so the team doesn't have to pull over on the side of the road and wait for the power company to show up.

Having the ScrumMaster chase down impediments keeps the team heads-down and moving forward without distraction.

One thing that the ScrumMaster *doesn't* do is tell everyone what to work on each day. Scrum is an all-volunteer endeavor. There is no "assigning" in Scrum. Those who have experience with traditional project management might struggle with this at first, since they may be used to orchestrating the various tasks of the development team.

To be an effective ScrumMaster, the shift needs to be made to *facilitating* the process as opposed to *directing* the process.

Traits of a Good ScrumMaster

The traits of an effective ScrumMaster are:

Disciplined. Following the rules is a critical part of Scrum, and the ScrumMaster is the one who ensures everyone on the Scrum team is adhering to the core 10 principles, as well as any innovations they've introduced as they've made the process their own. Human nature being what it is, there are times when the team may say, "Can't we skip the daily scrum today?" or "Do we really need to spend time doing sprint planning?" The ScrumMaster needs to always be the one to say, "We're sticking with it."

Helpful. The ScrumMaster is absolutely in a servant leadership role. Although they often pitch in to help move things along, their primary role is ensuring everyone *else* on the team has what they need. From resolving impediments to orchestrating communication among the product owner and the development team, they're always focused on being as helpful as possible.

A rule-follower. Related to being disciplined, the person who fills the ScrumMaster role should be one who loves to follow the rules and ensure the team does as well.

Creative. Since Scrum is by design incomplete, the team innovates to create their own flavor of the process. The ScrumMaster drives that innovation, constantly challenging the team to come up with new ideas. It helps if they are creative themselves, so they can contribute their own thoughts on how to do it better.

Diplomatic. One of the challenges of being a ScrumMaster is the need to be firm, while at the same time avoiding generating animosity among the team members. If the team comes to disrespect and undervalue the ScrumMaster, it will be tough for them to be at the top of their game.

Confident. The ScrumMaster owns the process for that Scrum team. Period. No one else can decide how the development team will get the work done. They certainly should do their best to get buy-in from the team, but if there is dissent, they are the final decision-maker.

Protective. The ScrumMaster is on a constant lookout for any distractions or outside influences getting in the way of the team getting things done. Having a feeling of ownership—of it being "their team"—can help drive this protective behavior.

Wants to improve. "I know we're killing it. But how can we do it even *better*?" That's what the ScrumMaster should be asking. They're always striving for perfection, knowing that they'll never attain it, but by God, they're going to try.

Sources of Good ScrumMasters

Some existing job titles to consider when selecting your ScrumMaster are:

Project managers. Project managers typically have the requisite skills to be on the lookout for impediments, keep track of the details, and nudge the team in the right direction. However, if they are the overbearing type that must always be in control, that might be a warning sign. A ScrumMaster is most definitely *not* in a position of control. Facilitation is the key word here. They won't be "managing" the work.

Business analysts. Also attuned to dealing with the details, a business analyst can make a good ScrumMaster. They typically understand the development process and what it takes to get a product built. If they have the right personality traits, they could be a good fit.

Quality assurance engineers. Some QA engineers I've come to know have aspirations of rising above testing. The ScrumMaster role might be a good fit for them. They're likely to be detail-oriented, and probably a rule-follower. If they also possess the other traits, they may excel in this role, given the right training.

Software engineers. On many teams, a software engineer takes on the role of ScrumMaster. The only thing I'd be careful about here is if they are so busy writing code that they don't pay enough attention to their duties as a ScrumMaster. Like with the QA engineer, I'd be careful to ensure they receive solid Scrum training, so they understand the fundamentals.

17.6 Don't Have One Person Be Both Product Owner and ScrumMaster

In the interest of perceived efficiency, some decide to make the product owner and ScrumMaster the same person.

This is a mistake.

These are two completely separate roles with no overlap. They have different responsibilities, require different personality traits, and it's important to have natural tension between them. (Cohn, 2014a)

If the team is really small and doesn't require a full-time level of effort for both roles, I'd much rather see two part-time people filling each role than one full-time person filling both roles.

Reasons to Separate the Roles

Has anyone in the history of Scrum put one person in both roles? Sure. In fact, I've done it in the past.

But it was messy. And now, looking back, I see how much we lost by not having two separate people.

With the significant drawbacks it introduces, I don't think it's worth the risk to merge these two roles into one person. I recommend you avoid it.

There are a few reasons to separate these two roles.

The roles have different responsibilities. The product owner typically spends their day splitting their time between meeting with stakeholders and end users to talk about what comes next, updating the product backlog, and answering questions from the team. The ScrumMaster is "behind the curtains," working the machinery of the development team to help them produce *right now*. The product owner lives primarily in the future, whereas the ScrumMaster is living moment-by-moment.

They require different personality traits. The product owner is the dreamer. The big-picture person. The cheerleader who gets fired up about what the team is building. They don't get mired down in implementation details and day-to-day challenges of the development team; they continue thinking about what else might be possible. The ScrumMaster, on the other hand, is all *about* the details. They are helping the development team keep all the balls in the air, facilitating their work, and resolving impediments. These are two different types of people.

A natural tension is important. It's the product owner's role to dream big, assuming no constraints on what is possible. They push for more out of the development team as often as they can, since they're responsible for the return on investment, and they often have stakeholders breathing down their neck for more.

On the other hand, the ScrumMaster is there to provide a balance of power and to act as an ambassador of sorts for the development team. They push back when the product owner gets get a little too overbearing or tries to break the rules. "Adam, I know you want more, but you can't change the scope mid-sprint. Let's see how the team does and maybe if they wrap everything up early they can sneak something else in at the end."

Have Each Role Report to Different People

One problem I've seen is when the product owner and ScrumMaster both report to the same person, for example, if they're both in the same department. This can get messy because you might have natural tension at the Scrum team level, but when that tension occasionally evolves into managers getting involved, it helps to have *them* be two separate people as well.

Especially at the beginning, the product owner and ScrumMaster will be figuring out how to work well together and agreeing to disagree when appropriate. They both need to push when required, but back off when it's obvious that going further would break the rules.

But sometimes people struggle with that. That's where the managers come into play.

The four of them—the product owner, ScrumMaster, and each of their managers—can sit down and talk it through. The managers, knowing and fully supporting the rules of Scrum, can help the team members work through their differences and help steer them back on track toward a healthy working relationship.

If they both report to the same person, this is not possible, and you'll lose out on this ability for them to leverage their "servant leaders" for help.

17.7 Assembling the Development Team

The development team is where the rubber meets the road. They are the ones who will do the work, executing on the vision owned by the product owner, while being guided along the process by the ScrumMaster.

Here are some key tips for selecting your development team:

Ensure there is at least one senior developer or architect. Ideally, select someone who has experience with test-driven development and continuous integration. This will ensure that at least *someone* won't be starting from scratch as the team comes up to speed with these concepts. This person's role is largely to help the developers and ensure the code is written well and in keeping with the overall technical goals of the company. They aren't typically sitting down and writing code all day long.

Include all the required skills. Ensure you have expertise included for each technology used to build the product. Ideally this includes full-stack developers, who can work on either the back end or front end of the product. It may also include just back-end or just front-end developers, but I would prefer full-stack developers on my team if possible.

At least one full-stack developer with more experience on the back end, and one with more experience on the front end would be the ideal combination. That way you get more flexibility, since they can work on either, but collectively there is deep experience in both.

Avoid very junior developers. Very junior developers end up sucking up all the bandwidth of the more senior developers, who are trying to pull them along. Leave them out of the club for now and let the mid-level and senior developers knock it out of the park. They can come along later on subsequent Scrum development teams.

Include DevOps capability, at least part-time. In Part II, I talked extensively about the technical underpinnings required to execute Scrum effectively. Managing source code, test environments, and continuous integration are all very important. If no one on the team has experience with these technologies, ensure you include someone from your DevOps group, even if part-time. It's critical that the development team can fully own their end-to-end process and all their environments, instead of relying on people outside the team.

Don't forget about QA. Remember that in Scrum, there is no "handing it over to QA" after the sprint ends. All testing and bug fixing must happen in the sprint, and the team needs to be capable of doing all of this work. You don't need a large number of QA engineers, since the whole team typically ends up pitching in with testing, particularly toward the end of the sprint. We typically have one full-time QA engineer on a team with four full-time programmers. I would recommend no more than two.

Keep the team size small. Remember that you are going to be teaching everyone on the team about Scrum and how to work together. Erring on the smaller side will reduce the number of people who need to get up to speed and learn how to work together.

I'd recommend: product owner, ScrumMaster, senior developer or architect, two to four full-time software engineers, and one QA engineer. That's six to eight people, right in the sweet spot of "seven plus or minus two," the typical guidance for the size of a Scrum development team.

Is This Enough QA Horsepower?

Many people are surprised when I talk about only one QA engineer on a team with as many as four full-time developers. They say, "Isn't the usual recommendation that a QA engineer can only support two, or *maybe* three developers?"

That was the guidance I followed pre-agile as well. However, I found that once we adopted Scrum, the QA engineers simply didn't have enough work to do—a nice problem to have!

There are a few reasons for this:

The software is dramatically more stable. Test-driven development, comprehensive unit test coverage, and consistent code reviews accelerate discovery and resolution of bugs. Therefore, the QA engineers have fewer bugs to find. Our teams produce software each sprint that's at a level of quality we only obtained after about six months of production use and bug fixing back in the waterfall days.

The amount of code is smaller. Because each user story is being driven to a shippable state, there's less code than the waterfall approach of dumping a bunch of work onto a QA team all at once. It's easier to keep up with testing, and the bugs tend to be smaller and easier to fix.

Requirements bugs are reduced or eliminated. Because the business is involved all along the way—embodied by the product owner—and because the entire Scrum team is helping to write and enhance user story acceptance criteria, it's much less likely that there are major requirements bugs. This dramatically reduces the QA effort.

Programmers can test. Part of what makes this work is every member of the development team does whatever is necessary to get across the finish line. Toward the end of each sprint, there's usually an "all-hands-on-deck" approach, with everyone testing the last story or two. QA engineers seldom have the experience to write production-quality code, but programmers are certainly capable of testing.

The ScrumMaster can pitch in. If the ScrumMaster on the team has the bandwidth—which is usually the case unless they're working with multiple teams—there's no reason they can't assist with the testing if it would help things move along.

Note that the product owner shouldn't test until the development team thinks the product is shippable. This helps keep their perspective fresh, so they can see things that the development team may have missed because they're too close to the work of the sprint.

17.8 Seat Your Co-Located Team Together

Most companies have their product people in one area of the office, project managers in another, and programmers and QA engineers in additional locations.

That's going to need to change if you want to get the best results.

Agile teams work because you get all the necessary roles together, empower them to make decisions, and get them communicating like they never have before. If everyone is sitting in a different location, that's very difficult. You might as well put them in five different buildings.

You have a *huge* advantage if all your Scrum team members are in the same location. Your co-located team will likely out-perform other teams that have members in multiple locales. To get the biggest bang for the buck, you need to sit them together.

Those who are used to a waterfall approach often don't appreciate just how much conversation happens throughout every day as the team works together. Because they're moving much more quickly than normal, at least some members of the team will need to coordinate their work almost continuously.

It's much easier to do this when they're sitting together. (Pietri, 2009)

This often involves working with the facilities team to relocate people and may involve reconfiguring existing work areas. I realize this is probably a pain and may involve you having to fight a bit to make it happen. This is another reason why it's so important to have buy-in at the highest levels. If you encounter resistance, upper leadership can often push it forward.

If you think this is just too much to deal with and threatens your ability to get your pilot team going, you can come up with other creative short-term ideas. I've seen some companies retire a large conference room and have the pilot team take it over as their shared workspace.

Just remember that this should be viewed as a temporary solution. As you roll out agile to the rest of the company, you'll need to tackle this challenge.

One drawback of the conference-room approach is it's difficult to collaborate. If two team members seated on opposite sides of the table need to collaborate on one of their screens, someone needs to walk around the table.

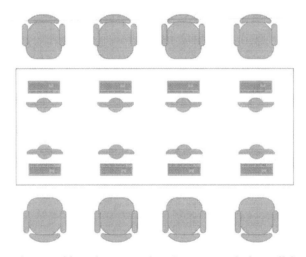

Seating around a conference table or face-on workstations can work, but collaboration often involves someone walking to the other side.

A pod-style arrangement is often a better option. The team works around the outside and there is open space in the middle. (Muldoon, 2014)

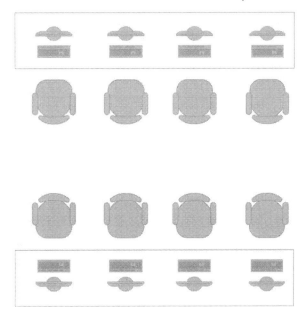

A pod-style arrangement typically works best for co-located teams, providing easier collaboration.

This allows the team to feel like they have their own "protected" space, it allows them to have a daily scrum right there in the middle, and they can easily wheel their chairs around to have a quick conversation or look at someone else's monitor to collaborate.

17.9 Distributed Teams and Multiple Time Zones

If it's likely that once you roll out agile to the entire organization, there will be Scrum teams where one or more members will be in different geographic locations, I suggest you consider making your pilot team at least partially distributed as well.

As I pointed out in Section 17.1, you want to create a team that is likely to be successful, so I'd play favorites here. For example, do your best to keep most of the team in one location, and pick strong individuals who are remote.

This will help you prove out the model of how Scrum will work at your company when team members aren't sitting right next to each other.

At Ascendle, 100% of our development teams are distributed, and they routinely out-perform any other development team I've ever seen. We've discovered a few key factors that make this work: time zone alignment, verbal communication, real-time written communication, and a strict adherence to Scrum guideposts.

Time Zone Alignment

Because of its focus on side-by-side teamwork, it's imperative that there are as many hours in the day as possible for the Scrum team members to work simultaneously. We've found that as much as a seven-hour time difference can be accommodated, but not much more.

One group shifts their work hours a little earlier and the other a little later, and they can overlap by four to six hours per day, depending upon how much they adjust. On time-intensive days, such as when sprint planning occurs, there may be more of a shift to ensure enough time to complete the process.

We've had team members offset by as many as 12 hours, but they adjusted their work day to keep that four to six hours per day of overlap.

I strongly discourage you to have members of the same team working on opposite sides of the clock with no work day alignment. The idea of having your offshore team members work while you sleep sounds romantic, but you introduce significant challenges without real-time communication. (Alzoubi, et al., 2015)

Verbal Communication

Some companies adopting Scrum with a distributed team discount the value of verbal communication. "We'll just send our daily scrum update via email or in the chat room." Remember *individuals and interactions* over *processes and tools* from the Agile Manifesto. If you avoid verbal communication in lieu of written updates, you're abandoning this key principle.

Our distributed teams use GoToMeeting for their Scrum ceremonies, and everyone participates. This brings another factor into play: verbal communication skills. If you have team members who struggle with being understood by others on the team, they likely aren't a good fit for your pilot team and may not be a good fit for *any* Scrum team in your organization.

This may sound harsh, but if the *entire* team can't effectively communicate in one spoken language, they are set up for failure. Verbal communication is too critical to the success of agile.

You *cannot* "make up for it" via written communication. That may have worked with waterfall, but it will not work with Scrum. (Melnik & Maurer, 2004)

Real-Time Written Communication

Communication doesn't stop when the daily scrum is over. Scrum requires an almost continuous stream of dialogue between the team members. This will often mean picking up the phone—or Skype or GoToMeeting—but much of the communication between team members tends to be quick, focused on answering brief questions or synchronizing their work.

For example, "Maria, I just committed that code you were waiting on," or "Ben, I fixed those code review comments. Can you take a quick look to see if it's what you were thinking?"

For a co-located team, this is easy. They just turn around in their chair and tell the person. However, if they're distributed, they need a way to facilitate this ad-hoc communication. A team chat room is an easy way to make this happen.

Tools such as Slack make this type of communication easy. If you have a distributed team, I highly recommend creating a team chat room.

There's one other thing to keep in mind. Keep others in the company from adding their own commentary in the Scrum team's chat room, which can be very distracting. If you *must* provide access to anyone not on the Scrum team, ensure they know it's a "view only" arrangement and have them keep their commentary to themselves.

To provide access to managers and mentors, I suggest a separate chat room. This is where team members can go to ping those outside the team for help, without adding noise to "their" team room.

To the greatest extent possible, keep the Scrum team's chat room a "safe place" just for them.

Strict Adherence to Scrum

I've already talked about how important it is to stick to the fundamentals, but if you slack off with a distributed team, you'll *really* feel the pain.

Co-located teams can often get away with cheating a bit. Although they'll still be hurting their ability to reach their full potential, things won't completely fall apart.

That's not the case with a distributed team.

Without physical proximity to fall back on, they'll quickly spin off in different directions and progress will likely grind to a halt. It's always important to stick to the rules, but with a distributed team the cost for failing to do so becomes much more severe.

Key Takeaways

- When choosing a pilot team, there's nothing wrong with stacking the deck a bit. Don't pick a bunch of absolute superstars who will succeed no matter what, but don't be afraid to bias your selections to ensure they can become a model for the rest of the company.

- Select a pilot team who will focus on a product that uses commercial software development technology such as Java or .NET. Avoid technologies that have weaker support for contemporary development practices, such as websites and Salesforce.com. Although Scrum can be used for those teams, there are some technical challenges you'll want your pilot team to avoid.

- Pilot team members need to be dedicated 100% to their Scrum team. Don't pick someone who needs to continue being involved with five other projects. Get *everything* else off their plate before putting them on the team. The only exception may be a part-time specialist such as a DevOps person if the developers don't have the necessary skills to maintain their test environments.

- The product owner is the make-or-break Scrum team member, so choose wisely. Often a product manager makes a great product owner, if they have the right personality. A project manager can also be a product owner if they have the right traits. Finally, some of the best product owners I've seen are user experience (UX) architects, who live and breathe the process of interpreting end-user requirements and creating a vision for how to solve their challenges.

- A traditional project manager can often become a ScrumMaster, as long as they can make the shift from directing the work to facilitating the process.

- Make sure you have the product owner and ScrumMaster roles filled by two *different* people. Combining them loses the ability for them to focus tightly on their role, and you'll lose the natural tension that's an important success factor.

- The development team should include a senior developer or architect, two to four full-time mid-level or senior developers, and QA and DevOps expertise. Avoid very junior developers and ensure you have enough collective experience to handle all the technology, for example, both front end and back end.

- Seat your pilot team together in the same physical spot in the office. A pod-style arrangement is most effective, but if you will encounter a large delay while you work with the facilities group, pick a temporary spot for them such as a large conference room that can be repurposed. This is really important for co-located teams; don't fall into the trap of thinking this is optional just because it's going to ruffle some feathers.

- If it's likely that the majority of your teams will be distributed once you roll out agile to the entire organization, include one or two remote members on the pilot team. This will help you prove out the model of how the process works with distributed teams.

- Key success factors for distributed teams include time zone alignment—ensuring four to six hours a day of overlap for the entire team—verbal communication, real-time written communication, and strict adherence to Scrum rules.

Chapter 18
Your Team's Path to Excellence

The only source of knowledge is experience.

- Albert Einstein

One of our team members was speaking to a group of business analysts the other day at a conference, teaching them how to write user stories. The audience was full of people struggling to figure out how they fit into this new agile world.

After the session, she was talking to a few folks who stayed after to ask some additional questions, and the topic of training came up. The attendee said, "We were just handed a book about Scrum and told, 'Read this and figure it out.' We tried, but we can't seem to make it work on our own."

Dismayed, our team member explained that what they need goes well beyond just reading a book.

Although I'd love to tell you that reading this book will fully prepare your team members to be successful, it's just one step in the process.

It's like saying, "Here's a book on how to play golf. Now go win your club championship."

There are some super-athletic people who can pick up the game and become really good, without any help or instruction. But most will need lessons, practice, and a heck of a lot of patience to become at least reasonably competent.

Golf is simple. I can explain it in two sentences: Whack a little white ball until it goes into a 4-inch cup. Try to hit it as few times as possible.

However, I think everyone would agree that golf is not *easy*.

Just like Scrum.

Unfortunately, this pattern of dramatically underestimating what it takes to become proficient repeats itself over and over as teams struggle to make agile work in their company. I hear about it all the time.

In fact, the most common scenario I've seen is a company that tried winging it and completely failed, abandoning agile altogether and going back to "the old way."

It wasn't for lack of trying. They bought some online training. They sent some of their people to two-day certification classes. They read some books. Everyone *really* wanted to make it work. But most are now scratching their heads about what to do to fix it.

You can definitely limp along with a just OK agile process. But what I've seen is there can be *so* much more in it for you and your company if you do it right. Attaining even a basic level of competency is likely going to be light-years better than what you're experiencing now.

18.1 Four Stages of Learning: The Conscious Competence Model

Before I talk about the best way to prepare your people, I'd like to discuss a model of learning that I've found very helpful in understanding how we as humans attain proficiency in a new skill.

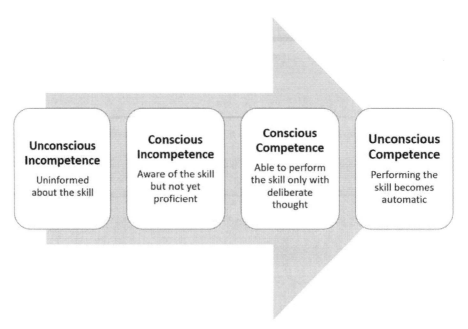

The conscious competence model has four stages of learning.

The model has four stages: (Chapman, n.d.)

1. *Unconscious incompetence.* This is the "blissfully ignorant" stage. There is a lack of awareness of the new skill, and the person may deny the relevance or usefulness of it. In general, they don't know what they don't know.

2. *Conscious incompetence.* The person is aware of the existence and relevance of the skill. They realize that if they improve their proficiency in this area, they will become more effective. Ideally, they make a commitment to learn and practice the new skill, to move to the next level.

3. *Conscious competence.* The new skill can be performed reliably at will. They can perform it without help but can't perform it well unless they're thinking about it. The skill isn't yet "second nature" or "automatic."

4. *Unconscious competence.* The person has practiced the new skill to the point that it enters the subconscious—it becomes "second nature." An example of this is when you drive to work while thinking of other things and you don't remember the trip. You were on "autopilot."

The exact origins of this model are debatable. Modern sources can be traced back to the 1960's, but some references to similar concepts go back thousands of years.

Most companies I've seen are somewhere between unconscious incompetence and conscious incompetence. Most managers and stakeholders are at the first level, and teams that are trying and failing are at the second.

I've occasionally seen teams that are at the third level—conscious competence—and sometimes I've discovered teams who are at the fourth level, just cranking out results sprint after sprint. But that's the exception.

Ascendle's development teams include team members who are all at level 3 or level 4. This is what you should expect to attain with your teams.

You *may* eventually be able to get everyone to the unconsciously competent level, but that's expecting a lot. That would be where everyone "just does it," without ever needing any reminders about how to stick with the process.

18.2 The Cognitive Apprenticeship Learning Method

Before schools, apprenticeship was the most common means of learning. This technique was used to transfer required knowledge to become an expert in fields from painting and sculpturing, to medicine and law.

Today, we still use similar methods in some cases. For example, to learn a new language. Through observation, coaching, and repetitive practice, the student at first stumbles, but over time they become better. Eventually, they can speak and write the new language independently, as they continue to practice and become even more proficient.

Cognitive apprenticeship embeds the learning of skills and knowledge in the social and functional context of their use. This is in contrast to most school-style instruction, which includes broad-based training that is often abstracted from its uses in the real world. (Collins, et al., 1989; Berryman, 1991)

This approach is a perfect match for the challenges of getting your people proficient with the agile process. You could sit them in a classroom for months, learning all there is to know about agile theory, but until it's applied in practice, that knowledge is not very leverageable.

This model can also result in teams that recognize a higher level of importance to using a process, as well as more motivation to solve problems—two critical factors to successfully adopting agile. (Walker, 2004)

The apprenticeship approach is a particularly good fit for Scrum, since at its heart there's a dependency on it being adapted on-the-fly in the context of a team in operation. A classroom-based training approach is impossible, since no one knows all the details until it's put into use in *your* team at *your* company.

18.3 Teaching the Fundamentals

Before diving into the apprenticeship approach, it's important to lay the groundwork with at least *some* background information. That way your team members have the required context to frame their experiential learning.

This is where traditional classroom-style learning can come into play, but not for months on end. This phase of the process typically takes two to three weeks, depending upon scheduling and availability. Team members spend about three hours each day attending training sessions.

You can see this approach illustrated in the sample adoption timeline in Section 16.6.

Who Needs Training?

It's likely fairly obvious that everyone on the Scrum team will need training, including the development team, product owner, and ScrumMaster.

However, the training shouldn't stop with them. You also need to provide training for everyone who is *not* on the Scrum team who will either be interacting with them or supporting them. They need to understand the rules, to avoid conflicts with the "old way" and the "new way."

Many companies fail in their agile adoption due to a lack of understanding and support from the top, as well as a general resistance at a cultural level to embracing agile principles.

(VersionOne, 2018) Paying attention to those surrounding the Scrum team is a critical way to limit risk and increase your likelihood of success.

There should be a determined focus on providing training to managers, upper leadership, and any other business stakeholders impacted by the work of the Scrum team. They'll need not only training on Scrum fundamentals, but ongoing check-ins to ensure their questions are addressed along the way.

Members of **upper leadership**, which could include members of the C-suite, need to understand the high-level concepts of Scrum. They require an awareness of inverting power within their company—those who are doing the work determine how it gets done, and everyone works in service of that goal. They also need to be aware of how the product gets built incrementally, so they know how important it is for them to attend sprint reviews and have their say about how the product is coming together.

Managers, to whom the members of the Scrum team report, need to learn how to make the shift from directing the work to supporting the work. They also need to learn how to defend their Scrum teams when others in the company question why they are being "allowed" to make their own process and technical decisions.

Other stakeholders, who have a vested interest in the work of the Scrum team, need to understand the rules of the road and how the product comes together. This may include senior architects, members of other groups or divisions in the company, and anyone else who is impacted by the development of the product.

Methods of Training

If you can hand everyone a copy of this book and you're comfortable that they'll read it and absorb the information, go for it. In my experience, however, not everyone is the type who can sit down and read a book cover to cover, then successfully apply the information.

As we've evolved our training process over the years, we've found lecture-style presentations work best to cover the fundamentals. A series of 60- to 90-minute classroom-style presentations, each focused on a specific area of agile and Scrum, gives team members enough information to get started, without overwhelming them.

This book can then be a detailed reference for team members to dive more deeply as they start using the process.

When your team members move from classroom-style presentations to applying new concepts through active learning, they'll tend to absorb the information more effectively and quickly become more competent. (Freeman, et al., 2014)

Important Topics to Cover

We've found that covering a series of key topics will get everyone to the starting line with enough knowledge to allow them to proceed to the apprenticeship phase.

This material should get everyone to the "conscious incompetence" stage of learning. They can't yet execute the process independently, but they have enough awareness to see the potential value and they are prepared to learn more by doing.

Suggested topics include the following:

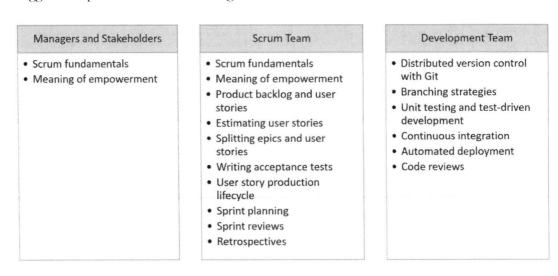

Managers and Stakeholders	Scrum Team	Development Team
• Scrum fundamentals • Meaning of empowerment	• Scrum fundamentals • Meaning of empowerment • Product backlog and user stories • Estimating user stories • Splitting epics and user stories • Writing acceptance tests • User story production lifecycle • Sprint planning • Sprint reviews • Retrospectives	• Distributed version control with Git • Branching strategies • Unit testing and test-driven development • Continuous integration • Automated deployment • Code reviews

Suggested topics for classroom-style training.

In the rest of this section, I'll describe a sample curriculum you could use with your team.

Managers, Upper Leadership, and Other Business Stakeholders

Agile and Scrum Fundamentals for Stakeholders. This is a high-level introduction to Scrum, with a bias toward the responsibilities of managers and leaders in the context of agile. A specific theme is what it means to have an "empowered" team and why it's in the best interest of everyone to make sure that empowerment actually happens.

Also included is what everyone outside the team can expect in terms of transparency, predictability, and accountability. Finally, there's a focus on the meaning of "servant leadership" and how that plays out day by day once the team is up and running.

The Meaning of Empowerment for Stakeholders. Often thrown around as a buzzword with nothing to back it up, this topic discusses what *true* empowerment looks like in practice. Questions such as, "How do we make sure they don't mess up if we let them make technical decisions?" are addressed, explaining how leaders help the Scrum development team by ensuring they have the information to make the best choices.

This topic also includes agile "anti-patterns" to watch out for—symptoms of empowerment failure.

Scrum Team Members: Product Owner, ScrumMaster and Development Team

Agile and Scrum Fundamentals for the Team. This is similar to the presentation for stakeholders, but from the perspective of someone on the Scrum team. It includes an overview of what it means for a team to be cross-functional, a discussion of each role, and an explanation of responsibilities and why the process works.

The Meaning of Empowerment for the Team. Again here, this is like the stakeholder presentation, but from the team perspective. The number one question from most teams is, "Are you sure they'll let us do this?" Unsure if they will truly be empowered by their higher-ups, this topic covers that question in-depth.

The rule that only the development team can determine how to get the product built will be explained, and why this means that the development team needs a lot more information. Included is an explanation that they need to ensure they're making the *right* decisions for them and their product, while also ensuring they support the company's overall strategy and goals.

The Product Backlog and User Stories. Most team members have some experience with "specs," but the concept of using lightweight user stories—and the fact that the entire team helps write them—is foreign to most. This topic explains the structure of the product backlog and takes an in-depth look at user stories and how to write them.

Estimating the Product Backlog. Story points, the Cohn scale, and velocity are covered in this topic, including how they're combined to create a schedule estimate. The mechanics of assigning story point estimates to user stories via the Planning Poker process are discussed, as well as an explanation of when estimating happens.

Splitting Epics and User Stories. When a product backlog is first created, it typically contains stories that are too large to fit into one sprint and must be split into smaller ones. This topic includes an explanation of why it's important to split stories and the various methods that the team can use to divide them, such as along functional boundaries, data boundaries, priorities, etc.

Writing Acceptance Tests. Part of ensuring each user story is truly ready for an end user is having a plan for ensuring it meets the expectations of the product owner. This topic discusses the behavior-driven development (BDD) style of writing acceptance test plans, and how in-depth they should be. It also addresses how to handle questions that come up about the desired behavior of a user story as the tests are written.

User Story Production Lifecycle. Before the Scrum team starts their first sprint planning session, it's important for them to understand how user stories typically move from the vision in the product owner's head to completed, tested, shippable functionality.

This topic includes a discussion about the different types of subtasks the team might include when they break down the required work to produce a user story. These include creating and reviewing acceptance tests, writing unit tests and code, performing a code review, and testing and fixing bugs prior to the product owner's final acceptance.

Sprint Planning. This topic brings all the prior presentations together, by giving the team a preview of the sprint planning process. It includes an overview of why sprint planning is so critical, which is important since most teams have a negative reaction at first. "Why are we spending all this time planning when we could be writing code?"

Sprint Reviews. Running effective sprint reviews is an important way to provide confidence to everyone outside the Scrum team. I've found that as soon as everyone can see real, working features that have been added in the last two weeks, skepticism evaporates. This topic provides an outline of the sprint review process, along with tips such as ensuring that the demo of the software takes center stage, and only showing functionality that's truly shippable.

Retrospectives. Some teams fall into the trap of wimping out on the retrospective process and missing a key part of Scrum—continuous improvement. This topic provides several suggested approaches to running the retrospective, and how to get more participation from quiet team members. Also included are tips on how to experiment with new ideas and adopt those that help improve the process.

Scrum Development Team

In addition to the Scrum-focused training outlined above, we've found that most development teams don't have a solid handle on contemporary software engineering techniques such as those I detailed in Section II.

A series of technical presentations can be used to address any knowledge gaps. If your development team is already well-versed in these concepts, some or all of these can be skipped.

Distributed Version Control with Git. Most technical team members have some experience with source code control, but it's typically with a centralized tool such as Subversion (SVN) or CVS.

This topic includes a discussion about distributed version control and why this newer technology is so much more powerful than the centralized approach. It also covers the fundamentals of Git, the most popular distributed version control system.

Branching Strategies for Agile Source Control. A critical part of making Scrum work is protecting the shippable product increment's code from half-complete, untested functionality. Branching strategies handle this problem gracefully, and this topic discusses various approaches and covers the Git Flow strategy in detail.

Unit Testing and Test-Driven Development. Today's developers would typically agree that unit testing is a great idea, but many don't know about best practices and how to get started. Fewer understand test-driven development and the benefits it can bring. This topic covers the fundamentals of unit testing, dependency isolation, and test-driven development, with a strong focus on, "Why you should care as a developer."

Continuous Integration. Unit tests are great but leaving it up to the developers to remember to run them can be a pitfall. This topic covers continuous integration fundamentals and includes some examples of different technologies the development team might consider.

Automated Deployment. Automated deployment is an important part of building efficiency into a Scrum development team. This topic covers how this technology works, and why it's so important to be able to deploy code with the click of a button or automatically with each code change.

Code Reviews. Inspecting code that someone else wrote is an important part of ensuring quality and knowledge-sharing among developers. This topic explains why it's so critical, what to look for during a code review, and the use of source code pull requests to facilitate reviews before code is merged into the main product.

Included is a discussion about what to do when issues are found, who should resolve them, and when code should be re-reviewed after updates are made.

18.4 Starting Your Team's Experiential Learning

Once the Scrum team and stakeholders have a good handle on the fundamentals, the next thing to do is get started. Be careful not to get stuck in a mode of "getting ready to get ready." Just dive right in and figure out the rest as you go.

The apprenticeship model, with its focus on hands-on learning, is a great way to reinforce agile concepts while at the same time figuring out how to adapt Scrum to work best for your organization.

We've experimented with a variety of approaches, and we've found the following works best. The next few chapters cover each of these topics in more detail.

Form the product backlog. The best way for most Scrum teams to begin learning about Scrum is to start with the process of creating the product backlog. Most of the time there is some sort of wish list for the product, but it's not usually in the form of a product backlog containing user stories in force-ranked order.

By having the entire team participate, they will start to understand the vision of the product more deeply. If the vision is a little hazy for the product owner, it will be forced into sharp focus through this exercise.

Estimate the size of the product backlog. Using Planning Poker, the Scrum development team will estimate the relative size of each user story and assign a story points number. This gives the product owner additional insight in case the relative priority of stories on the backlog needs to be re-thought if some are larger than expected. It also tells the team whether some larger stories near the top of the product backlog need to be split before their first sprint planning.

Split any stories larger than three points at the top of the backlog. In my experience, teams have a difficult time learning the process. Smaller user stories help them be successful by taking on just a little bit of functionality in their first sprint or two. This allows them to focus on learning the process while tackling bite-sized pieces of the product.

Splitting stories at the top of the product backlog that are larger than three story points—until there are five or six stories that are three points or smaller at the top—will help the team be more successful.

Lay the technical groundwork. While all the above is happening over the course of a few weeks, the development team—with the help of their managers and other technical leaders—can be laying the technical groundwork. Setting up test environments, configuring source code control, and getting continuous integration working will mean they can hit the ground running when they start their first sprint.

Start sprinting. Once the one-time setup work is done, there's nothing left to do but start the first sprint. As I outlined above, at first the development team will take on a very small amount of work—perhaps just two or three small stories of three points or less each. This is absolutely fine because the most important thing is to focus on doing the process well, while producing fully-tested, shippable functionality.

18.5 Agile Coaches

You're going to need some help orchestrating everything I'm talking about. You'll need either internal coaches or external coaches—or a combination of both—to move your team along.

Agile coaches can use a combination of the following techniques for knowledge transfer during this apprenticeship phase:

- *Modeling.* Coaches can temporarily take on various Scrum roles to model behavior. For example, one coach could act as the ScrumMaster and the other as the product owner, demonstrating how those roles interact with each other and the development team to facilitate the process.

- *Guiding.* As the Scrum team gets going with the process, coaches can keep a close eye on things and help answer questions and provide feedback along the way.

- *Overseeing.* Once the team starts to get the hang of it, the coach can become less involved with every aspect of the process and start to step back into an observer role. They can then allow the team to fail a little bit on their own and see if they course-correct. If they struggle, the coach is there to steer them back on course.

- *Mentoring.* Eventually the Scrum team will be fully capable of executing the process on their own. At this point, the coach can check in with them on occasion, including attending sprint reviews, but mostly be there as a resource and sounding board for the team to lean on.

- *Helping with technical topics.* A coach with a technical background—often called a *technical coach*, as opposed to a *process coach* who focuses on Scrum fundamentals—can help developers navigate technical hurdles as they figure out test-driven development, continuous integration, and configuring test environments.

The Benefits of an External Coach

Those of us who are parents know that it's difficult to teach your own children. They tend to listen to others more closely—and lend more credibility to what they say. (LeBolt, 2015)

Having an external coach can provide the same benefits. If someone comes in from outside the company, what they say is likely to carry more weight than if team members hear the same thing from an internal coach.

Another huge benefit of an external coach is their experience with other companies. They're more likely to have seen the same situation at another company that you're facing today, and can more rapidly come up with a solution for you.

How Many Coaches?

Each situation is different, but a rule of thumb you can start with is each process coach or technical coach can typically focus on one to three Scrum teams.

If a team is particularly challenged with getting up to speed, they may need a full-time coach dedicated to helping them get up and running. As they get used to the process, they'll need less time and coaches can jump from team to team to help them out.

If you have a large organization and want to get a lot of teams up and running quickly once your pilot team has stabilized the process, you may need quite a few coaches.

18.6 What About Agile Certifications?

My son is 15 ½ years old, and in New Hampshire that means he can attend a driver education course in preparation for getting his license. He's under the impression that once he gets it, he'll be ready to hit the road with no limitations, and full independence.

My wife and I beg to differ—as does the state of New Hampshire, which imposes restrictions on new drivers.

We've explained to him that getting his license means he's met the *minimum* standard for competency behind the wheel, and marks the beginning of his learning, not the end.

Agile certifications are similar. They tell you that your team member has a minimum level of knowledge about a specific Scrum role, but they may not be ready to execute independently quite yet; they likely have more to learn.

Don't skimp on coaching for your team members, even if they have a newly-minted certification.

Key Takeaways

- Humans go through four stages when learning a new skill. Unconscious incompetence is when they don't know what they don't know. Conscious incompetence is when they know about the skill, but don't yet possess the ability. Conscious competence is when they have learned the skill to the point where they can do it when thinking about it. Finally, unconscious competence is when they can perform the skill without thinking about it.

- Cognitive apprenticeship is how skills used to be taught and is an effective approach for your team members to learn Scrum. This experiential learning technique is especially helpful since by design Scrum is incomplete, and everyone will be figuring out the specifics of how the process works best at your company as they go.

- Before starting their first sprint, your Scrum team should be taught the fundamentals. In addition to the team, it's important for their managers, upper leadership, and other business stakeholders to also understand the fundamentals. Especially important is the concept of an empowered team, so everyone can move toward becoming servant leaders for team members.

- Steps to begin include: forming the product backlog, assigning story point estimates, splitting larger stories near the top of the list, and laying the technical groundwork.

- Once these steps are complete, the next thing to do is to get the Scrum team to start sprinting. Don't spend too much time "getting ready to get ready." Instead get the team going and make adjustments as you go along.

- Agile coaches can help in a variety of ways, including modeling Scrum roles and providing close supervision for the team. Over time the coach can move to a mentor role, spot-checking the team and answering questions as they come up.

- As a rule of thumb, each coach can work with one to three Scrum teams. As teams are just starting, they'll likely need more attention as they come up to speed with the process.

- *Process coaches* focus on Scrum fundamentals and *technical coaches* help with topics such as test-driven development, continuous integration, and setting up test environments.

- An external coach can help lend more credibility to what they're telling your team members. They can also bring a unique outside perspective and leverage their experience with other companies who've faced the same challenges as you.

- Agile certifications are great but be careful not to assume that once they have the piece of paper, your team members are ready to execute independently. Treat certifications as a "license to learn," and provide coaching until those team members demonstrate competency.

Chapter 19
Creating the Initial Product Backlog

You've got to be very careful if you don't know where you're going, because you might not get there.

*- **Yogi Berra**, American baseball player, manager and coach, and fifteen-time All-Star, three-time American League MVP Award winner, and ten-time World Series champion.*

Your pilot team may already have some sort of specs, to-do list, or "backlog" that's been guiding their work to date. However, it may not be in the best format to support Scrum concepts, and it's unlikely that the development team has complete familiarity with the overall vision for the product.

It's also likely that the existing feature list hasn't been force-ranked by business value with the involvement of the appropriate stakeholders.

Even if you think you're ahead of the curve with your current feature list, I encourage you to step through this chapter and take a clean-sheet approach. Have the pilot team create a brand-new product backlog from scratch.

You won't be throwing away any existing work. New user stories can reference any detailed specifications that have been created over time, but the product backlog itself must be lightweight and streamlined—not weighed down by extra details.

Note that although I use the word "you" throughout this chapter, everything I describe should be completed with the entire Scrum team present—product owner, ScrumMaster, and development team—unless otherwise noted. This initial creation process is a key part of "programming the collective team's subconscious" about the vision for the product and starting them down the road to becoming a cohesive unit.

19.1 The Backlog Creation Process

Over the years, I've experimented with various ways to create a product backlog. What I've found works best is the following process:

1. *Create a list of user roles.* Whether you call them roles, actors, personas, or something else, it's important to first think about putting yourself into the shoes of those who will get value from your product.

2. *Brainstorm features.* For each user role, think about what they want to accomplish in your product. Write down a short one- to five-word description of each. Shoot for no more than about 100 features in total.

3. *Convert roles and features into user stories.* Combining each role and feature, and adding the "why," create a list of user stories using the format I describe in Chapter 4.

4. *Group user stories into three buckets.* You'll force-rank the user stories later, but taking an initial pass is helpful to identify any low-priority user stories where the effort to fully detail them can be deferred until down the road. Group stories into *must have, nice to have,* and *someday maybe.* You'll end up putting all of them on the product backlog, but you'll pay the most attention to the "must haves."

5. *Prioritize the backlog by business value.* Rearrange the product backlog to order the user stories by business value. The most important story will be first on the list, followed by the second most important story, and so on.

6. *Write acceptance criteria.* For all the must have and nice to have user stories, write three to ten bullet points that describe the expected behavior once the user story is implemented.

Once you complete this process, you'll have a fully-formed product backlog that is ready for the team to estimate. Because it's been prioritized, you know that more attention must be paid to the user stories at the top of the list, and those near the bottom can be ignored for now.

19.2 Create a List of Roles to Understand Your Users Better

It's difficult to put yourself in the shoes of your users if you don't know who they are. As a team, brainstorm a list of user roles and write a short description of each.

For example, if you are building an e-commerce web application, you might come up with roles such as *Shopper, Catalog Manager,* and *Shipping Clerk.*

Catalog Manager   **Financial Analyst**   **Shopper**   **Shipping Clerk**   **Customer Support Rep**

Example roles for an e-commerce web application.

Generic User Roles

Do your best to brainstorm at least several different roles, as opposed to just writing down one role such as "System User." This will ensure you get more value than every user story starting, "As a System User…"

If you have only one role, you'll lose the value of being able to think about what each different type of user needs from the product. (Cohn, 2004)

There *are* times when it helps to have roles that are general in nature.

For example, it probably doesn't make sense for me to write: *As a Catalog Manager or a Shopper or a Shipping Clerk or a Financial Analyst or a Customer Support Rep, I want to log in, so I can access my account.*

In this case, logging in is something that applies to every role, so I could selectively use a generic role to represent a broad set of more-specific roles.

This would let me write: *As a System User, I want to log in, so I can access my account.*

The takeaway here is to use generic roles when it makes things simpler but use specific roles whenever possible.

User Roles for Other Systems

Many software products these days must support interaction with other software systems. For example, we might need to provide the ability to access our product via an application programming interface (API).

In this situation, simply define a user role that describes that other system.

I could then write a user story along the lines of: *As an External System, I want to retrieve order information, so I can perform analytics on the data.*

The acceptance criteria could go on to explain what is expected, which may include details that are more technical than other user stories. Examples might include, "I can access the API from within our cloud environment" and "I must authenticate my requests to the API for security purposes."

In this case, the story is technical, so technical details are required.

Note that this doesn't break the rule of, "The product owner can't tell the development team how to build it." Because the product owner wouldn't be happy if the team built an unsecure API, that *must* be stated as one of the acceptance criteria. The development team is still free to select which technology to use to build it and how they write the code.

19.3 Brainstorm Features for Each User Role

Now that you have a list of roles, it becomes easier to think about features. Just put yourself into the shoes of each of the roles and think about what they need in the application.

Focus on rapid-fire brainstorming here, with the entire team participating. Don't get bogged down discussing the requirements of each feature—that will come later.

For our fictional e-commerce web application, we might come up with features for the Shopper role such as *Shop*, *View cart*, and *Check out*. For the Catalog Manager, we may have *Manage catalog items* and *Put products on sale*.

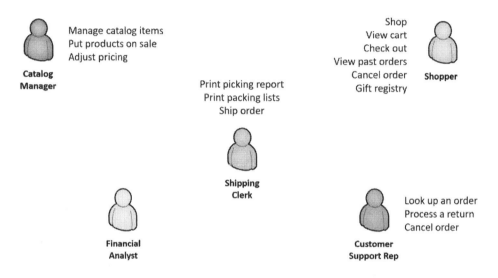

A brainstormed list of features per role for a fictional e-commerce web application.

Keep it to 100 Features or Fewer

To keep the product backlog from becoming too unwieldy, shoot for no more than 75 to 100 features at this stage in the process.

Some teams responsible for very large products complain to me that this isn't possible. I explain to them it's all about the size of those features.

Anything can be described in a small number of features, if those features are appropriately sized.

Let's say I'm going to build a new space shuttle—an extraordinarily complex endeavor. I can describe it in five features:

- Launch from Earth into space.

- Carry up to seven people.

- Carry a payload into space.

- Land like an airplane back on Earth.

- Re-use the shuttle for more missions.

These are pretty large features, which over time will need to be split into many more. But right now, if I needed to get a really high-level view of what needs to be done, I can abstract the requirements in this fashion.

Keeping your list of features short right now will lead to fewer stories to write, fewer to estimate, and fewer to prioritize and manage.

Before the first sprint, the team will split the stories at the top of the backlog into smaller bite-sized pieces, but the rest of the backlog can remain at a high level.

Over time you'll likely end up with hundreds of user stories, but you don't need that level of detail initially.

19.4 Convert Roles and Features into User Stories

You now have the building blocks for creating user stories in the format: *As a [role], I want [capability], so I [benefit]*. You've identified the roles and capabilities, so now you just need to add the benefit.

User stories include a role, a capability, and a benefit.

One by one, go through your feature list and expand each into a user story. Think carefully about the benefit. What's the reason this provides value to the specified role? Keep it short and meaningful.

Converting the features for the Shopper role may result in a list such as the following:

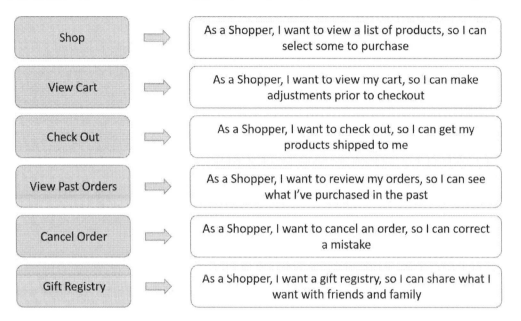

Example features for the Shopper role, converted into user stories by adding a benefit for each.

19.5 Group User Stories by Priority

To focus your effort on the most important stories, the next step is to do a rough prioritization of the list into three buckets:

Must have. These are user stories that need to be in the product for it to be usable by *someone*. If any one of these stories was omitted, it would render the product useless. This doesn't necessarily mean all of your customers will be happy once these stories are complete, but the product will provide *some* degree of value to *some* customers.

Another way to think about this is determining what's needed for your "minimum viable product" (MVP), which represents the smallest feature set that lets you start learning more about how your product will be used in the real world, and ensuring someone will pay for it. (Ries, 2011)

Nice to have. It would be great to have some of these in the product if there's time, but missing them won't prevent users from getting value. If things are going great, or you decide to extend the ship date to sneak a few more stories in, this is where you'll go first to pick and choose.

Someday maybe. These are your "dream stories." If you could get everything you wanted, or your approved budget just tripled, you could think about adding some of these. But, it's likely they're far off in the future unless business conditions change and they become more important.

You'll add details and story point estimates to only the *must have* and *nice to have* user stories and leave the *someday maybe* stories until later.

Must Have	Nice to Have	Someday Maybe
Necessary to be usable by *someone*	Include if there's extra time	Add at some point in the future

Doing an early prioritization of user stories into three buckets helps focus the Scrum team's effort.

Don't worry about this process being perfect. The primary goal here is to make sure you give yourself "permission to ignore for now" the low-priority user stories that you can worry about down the road, focusing effort on only what's likely to be in your near future.

Note that all the stories you've identified should be on your product backlog. You always want everything you think you might include in the product at some point to be on there. The must haves will be at the top, the nice to haves will be in the middle, and the someday maybe stories will be at the end.

An Alternative: The MoSCoW Model

Another way you can do a rough prioritization is using the MoSCoW model, named based on the first letters of its four categories: *must have*, *should have*, *could have*, and *won't have*.

This effectively splits my *nice to have* box into two—*should have* and *could have*.

I like the three-bucket system I propose because it fits nicely into the concept of the must haves going into the MVP version, nice to haves being considered for inclusion in a series of "Version 1.x" releases sometime after MVP, and the someday maybes in Version 2, Version 3, etc.

I encourage you to use whatever model works best for you. The key is to perform a rough prioritization at the beginning to help focus effort on the more important user stories.

19.6 Prioritize the Backlog by Business Value

Now that you've completed the rough prioritization, the next step is to force-rank the stories into a specific order based on business value.

Although you can complete this process for the entire product backlog, it's most important to focus on completing the process for the user stories in the *must have* group, since the team will be starting at the top and working their way down.

You'll have time later to force-rank stories lower on the list.

What is "Business Value?"

Many product owners and team members new to Scrum scratch their heads at this point. They wonder, "What exactly do you mean when you say, 'business value?'"

What's a little tricky about this is I can't *tell* you what business value means, exactly, because it depends on your specific context. If you're building a mobile app that relies on in-app purchases to drive revenue, business value might be measured by how many features you can add that make users want to buy more widgets.

If you're creating a web application for professional photographers, business value might be measured by how much time you can save them in their client workflow.

The best tip I can give you is to keep asking yourself, "What are the most important things the team can build right now to help us achieve our business goals?" This might include:

- Getting more customers.

- Increasing revenue.

- Enhancing reputation.

- Increasing user satisfaction.

One other thing to keep in mind is business value changes over time. For example, when first developing a product you might be focused on getting as many new customers as possible. Later your focus will likely shift toward making sure those customers are getting the enhancements they're asking for. (Schuurman, 2017)

If You Could Only Have One Thing, What Would It Be?

Many Scrum teams struggle with the force-ranking concept. Developers typically think very linearly, so they'll often say, "Let's start with login."

But that doesn't provide much value to an end user. Picture your team saying to a customer, "Here's our new product! You can log in!"

The customer would likely reply, "What can I do once I log in?" If the answer is, "Nothing," they probably won't be reaching for their wallets to buy your product.

As an illustration, if I was building a new e-commerce app, and I wanted to compete with Amazon, I wouldn't start with login.

Amazon's real innovation is their purchasing process. They make it *way* too easy to buy a bunch of stuff you don't need. Trust me, I know. My impulse purchases are rampant.

Login certainly may come along fairly quickly, since it will be needed to support features such as viewing my past orders, but it wouldn't be the *very first* user story. I'd start with the checkout user story instead. *That's* where I'd focus my initial energy.

Telling a Story About the Story

Your reaction to this might be, "That's a little silly. We can't possibly ship a product that *just* has a checkout process. We'll need to let the user browse the product catalog, add items to the cart, review their cart, and *then* complete their purchase."

The product must be usable at the end of each sprint. How is this possible if the only feature completed to date is checkout?

I call this, "Telling a story about the story." You need to fabricate a fictional scenario that allows you to argue that product would, in fact, be shippable even though there's no way you would actually ship it with just checkout and nothing else.

This technique allows you to ensure that you stick to the rules without slipping back into a waterfall mentality where you stray from the concept of a shippable product at the end of each sprint.

The "story" I'd tell about this particular user story would go something like this: "OK. So, we have one product in our catalog, and every one of our users wants just that one product.

"Since we don't have the shipping feature yet, and also because we realize payment processing wouldn't quite fit into the sprint, we'll just have each customer drive to our warehouse with some money and pick up their product."

Why This Is Important

At this point, I may sound like a complete lunatic. "One product? And customers are going to *drive to our warehouse to pick it up?* What the hell are you talking about?"

There's a method to my madness. Bear with me.

First, remember that I'm not saying that you would *actually* ship this product. It's not yet reached a minimally-viable state—a critical mass that lets it actually be used in the real world.

All I'm talking about here is a way to abandon conventional linear thinking about building products, and instead focus solely about business value.

I realize prioritizing by business value isn't easy and may fly in the face of what most development teams are used to. Keep asking yourself, "If I could only have one thing…" and, "If I could only have two things…" etc.

It's like building a new house and being able to first build the kitchen. Then maybe the master bedroom and master bathroom. Then the family room, and so on.

That's not possible when building a house, but it's absolutely possible with software, and there are several benefits.

It forces thinking about the most important things early. In my example, checkout is the crucial feature in the product. If the checkout process stinks, it's dead in the water. By focusing effort on this area first, the team is forced to think through how it should work the best.

It accelerates risk. Let's say the development team starts working on the checkout process, then they dig in on payment processing. They then realize the way they were planning on processing credit cards won't work. It's much better to discover this early in the process than at the end.

It lets everyone live with it for a long time. By completing the most important parts of your product first, that functionality is exposed to real use for the longest amount of time. Everyone who gets their hands on the product after the conclusion of each sprint will be able to put it through the paces and identify issues.

A month after completing the checkout feature, someone from marketing might say, "Hey, this part of the process is a little confusing," or "I think I found a bug." You want to know about those issues *now*, not two weeks from shipping or—even worse—two weeks *after* shipping, when your customers find them.

It's more likely to get deliberate attention. As much as Scrum works to eliminate it, human nature is such that there's a tendency to rush near the end. By working on the most critical user stories first, they'll get the most careful thought and attention.

You probably don't have enough time. Anyone who has spent any time developing software has discovered there's never enough time to finish everything you want. If it turns out there isn't enough time to get everything done—and it's highly likely that's the case—the user stories that get cut are those at the end of the list. Because you've prioritized by business value, the stories that don't make it into the initial release don't hurt as much.

You can ship early. When's the last time you heard of a software product shipping *ahead* of schedule? With this prioritization approach, it's absolutely possible. Instead of running out of time, the product owner makes a conscious decision to defer some user stories to the next release and put the product into production earlier than originally planned. This would be impossible if the most valuable user stories weren't at the top of the list.

19.7 Write Acceptance Criteria

The final step in preparing your product backlog is to write acceptance criteria for each user story. Don't worry about the stories in your someday maybe bucket. Just focus on the must have and nice to have stories.

Work from top to bottom, so you ensure you're completing acceptance criteria for the most important user stories first.

Shoot for no more than about five to ten bullet points. It's most important to get through all the user stories than to make all the acceptance criteria comprehensive right now.

Remember that the Scrum team will be reviewing and discussing user stories every sprint as they refine the product backlog together.

Review Sections 4.2 and 4.3 for more tips on writing acceptance criteria.

Example: View Cart

As a Shopper, I want to view my cart, so I can make adjustments prior to checkout

- I can see the items I've added to my cart.

- I can see the quantities I've specified.

- I can see a total price excluding shipping and tax.

- I can see an updated total price if I make changes.

- I can adjust the quantities.

- I can remove items from the cart.

- I can navigate to the detailed product page for an item in the cart.

Example: Check Out

As a Shopper, I want to check out, so I can get my products shipped to me

- I can see the items that I'm purchasing.

- I can enter shipping and billing addresses.

- I can select a shipment method.

- I can see the total shipping cost.

- I can see the total amount I'll be charged.

- I can adjust quantities of items in my cart.

- I can enter a credit card number.

- I can confirm that I'm ready to place my order.

- I can see a confirmation that my order was placed.

- I receive an e-mail with order details.

Add References to Existing Specs

If you have comprehensive specs that already exist, add a note to each relevant user story as a reference to that detailed information. For example, "See *Phase 2 Spec.docx*, pages 34-41."

Do *not* copy all the details into each user story. You don't need that level of detail until the story is ready to be implemented, and by then it's likely the details will be different based on how the product has come together to that point.

Remember that one of the key productivity gains with Scrum comes from, "permission to ignore for now." Leave the nitty gritty details alone until you absolutely need them.

Key Takeaways

- Even if you have a to-do list, feature list, or specifications for your application, creating a product backlog in a format that best supports Scrum is an important part of laying a solid foundation for the team.

- The entire Scrum team should participate in as much of the backlog creation process as possible, so you can start to get the vision for the product into their collective subconscious.

- The process I've seen work best is: 1) creating a list of user roles, 2) brainstorming the features each role cares about, 3) converting roles and features into user stories, 4) grouping stories into *must have*, *nice to have*, and *someday maybe* buckets, 5) prioritizing by business value, and 6) writing acceptance criteria for the must have and nice to have stories.

- Avoid creating one generic role such as "System User" and using it for every user story. Be as specific as possible. That said, it might make sense to have a generic user for some broadly-applicable user stories, such as logging in, which applies to every type of user.

- Keep your list of features small at this stage. Shoot for no more than about 100. Use larger features if necessary to get your list to this size. Keeping it shorter at this point will help you complete the rest of the process. Over time, user stories will be split into smaller stories as necessary, but right now you don't want the product backlog to get too unwieldy.

- Combining each role and feature and adding a benefit allows you to expand them into user stories.

- Some user stories might describe providing access to your product by other software systems, for example via an API. In this case, you could use a user role such as "External System." A user role doesn't need to represent a human.

- Grouping user stories into three buckets lets you take a first pass at a rough prioritization. Must have means you need the user story in order to provide at least some value to some portion of your customer base. This is often referred to as the "minimum viable product," or "MVP." Nice to have stories are those you can add if you have time, and someday maybe stories are off in the future.

- Every story—even the someday maybes—will be on your product backlog, which represents everything you envision adding to the product now or in the future.

- Prioritizing the backlog by business value gets the most important features into the hands of stakeholders as early as possible. This gives you more time to refine how they work and discover bugs the team may have missed. If time runs short—which almost always happens—the user stories that end up on the chopping block will be the least important.

- Add acceptance criteria—starting from the top of the list and working your way down—comprised of no more than five to ten bullets. You can add more detail later as the Scrum team refines the backlog.

- If you have comprehensive specs that have already been created, don't copy them into your user stories. Include a reference to the relevant portion of the specs and ignore the details until the story is ready to be completed in a sprint.

Chapter 20
Estimating the Size of the Product Backlog

It is very difficult to make a vigorous, plausible, and job-risking defense of an estimate that is derived by no quantitative method, supported by little data, and certified chiefly by the hunches of the managers.

*- **Fred Brooks**, The Mythical Man-Month*

Years ago, I was sitting in my office when my business partner walked in. He said, "I need a rough estimate for a new feature a prospective customer is asking about."

He went on to describe what the customer was looking for. I thought for a minute or two and said, "I don't know, maybe three or four days?"

He said, "Thanks," and headed back to his office. Not thinking any more about it, I put my head down and got back to work.

When it came time to implement that feature, it turns out I was off on my estimate.

Way off.

We ended up spending about six *weeks* coding and testing. It turned out there were all kinds of things I hadn't thought about with my off-the-cuff answer.

This was a continuing challenge for me. I spent *years* stuck in a repeating pattern of poor estimation. It seemed like the only way to get an accurate estimate was to lock my team in a room for a month to estimate the next three months of work. Needless to say, that wasn't a workable solution.

Shortly after I started experimenting with Scrum, a colleague introduced me to agile estimating techniques, and they completely eliminated the problem. Using a combination of expert opinion and evidence-based scheduling, I now know how to predict software schedules to within plus or minus 10%.

Estimating now takes days rather than months, and the results are dramatically better.

In this chapter, I'll explain relative size estimation using story points and Planning Poker, a technique to quickly create accurate estimates. In the next chapter, I'll walk you through how to create an initial rough schedule forecast even before work begins.

20.1 The Power of Relative Size

In general, humans suck at estimating.

Have you ever played that game where you need to guess how many jelly beans are in the jar? How well did you do?

If you were with a group of people, were all your guesses about the same or were they all over the map?

Guessing how many jelly beans are in the jar is tough for us humans because we aren't very good at absolute estimation.

Chances are, your estimate was at least somewhat off the mark, and your group likely had a wide range of guesses, which is consistent with academic research. (Berndt, et al., 2006)

Here's another example. If you looked at the cup shown below, can you guess how many ounces or milliliters it holds?

Can you guess how many ounces or milliliters are in this cup?
It's very difficult without a sense of scale.

I've shown this picture to a variety of audiences at my speaking engagements, and answers range from 8 ounces to 64 ounces! That's not very accurate.

We Already Know How to Do Relative Estimation

Humans are really bad at *absolute* estimation, such as guessing how many jelly beans are in a jar or the capacity of a coffee cup. However, we're really good at *relative* estimation—comparing things to each other and determining how much larger or smaller they are.

To illustrate this, look at the picture of the three coffee cups below. If I told you the smallest cup holds 8 ounces, it's likely you'd be able to guess at least fairly accurately about the capacity of the larger cups.

Humans are much better at relative estimation. If I told you the first cup holds 8 ounces, you'd likely be able to guess the capacity of the others fairly accurately.

This is the technique you'll use to estimate the relative size of each story on the product backlog.

You'll first select two user stories to use as "anchors," assigning story points to them such as 2 and 5, or 3 and 8. Then you'll compare other stories on the backlog, determining if they are larger or smaller than the anchor stories, and by how much.

I'll explain this in detail in Section 20.4.

Absolute Estimation Doesn't Work for Software

Absolute estimation is when a developer is asked, "How long do you think this will take?" and the answer is expressed in a definitive measure: time.

There are three fundamental problems with attempting to use absolute size for estimating software development, which relative estimation eliminates:

It's hard to do it well. It's difficult to estimate accurately unless you break the work down into tasks of no more than about two days of effort. If you were instead to break it down into week-long tasks, you're not forced to think through things in enough detail, and there will be too many surprises. That week will likely turn into three weeks. (McConnell, 2006)

It takes too long to do it right. There isn't usually enough time to do the amount of work necessary to break down the entire product backlog into chunks of two days or less—that would probably take months. Plus, some stories typically never get developed due to changing priorities and user feedback during development. Over-investing time to create a detailed estimate up front would be a waste.

The answer varies. The time a developer needs to code a user story can vary by as much as 10 to 1, depending upon their familiarity with the product and technology, level of experience, and natural ability. (McConnell, 2008). This means if you ask Ellen how long you think it will take she may say, "Two days." If you then ask Ben the same question and he answers, "Four weeks," *they may both be correct.*

It would be great if Ellen the superstar could code the whole product, but that's unlikely. There needs to be a way to come up with an answer that's independent of who will end up doing the work.

20.2 Story Points: An Abstract Measurement of Size

Once you decide to adopt relative estimation, you need a way to assign a size to each user story.

This can be done using t-shirt sizes or other abstract techniques, but I've found using numeric story points gives you the most power. It's difficult to add t-shirt sizes, but it's easy to add numbers together.

The story points technique provides an abstract measurement of relative size, using numbers from 0.5 to 100. A modified Fibonacci sequence is used, where the gaps between numbers grow as they increase.

The Cohn Scale

The numeric sequence used is often called the *Cohn Scale*, named after Mike Cohn, who created it.

This accounts for an increasing degree of uncertainty about the size of user stories as they grow larger.

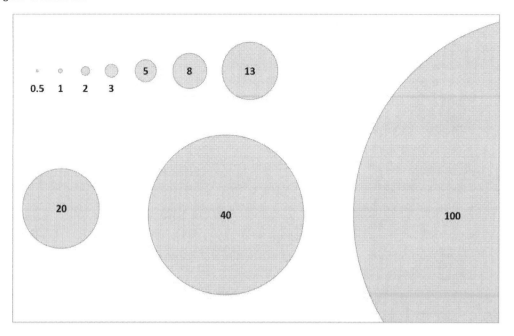

The Cohn Scale for story point estimates, which is a modified Fibonacci sequence.

It's easy for a team to differentiate between 3 and 5. But it would be difficult for them to choose between 40 and 42. This is the reason for less precision at the top end of the range, which includes 13, 20, 40, and 100.

The numbers are arranged so the space between each number allows wiggle room of approximately plus or minus 50%. Some stories will turn out to be larger than what the team estimated, and others smaller.

Once added together, however, the overall story point estimate of the product backlog is fairly accurate. This is because the errors tend to cancel each other out.

How Story Point Estimates Are Leveraged

Story point estimates provide a lot of power, in a few ways:

Clarity of communication. Software estimation has a long history of a disconnect between what the development team *said* and what they *meant*. Communication issues often arise between the team and business leaders, leading to stress and mistrust. Once business leaders understand story points, there is a shared understanding and a clear way to communicate when the team is asked, "How big is this?"

Insight for the product owner. Once the product backlog is estimated, the product owner gains a tremendous amount of power. They can look at stories with large estimates and ask, "What makes this so large?" It could be that one small part of the story caused it to be 13 points instead of 5. Once the product owner understands that, they can think about whether to defer or eliminate the time-consuming part of the story, saving time.

The product owner can also make prioritization changes based on story point estimates. If they have a 13-point story near the top of the list, they may decide to move it down and instead get two 5-point stories and a 3-point story.

What-if scenarios. Once coupled with the schedule estimating techniques I'll explain in the next chapter, the product owner can play around with the stories included in the next product release. They can add and remove stories and see the effect on the schedule. It puts the power to control the schedule directly in the hands of the most-appropriate person: the representative of the business.

20.3 Rapid Estimation with Planning Poker

You could certainly just ask your most senior developer to run through the product backlog and stick a point estimate on each user story. The problem with that approach is you'll risk the same trap I fell into when I gave my business partner an off-the-cuff estimate—you're leveraging just one person's opinion, without forcing any discussion about everything that's involved.

Regardless of the technique, more brains on the problem will result in a more accurate estimate. As few as three to five people with varied experience will produce dramatically better results than just a single estimator. (Jørgensen, 2004)

Planning Poker, a technique created by James Grenning and popularized by Mike Cohn, is a process that involves everyone on the team mining their collective expertise to create accurate estimates. (Grenning, 2002; Cohn, 2006a)

The product owner discusses each user story and then each member of the development team votes what they think the appropriate points should be, based on comparing it to other stories in the product backlog.

The team discusses the votes and repeats the process until a consensus is reached, or any outliers agree to go with the majority opinion.

Benefits of Planning Poker

There are multiple benefits to this technique.

It's fast. Once your team becomes familiar with the process, they'll get really fast at banging out estimates without losing accuracy. Our development teams can typically estimate roughly 6 to 12 months of work in three to six, two-hour sessions. I'll provide some rough guidelines in Section 20.4 to determine how long it will take to estimate your product backlog.

It involves everyone on the team. Estimates are dramatically more accurate when multiple people are involved, especially when those people have a variety of backgrounds and roles (McConnell, 2006). Because everyone on the Scrum development team is required to participate, no one can just sit back and daydream.

It's democratic. Nathan, who has been at the company for 15 years and wrote most of the company's software, is likely going to be viewed as the resident expert. But Olivia, who was just hired two months ago, has extensive experience from outside the company and a different perspective. Using Planning Poker, both their voices are heard, and their collective experience and knowledge are leveraged.

Without Planning Poker, it's likely everyone would stay quiet and just "go with what Nathan says," but that would lead to a less-accurate estimate.

It eliminates dependencies on individuals. When only one developer does the estimating—because they're the "expert"—all hell can break loose if that developer isn't available when it comes time to code that user story. By working as a group to create estimates, the dependency upon the most-qualified developer doing the work is eliminated.

It forces everyone to really understand the user story. I've always been amazed at how much smarter a developer appears to get when asked what they think the story point estimate should be. Planning Poker really makes team members think about what's involved and ensures the product owner gets peppered with questions if anything is unclear.

It adds clarity to each user story. Although the entire Scrum team should be involved in writing user stories, that's not always possible. The product owner will often write at least a subset of the stories on the backlog on their own.

Because they don't usually have the same technical experience as the collective team, they may have some holes in their thinking that will threaten the ability for the story to be easily implemented. During the estimating process, the development team can help tighten up any holes in user stories, resulting in quicker and easier implementation.

It drives the collective understanding of the product backlog. One of the foundations of Scrum is the reliance on verbal discussions and the collective understanding by the development team of the makeup of the product backlog, as opposed to comprehensive documentation. This style of estimating forces the entire Scrum team to a much higher level of understanding of the product backlog and makes it theirs as opposed to only the product owner having in-depth knowledge of what's in there.

It avoids a conflict of interest. One of the rules of Planning Poker is only those who will be turning user stories into shippable functionality are allowed to estimate. Though the product owner participates in the process, explaining each user story and answering questions, they don't get a vote. The ScrumMaster doesn't estimate either unless they are also a member of the development team. This avoids the product owner from having too much power to steer story point estimates in a way that may support their agenda—usually trying to get lower story point numbers—but doesn't represent the reality of the situation.

It can shorten the schedule. One of the challenges with traditional waterfall development is the disconnect between those who write the specs and those who write the code. Although the product owner isn't allowed to vote, they can ask for information if an estimate surprises them.

For example, if the team votes 40 for a certain story, but the product owner was thinking it might be more like a 13, they can ask, "What makes this story so big?"

The development team explains that a certain part of the story is tricky and increases the effort quite a bit. The product owner could then ask, "What would it be if I pulled that part out?"

The team re-votes and they come up with 20 points without it.

The product owner, thinking that portion of the story is not worth an extra 20 points, can then say, "I'm going to pull that part out and put it in a new user story down in the someday maybe section."

The product owner didn't break the rules by trying to strong-arm the team into arbitrarily reducing their vote. She just asked for some insight and for the team to examine a quick "what if" scenario. However, she just cut the time in half for that story because she was there, doing her job of owning the ROI of the product.

This is not possible with waterfall; the team will build everything as written. This is one of the many ways agile shortens software schedules and mitigates risk.

20.4 Preparing to Estimate

Before the development team can play Planning Poker they need a way to vote for a story point value, and they need to establish a baseline for comparison by selecting two *anchor stories*.

Planning Poker Cards

Physical Planning Poker cards can be used by co-located teams. I happen to like those sold by Mountain Goat Software. Each deck includes enough cards for four estimators and are inexpensive at only $2.50 each at the time of this writing.

Scrum Planning Poker cards.

You can purchase them at:

* http://bit.ly/PlanningPokerCards

There are also mobile apps you can download that allow selecting a virtual card. The development team member using the app selects their value, then places their smartphone face-down on the table in front of them until everyone has voted.

At that point, whoever is facilitating the meeting—often the ScrumMaster—tells everyone to flip their phones over so everyone can see the votes, just like when using physical cards.

An app I've used in the past is called Scrum Poker Cards, which is available for both iOS and Android. Here are links to the listing in the respective app store:

- iOS version: http://bit.ly/ScrumPokerAppiOS

- Android version: http://bit.ly/ScrumPokerAppAndroid

Distributed Teams

For distributed teams, there is no option to play with physical cards or a phone app. But Planning Poker can still take place.

None of our teams are co-located, but every one of them uses Planning Poker.

There are a few options for your distributed team:

Vote verbally. Some development teams use a tool such as GoToMeeting or WebEx to get on a call, discuss stories, and announce their votes verbally. The problem with this form of voting is it happens one team member at a time. The junior developer may hear the senior developer's vote and think, "He must know what he's talking about. I was going to say 5 but now I'll say 3 to match his vote."

This defeats the democratic aspect of the process and you lose the benefit of forcing the team to discuss their different viewpoints. I do not recommend this approach.

Use an instant messaging tool. The development team discusses a story, and everyone types in their vote into the chat window in GoToMeeting or WebEx, or their team chat room in a tool such as Slack. When everyone is ready, the facilitator—typically the ScrumMaster—says "go." At this point, everyone presses the enter key on the keyboard and all the votes show up in the chat window.

In my experience this works OK, but I'd recommend it only if you have one or two stories to vote on and you find it's more efficient than the next option.

Use a Planning Poker web app. The development team signs into a cloud-hosted web app specifically designed to facilitate playing Planning Poker. I prefer planningpoker.com.

I've found this third option, using a web app, works the best. At the time of this writing, planningpoker.com is free for up to five players and supports logging in as an observer only, for use by the product owner and ScrumMaster.

When setting up a game, be sure to pick the *modified Fibonacci* set of story points to match the numbers in the Cohn Scale.

See http://bit.ly/OnlinePlanningPoker for more details.

Special Planning Poker Cards

If you purchase Planning Poker cards or use a mobile app, you'll often find some special cards in addition to the values from 0.5 to 100.

Zero-point card. Although it may not happen at the start of the process, sometimes your product backlog evolves to include a user story that's very straightforward. The team believes it will only be a few minutes of work, plus a few minutes to test.

For example, there may be some feedback from the sales team that they want to highlight products that have free shipping. The app already shows "$0" for shipping, but the team needs to add code that shows "FREE!" instead of $0.

In this case, assigning 0.5 story points may artificially inflate the team's velocity, so they may opt to assign 0 to that story. They don't want to take an inflated amount of credit for doing a trivial amount of work. (Cohn, 2015b)

Question mark. Sometimes a team member really has no idea what to estimate, even though they heard the discussion about the user story. By using the question mark card they're saying, "I have absolutely no clue what to estimate." In this case, the team should discuss the story further and re-vote. If the team member who voted with a question mark voted again, you can ask them if they're comfortable with the rest of the team voting and proceed without them if they're OK with it.

Avoid the trap of one person on the team throwing down the question mark for every story, just because they don't feel like they're qualified to vote. Even those who are less technical—such as a user experience architect or testers—can provide great insight. Don't under-value their opinion and don't let them self-select out of the process. It's important that everyone participates.

Infinity symbol. Sometimes a story is so large that it won't fit into even the maximum value of 100. This may be a story so big, undefined, or risky that a team member doesn't feel comfortable placing any sort of story point value on it. They're effectively saying, "I don't think this is possible."

For example, consider the user story: As a CAD Designer, I want a new rendering engine, so my drawings will appear sooner. Some development team members understand this to mean, "Re-write the entire core framework of the application that we just spent the last five years creating."

This type of story either needs clarification—for example with the product owner saying, "I didn't mean re-write the whole core of the app!"—or the story needs to be split into smaller stories.

Coffee cup. Sometimes team members get a bit tired and need a coffee refill, food or bathroom break. Maybe they've been too polite to say something, or they have made the suggestion a couple of times and the rest of the team doesn't seem to be listening. They can throw out the coffee cup card as a crystal-clear indication that they are ready for a break.

Selecting "Anchor" Stories

Because the Planning Poker estimating technique is *relative* as opposed to *absolute*, your team needs to be able to compare user stories to each other. The problem is, at the start of the process there are no points on any stories, so there's nothing to compare to.

The best way to address this is to choose *anchor stories*. These are two stories selected by the development team that are then assigned specific story point values without voting.

At that point, the team can then compare other stories to the anchor stories.

How this works is the development team looks down the list and selects a story that seems like it should be 2 points, and another that seems like it should be 5.

An alternative is to use 3 points and 8 points.

Many teams struggle with this, not knowing how they should choose. Here are some tips that I've found work well:

- Have the team review the available story point values on the Cohn Scale, ranging from 0.5 to 100, and have them find a user story in the product backlog that seems very straightforward. It's likely there's at least one or two. Have the team decide to assign either 2 or 3 to that story, based on how they feel about it. This will be the first anchor story.

- Have the team then look through the backlog and select a story that seems to be a little more than twice as big as the first anchor story. If the team selected 2 for their first story, have them assign 5 to the second. If they selected 3, then have them assign 8.

Note that I'm not saying the team can only limit their votes for the rest of the product backlog to something less than 5 or 8 points. This is just a technique to put stakes in the ground to establish a baseline reference. It's likely the product backlog will contain stories with estimates that are all over the map.

The reason for picking 2 and 5 for your anchor stories, or 5 and 8, is because studies have shown that we're best at estimating things that fall within one order of magnitude—between a number and ten times that number. We're much better at estimating on a scale of 1 to 10 than a scale of 1 to 100, because our ability to accurately discriminate size diminishes as the difference between the stories becomes larger. (Cohn, 2006a; Miranda, 2001)

At this point, the Planning Poker process can commence. Once story points are assigned to a few additional stories, the team will have more to use for comparison as they continue their estimating process.

Remember to keep the team focused on *relative* estimating. Have them continue to compare stories to each other and thinking, "Is this larger, smaller, or about the same? If larger or smaller, by how much?"

20.5 Story Points Are Not About Time

When starting with this process and choosing their anchor stories, new teams often ask me something along the lines of, "How many days should it take us to finish 2 story points? Can we say that 2 points is the same as two days?"

My answer to this question is, "I have no idea. Story points have nothing to do with time, just your overall estimated level of effort. How much time it will take depends on how fast you can complete the work."

You don't know yet if a two-point story will take two days, four days, or half a day. Time depends upon way too many factors that are difficult to predict at this stage.

That said, the reason you're using story points is to create a schedule forecast, but that only comes when velocity is introduced into the mix. Velocity is how many points the team can complete each sprint.

I like to say that story points are connected to time *only* through velocity. It's OK after the team has gotten up to speed to say, "Based on what they've completed in the past few sprints, it looks like this team can complete about 25 story points per sprint." That's their velocity, which allows a connection between story points and time.

Where danger comes into play is when management says something like, "Each development team member provides enough capacity to complete 8 story points in a two-week sprint. Since we have four developers and one tester on this development team, they should be able to complete 40 story points per sprint."

That is directly connecting story points to time and has absolutely no basis in reality. No one has ever built *this* product with *this* technology with *this* team. You have *no idea* how fast they can move.

In the next chapter, I'll give you some techniques you can use to create a *rough approximation* of what the team's velocity *might* be, but the only way to know for sure is to run a few sprints and see what they can do.

I encourage you to avoid discussing time altogether when talking about story points at this stage. They will eventually *turn into* time, but do not have a *direct connection* to time. The only way story points are tied to time is via velocity.

20.6 The Planning Poker Process

Planning Poker creates an environment of open discussion, transparency, and everyone's opinion carrying the same weight.

Ideally, the entire development team participates, but if scheduling becomes a big problem, it's OK to proceed with the majority of the development team present. However, be careful to include the entire team whenever possible.

It's important that the product owner attends, even though they are not allowed to vote. Remember that acceptance criteria serve only as a reminder of conversations that have taken place, so having the product owner available for clarification is critical. (Mahnic, 2011)

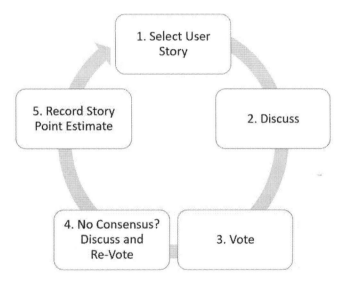

The Planning Poker process.

The ScrumMaster often facilitates the process, though they can't vote unless they're also a member of the development team.

Here's how Planning Poker works:

1. *Review the story.* The product owner reads the user story sentence and reviews the acceptance criteria with the development team.

2. *Discuss the details.* The development team discusses the story, asking the product owner questions as necessary.

3. *Compare to other stories.* Once the discussion is complete, each development team member compares the story being discussed against the other stories in the product backlog, to get a feel for the relative size of the story as compared to others that already have estimates.

4. *Vote.* Each team member selects a card out of their deck and places it *face-down* in front of them. This is important because this process depends on each person's card being secret until everyone has voted. This ensures everyone is engaged and the vote is democratic.

5. *Flip the cards.* Once everyone on the development team has voted, the facilitator—often the ScrumMaster—tells everyone to "flip," at which point everyone turns their cards over.

6. *Discuss if necessary.* If everyone voted the same number—which occasionally happens— that's easy; the number everyone voted is the story point estimate, and the team moves on to the next story. If there is a range of votes, which is typical, I recommend you ask the low person to explain their thinking, and the high person to explain their thinking. Then encourage additional discussion from the rest of the group. This "high and low" technique is just a way to get things started.

Do *not* just average the votes and assign a number. The discussion from different points of view is a critical part of increasing the team's knowledge. (Jørgensen, 2004)

1. *Drive to consensus.* Everyone takes their cards back and they re-vote until there is a consensus. Occasionally there will be a couple of outliers, and the ScrumMaster can ask if they are OK going with the majority vote, or if they want to "fight for" their number.

2. *Record the estimate.* The facilitator records the story point estimate.

3. *Repeat for the next user story.* The development team repeats this process for the next user story.

Note that the product owner is *not allowed to vote,* and the ScrumMaster should vote only if they are also a member of the development team. That is, they will be doing work to produce the shippable product increment each sprint.

Only Estimate "Must Have" and "Nice to Have" User Stories

One of the reasons I described the high-level prioritization process in the last chapter is to limit the amount of time your development team needs to spend estimating stories.

I suggest focusing your estimating process solely on the must have and nice to have stories. The someday maybe stories can be estimated later, if they move to a higher priority or if the product owner wants to know how big some of them are.

It's About Effort, Not Complexity

Some teams get confused about the story points concept and will assign higher values to user stories that are complex, even if they won't involve a lot of effort. Complexity is certainly a factor that contributes to size, but it's not the *only* factor.

It's about the overall effort, which can be influenced by complexity, risk, and uncertainty. (Cohn, 2014b)

Let's look at two examples, by pretending your team has been working on the product for a while prior to adopting Scrum and creating their backlog.

In one case, a user story specifies some encryption that needs to be added to part of the product. Encryption is pretty complex—most developers need a solid computer science background or a lot of experience to understand all of its idiosyncrasies. But the team's development technology has built-in functions to deal with encryption, so it's actually pretty easy to implement what's needed with a few lines of code, and testing is simple. The data will either be encrypted after this story is implemented, or it won't.

In another case, there's a story to enhance the user experience in the application to support 508 compliance, providing accessibility for disabled users. This is a pretty major effort because accessibility wasn't considered with the work the team has done to date, and the entire application is affected. They likely will have to make small adjustments to most of the screens, and test everything on multiple browsers. This isn't complex work. But it's a lot of development and testing effort.

The development team might estimate the first story as 3 points. They second one they may call 40 points. The first story is more *complex*, but the *level of effort* is much higher for the second.

Have your team keep in mind that their estimates are about the entire effort to drive a user story from start to finish, including technical design, unit tests, coding, testing, and bug-fixing. This may or may not be directly tied to complexity.

Their estimates should also consider any risk factors they think may drive the level of effort higher. For example, if a story represents interacting with a third-party API that no one has experience with, that often means more effort due to learning as they go. The development team should take that into account and put a larger number on the story.

Finally, the level of effort required to properly test the user story should be considered. If a story is going to require a lot more testing than other stories, or if it's particularly difficult to test and needs a lot of manual effort, this should also be reflected in the story point estimate. This is one reason the *entire* development team—including testers—does the estimating.

It's about the all-in effort, which is influenced by complexity and risk, but not solely one or the other.

Round Up

Often, when teams get together to estimate, they'll think about a number that's not one of the options available on the Cohn Scale. For example, they may think, "This feels like a 10." The closest numbers are 8 and 13. Which should they choose?

When the team feels like a story is larger than one of the values, round up. There's a risk that it's even bigger than they think. Introducing a slightly pessimistic bias will help counter the tendency for developers to be too optimistic. (Cohn, 2015a)

20.7 How Long Should Estimating Take?

When a team starts the Planning Poker process, they'll be a little slow since they are learning the technique. If any members of the team are not familiar with the product, that may slow things down as well.

The good news is they'll get faster over time.

Once the team is up to speed, it's important to focus on keeping the discussion and voting process for each user story fairly short. Though the development team needs to understand the vision for each, they don't need to talk through exactly how they'll implement every story.

Early on, the team might need 10to 15 minutes to talk through each story, do the estimating process, discuss their votes, and decide on the right story point value. They might need this much time for the first estimating session or two.

As the team gets better, they should get their discussion for each story down to no more than 3 to 5 minutes.

Experience shows that if the development team spends a short amount of time on a user story, no more than 5 to 10 minutes, they can come up with an estimate that's nearly as good as if they spent a lot more time thinking about the story. (Cohn, 2006a) Don't worry if the team doesn't discuss every detail. Their estimates are still valid.

This Amount of Estimating Is a One-Time Investment

One thing to keep in mind is this initial estimating process for the product backlog is a one-time investment. Once the must have and nice to have user stories have been estimated, from that point forward the development team will only need to estimate a few stories at a time.

This is part of keeping the backlog refined, either in an ad-hoc manner or via a backlog refinement ceremony such as what I described in Section 6.5.

Initial Estimating	Backlog Refinement
• Happens only once, at the beginning • Entire product backlog • Starts with "anchor" stories • Multiple sessions, likely over several weeks	• Happens every sprint • A handful of stories • New or split stories, or those moved up from *someday maybe* portion of the backlog • Usually one session per sprint

One-time initial backlog estimating, versus backlog refinement, which happens throughout development.

Additional estimating during backlog refinement is typically needed when:

- *User stories are split.* Larger user stories often need to be split into smaller ones before they can enter a sprint. When the new stories are created, they need to be estimated. Note that it's not necessarily the case that the total points for the split stories will add up to the original estimate, though they should be roughly the same. (Cohn, 2015a) See Chapter 22 for more details about splitting stories.

- *New user stories are added.* Because requirements are emergent, the product backlog is in a constant state of change. When new requirements are discovered, the product owner will create a new user story and add it to the backlog. The development team then helps add details and determines a story point estimate.

- *Priorities change.* I suggested earlier in this chapter to spend time estimating only the must have and nice to have stories, and don't bother with those that are someday maybe. If any of those become more important over time and moved up in the product backlog, they'll need a story point estimate. There may also be times when the product owner would like an estimate so they can determine how many points would be added if they add a someday maybe story to an upcoming release.

It may feel like the team is spending a *lot* of time in these initial estimating sessions. Encourage them to stick with it, but limit the time spent on each story.

One thing to keep in mind is that it's OK for the initial backlog estimating to continue into the team's first sprint. As long as the top of the backlog is estimated and in good shape, they can get started and continue to chip away at the estimating.

You don't want the process to stretch on *too* long, because no one will understand the overall size of the backlog. In a worst-case scenario, strive to get the must have and nice to have stories estimated by the end of the first sprint, or *maybe* the second sprint if absolutely necessary.

Don't Try to Figure It All Out

Some teams get sucked into long, drawn-out discussions about each user story, trying to figure out *exactly* how they'll build it. This typically results in estimating taking a long time, and people losing interest and energy.

It's OK to discuss the major moving parts about what would be involved to get something done, but avoid designing the entire solution.

For example, let's say we have a user story: *As a Shopper, I want a text message when my order ships, so I know when to expect my products.*

Before voting, Emma might ask, "Do we already have a solution for sending text messages? Did we solve this for other products?"

David responds, "We haven't, but a few weeks ago I was playing around with Twilio, a cloud-hosted SMS service which is pretty popular. I think we could use that. I don't think we need to write it from scratch."

Olivia asks, "Is it compatible with Microsoft Azure, since that's where we're hosting our application?"

"I just Googled 'azure twilio' and I saw some results, including some developer guidance from Microsoft," responds Alice, "Should I dig in some more to figure out exactly how it should work?"

The ScrumMaster, Ben, jumps in. "Let's not get too far into the 'how' right now. How about I make a note in the story that you guys are thinking you can use Twilio, as opposed to writing something from scratch? Is that enough information to vote?"

The development team nods their heads. "Great," says Ben, "How about you guys vote, and we'll see if you're all on the same page?"

In this case the development team was thinking, "If we have to write this from scratch, that's much different than using something off the shelf. And if we've already solved this problem for another product, that will make things even simpler. We can just steal what we did and use it for this product."

Then they went on to discuss other potential "gotchas," such as making sure the tool they're talking about will work with Azure.

Ben, the ScrumMaster, did a good job of jumping in when it looked like the team might get sidetracked by figuring out exactly how it will work.

The team needs enough information to cast a reasonable, informed vote—that's it. Anything more than that can be deferred until the story is getting close to the top of the product backlog.

During estimating, be sure to keep an eye out for the team getting sucked to far down into the "how."

Using a Sand Timer

Some teams have found that using a two-minute sand timer—the kind that comes with many board games—can be helpful to keep things moving along. (Cohn, 2006a)

Place the sand timer in the middle of the table. At any point when someone thinks the discussion is getting too deep into the details, they reach over and flip the timer. When time runs out, discussion stops, and everyone votes.

If an agreement isn't reached, the timer can be used again. Usually, it doesn't need to be used more than once.

For virtual teams, anyone can post a chat message saying, "Two minutes." Whoever is facilitating the estimating process—often the ScrumMaster—then starts a timer. When the time is up, they notify the team and everyone votes.

Key Takeaways

- Humans aren't very good at estimating absolute size but do well at estimating relative size based on comparison.

- Instead of attempting to estimate in hours, days, or weeks—which would be an absolute size estimate—story points provide an abstract measurement to facilitate relative size estimation.

- Estimating software using absolute size is especially difficult and time-consuming, since you'd need to break everything down into tasks no larger than about two days.

- The Cohn Scale is a modified Fibonacci sequence, which provides a range of story point values for the team. Ranging from 0.5 to 100, the space between the numbers increases as they grow larger, accounting for larger estimating errors for more substantial user stories.

- Story point estimates provide insight for the product owner and stakeholders by increasing communication, helping guide prioritization, and facilitating what-if scenarios.

- Planning Poker is a rapid estimating technique that utilizes the collective experience of everyone on the development team to come up with accurate story point values. The process also reinforces the team's knowledge of the product to be built, speeding development.

- Co-located teams can use Planning Poker cards or a mobile app, while distributed teams can use an online tool such as planningpoker.com.

- To start the process, the development team selects *anchor stories*, picking two that seem like 2 points and 5 points, or 3 points and 8 points.

- Initial estimating of the full product backlog is a one-time investment. Additional estimating needs to occur only when stories are split, new stories are added, someday maybe stories move up in priority, or the product owner wants to know the size of a someday maybe story.

- To keep things moving along, a two-minute sand timer can be used. Any time someone thinks the discussion is moving along too slowly, they can flip the timer in the center of the table. When time runs out, everyone votes.

Chapter 21
Creating an Initial Schedule Projection

Even though the future seems far away, it is actually beginning right now.

- **Mattie J.T. Stepanek**, *American poet.*

If you've ever been asked the question, "How long will this take?" or, "When will it be done?" you know the challenges involved in software estimating.

Many different estimating techniques have been created over the years, and I'm guessing all of them have been applied to software at one point or another. I certainly tried a bunch of different approaches throughout my career.

The problem is that none of them worked. Whatever I tried, my schedules were wildly inaccurate.

I'm not the only one who's had challenges estimating software projects. One dramatic failure in recent history is Healthcare.gov. Originally estimated to cost $93.7 million, the budget soared to hundreds of millions of dollars. Although the website launched on schedule, it was plagued by crashes, errors, and performance issues that took months to fix, and security problems continue to this day. (U.S. Government Accountability Office, 2014; Reuters, 2018; Bleiberg & West, 2015)

The good news is there is a solution. Following the steps in the last chapter, your product backlog's user stories now have story point estimates, so you have the answer to, "How big is this?"

Now you just need to know, "How fast can the team complete story points?"

To understand that, you need the team's *velocity*—the number of story points they can drive to "done" each sprint.

21.1 The Chicken and Egg Problem: What's the Velocity?

Before the Scrum team starts sprinting, you have a problem. Velocity is a measure of how fast the team can go, but they haven't completed any sprints. They don't have any track record yet.

If you need to provide some sort of schedule estimate in order to get budget approval and green-light development, what do you do?

If you had a velocity number in hand, you could apply it to the size of the product backlog to determine how many sprints it will take to complete. Multiplying the number of sprints by the duration of each sprint gives you the total time.

For example, if the product backlog contains stories that add up to 100 story points, and you estimate the velocity of the team as 20 points per sprint, that's 5 sprints. Multiplying that by a sprint duration of 2 weeks gives you 10 weeks.

21.2 Options to Predict the Team's Velocity

So how do you predict the team's velocity?

There are three options at this stage of the game: (Cohn, 2006a)

- *Use historical information.* You look at what this development team or a similar team was able to achieve for velocity on another product and use that number.

- *Run a few sprints.* The Scrum team starts sprinting, and you see how many story points they can complete in the first few sprints to estimate their velocity for the remaining work.

- *Break down a few stories into subtasks.* The Scrum team selects a few stories from the product backlog and does micro-planning. They determine the work to design, code, test, and fix any bugs to drive each story to "done." By breaking each story down into subtasks—each with an hour estimate—they determine the required time. They then figure out how many of their selected stories they could complete in the hours they have available in a typical sprint, then use the total story points as their estimated velocity.

The first option, using historical data from another product's development, is risky. Unless there is a strong correlation between the type of work and individual team members, it's unlikely the new team will achieve the exact same velocity on the new product.

I'd only recommend this approach if the business problem, technology, and team are the same or at minimum, very similar. Otherwise, it's likely going to be an apples to oranges comparison.

The second option, running a few sprints, is ideal. This approach will allow you to see how *this* team can perform when building *this* product using *this* technology.

Ascendle is a professional services company, which usually means it's difficult for us to run a few sprints. It would be a little awkward if we told our client, "We don't know how long this will take to build, or how much it will cost, but can we just get started and we'll tell you in a few weeks?"

If you're faced with a similar situation, where it's not possible to run a few sprints, choose the third option: breaking down some user stories into subtasks.

The process takes a short amount of time and although your schedule estimate will be less reliable than running a few sprints, it will give you a less-risky answer than using historical velocity numbers which may be completely inapplicable.

21.3 Breaking Down Stories into Subtasks to Estimate Velocity

Having the Scrum team spend time to think through what it would take to complete a handful of user stories is a great way to estimate velocity. It's also a good way to get the development team to practice the same type of micro-planning that is crucial for effective sprint planning.

This is how the process works:

1. *Determine gross capacity.* For a typical sprint, determine how many hours the development team members can spend focused *solely* on this product.

2. *Determine net capacity.* Subtract Scrum ceremony time from the gross capacity number to come up with the net capacity—the total number of hours the team can spend heads-down working on subtasks.

3. *Select stories from the product backlog.* Select a handful of stories from the product backlog that have different story point size estimates. For example, a 5, a 13, an 8, and a 3.

4. *Break down a user story.* Brainstorm the subtasks that are required to drive the first story to "done," each with an hour estimate. To ensure the right level of detailed thinking, each subtask should be sized to about one day or less.

5. *Repeat.* Repeat the process until the net capacity hour estimate is consumed.

6. *Determine velocity.* Add up the points from the stories that "fit," and use that as your estimated velocity.

Determine Gross Capacity

It's important to consider how much time the development team can spend focused on product work during a typical two-week sprint. Although it would be great if everyone could come into work every day and ignore everything except what they need to get done on the product, that's seldom realistic.

There are unrelated meetings to attend, email, lunch, taking breaks, and more. In an eight-hour day, you might find that team members are lucky to get in six hours of uninterrupted work.

In addition, although not ideal, some team members might be shared with another team, so some of their time will be spent focused on *their* needs.

The development team members should talk through how much time each of them can spend focused solely on this product during each sprint.

Although things such as personal days, vacation time, and other unrelated meetings will be considered when the team plans each "real" sprint, at this stage they can ignore those factors. This is an "ideal" sprint, so they should do their best to estimate what will be typical.

For example, if the senior developer on the team knows he'll get pulled into a one-hour meeting with the enterprise architect every week, he should subtract that from the time he has available. But if he has two days off next week, he would ignore that for this exercise.

Include *only* the availability of the development team members. Omit the product owner and ScrumMaster unless they will be spending part of their time working on producing the product. For example, if your ScrumMaster is also a programmer. In that case, only include the time they'll be able to realistically spend working on subtasks.

An example is shown below:

Team Member	Hours per Week	Other Projects	E-mail & Other Meetings	Gross Capacity
Emma	40	15	5	20
Ben	40	10	5	25
David	40	-	10	30
Maria	40	5	5	30
Lucas	40	-	15	25
			Total	130 hrs per week
				260 hrs per sprint

Calculate the gross capacity for the development team, which is the time they can spend focused on the product.

Determine Net Capacity

Part of working on the product is the care and feeding of Scrum that's necessary to get the results you expect. You subtract time for Scrum ceremonies from the gross capacity number to determine *net capacity.*

At this point, some people get hung up on this concept. I'll hear things like, "It seems like Scrum has a lot of overhead. I mean, look at all the time we'll be spending in meetings!"

As I pointed out in Section 6.7, attending Scrum ceremonies is *part of doing the work*. Does that mean the team will spend time talking to each other instead of writing code or testing? Yes. However, keep in mind that if they don't communicate effectively, they'll waste a lot more time by working in an uncoordinated fashion.

Net capacity is calculated by subtracting ceremony time from gross capacity.

Once you subtract Scrum ceremony time from the gross capacity number to determine net capacity, you'll arrive at the total amount of time the team can spend working on driving stories to "done."

Team Member	Gross Capacity (Sprint)	Sprint Planning	Daily Scrums (10)	Backlog Refinement	Sprint Review	Retrospective	Net Capacity
Emma	40	4	2.5	2	1	1	29.5
Ben	50	4	2.5	2	1	1	39.5
David	60	4	2.5	2	1	1	49.5
Maria	60	4	2.5	2	1	1	49.5
Lucas	50	4	2.5	2	1	1	39.5
						Total	207.5 hrs per sprint

Net capacity is gross capacity less Scrum ceremony time.

Select Stories from the Product Backlog

Looking at your product backlog, the next step is to pick a handful of stories—three to four—with a range of story point estimates.

Select stories at the small end of the scale, since breaking down the work will be easier. I recommend keeping within a range of 2 to 13 story points.

Break Down a Story

Now is when the fun work begins. The development team sits down and brainstorms *everything* that will be required to drive the story to "done."

This includes technical design, writing unit tests and code, code reviews, testing, fixing bugs, product owner acceptance, and anything else that's necessary.

For example, if your product needs end-user documentation in order to be considered "shippable," include the time needed to outline, write, edit, and correct any mistakes.

Sample Subtask Breakdown for a Story

Here's an example breakdown for a fairly small user story:

Subtask	Hours
Write acceptance tests, review, and make edits	2
Write online help, review, and make edits	4
Create technical implementation strategy and review with team[3]	6
Create feature branch in source code repository	0.25
Create user interface layout including style edits	4
Write unit tests and code for front end	4
Write unit tests and code for back end – framework of the story	4
Write unit tests and code for back end – additional functionality	4
Insurance for unexpected coding issues	4
Run acceptance tests	2
Fix bugs	4
Peer code review, edits, and merge feature branch	2
Product owner review	2
Adjustments from product owner review	2
Total	**44.25 hrs**

Example of a user story broken down into all the required subtasks to drive it to "done."

Be sure to keep the subtasks sized small enough that they can be completed in one day or less. This ensures the team is forced to carefully think through a fine-grained plan. If they are not detailed enough, they're more likely to miss some things.

---

[3] The hour estimate includes one hour to write the strategy, and a one-hour discussion with the five-person development team. Whenever multiple team members are involved with a subtask, it's important to include the total time for everyone.

It's also good practice for what they'll be doing soon—sprint planning. I've found if subtasks are sized to no more than one day, it's much more likely that a) the team avoids "gotchas" when they forget about things that will need to be done and b) there's more of a feeling of momentum as each team member knocks down at least one subtask every day of the sprint.

Our teams assume each member has a maximum of six hours per day when taking into account meals, breaks, email, and other distractions. This would lead you to believe that six hours is a good maximum size for a subtask.

What we've discovered is there are times when a six-hour subtask is under-estimated and takes more like eight or nine hours to complete, meaning it won't fit into one working day. Because of this, we now break down subtasks into no more than four hours each, which leaves more wiggle room.

Identifying all the Subtasks

Keep in mind that it's likely your development team has never been forced to think about *everything* that needs to be done, start to finish, to complete a user story. Be patient as they talk their way through it and ensure that everyone participates. You can act as a facilitator to ensure the process goes as smoothly as it can until they get the hang of it.

Here's a trigger list you can use to help the team think through everything that might be required for the user story:

- Specifications that need to be created or clarified. For example, UX mockups, calculation spreadsheets, "seed" data to be used for testing, etc.

- Technical design work, for example, writing a technical implementation strategy and reviewing it with the development team. Be sure to include the total time for all participants. For example, a five-person development team spending an hour together reviewing the strategy would be five hours.

- Acceptance tests to write and review.

- Updating the code that generates seed data in the database.

- Required development subtasks, including both back-end and front-end code and unit tests.

- Writing and testing database update scripts to modify its structure as required by the user story.

- Insurance for unknown coding work that might come up while completing the user story.

- Code reviews and the associated work to update the code based on reviewer feedback.

- Running code coverage tools to ensure proper unit test coverage and addressing any issues that are found.

- Running acceptance tests specific to the story.

- Running general acceptance tests used for every story in the product. For example, responsive user interface testing, performance testing, localization, or security.

- Fixing bugs and re-testing them.

- Product owner review for accepting or rejecting the user story.

- Addressing any issues the product owner discovered during their review.

Repeat the Process Until Net Capacity Is Consumed

The development team repeats the process of breaking down each user story until adding one more would go over their estimated net capacity total.

The team might choose to not fill the entire estimated net capacity, even if they could "squeeze one more story in." If they feel like the amount of work they've broken down for the sprint "feels about right," they can conclude.

Determine Velocity

Add the total points for the user stories that fit into the net capacity. This is your velocity estimate.

As a Shopper, I want to review my cart, so I can make adjustments prior to checkout **5**	As a Shopper, I want to view a list of products, so I can select some to purchase **13**	As a Shopper, I want to review my orders, so I can see what I've purchased in the past **3**

Estimated Velocity: 21

The total points from the user stories the team was able to "fit" into the net capacity is the velocity estimate.

21.4 Using the Cone of Uncertainty to Anticipate the Unknown

Once you complete the process of estimating your velocity, you can apply it to the total story points in your product backlog and come up with an answer for, "How long will it take?"

For example, if you have 100 story points identified for the initial "minimum viable product" release, and you estimate a velocity of 21 story points per sprint, it's easy to do the math:

100 story points / 21 story points per sprint = 4.8 sprints

If you round up to five sprints, you can then determine the total timeframe:

5 sprints x 2 weeks per sprint = 10 weeks

You'll be tempted to proudly walk in and tell the boss, "We'll definitely be done in 10 weeks, guaranteed!" I encourage you to keep reading, because you have more work to do.

Is it Really That Easy?

The estimating technique of leveraging expert opinion to create story point estimates, then using those same experts to come up with an estimated velocity *is* in fact that easy. But walking into the boss's office and giving her an iron-clad guarantee that you've correctly predicted the future isn't.

There are all kinds of things that might happen as the team starts working. They might have:

- Overestimated how many hours per week they can focus on the product.

- Underestimated how long it will take to complete each of the subtasks they identified.

- Missed some subtasks that will be required to get stories to "done."

Then there are the realities of them coming up to speed with the Scrum framework, as well as the technical challenges they'll face when asked to produce shippable software faster than they ever have before.

They'll likely start off more slowly than you think, then ramp up over time.

Addressing the Unknown

An important part of this process is acknowledging that early in your team's agile journey, there will be a high degree of uncertainty around just how fast they'll be able to go. They have *zero* track record, so the estimated velocity might be off by quite a bit.

The good news is as they get more experience, they'll establish a proven track record and uncertainty will be reduced. But they're not at that stage yet.

Instead of promising your boss, "This will definitely be done in 10 weeks," you can instead provide a range. For example, you could say, "At this stage of the game we have a *very* rough estimate, but it at least gives us a general order of magnitude of understanding what this will take. Once we run a few sprints, we'll know more about how fast the team can move, and this estimate will get more accurate."

A model you can use to address this challenge and determine what the range should be is the *cone of uncertainty*.

The cone of uncertainty was initially created by Barry Boehm and later made popular by Steve McConnell for waterfall projects. It was then adapted by Mike Cohn for agile. It allows you to scale your estimated velocity based on how many sprints the team has completed. (Boehm, 1984; McConnell, 1998; Cohn, 2006a)

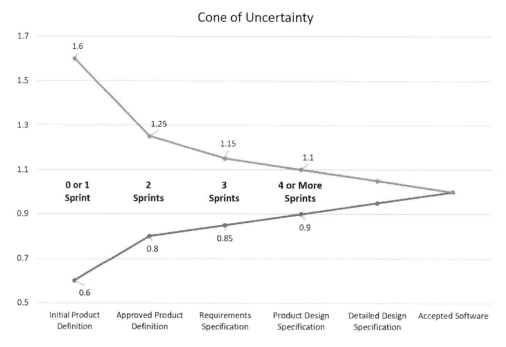

The cone of uncertainty—originally developed for waterfall projects and now applied to agile—allows you to scale your estimated velocity based on the number of sprints the team has completed.

Using scaling factors based on how many sprints have been completed, you can adjust your estimated velocity to create a range of completion timeframes.

For example, if you haven't started any sprints yet, the cone of uncertainty says you should use factors of 1.6 and 0.6.

Using these values, you can create both an *optimistic* velocity, based on the team going faster than estimated, and a *pessimistic* velocity, based on them going slower:

Optimistic velocity = 21 x **1.6** = 33.6 story points per sprint

Pessimistic velocity = 21 x **0.6** = 12.6 story points per sprint

Using these adjusted velocities, you can now calculate a time *range*:

Optimistic duration = 100 story points / **33.6** = 3 sprints x 2 weeks = 6 weeks

Pessimistic duration = 100 story points / **12.6** = 8 sprints x 2 weeks = 16 weeks

Estimated duration: 6 to 16 weeks

As the team executes sprints and establishes a track record, this range narrows:

Sprints Completed	Uncertainty Factor	Velocity Range	Duration Range
0 to 1	0.6 to 1.6	12.6 to 33.6	6 to 16 weeks
2	0.8 to 1.25	16.8 to 26.3	8 to 12 weeks
3	0.85 to 1.15	17.9 to 24.2	8 to 11 weeks
4 or more	0.9 to 1.1	18.9 to 23.1	9 to 11 weeks

Using an estimated velocity of 21 story points per sprint, the cone of uncertainty allows you to scale your time estimate based on how many sprints have been completed.

Note that this is a simplified model. Once the team gets started, the product backlog will be in a constant state of change as adjustments are made by the product owner and the team completes user stories.

The illustration above assumes 100 story points for every calculation, and duration has been rounded to the nearest week.

When you use this technique moving forward, you'll calculate the total story points remaining at a specific point in time—often the end of each sprint. You'll then use that total, the average velocity of the team, and the appropriate cone of uncertainty factors to update the forecasted completion date range.

Early in the process—when the degree of uncertainty is very high—you'll come up with a very wide range. As the team gains experience and completes more sprints, uncertainty is reduced and the range narrows accordingly.

Notice, however, that you never reach perfection. There will *always* be a degree of uncertainty, so your estimates will never get better than plus or minus 10%.

What if My Boss Won't Be Happy with This Answer?

When I explain this concept to attendees of my talks, they sometimes say, "I'd get laughed out of the room if I showed that to my boss. It's too wide a range. She'll think I don't know what I'm talking about."

Before I address this, I want to emphasize that *this is as good as you can get* at this point. Be careful not to fool yourself into believing that you can be more accurate than this.

You can't.

Most estimation failure that I've seen over the years has been due to guesswork and "feelings."

"It feels like this should take about *this* long" has nothing to do with reality.

The beauty of this estimating technique is it's based on *empirical data*. Sure, there's expert opinion involved by those who will do the work, but there's a scientific, step-by-step process. And once you start running sprints, you'll be able to point to *evidence*: how fast the team can, in fact, move.

Even if you decide you want to give your boss a narrower range, you should remember that the precision of your estimate won't magically improve. It's simply not possible; you don't have enough information quite yet.

If you do insist on reducing your estimated timeframe, be sure you select the *more pessimistic* end of the scale, not the *more optimistic* end.

For example, if your range is 6 to 16 weeks, you could tell your boss, "Our current estimate is 11 to 16 weeks."

I would *not* recommend you tell your boss, "We'll definitely get it done in 6 to 11 weeks."

Key Takeaways

- To convert story points to time, you need *velocity* which is the number of points the team can drive to "done" during one sprint.

- The best way to estimate velocity is by running a few sprints. If that's not possible, you can compare the velocity to work on another product or break down a few stories into subtasks to determine how many story points might fit into a sprint.

- Breaking down some stories is usually a better option than using the velocity from another team that may not be applicable to *this* team, *this* product, and *this* technology.

- To determine an estimated velocity using the "break down some stories" method, the team calculates how many hours they can work on stories during a typical sprint, then they determine how many stories they think can be driven to "done" in that timeframe.

- The cone of uncertainty acknowledges that it's difficult to accurately predict velocity before the team has started working on the product. It allows you to establish optimistic and pessimistic velocity estimates, which then let you create a range of completion timeframes.

- As more sprints are completed, the cone of uncertainty narrows, as do your completion timeframe estimates. However, it never narrows to less than plus or minus 10%.

- If you're nervous about providing a very wide range of estimates, you can make the range narrower. I encourage you to select the more *pessimistic* end of the range, however, and not the more *optimistic* one.

Chapter 22
Splitting User Stories for Increased Momentum

Nothing is so fatiguing as the eternal hanging on of an uncompleted task.

- **William James**, *American philosopher and psychologist.*

We've all been faced with a daunting challenge that seems almost too big to tackle. Creating PowerPoint slides for the group presentation next week, on a topic unfamiliar to you. Writing a report documenting two months of painstaking research. Hiring and training a new employee in a tight job market.

All of these have one thing in common: they can become overwhelming if you think about them as one item on your to-do list. You drag your feet and never quite get started early enough because it's too much to think about. Late nights and cutting corners are often inevitable.

To make these types of large challenges more do-able, most of us will break them down into bite-sized pieces. It's much easier to get motivated when the barrier to entry is lower. Once you start, you suddenly have a feeling of momentum. The process builds on itself until you're done, at which point you look back and think, "What was the big deal?"

Scrum teams face this same type of challenge when tackling user stories that are too large. Although they do have a way to break down the work using subtasks, stories that take an entire sprint or more to complete cause problems for the team.

Large stories make it difficult for the team to feel a sense of momentum, and they can cause an even worse problem: not quite getting them done by the end of the sprint. Showing up to sprint review and having to explain *again* why they didn't complete their stories can demoralize a development team.

Finally, by keeping user stories small, it's much easier for the team to do *a little bit of everything all the time*, a key principle of Scrum. By completing a user story every two to three days, it's easier to have simultaneous design, coding, testing, and fixing bugs.

22.1 Avoid "Traveling" Stories by Splitting Them

I like the term *traveling stories* to describe those that get carried from sprint to sprint in a partial state of completion, because they were too large to complete within a single sprint. (Gottesdiener, 2013)

The cure? Split large stories, thin-slicing them into smaller, more "do-able" chunks that the team can drive to completion within one sprint.

This is especially important for a team that's new to Scrum, since they will be learning the process while simultaneously attempting to complete everything within what may seem like an impossibly short amount of time.

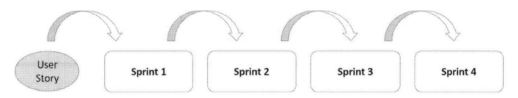

User stories that are too large never quite get done and "travel" from sprint to sprint.

Split Stories at the Top of the Product Backlog

Since the problem only comes into play when too-large user stories are introduced into a sprint, you only need to focus on splitting stories at the top of the backlog.

This helps you avoid two problems:

- *Wasting time.* The product backlog is in a constant state of change, and the further into the future you go, the less sure you are about where a user story will end up on the list. If you go too far down the backlog, you may spend time and energy splitting user stories that may never be added to the product.

- *Making your product backlog unwieldy.* In Chapter 19, I recommended you keep the initial product backlog to about 75 to 100 user stories. If you start splitting every story in the backlog, you'll rapidly eliminate the benefit of having a shorter list to manage.

As a rule of thumb, only worry about splitting enough stories to fit into the next sprint or two.

22.2 The Six-Way Model for Splitting User Stories

Splitting stories, especially for first-time product owners, can sometimes be challenging. One of the requirements for stories is they remain self-contained, and each delivers incremental value.

If you think about a large user story as big piece of multi-layer cake—with a data layer, business layer, presentation layer, and so on—it's important to slice the story into smaller pieces *vertically*. Serving just one layer of the cake—for example, just the database and no user interface—doesn't provide value to the user. This is important because many developers often like to focus just on one layer at a time. (Wake, 2003)

This is something to keep in mind as the team comes up to speed with this process. Many developers have a difficult time getting their brains wrapped around user stories that don't align with a layer-by-layer approach. Spend time to help them understand that the resulting, smaller stories still need to each provide incremental value to an end user, which is why they need *every* layer.

To make it easier to split the stories in the right way, you can use the following list and think about which strategy, or combination of strategies, might work best. (Cohn, 2006a)

- Data boundaries

- Operational boundaries

- CRUD operations

- Cross-cutting concerns

- Performance

- Different priorities

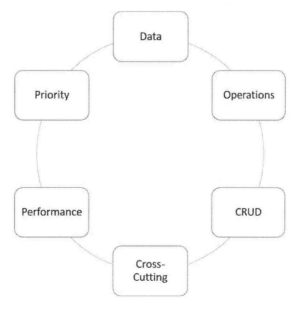

Six strategies you can use to split user stories.

Data Boundaries

Many large user stories deal with different types of data. For example, if you are building a banking app, you might have a story along the lines of: *As a Customer, I want to view my checking account online, so I can get information without having to call the bank.*

This story might include viewing recent transactions, viewing the details of a check, and viewing monthly statements.

Using the data boundaries strategy, it could be split into:

- As a Customer, I want to view a list of recent transactions, so I can see the activity in my account

- As a Customer, I want to view the front and back of a check, so I can see its details

- As a Customer, I want to view my monthly statement, so I don't need a paper statement

Notice how any of these user stories could be independently delivered to the end user, because each provides incremental value. You may choose to wait until they're all done to ship, but they aren't tied to each other.

I'll talk more about how to ensure each of your new stories support this concept in Section 22.5.

Operational Boundaries

This approach is what I call, "Make it work, then make it fancier." You start by thinking about the simplest version of the user story that could possibly deliver value to the user, and make that your first story. Then put additional "fancy" functionality into one or more additional stories.

As an example, pretend you're creating a new streaming music app. The large story is: *As a Listener, I want to listen to streaming music, so I don't have to purchase and download music.*

In this case, the simplest thing that could *possibly* deliver value to *someone* is simply listening to a random selection of music.

That story might be written: *As a Listener, I want to listen to a random selection of music, so I can be entertained.*

Additional stories each add incremental value:

- As a Listener, I want an automatic playlist based on an artist I specify, so I can listen to similar music

- As a Listener, I want to create my own playlist, so I can select the songs I'd like to listen to

- As a Listener, I want to share my playlist with others, so I can expose my friends to my favorite music

An additional benefit to splitting a user story along operational boundaries is it allows the development team to focus on getting *something* working, which is often the biggest challenge with a new story. They can then add additional capability onto the base functionality.

By giving them "permission to ignore" the fancy stuff up front, they are often more productive, simply by allowing them to focus on the basics.

CRUD Operations

The acronym CRUD stands for the typical operations a user can do with data: **c**reate, **r**ead, **u**pdate, and **d**elete. Although you don't want your initial product backlog to be filled with separate user stories for every CRUD operation in the entire product, it's a powerful splitting strategy.

On our Ascendle teams, we often use this approach when building new applications for our clients, especially for the first batch of CRUD screens. Later stories typically progress faster since the patterns become more well-established, so we often don't need to split subsequent stories along CRUD boundaries.

For a multi-tenant web application, a user story could be: *As an Administrator, I want to manage customers, so I can control access to the application.* The split stories could be:

- As an Administrator, I want to view a list of customers, so I can see who has access to the application

- As an Administrator, I want to view the details for one customer, so I can see all their information

- As an Administrator, I want to create and edit customers, so I can manage the list

- As an Administrator, I want to disable a customer, so I can restrict access to the application

You might wonder how these stories can be tested independently. For example, how can you build the list story first if you don't have the ability to create customers yet?

The technique I like to use is to add *seed data* to the database during the deployment process, providing a set of demonstration customers. This permits working with a list of customers without requiring the create and edit story to be completed prior to the list story.

It's also helpful for testing, since you don't have to create a bunch of data by hand every time a new build is deployed.

Cross-Cutting Concerns

Functionality that applies to most or all the user stories in the application are referred to as *cross-cutting concerns*.

Examples include:

- Security

- Validation

- Error handling

- Logging

- Encryption

It's often acceptable to delay the implementation of one or more of these as a way to split a story.

Take security for example. A feature can be implemented in a "wide open" fashion, with no security restrictions. Then later, the required security enhancements are added via a separate story.

For example, consider the following user story for a human resources application: *As a Human Resources Specialist, I want to manage salary information for an employee, so I can track their salary history.*

This might be split into two user stories. The first user story has the same title as the original story, but the security-related acceptance criteria have been pulled into a new, second story:

- As a Human Resources Specialist, I want to manage salary information for an employee, so I can track their salary history

- As an Administrator, I want to restrict access to salary information to specific user roles, so I can control who sees sensitive information

Would you ship the product after the first story is done? No, but your development team will likely get the fully-shippable feature done more quickly by splitting it in this way.

Performance

A well-known saying in software development is: *make it work, then make it fast.* (Lampson, 1983; Johnson, 1983) Splitting performance into a separate story is another technique you can use.

First, the development team focuses on building the basic functionality, with no consideration for performance ("make it work"). Then, in a separate story, they optimize the code to meet performance requirements ("make it fast").

For example, imagine you're creating an internet of things (IoT) web application that monitors the temperature in refrigerated tractor trailers that transport food or medicine. The original user story is: *As a Fleet Manager, I want to monitor the temperature in transit, so I can know if there were any unacceptable variations.*

You determine that when this feature is fully implemented, it should be able to handle 500 trailers, which will address the first year or two of customers. But initially, the development team can focus on a much smaller number.

This story could be split into two:

- As a Fleet Manager, I want to monitor the temperature of up to five trailers, so I can know if there were any unacceptable variations.

- As the SureTemp Product Team, I want the product to handle up to 500 trailers, so we can support the expected customer base for the first year or two.

The second user story is written using an internal role—that of your product team. An individual customer has a maximum of 20 trailers, so the only role who cares about supporting 500 trailers across the entire application is the team responsible for the SureTemp product.

This Strategy Avoids Early Optimization

One benefit of this splitting strategy is it avoids *attempting to optimize too early.*

Programmers are famous for trying to make their code as efficient as possible, but they often spend a lot of time trying to make the wrong code run more quickly. They spend hours on non-critical parts of the application, optimizing code that is unrelated to any performance issues.

They tend to focus on the 97% of the code that has zero impact on performance issues, instead of concentrating on the 3% that does matter. The only way to identify the slow code is to *run the completed, working code* and use performance analysis tools to identify the 3% that's causing the slowdown. If programmers guess at what parts of the application will be slow, they're likely to guess incorrectly. Remember that *premature optimization is the root of all evil.* (Knuth, 1974; McConnell, 2004; Knuth, 1971)

Splitting along performance boundaries allows you to give the development team permission to ignore performance until the code is working. They'll then have a much better chance of spending the minimum amount of time optimizing code, focused on the small percentage that's causing the slow performance.

Different Priorities

The last splitting technique is to pull out any portions of a user story that can wait until later. The split user story or stories can then be pushed down lower on the backlog.

Let's say you have a user story along the lines of: *As a Shopper, I want to see information in my local language, so I don't have to have solid English skills to use the product.*

You've studied your target market and determined you need to support three languages in addition to English: Mexican Spanish, French, and German. However, based on your company's marketing plans, Mexican Spanish is the most important, followed by French in the next release, and German can wait until some future release. You could split the stories into:

- As a Shopper, I want to see information in Mexican Spanish, so I don't have to have solid English skills to use the product

- As a Shopper, I want to see information in French, so I don't have to have solid English skills to use the product

- As a Shopper, I want to see information in German, so I don't have to have solid English skills to use the product

Any time you think, "This part of the story can wait," consider splitting it by priority and push the less-important stories down in the backlog.

Don't Be Afraid of Combining Strategies

Many stories can be split with just one of these strategies, but don't be afraid of leveraging more than one.

For example, I may have a user story such as the following: *As an Author, I want a spell checker, so I can prevent spelling errors in my document.*

It might include acceptance criteria such as:

- I can check spelling in English.

- I can check spelling in Spanish.

- I can see a wavy line under misspelled words.

- I can see suggestions for the misspelled words.

- I can add a word to the dictionary.

I might use the *priority* strategy to separate checking spelling in Spanish, moving it down the product backlog in a new story. Then I could use the *operations* strategy to pull out word suggestions and adding a word to the dictionary into two additional stories.

22.3 SPIDR: An Alternative Method for Splitting Stories

I've have had a lot of success with the six-way strategy I outlined in the previous section, both when splitting stories myself and teaching others what really is more of an art than a science. However, you may find that it doesn't work for you and you'd like an alternative.

In the interest of completeness, in this section I'll describe another method for splitting user stories: SPIDR. (Cohn, 2017a; Lattenkamp, 2017)

The acronym stands for:

- **S**pikes

- **P**aths

- **I**nterfaces

- **D**ata

- **R**ules

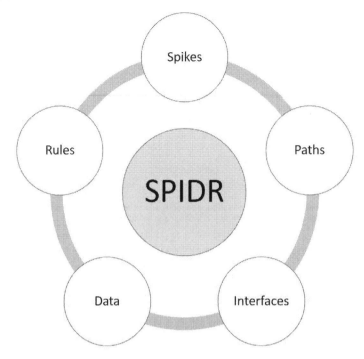

SPIDR is an acronym for an alternative set of user story splitting strategies.

Spikes

In agile terminology, a *spike* is research conducted to make the development team smarter about what it will take to implement a user story. In some cases, a story is large because there are a lot of technical unknowns.

I faced this the first time we built a product that used Stripe for payment processing. A cloud-hosted payment system, Stripe turned out to be robust and easy to use. However, at the beginning, there were a lot of unknowns because no one on the team had used it before. They estimated the user story quite large to account for this risk.

Don't Create a User Story

What's a little confusing about this part of the SPIDR acronym is you *should not create a user story for the spike*. A spike doesn't deliver any value to the product owner and, by extension, other business stakeholders. It provides direct value to the development team—by making them smarter about how to get a user story done—but delivers only *indirect* value to stakeholders.

Therefore, you shouldn't create a user story which, by definition, must deliver business value to stakeholders.

To represent the work of the spike on the product backlog, I use the term *task*, which aligns with the terminology in Jira, the most popular agile management tool. In this case, the product owner adds a task to the product backlog and the development team pulls that into the next sprint.

Don't Reduce the Story Point Estimate

You might think that by pulling out the research work from the user story, the original story point estimate should be reduced. I don't advise that because you aren't doing less work. You're just splitting the work into multiple sprints.

The benefit of the spike is to either eliminate the technical risk—meaning the user story can then be completed within one sprint—or to help the development team understand more clearly how the work can be split into smaller stories.

How You Know You Need a Spike

My rule of thumb for determining when you need a spike is if the development team doesn't have enough information to break down a story into subtasks during the splint planning process.

They complete the spike in one sprint, then the following sprint, they can pull in the related user story and break it down into subtasks, leveraging the knowledge they gained by completing the research.

Use the Other Options First

Although *spikes* is listed first in the SPIDR acronym, this technique should be considered only after the other techniques have been evaluated, since ideally any technical research should be performed within the same sprint as the user story.

Paths

Sometimes a user story is large because the user can take multiple paths through the functionality. For example, in the case of checkout, a user might complete their purchase using a credit card or using a gift card purchased by someone else.

In this instance, there could be one story for purchasing with a credit card, and another story to support the use of a gift card.

Interfaces

In this case, you split the story based on user interfaces or technical interfaces.

For example, you can split a user story into support for different device types. For a web application, this could be one story for desktop browsers, one story for Android devices, and one for iOS.

Another example is first creating a simple user interface, then a subsequent story that makes the user interface fancier. For example, the first version of a screen doesn't support drag and drop, and that's represented by the first story. The second story adds the drag and drop functionality.

Finally, a user story for exporting data might initially include two different targets, for example, Word or Excel. That story could be split into one for exporting to Word and another for exporting to Excel.

Note that in this scenario, the first story will likely be larger than the second, since the heavy lifting of getting the export to work for *any* format needs to be completed first. Adding the ability to output to a different file format is likely a smaller amount of effort.

Data

You can often implement a simpler version of a user story with a subset of data. For example, if you are building a human resources application, the user story for managing employees could be split into managing the text information for the employee—name, hire date, position, etc.—and another to add a picture of the employee.

Rules

Many user stories have a variety of rules to make the associated functionality robust. A splitting option is to relax the rules for the first user story and handle them in a subsequent one.

Examples include:

- *Performance.* You can build the first user story, then worry about adhering to performance requirements in one or more subsequent stories.

- *Validation.* The initial story can be "open," allowing any sort of data entry. Then a later user story can add validation to enforce maximum lengths, required fields, etc.

- *Standards.* The first story is completed without adhering to standards, and a subsequent one can address them. For example, the feature is built with no encryption at first, then encryption is added in a later story.

22.4 "There's No Way to Split This User Story"

Sometimes when I'm helping a newer development team they'll struggle with the splitting process. They'll come upon a user story and say, "We can't split this story. It has to stay as-is."

First let me say, I've never met a user story I can't split. However, sometimes a lot of creativity is required when applying the splitting techniques in this chapter.

As an example, a team recently had a user story, *As an Operations Specialist, I want orders to be transferred to the back-end system, so I can fulfill them.*

Acceptance criteria included a variety of things, such as transferring the order, transferring order line items, handling errors from the back-end system's API, and storing the transfer date in the database if it was successful.

The team felt like they had to do all of this at once; there was no way to split the story.

The trick to tackling this is to think about the smallest pieces of individual functionality that provide some sort of value and can be completed, tested, and demonstrated.

Here are some leading questions I asked the team to help them think about how to create a smaller story. Anything that didn't make it into the first story would be placed in subsequent, split stories:

- What if you just sent the order information and no line items to the API?

- If that's too much, how about just one or two values from the order, such as Order Number and Customer ID?

- What if you didn't handle any errors from the API yet?

- What if you don't store the transfer date yet? Or just assume the transfer always succeeds and store the current date?

The key point to remember is that when splitting stories, *there is no assumption that the product* must *be shipped when the first split story is completed.*

Remember, as I talked about at the beginning of this chapter, the reason you want to split stories is to increase momentum and avoid "traveling" stories. If you split a user story into *very* basic components, that's OK.

Just remember to complete each user story as a thin *vertical* slice, not a *horizontal* slice.

22.5 Use INVEST to Ensure the Quality of Split Stories

When splitting a user story, it's sometimes easy to fall into the trap of the resulting stories being not quite right. For example, you may end up with stories that slip back into a waterfall approach, with one story focused on coding and another on testing.

To help ensure the split stories are still "agile friendly," I have another acronym for you: INVEST. (Wake, 2003)

- **I**ndependent

- **N**egotiable

- **V**aluable

- **E**stimable

- **S**mall

- **T**estable

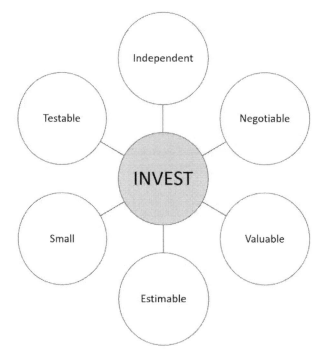

The INVEST mnemonic helps ensure high-quality user stories.

Independent

Ideally, user stories shouldn't be tied to one another. You should be able to implement them in any order.

This is helpful to the product owner so he can reorder the product backlog as necessary. It also means more effective development because there will be less "stepping on each other" if the team is dividing and conquering to work on more than one user story at the same time.

For example, if you split a story into one for the functionality and another for performance, it only makes sense to do the performance story once the functionality story is completed.

It's common that there will be *some* order dependency in your product backlog but try to keep it to a minimum.

Negotiable

A good user story provides a high-level overview but doesn't include every possible detail. This provides more flexibility for the development team to work collaboratively with the product owner during the sprint.

Using a lightweight list of five to ten acceptance criteria and avoiding pages and pages of specifications for each story is a good way to keep stories negotiable.

As each story nears the top of the product backlog and is discussed with the team, additional details are often added, but they're not needed until it nears development.

Valuable

Every user story must provide at least some value to the end user. This is what prevents you from creating stories representing horizontal slices—the data layer, the business layer, the presentation layer, etc.

Once completed, a story might not deliver enough functionality to warrant a new release of the product, but incremental value is provided, and the functionality is usable.

For example, you might have a user story to provide a basic implementation of browsing products for your e-commerce application: *As a Shopper, I want to browse products, so I can select some to purchase.*

This story just lists all the products you sell, with no filtering or any additional functionality. It delivers value to the user; they can, in fact, browse your products. But you likely wouldn't ship this feature until additional user stories are done such as: *As a Shopper, I want to browse products by category, so I can find those I'm looking for* and *As a Shopper, I want to filter products by average customer review, so I can find the best products.*

Estimable

A user story needs enough detail to allow the development team to assign a story point estimate. As I discussed in Chapter 20, the estimate doesn't need to be perfect, so you don't need a *lot* of information. But there needs to be enough detail to allow the team to compare it to other stories.

In some cases, a story might be vague or involves technology or techniques that are unfamiliar to the team. In this case, they could assign an inflated estimate, as a way of saying, "We're not sure about a lot of this."

If the product owner needs a better estimate, the team might need to use a *spike* to do some technical research to better understand what's involved. I talked about spikes in Section 22.3.

Small

Although stories lower down on the backlog can be larger, those near the top need to be small enough to accomplish in a sprint. I recommend that you split stories to a size that three to four of them can fit into a sprint.

My rule of thumb is to split stories to no larger than 25% to 33% of the team's average velocity from the previous three sprints. If the team hasn't completed three sprints yet, I recommend splitting stories so they're no larger than three points.

If stories are larger, for example if only one or two can fit into a sprint, it's difficult for the team to get a feeling of momentum. It also increases the risk that if something goes wrong, the team won't be able to get the stories done.

Testable

If no one can figure out how the user story will be tested once implemented, that's a warning sign. The story may not be clear enough, or it may not deliver value.

This is one reason I recommend writing acceptance tests early in the sprint. They serve to "beta test" the story, to ensure it is in fact testable. See Chapter 14 for more details.

22.6 Who Splits User Stories and When?

I won't lie to you. Splitting stories is an art form, and an acquired talent. It will take practice for you to get it right. This is a great place to get help from either more experienced team members within your company or external coaching expertise.

Because it's tricky to learn, it's not always the best idea to have the *entire* Scrum team participate. In some cases, the product owner can split stories on their own. The risk is they may not have enough technical insight to choose the best technical dividing lines.

Use a Small Group to Split Stories

In my experience, the best way to split stories is to take an initial pass with a small subset of the team, including the product owner, ScrumMaster, and one of the senior developers.

The product owner is in charge of the product backlog, so they absolutely should be involved in any splitting process. They'll be able to make key decisions, especially when splitting stories by priority. They can select where in the backlog the lower-priority stories belong.

The ScrumMaster, as the embedded Scrum coach on the team, can help move the process along. If they don't have a lot of experience splitting stories, working through this process will give them more exposure to this skill and increase their value to the company.

Finally, involving a senior developer or two is helpful because there are often ways to split stories that make it easier or harder to develop. Having a technical perspective can ensure that you apply the most implementation-friendly breakpoints between stories. They can also help ensure each split story represents a vertical slice through all the layers of the application, avoiding those that don't deliver value to the end user.

Note that once the stories are split by this small group, they should *not* assign story point estimates. That should be done by the entire development team whenever possible during backlog refinement.

There is no formal ceremony for this splitting process; it's just part of the product owner's responsibility to keep the backlog in good shape. You can choose the best time to do this process, typically during the sprint prior to when the split stories will be added to a sprint.

Assuming you have a backlog refinement ceremony with the entire Scrum team, make sure you take time to split stories before that ceremony happens.

Get the Development Team Smart About the New Stories

Although a smaller group is often the most efficient way to perform the splitting process, it's critical that the entire development team reviews the newly-split stories. Backlog refinement is a great time to do this, since they'll also need to estimate story points for the newly-split stories using the Planning Poker process.

As I talked about in Chapter 20, story points are an important output from the backlog refinement process, but more important is getting the entire development team smart about the stories.

Do the New Story Points Need to Add Up to the Original?

Sometimes you have a large story that gets split into smaller ones, and when the development team assigns story point estimates, they won't add up to the original number.

For example, you may have a 13-point story that gets split into three 5-point stories, totaling 15. Or it may get split into one 5-point story and two 3-point stories, which adds up to 11.

This is perfectly acceptable and expected. When stories are split, a by-product is the development team tends to understand them better, and when using smaller story point numbers, there is more precision than larger numbers.

If a 13-point story gets split into ten 5-point stories, that should be a reason to take a step back and ask, "What's happening here?" Was the development team too optimistic when they assigned the original 13-point estimate? Is it possible they didn't really understand the story until the splitting process happened and more detail was added? Or are they being overly pessimistic with the split stories?

As a rule of thumb, the split stories should add up to approximately plus or minus 50% of the original story, which is in the margin of error of the story point estimating technique. (Cohn, 2006a)

For a 13-point story, the split stories, should add up to a total roughly the range of 6 to 7 points on the low end, and 19 to 20 points on the high end.

Stories that Are Too Small Can Introduce Excess Overhead

Having stories that are too large is one problem, but it's also an issue if stories are too *small*.

There is a certain amount of overhead involved in managing a user story. It needs to be discussed, estimated, and its priority order managed. When it's pulled into a sprint, it needs to be designed, coded, and tested.

Having 20 stories in a sprint is often as risky as having just 1 story. In a two-week sprint, with 10 working days, that means the development team needs to design, code, test, fix bugs, and have the product owner review *two stories every day*, including on sprint planning day! That's a lot to ask.

For two-week sprints, use a rule of thumb that your split stories should be no more than 25% to 33% of the team's average velocity from the last three sprints. This means you'll end up with three to four stories in each sprint.

One nice side benefit of this is as the development team speeds up, you'll end up with larger stories, because their velocity will be higher.

For example, if the team is just getting going, their average velocity might be 15 story points per sprint. In this case, split stories should be no larger than 3 to 5 points.

As the team speeds up, they may reach a velocity of 30, in which case they should split stories to 8 points or less.

For a brand-new team with *no* established velocity, experiment with stories no larger than 3 story points until they have a track record of how many story points they can drive to "done" each sprint.

Key Takeaways

- Especially for new teams, driving a user story to *really* done—to the point it's at a shippable level of quality—is very difficult to do during a sprint. To help the team be more successful, make the user stories very small at first so that they can drive them to done.

- Stories that don't quite get done are often called *traveling stories*, since they travel from sprint to sprint. If most of your stories are traveling, then you're not really doing Scrum. Making stories smaller helps address this problem.

- When you split stories, focus only on the top of the product backlog. Stories lower on the product backlog, that aren't going to be added to the next sprint or two, can stay as-is. This keeps your product backlog smaller and easier to manage, and avoids wasting time on splitting stories that may end up getting re-prioritized lower on the backlog.

- The six-way model for splitting stories provides a variety of methods you can use. One or more can be applied to each large user story. They include data boundaries, operational boundaries, CRUD operations, cross-cutting concerns, performance, and different priorities.

- An alternative approach is SPIDR, which stands for spikes, paths, interfaces, data, and rules. I find the six-way model easier to use, but you may like SPIDR better; it's a personal preference. Use what seems to work best.

- INVEST is an acronym to test the quality of your user stories. User stories should be independent, negotiable, valuable, estimable, small, and testable.

- Although the entire Scrum team can work together to split user stories, I find it's often easier for a smaller group to complete the process. The product owner, ScrumMaster, and a senior developer or two is often more efficient. This group should *not* assign story point estimates.

- Although the smaller group is often the best way to complete the splitting process, the entire development team needs to get familiar with the split stories. This is usually best done through a backlog refinement ceremony when they'll review and estimate the story points for the split stories using Planning Poker.

- The total story points of the split stories don't need to add up to the story point estimate of the original un-split story. However, the total shouldn't be *too* far off. Use a rule of thumb that the total of the split stories should be roughly plus or minus 50% of the original user story estimate. If it's far outside that range, discuss it with the development team to ensure it makes sense. This can happen, especially if the team was less experienced when the original story was estimated, or the story was much different to what they initially thought now that they see it broken down into smaller stories.

- Making too many tiny stories can often be as bad as having stories that are too large. They add a lot of noise to the product backlog and incur additional overhead since the team needs to design, code, and test each of them start-to-finish within the sprint. A rule of thumb you can use is to make stories no larger than 25% to 33% of the average velocity of the team's last three sprints, so about three to four of them are added to each sprint. As the team speeds up, their split stories can be larger, since their velocity will be higher

Chapter 23
Final Preparations Before Your First Sprint

The temptation to take the easy road is always there. It is as easy as staying in bed in the morning and sleeping in. But discipline is paramount to ultimate success and victory for any leader and any team.

- **Jocko Willink**, *American podcaster, author, and retired United States Navy SEAL commander.*

At the heart of Scrum is the sprint, during which a "done," usable, and potentially releasable product increment is created. (Schwaber & Sutherland, 2017)

The problem is most teams new to agile can't realistically accomplish this goal. They aren't set up to handle the rapid production of new, fully-tested code in a matter of weeks.

Before they dive into their first sprint and realize half-way through that they're stuck and unable to produce a usable product increment, they should do some preparation to lay the groundwork.

I'm a big fan of avoiding "getting ready to get ready," so if you read through this chapter and think, "We've totally got this under control *now*," then by all means, skip ahead to the next chapter and light the fires!

However, if you see that the team needs time to ensure they can, in fact, produce a product increment during their first sprint, have them do it now. This is a great example of "slow down to speed up."

One thing to remember is the first Scrum team at your company is forging ahead into uncharted territory. They are the pioneers, and everyone—both the skeptics and the supporters—will be watching. The last thing you want is for the team to complete their first sprint and produce…nothing.

When the Scrum team says, "We're running a sprint," they're making an implicit promise to create something of value—a usable product increment—by its conclusion.

Does this mean you're not allowed to use the Scrum framework to manage the work I outline in this chapter? No. Just don't call what you're doing a "sprint." I talk about this more toward the end of this chapter in Section 23.12.

23.1 What You Should Have in Place Before Starting Your First Sprint

I've found that if you have a handful of things in place before starting your first sprint, you'll have a dramatically higher likelihood of being able to create a shippable increment by the end.

Remember that your team is most likely going to struggle their first time at bat. If they haven't done it before, learning how to work on just a small part of the product—including making it completely shippable—is *hard*. You want to avoid any and all distractions.

Most of what's necessary is outlined in Part II Understanding Agile Software Construction. Here's a summarized to-do list:

- Complete initial user experience (UX) design.

- Deploy agile tools.

- Define Scrum and technical standards.

- Configure developer workstations.

- Set up source code control.

- Create an initial code framework: the "walking skeleton."

- Configure continuous integration.

- Provision team test environments.

- Establish continuous deployment.

- Research production deployment considerations.

What if We Can't Get All of This Done, but We Want to Start Our First Sprint?

Is it the end of the world if a few of these aren't quite ready and you want to start your first sprint? No, but having as many in place as possible will dramatically increase your team's chances of success as they get going.

Note that some of what I outline may not apply to you and your team. For example, if you're working on the development of a marketing website with a content management system

(CMS), continuous deployment may not be supported by the technology. Just ignore any suggestions that aren't applicable.

If you do choose to start your first sprint without some of these done, I encourage you to wait at least until you feel like they can be wrapped up within a few days of starting the sprint if possible. Otherwise, your team will start with a big distraction from getting work done on the product.

There's also something to be said for a little bit of pressure to get things done, both for your team as well as others who are helping them get everything in place.

For example, if a separate DevOps group holds the keys to the kingdom and they're telling you, "It will be six weeks until we can even think about working on this for you," some higher-ups might need to get involved to think creatively about how to work around that limitation. "Look, these guys can't start working until we get them some sort of test environment. What can we do to move this along?"

23.2 Complete Initial User Experience (UX) Design

Many user experience (UX) professionals become a little perplexed when they learn that the development team is going to start building the product very soon. They're typically used to a phased, waterfall-like approach, involving months of customer research, ideation, and thorough user experience design of the entire product.

With agile, the user experience design process needs to be adapted to fit the iterative and incremental nature of development.

It's often the case that initial customer research will still happen up front. For example, some work may be required to support the decision to build the product. However, if the "go" decision has been made, the Scrum team will typically get started fairly quickly—often measured in weeks, not months.

Wherever they are in the process, the UX professionals need to shift gears to the care and feeding of the Scrum development team. This is where the prioritized product backlog comes into play. Instead of attempting to design the *entire* product, the UX architects and visual designers can focus on the top-priority user stories.

What's needed at this point to support the agile process is to complete the "simplest UX process that could possibly work," so the development team can start building. This usually means the UX team is designing just a few screens at a time, as opposed to the entire product end to end.

Over time, subsequent UX work is adjusted based on how the product is coming together.

This is important because the traditional "design the entire product" approach to UX may result in extensive rework, due to changes during construction. For example, the product owner may decide to simplify a feature when it turns out that the original design would be too time-consuming to build.

If the UX work was already done for the entire product, that change may mean that major portions of the rest of the UX design no longer work and need to be re-thought.

To avoid this, a strategy that keeps UX closely aligned with the work of the Scrum team is important.

One option is to embed a UX specialist right in the team. This is the best option, as they always understand the complete context of how the product is being built.

An alternative is for the product owner to work closely with UX team members outside the Scrum team, utilizing them as "external resources."

In either case, the key strategy for UX is to focus on designing just what the team needs for the next sprint or two, keeping the design work as agile as the development work.

23.3 Deploy Agile Tools

When brainstorming roles and features and creating the product backlog as I described in Chapter 19, you may have used tools such as Microsoft Word, Excel, or even a wiki such as Confluence.

As you embark on adopting the Scrum framework to help orchestrate the team's day-to-day activities, it's important to move to a purpose-built tool designed for agile.

You Need a Scrum Software Development Tool

If you don't have one, it's time to deploy a tool such as Atlassian's Jira, which will let you manage various Scrum artifacts and support required communication within the team.

An agile tool allows you to easily manage the product backlog, a way for the team to plan the work of the sprint, and a sprint task board to visualize and coordinate the day-to-day work. It also provides reports such as a sprint burndown chart and release burndown.

When in Doubt, Try Jira

I selected Jira for Ascendle when I started the company almost six years ago, since it was the most popular tool at the time. It continues to be the leader, with 58% of the market. (VersionOne, 2018)

Our team members have worked with a bunch of other tools over the years, so we've seen a wide variety. The bottom line is you can make Scrum work with almost any tool. However, I've found Jira to be the easiest to use and most comprehensive. If you already have something that supports the fundamentals of Scrum, great. If not, give Jira a try.

One additional benefit of Jira is new team members you hire will likely have at least some experience with it, due to its popularity. This reduces their required training time.

I don't have any financial interest in your decision. I just want you to have a solid application that supports the process well and gets out of your way as much as possible. The last thing you want is your team learning a new process *and* being distracted by a tool that's the wrong fit.

23.4 Define Scrum and Technical Standards

Now is a good time to have the team work out a few different standards to help increase communication, start Scrum ceremonies on time, and ensure a high level of code quality.

Definition of Done

Creating a *definition of done* ensures everyone knows what the team means at the end of a sprint when they say, "These stories are done."

See Section 9.4 for more details and an example.

Definition of Ready

Your team may also want to create a *definition of ready*, which can serve as a reminder to everyone about what's required for a story to be considered for inclusion in the current sprint.

For example, the user story needs to be small enough to fit into the sprint, and the development team needs to have enough knowledge in order to break the story into subtasks.

Late Penalty or On-time Incentive

In many companies, there is rampant abuse of meeting start times. People wander in a few minutes late for the 9 a.m. meeting, see that there are still a few stragglers that haven't shown up yet, and start chatting with their neighbor. Eventually everyone arrives, and the meeting begins. It's 9:08 a.m.

Scrum is all about *producing amazing results quickly*. Part of the process is being extremely efficient and not wasting any time. Showing up late to a ceremony burns time very quickly.

If you have nine people in a room and a meeting starts eight minutes late, they just wasted *an hour and twelve minutes*.

There's another consideration, especially for the daily scrum. Once your team gets the hang of the process, it's not unheard of for it to be very short.

For example, everyone goes around the room, spends about 30 seconds giving an update, and with no issues or impediments to discuss, they conclude. Even with the maximum development team size of nine people, this takes *four and a half minutes*.

If you're eight minutes late to a four-and-a-half-minute meeting, you might as well have not even bothered showing up.

Whenever you get the entire Scrum team together for a ceremony, be very sensitive about time. The clock is ticking, and the end of the sprint is coming faster than anyone would like.

I encourage you to have your team members show up 5 to 15 minutes *early* for chit-chat, and start your Scrum ceremony precisely on time. If the team doesn't have room to meet in their work area, reserve the conference room for that same amount of time—5 to 15 minutes before the scheduled start.

Many teams find that setting a *late penalty* helps underscore this philosophy, especially for the daily scrum. If you're late, you pay the price.

Late penalties vary, but examples include paying $1 into the "pizza jar," singing a song for 10 seconds, telling a joke, etc. It's up to the Scrum team to decide on their penalty as a group.

Other teams decide to use an incentive instead of a penalty. For example, the first person to arrive gets a small treat. Or if the entire team is on time for all ceremonies during the sprint, the team gets a reward such as a company-paid lunch, leaving the office early to see a movie together, and so on. (Cohn, 2016b)

Coding Standards

If you have coding standards that are in common use, great. Keep on using them. Having and following coding standards is an important way to drive consistency and increase the team's success. (Dorman, 2007)

If you have coding standards, but few know they exist and they're not being followed, it's time to dust them off, and review and adjust them if necessary. This is a great way for the development team to start feeling a sense of ownership over the process. They can drive coding standards and solicit input from other teams and architects.

Finally, if you don't have any coding standards at all, it's time to create them.

See Section 15.7 for more about coding standards.

23.5 Configure Developer Workstations

In many cases, your developer's workstations will be set up and ready to go. However, some work may be necessary.

Every developer on the team needs to be able to:

- Get the code from source control for the entire product, compile it and use the product on their machine.

- Run all unit tests locally on their computer.

There are a few reasons this may not be possible. If any of these issues are present on any of your team's developer workstations, they'll need to be remedied before you start your first sprint. Your developers will be able to tell you whether any of these problems exist, and let you know what help they may need getting their workstations up to spec.

They have only some of the development tools. A front-end developer might only have tools to work on and run the front-end code. A back-end developer may be in the same boat.

In either case, they'll need additional tools so they can run the *entire* product locally on their machine. This allows them to ensure the product works from top to bottom, which accelerates the discovery of problems. It also makes them more flexible by being able to work on any part of the product. Sometimes the front-end person will need to help with back-end coding, and vice-versa.

They don't have a local database. Using a shared database is common on many teams, but this often leads to developers stepping on each other as they move development forward. If your technology supports a local database, I strongly encourage you to configure one on each developer workstation.

They don't have all the product components. When working on a larger product with many components, developers might need parts of the product developed by other teams installed on their machine. This is common on teams where developers can only run code on a shared "dev" environment, but not on their own workstations. This type of arrangement will kill your team's productivity and needs to be remedied.

They can't execute all the unit tests. It's critical that developers have what they need to run *all* the unit tests in the product. Relying solely on the integration server to run unit tests delays detection of issues. It's important for developers to be able to run unit tests *before* they commit their code changes to the central repository.

23.6 Set Up Distributed Version Control

As I talked about in Chapter 12, having a contemporary source code version control system in place that supports flexible branching is a critical success factor.

Git is the most widely-used source code management tool, with over 87% of respondents to the Stack Overflow 2018 Developer Survey using the technology, compared to second-place Subversion at 16.1%. (Stack Overflow, 2018)

Developers have a variety of Git tools to choose from to use locally on their computer, and they may each have their own favorite.

You'll also need a centralized storage area for source code, and in this case, you need to pick one tool. Options include Bitbucket, GitHub, Team Foundation Server, Azure DevOps (formerly Visual Studio Team Services), and more.

Once you have a tool installed, the development team should configure it to support their chosen branching strategy. For example, if they use Git Flow as I described in Section 12.5, they'd configure a Master branch and a Develop branch as a starting point.

23.7 Create an Initial Code Framework: The "Walking Skeleton"

If your development team is starting from scratch at the beginning of their first sprint, they may rush to get something—anything—in place and working. That may mean little time is spent thinking about critical decisions about technology and architecture such as what I described in Chapter 15.

Accelerating these decisions and creating a basic framework of your product will help reduce risk. In programming circles, this is often called a "hello world" application, because all that you can do is navigate to the home page and see, "Hello, world!" on the screen.

However, unlike many hello world applications—which are often just slapped together to get something working—in this case, the "walking skeleton" application is at a production-ready level of quality. It's structured correctly, it has unit tests, and is ready for real product functionality to be added.

The term *walking skeleton,* first coined by Alistair Cockburn, is described as a "tiny implementation of the system that performs a small end-to-end function." He goes on to explain that, "The architecture and the functionality can then evolve in parallel." The walking skeleton is a great way to jump-start your team's work as well as support the concept of emergent architecture that I described in Chapter 15. (Cockburn, 1996)

A side benefit of this approach is you'll have code and unit tests you can work with to ensure the version control system is working, and you'll have something to use as you set up continuous integration and continuous deployment to your test environments.

Proving that the technology works end-to-end before starting your first sprint puts you dramatically ahead of the game. It provides the team with a working application, so they can focus on producing the shippable increment when the sprint commences.

23.8 Configure Continuous Integration

Proving that you can get the latest source code, run unit tests, and broadcast any test failures to the team—all in an automated fashion—is the next step in the process.

Again here, you don't want your development team distracted by fooling around with the continuous integration server during their first sprint. You want it to "just work," so they can put their heads down and crank out code.

See Section 13.3 for more details about continuous integration.

23.9 Provision Team Test Environments

It makes no sense to start your first sprint if the development team can't test anything.

Be careful to avoid the trap of, "We'll just have them test on their developer workstations for a while." This may seem at first like a great solution, until the team attempts to deploy the product to an environment for the product owner to use and nothing works right.

Also, avoid thinking that they can test using an environment shared with other teams. Your team will need to deploy new code frequently, to multiple test environments. They'll slow to a crawl if they have to coordinate with other teams.

Bite the bullet *now* and figure it out.

See Chapter 11 for extensive guidance about team test environments. Pay particular attention to Section 11.4, where I talked about the challenges you may face and ideas of how to work around them.

23.10 Establish Continuous Deployment

If the code is difficult to deploy, your development team is unlikely to fully leverage their team test environments. When faced with a choice between a long, tedious manual deployment process and just testing on their developer workstation, they'll likely choose the latter.

Configuring continuous deployment allows you to connect a source code branch directly to an environment and automates the steps to deploy code. Because the process is so streamlined, the time your team would otherwise spend fooling around with a manual deployment process can be spent producing more shippable functionality.

At this stage in the process, the best way to get continuous deployment up and running is by configuring the product owner acceptance environment to be directly connected to the Develop branch. Once the team gets it connected and deploying properly, they can make a small change to the code in the Develop branch and ensure it gets automatically deployed to the product owner environment.

Once they get that working, they can configure additional team test environments.

There are a variety of tools that can be used for this purpose. Microsoft Azure has built-in support for continuous deployment from a source code repository to an app service. Other tools include Jenkins, Bitbucket Pipelines, Bamboo, Azure DevOps (formerly Visual Studio Team System), and more.

If the development team can't get continuous deployment working, or it's not supported with the development technology they're using, at minimum they should create automation that can be triggered manually to deploy the code into a test environment.

The minimum standard they should meet is, "Click one button and the code is properly deployed to a team test environment and the product can be used in that environment."

See Chapter 11 for more about team test environments and automated deployment.

23.11 Research Production Deployment Considerations

I've worked with companies who spend a lot of time, effort, and energy coming up to speed with agile concepts, getting their development team over the hurdle of learning how to produce a shippable product increment each sprint, only to stop dead in the water when it comes time to deploy the product to production.

The Challenge

Most companies moving from waterfall to agile are simply not set up in a way that supports releasing a product to a production environment quickly and easily. I talked about the challenges you might face getting your team test environments set up in Section 11.4. When it comes time to get a production environment ready, those challenges can become even more severe.

The solution is to start working on that problem *now*. You don't want to be three sprints from finishing your MVP only to find that it will take three months to work through the red tape of getting approval to configure a new cloud production environment.

"The way we've always done it here" is likely going to have to change if you want to deliver the right amount of business value to the company. Otherwise, you might have a nice, shiny product ready to go, but no one can use it because you hit a roadblock.

Questions to Start Asking

Here are some questions you can start asking right now:

- What's involved in getting a production environment configured? Who do we need to talk to about the process?

- Have we deployed other products to this type of environment—for example, the cloud? If so, what are they and who can we talk to about their process?

- What security requirements does the product need to satisfy?

- Is penetration testing required before we can deploy our product to production? Who does the testing and how long does it usually take?

- What other departments, products, technologies, etc., may be impacted by the production deployment of our product?

- Are there new DevOps processes that will be required? If so, who needs to be involved with creating them?

- Is there any approval process for production deployments?

- Are there any other restrictions related to production deployment we need to be aware of?

Asking these questions right at the start of the process will help limit schedule risk for your development effort. Many of these questions aren't hard to answer, but there may be long calendar times involved to go from where you are today to where you need to be.

You'll need to work through existing machinery that's in place that may not be tuned for agile development and rapid deployment, so don't wait. Get started now.

23.12 Should We Use a "Sprint Zero?"

Many Scrum teams use a "sprint zero" to manage the work that's required to get everything ready to start producing a shippable product increment. They use the term *sprint zero* or *sprint 0* and utilize the Scrum framework for getting the work done.

There are a few issues with "sprint zero": (Cohn, 2013)

- *Using the word "sprint" is misleading.* In Scrum, if you say the team is going to run a "sprint," there's a specific implication: *they will produce a shippable product increment at the end of it.* If the team has no intention of doing that, the term gets watered down and it establishes a precedent that certain types of sprints have special rules.

- *The team may need more than one "sprint zero."* Although the goal should be to get everything I outline in this chapter done as quickly as possible—ideally within one or two weeks— sometimes things don't happen that quickly. If the team still doesn't feel comfortable that they're ready to create a shippable product increment, what happens? Is there a sprint zero point one?

I love the idea of using Scrum to manage the required work, and that is exactly what our Ascendle teams do at the start of a new client development engagement. They add tasks to their product backlog to track the work that needs to be done and use Scrum tools and techniques to get everything done. They then have a sprint planning ceremony to break down the tasks into subtasks and run a daily scrum to keep the ball rolling.

As a reminder, *tasks* represent work that's important for the development team to complete but don't provide the kind of direct benefit to the product owner and stakeholders provided by user stories. See Section 3.1 for more details.

This approach is great because it gives the team an opportunity to get a taste of what it's like to use the mechanics of Scrum without the pressure of producing a shippable product increment. This provides a great staged-learning opportunity. First, they learn how to use the project management features of Scrum to keep track of the details, then later they apply those techniques to producing product features.

When it comes time to name the iteration in the agile tool, just call it "Prep work" or "Setup" or something similar. This avoids conflict with the word "sprint."

Plus, you can always add "Prep work 2" if things don't get done and you need to run another iteration.

Key Takeaways

- In an ideal world, the Scrum team can just start a sprint and produce a shippable product increment right away—even if it has just a small bit of functionality. However, most teams will need some time to get things set up before they can realistically accomplish this goal.

- Most of the required setup is technical in nature. For example, configuring team test environments, continuous integration, and ensuring developer workstations are able to run the entire product and unit tests.

- This is a good time for any required initial user experience (UX) architecture and visual design work. It's often difficult to complete this type of work simultaneously with coding and testing of related user stories, so completing UX work ahead of the development team can be a great solution.

- If you don't have an agile tool in place, try Jira. It has comprehensive support for the Scrum framework. Because it's the most popular tool in use today, it's likely new team members will have at least some experience with it, reducing their training time.

- A *definition of done* should be nailed down at this point. Teams can also create a *definition of ready*, which makes it clear when a user story can be added to a sprint. Finally, they can decide on either a penalty or incentive to help ensure an on-time start for all Scrum ceremonies, which is important to avoid wasting time and slowing things down.

- Creating a "walking skeleton" of the application, to which functionality can be added, is a great way to jump-start the process and limit risk. This can then be used as the team configures continuous integration to run the unit tests automatically, as well as the team test environments.

- Source code version control, continuous integration, team test environments, and continuous deployment are all important to configure at this stage of the game. You don't want your team distracted by these as they focus on coding and testing user stories.

- Starting the conversation *now* about what it will take to get the application into production will help reduce risk if you face long calendar delays. Whether it's security requirements, provisioning the production environment, or simply figuring out how to make the production deployment process more agile, it's likely it will take some time. The last thing you want to discover when you're a few weeks from completing the MVP version of your product is that it will take three months to jump through the appropriate hoops.

- Some teams use a *sprint zero* to manage this up-front work. Although I love the idea of using Scrum to support the work I describe in this chapter, I don't recommend the use of the term "sprint zero." You can call it "Prep work" or "Setup" or something similar, but avoid the use of the word *sprint*. This prevents having two types of sprints—those that produce a shippable product increment and "special" sprints that do not.

Part IV
Building the Product

A journey of a thousand miles begins with a single step.

\- **Lao Tzu**, *Tao Te Ching*

Chapter 24
Determining Sprint Logistics

Football is a game played with arms, legs and shoulders but mostly from the neck up.

*- **Knute Rockne**, Norwegian-American football player and coach at the University of Notre Dame, regarded as one of the greatest coaches in college football history.*

You're ready to kick off your first sprint. Congratulations! It's time to consider some logistics about the best way for the sprints to run.

The first thing to determine is the length and cadence of your sprints. Choosing a sprint length is typically tied to how long the business can go without making any changes to the priorities of the team, since once a sprint starts, the scope remains fixed.

With Scrum, a new sprint starts immediately after the conclusion of the previous sprint, with no large gap in between. (Schwaber & Sutherland, 2017) Because of this, it's ideal if you can set up your sprint to end just before a weekend so the development team has a chance to catch their breath.

Ending a sprint in the middle of the week and starting a sprint the next day can make it more difficult to achieve one of the goals of Scrum: maintaining a work pace that can be sustained indefinitely. (Beck, et al., 2001b; Agile Alliance, n.d.)

The next step is to get the first sprint planning ceremony scheduled. Because all Scrum ceremonies are contained within the sprint, the start of the sprint planning is the kickoff of your sprint.

This chapter walks you through the process from start to finish.

24.1 Selecting the Best Sprint Duration

Scrum says sprints should last one week to no more than a calendar month. But how do you choose what will work for your team?

Long Enough for Momentum—Short Enough to Respond to Changing Business Conditions

The key is to keep your sprints as long as possible, so the development team can gain as much momentum as they can. That gives them an opportunity to get a lot done before they take a short breather and start the next sprint, beginning with the next sprint planning ceremony.

So why doesn't everyone just run one-month sprints?

The challenge is the rule of Scrum that says *you can't change scope once the sprint begins*. This prevents the product owner from yanking the rug out from under the development team just when they're making progress on their plan, killing their productivity.

There are times when the development team and product owner will clarify and occasionally renegotiate the details of the sprint as more information becomes known, but to the greatest extent possible, scope is *locked in place* once it begins. (Schwaber & Sutherland, 2017)

Because of this, a way to choose the duration of a sprint is *the longest the business can go without responding to changing business conditions*. (Cohn, 2006b)

For most teams, this means using a sprint duration of less than one month. Otherwise, there's a tendency to break the rules because it turns out the business really *can't* wait a month to adjust the priorities of the development team. (Levison, 2013)

Two Weeks Is the Sweet Spot

I recommend selecting a sprint length of two weeks. This strikes a nice balance between giving the development team enough time to hit their stride and get a lot done while remaining agile enough to respond to changing priorities.

A shorter duration also provides two additional benefits:

Avoiding student syndrome. Remember when you left finishing that paper until the night before it was due? A caffeine-fueled marathon session well into the night was likely the result. This is student syndrome. (Project Management Learning, 2010)

With a longer sprint, there's more time for team members to drag their feet until the end of the sprint. With a two-week sprint, the deadline is more imminent, helping to generate the positive stress—*eustress,* which I described in Section 5.2—that helps drive progress in an effective fashion.

Driving faster innovation. One thing to remember is no one yet knows the best way for Scrum to work within your organization. The retrospective at the end of each sprint is when the team looks in the mirror and discusses how to improve their process. A two-week sprint doubles the pace of inspecting and adapting as compared to a one-month sprint.

Scrum also drives *total transparency,* especially as it pertains to problems. As uncomfortable as it may be, the team will be forced to acknowledge and fix any issues that are getting in the way of them executing and creating a shippable increment each sprint. Keeping the sprint shorter reduces the amount of time those problems potentially go unacknowledged and unsolved.

Use One-Week Sprints for Very Short Projects

The only exception I've found to this rule of thumb is if you want to use Scrum to manage a very short project, which I define as having a total duration of five weeks or less.

For this kind of quick effort, I recommend a sprint length of one week. This will give you more fine-grained milestones—the end of each sprint—which will help keep things on track and allow pivoting as necessary as everything comes together over the course of the project.

If you are thinking, "Why not just do one big sprint," there's a big risk of getting to the end, showing the result to stakeholders, and having them say, "That's not what we wanted." By definition, a very short project doesn't give you enough time to recover from this kind of situation. Weekly feedback ensures the team is on the right track all along the way.

One other thing to think about is selecting the team for this kind of quick project. This is probably not the best time to pick team members who are learning Scrum from scratch.

As I talked about in Section 16.5, my rule of thumb is it takes 13 to 16 weeks for a brand-new team to get fully up to speed with this way of working. Five weeks or less doesn't provide enough time for inexperienced team members to learn the ropes, so I recommend choosing team members who have at least some experience with Scrum.

24.2 Picking the Best Day of the Week to Start a Sprint

Before you pull the trigger on scheduling your first sprint planning session, it's worth taking a few minutes to think about when you want the sprint to start and end.

Why is this important?

Toward the end of a sprint, the team will be nearing their deadline. As with any deadline, it's typical that there will be some scrambling as everyone realizes a few days before that the amount of work that remains is more than the time they have left. They'll likely be in a more focused and high-energy mode of working and may end up staying late at the office to get everything done.

They'll need a break.

If you have a sprint end and *immediately* roll into another sprint the next morning, there's typically not enough time for the team to take a breath, reset, and be ready to dive in again at a high level of productivity. Ideally you want to give the team a little more time.

One of the principles of Scrum is that a team should be able to produce at a high level of throughput *forever*. This means there are no more *death marches*, with everyone working 80-hour weeks for months on end to get the product out the door. But there will be pressure on the team as the end of the sprint approaches.

In this section, I'll talk about the best cadence for your sprint. Because they run back-to-back with no break in between, selecting the starting day for your first sprint will set up how the subsequent sprint aligns with the end-of-sprint deadline.

Best Option: Start on a Monday, End on a Friday

Monday is a natural "get going" type of day and is a good choice for sprint planning. You can kick off the week with forming the plan, and the team can dig right in. Assuming it's a two-week sprint, you'll end with the sprint review ceremony on the second Friday. Then you can roll into the next sprint on the following Monday.

Sun	Mon	Tue	Wed	Thu	Fri	Sat
	Sprint 1 Starts					
					Sprint 1 Ends	
	Sprint 2 Starts					
					Sprint 2 Ends	

Starting a sprint on a Monday builds in a natural break for the team. After the sprint ends on the following Friday, they can forget all about the product over the weekend and come in fresh the following Monday to start the next sprint.

What's nice about this approach is you build in a break for the team. They can go home after sprint review on Friday and *forget all about the product*.

It's likely that they'll be thinking at least a little bit about work during that middle weekend, since they're in the midst of an active sprint. But they'll have a great feeling of relief and a weight lifted off their shoulders once the sprint ends and they can have a "carefree" couple of days off.

It also provides a nice time for the team to knock off a little early that Friday afternoon and maybe grab a beer together to celebrate a particularly successful sprint.

Second Best: Start on a Friday, End on a Thursday

Sometimes schedules won't allow for the ideal alignment of the sprint with calendar weeks. Perhaps stakeholders aren't available to get together for the sprint review every other Friday, or there is some other conflict.

The second-best option is to get sprint planning done on Friday, start cranking away at work for the sprint that afternoon and come in Monday morning with a vengeance, ramping up momentum for that first full week.

Planning on Friday still allows the team to get some much-needed mental rest over the weekend, since they will have just started that afternoon and their brains are likely not fully engaged with the work of the sprint.

Although the sprint is active, they haven't ramped up quite yet. The focused work will begin Monday morning.

Sun	Mon	Tue	Wed	Thu	Fri	Sat
					Sprint 1 Starts	
				Sprint 1 Ends	Sprint 2 Starts	
				Sprint 2 Ends	Sprint 3 Starts	

Second best is planning the sprint on Friday. The team can still get a mental break over the weekend since they won't be fully engaged with the work of the sprint quite yet.

Third Best: Start on a Thursday, End on a Wednesday

The third best is to start on Thursday. The team will spend a full work day focused on sprint work that Friday, but it's likely still early enough in the sprint that they won't be fully engaged.

Sun	Mon	Tue	Wed	Thu	Fri	Sat
				Sprint 1 Starts		
			Sprint 1 Ends	Sprint 2 Starts		
			Sprint 2 Ends	Sprint 3 Starts		

Third best is starting the sprint on Thursday, but this is on the border of what I'd recommend.

This is the earliest start day that I'd recommend because you'll be bordering on the team having a low-energy day that Friday. Remember, they will likely be tired from completing the *prior* sprint, so they may be dragging a bit. You might start to lose some throughput on that day, and it will affect productivity at that point in *every* sprint.

Avoid Starting on Tuesday or Wednesday

If you start a sprint on Tuesday or Wednesday, I think you'll run into sustainability issues.

Here's the problem: if you start on Tuesday or Wednesday, the sprint will end on Monday or Tuesday, with its accompanying deadline. That means *every weekend* will be one where there is an active sprint in full operation. The team will never have any time to completely relax and forget about work.

Sun	Mon	Tue	Wed	Thu	Fri	Sat
		Sprint 1 Starts				
	Sprint 1 Ends	Sprint 2 Starts				
	Sprint 2 Ends	Sprint 3 Starts				

The worst-case scenario is starting a sprint on a Tuesday, which means it ends on a Monday.

Plus, if things are off track, it's likely that at least some team members will end up working during that last weekend of the sprint.

This will tend to erode your sustainability over time. Everyone needs time to recharge. Even if the development team is not *doing work* on the weekend, they'll probably be *thinking about work* if there's an active sprint.

If you have absolutely no choice, you can experiment with a Tuesday or Wednesday start, but personally, I'd avoid it if possible.

Avoid a Gap Between Sprints

If you introduce a few days off between sprints, you'll lose the effectiveness of your team. They won't know it until they've experienced Scrum for a while, but once they attempt to get things done without the framework of a sprint backlog and a daily scrum, it becomes obvious that their ability to effectively drive work forward in a coordinated fashion is difficult.

This is why one of the rules of Scrum is the next sprint begins at the conclusion of the previous sprint. That said, if you wrap up your sprint review and retrospective at 2 p.m. on a Friday, I wouldn't suggest diving right into sprint planning that afternoon. Give the team a short break so they can recharge for the next sprint, at which point they'll need to hit the ground running again.

Sometimes you'll decide to shift your sprints, for example if you've been starting them on Fridays and you want to change to start them on Mondays. If you need to do this, I encourage you to extend one sprint and shorten the next, or vice-versa. Don't introduce a break between them where you'll be operating without a safety net.

Accommodating Key Stakeholder Availability

You may get all excited about setting up your sprint with the *perfect* schedule. You start on a Monday, end on the following Friday. Life is good.

Then you find out the product manager for the entire product line your team is working on is tied up in strategy meetings every Friday.

It doesn't make a lot of sense to have a sprint review without one or more key stakeholders attending. That would defeat the purpose of providing transparency, visible progress through a demonstration of shippable features, and getting regular feedback.

As you think about the cadence of your sprints, talk to your key stakeholders to ensure they'll be available for the sprint review. Otherwise, you won't get the benefit of the business getting excited about how "This Scrum thing is really working well."

24.3 Scheduling the Sprint Planning Ceremony

Once you choose the starting day of the sprint, the next step is to get the sprint planning ceremony scheduled. Sprint planning marks the start of your sprint; it doesn't come before the sprint begins.

If you decide to start the sprint on Monday, for example, that's the day of sprint planning.

Time of Day

You can schedule sprint planning for any time that day, but I recommend first thing in the morning. Everyone will be fresh and have more energy and focus to bring to the planning process. Check with the team members to determine how early everyone can make it.

Sprint Planning and Multiple Time Zones

If you have team members in multiple time zones, this is something you should consider. Some team members may need to meet earlier or later than their normal working hours to ensure enough overlap to complete the entire planning session. This isn't something that's usually required every day; Scrum ceremonies can be adjusted to a time of better overlap with everyone's work schedule. But sprint planning is typically the longest ceremony of the entire sprint, so there may need to be some flexibility for this crucial ceremony.

Do *not* fall into the trap of thinking you can "get by" with a portion of the team attending only half of sprint planning. This ceremony is the most critical as it lays the groundwork for the entire sprint; find a way to get the whole team to participate simultaneously if at all possible.

See Section 6.1 for the duration of the sprint planning ceremony. For a typical two-week sprint, it's capped at four hours.

The ScrumMaster Is Usually the Best to Send Meeting Invites

Many teams find that having the ScrumMaster handle all scheduling is a nice way for them to help facilitate the ceremonies. There's nothing wrong with rotating this duty throughout the members of the Scrum team, but if one person always owns getting the calendar appointments sent out, it can avoid the potential confusion of, "I thought *you* were sending the meeting invites!"

That said, it's not the sole responsibility of the ScrumMaster to make sure the process is facilitated; it's up to the entire Scrum team. Team members need to be careful to avoid slipping back into an anti-teamwork attitude of, "Well the ScrumMaster didn't send out the calendar invites, so how was *I* to know I was supposed to show up for daily scrum at 9 a.m.?"

For example, if the ScrumMaster is going to be out of the office on vacation and meeting invitations need to be sent, someone else on the team must volunteer to take this on.

Attendees

It's critical that the product owner, ScrumMaster, and the majority of the development team attend the entire sprint planning ceremony. There will be times when one or two members of the team won't be able to make it but do your best to ensure the entire Scrum team is there.

The product owner is a critical attendee, since they'll need to clarify any questions from the development team that are discovered as they break down the product backlog items into subtasks.

What If the Product Owner Is on Vacation?

If the product owner is on vacation, or they got sick or they're out of the office for some other reason, the show must go on. This is not an ideal situation for your *first* sprint planning ceremony, but it may happen.

If the product owner can't make it, someone else on the Scrum team can act as a proxy for them, likely the ScrumMaster or a senior member of the development team. They should spend time with the product owner prior to them leaving on a planned vacation to get familiar with what's required.

If the product owner is out unexpectedly, the team should do their best to complete sprint planning without them.

Once the product owner is back, they can help with any minor course corrections if there was any confusion, or if the development team went in the wrong direction on one or more user stories.

I do *not* recommend rescheduling sprint planning around the product owner's vacation. This will throw off the sprint cadence and risk introducing a gap between sprints, which will hurt productivity as I talked about earlier in this chapter.

What If the Product Owner Keeps Blowing Off Sprint Planning?

Sometimes product owners will schedule other meetings at the same time as sprint planning, claiming they are more important. I don't think they're trying to be malicious—it's more likely they just don't understand how critical their attendance is at sprint planning.

Nothing is more important than the product owner's commitment to their Scrum team when they are desperately needed, and sprint planning is one of the most important ceremonies for them to attend.

If there's a conflicting department-level meeting, it needs to be rescheduled around the sprint planning ceremony if the product owner can't skip it.

This is an area where the ScrumMaster can help coach the product owner. Support from higher-ups may be necessary as well, acting in their role as servant leaders.

If the product owner is not put in a position to attend the sprint planning ceremony, *the organization is setting up the Scrum team to fail.*

The Meeting Space

Many Scrum teams have their own work area, but it's often an open-plan space with little privacy. It may be fine to have a 15-minute daily scrum in that spot, but a four-hour sprint planning ceremony might get distracting for other employees in that area.

With this in mind, it's likely going to be better for everyone to meet in a conference room. There should be seating for everyone and a projector where product backlog items can be reviewed and the team can collaborate on breaking down the work.

Keep an eye out for team members not paying attention, distracted by their laptop or phone. If you see that people aren't attentive or aren't engaged, consider an "electronics ban," meaning all electronics must be shut off or in airplane mode—or better yet, left at their desk. Five-minute breaks can be used every hour or so to allow people to check in for any crises that may have come up.

Everyone's natural tendency is to be distracted by their electronics, so I recommend experimenting with banning them and seeing if sprint planning goes more smoothly. (Gorlick, 2009)

24.4 Preparing for the Sprint Planning Ceremony

As the team goes into their first sprint planning ceremony, one thing to keep in mind is one or more of them may be a little pessimistic. "We have to sit in this room for *four hours*? This is stupid. I should be coding."

If the product backlog isn't in a good state or the agile tool isn't configured yet, things may get off to a rocky start, which may erode the confidence of the team and reinforce whatever negative feelings they may have.

Here's a quick checklist of best practices to help your sprint planning ceremonies run more smoothly:

The room is reserved 15 minutes early and 15 minutes past the projected end time. Another momentum-killer is when the entire Scrum team is waiting in the hallway for the group who had the room booked before them to finish up. Sprint planning then starts five or ten minutes late, after a mad scramble. Block out some extra time to ensure you can start on schedule.

Make sure everyone knows that "early is on time and on time is late." I recommend telling everyone to plan on arriving 15 minutes early. This will help accommodate any stragglers who arrive 5 minutes "late"—which will still be 10 minutes before your actual start time. This also provides for some chit-chat and settling in, so you can begin precisely on time. This is a great way to start the team down the path of understanding that with Scrum, you always start on time, as I talked about in Section 23.4

Stories at the top of the product backlog are small enough. The first five to ten user stories at the top of the product backlog should be no larger than three story points each, which is the size I recommend for a team that has no past velocity history.

If the team has a historical velocity—for example if they just completed a product and are starting a new effort—the user stories should be sized to no larger than 25% to 33% of their average velocity from their last three sprints. See Chapter 22 for more details.

The development team has a general understanding of the top of the product backlog. This should be automatic, since the development team should have been involved in estimating the story points for the stories at the top of the backlog. If for some reason they haven't discussed the top of the product backlog in the last few days, I suggest they spend a little bit of time reviewing it with the product owner *before* launching into sprint planning.

In the interest of keeping everyone "fresh," I would do this a day or two before sprint planning day. I wouldn't, for example, expand a four-hour sprint planning session to five hours, the first hour of which is spent reviewing the top of the backlog.

This doesn't mean that everyone must have an exact plan in their head when they walk in the room of how they'll break down the work. However, you don't want a situation where the product owner realizes they're starting from square one when someone says, "Wait. I have no idea what this story is about. Can you explain it to us?" There's not enough time for that.

The team has prepared others for their absence. One of the worst things that can happen during sprint planning is for a team member to be pulled out of the room. "Sorry, guys. I have to go help Betty with something. I'll be back in 20 minutes." This sort of thing will kill momentum and threaten the team's ability to get through planning as quickly as possible.

Any team members who have responsibilities outside the Scrum team should notify the appropriate people that they will be unavailable for the duration of the sprint planning ceremony. A quick email a day or two before with a heads up can work wonders. No one wants to leave a coworker hanging; a little communication can go a long way to address issues so they don't interrupt the sprint planning process.

The agile tool has been configured. Some teams like to plan on paper or a whiteboard. I prefer to work directly in the agile software tool used to manage the product backlog and sprint backlog, such as what I described in Section 23.3. Even if you plan outside of the software, it's going to be important to get the sprint backlog plugged into the tool immediately following sprint planning, so you should ensure it's ready to go at least a day or two prior to starting the session.

The ScrumMaster is familiar with how sprint planning works. The ScrumMaster is responsible for facilitating the sprint planning process—helping the product owner and the development team on how the process works and guiding them through the session. If they're not familiar with how sprint planning works, ensure they read this chapter and the next from start to finish.

24.5 A Sample Sprint Planning Agenda

Many new Scrums teams struggle with their first sprint planning session. They're not quite sure how everything will work, and they don't understand yet what, "Break down the work to create a plan" actually means.

One thing that may be helpful is providing a written agenda, to help everyone get a vision in their head of how it might unfold. On the next page is a sample agenda for a four-hour sprint planning session, which assumes a two-week sprint, and the development team taking on four user stories.

Since the actual number of user stories may vary—perhaps between three and five for a two-week sprint—and the amount of time required for each story may differ, this agenda may not *exactly* match what will actually happen. But it should provide some good guidance.

I'll go into more detail about each of the agenda items in the next chapter.

Description	Duration
Determine development team net capacity	20 min
Identify subtasks/hour estimates for user story 1	45 min
Break	5 min
Identify subtasks/hour estimates for user story 2	45 min
Break	5 min
Identify subtasks/hour estimates for user story 3	45 min
Break	5 min
Identify subtasks/hour estimates for user story 4	45 min
Break	5 min
Determine schedule for Scrum ceremonies	15 min
Initial daily scrum	5 min
Total	**4 hours**

A sample agenda for a four-hour sprint planning ceremony. This assumes a two-week sprint, and the development team taking on four stories.

One trap that teams seem to fall into is trying to figure everything out during sprint planning. They get sucked into talking about the design of the tables, how the different components will communicate to each other, and all kinds of other technical details. The result is they reach the end of the sprint planning timebox and they've planned…one story.

The timeframe I've outlined for each user story should help everyone understand that although it's important to talk through a plan, they don't need to answer *all* the questions now. That's what the work of the sprint is for—executing the high-level plan and figuring out the rest "on the ground," as they make their way through the sprint.

Key Takeaways

- The sprint length should be as long as possible, but no longer than the product owner can go before adjusting the priorities of the product backlog in response to changing business conditions.

- Most teams find that two weeks strikes the best balance between giving them enough time to gain momentum while keeping the sprint short enough to respond to the needs of the business in an agile fashion.

- The next sprint starts immediately after the conclusion of the current sprint, so it's important to give the development team a break. The best way to do this is by starting the sprint on a Monday and ending the sprint on a Friday, so they have the weekend to forget about the product and recharge for the next sprint.

- Second best is starting on a Friday and ending on a Thursday, and third best is starting on a Thursday and ending on a Wednesday.

- Avoid starting sprints on Tuesday or Wednesday which results in them ending on Monday or Tuesday, preventing the team from getting a "brain break" during a weekend. This also risks the team feeling like they have to work over the weekend immediately prior to the end of the sprint.

- Start your sprint planning ceremony in the morning if possible, when energy levels are high.

- Book the meeting room 15 minutes before the scheduled start and 15 minutes after the scheduled end, to leave some wiggle room. Ask the team to arrive 15 minutes before the scheduled start to ensure you can begin precisely on time—you have a lot of work to do, and no time to waste.

- The product owner, ScrumMaster, and the development team attend sprint planning. The product owner is extremely important; don't attempt to plan a sprint without having them present to answer questions and help the team plan in real time.

- If the product owner is on vacation or otherwise unavailable, someone on the Scrum team needs to fill in for them. The ScrumMaster can often fill this role by talking with the product owner before they go on vacation. The team should do the best it can and course-correct as necessary once the product owner returns. They should *not* delay the start of the sprint just because the product owner is not available; there should be no "days off" between sprints.

- If team members are distracted by laptops or smartphones during sprint planning, consider an "electronics ban," preventing all use of electronics except during breaks. The one exception is if the ScrumMaster is using a software tool in real time to facilitate the planning process.

- Ensure the top of the backlog is prepared, the agile tool is ready, and the ScrumMaster is prepared to facilitate the sprint planning ceremony.

- Ensure Scrum team members have let others in the organization know they'll be tied up. You want to avoid interruptions and people being pulled out of the room to deal with something that comes up because others didn't know they were going to be unavailable.

Chapter 25
Planning the Sprint

Plan your work and work your plan.

- ***Napoleon Hill**, American self-help author, best known for the book* Think and Grow
Rich, *which is among the 10 best-selling self-help books of all time.*

I've seen some teams sit down for 20 minutes, pick a few user stories off the product backlog, and leave the room to start coding.

That didn't turn out too well.

If you charge off into the forest without a map and a compass, you'll likely walk in circles for a few hours until you finally emerge back out of the woods, 100 yards from where you started.

This is what happens when teams believe they can effectively execute without a plan, simply because they think it takes too much time to create one. They usually get *something* done, but it's often based more on luck than a deliberate effort as they stumble their way through the sprint.

In contrast, a team that spends time thinking up front about what they need to do will rip through the work, guided by a solid plan of attack.

Sprint planning facilitates this type of thinking, in a structured and efficient fashion. Those who will do the work—the development team—spend time to collaborate, talking through the details of how they'll turn a handful of product backlog items into a product increment.

There are three big reasons to invest time in this type of planning: (Project Management Institute, 2013)

- Additional information is discovered as the team talks through the "how" of the work.

- Because every team member is involved in the planning process, their commitment toward completing the work increases.

- A plan acts as a roadmap for the team, allowing everyone to know what needs to be done first, second, and third, and permitting them to track their progress over the course of the sprint.

By spending time thinking strategically at the beginning, it's easier for the team to put their heads down and *go*, focusing on designing, coding, and testing the product through ruthless execution of their plan.

25.1 Setting the Stage for the Team

Before diving into the mechanics of sprint planning, it's often helpful for the ScrumMaster to talk with the team about Scrum values.

Successful use of Scrum depends on everyone becoming more proficient in living these five values. Once they are, the pillars of *transparency*, *inspection*, and *adaptation* come to life, and everyone gets the most from the Scrum framework. (Schwaber & Sutherland, 2017)

The five Scrum values are:

- *Commitment.* Everyone personally commits to achieving the goals of the Scrum team. The first step is committing to the sprint planning process.

- *Courage.* Team members have the courage to do the right thing and work on tough problems. They are going to "just say it" when they have something on their mind and ask for help when they need to.

- *Focus.* Everyone focuses on the work of the sprint and the goals of the Scrum team. Starting with sprint planning, everyone will focus on the process of thinking through the work of the sprint, avoiding getting distracted by their phone or laptop.

- *Openness.* The Scrum team and its stakeholders agree to be open about the work they are doing and the challenges they face while completing it.

- *Respect.* Team members respect each other to be capable, independent people.

Starting with this type of high-level conversation can help to get everyone on the same page and ready to dive in with a positive attitude.

25.2 Estimating the Team's Capacity for the Sprint

The first thing to figure out is, "How much work can we take on?"

This may be a foreign concept, since many development teams are used to being *told* what they can do in a certain timeframe. As shocking as it may be, Scrum says we should ask the *development team* to decide how much they think they can accomplish during the sprint.

To figure out how much work they should take on, the best first step is to answer the question, "How much time do we have?" And not only how much time they have in general, but how much time *in these next two weeks*, assuming a two-week sprint.

This is important because the development team shouldn't just blindly take on a bunch of work, only to realize they forgot about the company party next Tuesday afternoon, that Emma is out this Friday, and that Noah is on vacation next week.

At a high level, the process includes two steps:

- *Determine gross capacity.* Everyone on the development team looks at their calendars and determines how many hours they can dedicate to the Scrum team, starting with the beginning of the sprint planning ceremony through to the end of the retrospective on the last day of the sprint. Adding up everyone's total hours for the duration of the sprint gives you *gross capacity*.

- *Determine net capacity.* The time for various Scrum ceremonies is subtracted from the gross capacity to determine *net capacity*. This is the total amount of time available to work on the subtasks in the sprint.

See Section 21.3 for a detailed explanation of how to calculate gross capacity and net capacity, including examples.

25.3 Determining How Much Work Can Be Done and the Plan of Attack

Although some teams simply discuss a plan to complete product backlog items at a high level, I've found this is insufficient. I recommend decomposing each product backlog item into *subtasks* representing the steps required to complete it, each sized to about one day or less.

The process of creating a plan answers two important questions: (Schwaber & Sutherland, 2017)

- *What will fit into the sprint?* By breaking down product backlog items, the Scrum team understands how much work will fit into the sprint by summing the total hours of the subtasks. They can then ensure they don't take on more work than can be completed with the time they have available—their net capacity.

- *How will we do it?* Breaking down the product backlog items into a plan allows everyone to understand how the work required to deliver the product increment will be achieved.

Subtasks represent *all* the work required, such as technical design, coding, testing, fixing bugs, and the review by the product owner. They're typically written in a sequential order, forming a step-by-step strategy for getting the user story to done.

See *Break Down a Story* in Section 21.3 for more details about creating a complete list of subtasks required to produce each user story.

Planning Generates Questions

One of the reasons why it's so important that the product owner participates in the sprint planning process is because questions will come up as the development team talks through the details of how the work will get done. Often, it's not until the developers think through how they'll code and test a user story that they realize they don't have all the answers.

Their questions might be along the lines of desired behavior, such as, "When the user does *this*, what should happen?" They can also identify missing requirements, for example asking, "Do we have to do any validation on this screen?" The product owner can address these questions immediately as they come up.

Planning Identifies Costs That Are Too High

Back in the waterfall days, the product people who put together the spec were far removed from the developers coding each day.

This is one of the reasons why products took so long to build; no one was around who could say, "That's too fancy" or "That will take too long. Can you do it another way?" Developers just put their heads down and spent whatever time was necessary, regardless of whether it was worth the effort.

With the product owner involved with sprint planning, that problem goes away. As they listen to the developers talking about how they'll code and test a story, including how long it's going to take, the product owner can be on the lookout for stories that will cost too much. That is, the amount of time involved in producing it outstrips its business value.

Although the product owner isn't allowed to tell the development team how to turn product backlog items into the product increment, they *can* say, "Wait a minute. That seems like it's a lot of time for something that's not that valuable. Can you tell me what about this story makes it so tricky?"

The developers usually say something like, "It's *this* one part of the acceptance criteria."

Usually what happens at that point is the product owner says, "Huh. OK. I didn't think that would be that hard. I'm going to pull that out into a new story on the product backlog. Maybe we'll get to it down the road, but I don't want you guys spending *two days* to get it in there right now."

In this example, just by being there, the product owner identified a risk that he wasn't comfortable with, and by deferring it he shaved two days off the schedule. You don't have that kind of power with waterfall.

Avoid Getting Too Much Into the "How"

Although getting into the "how" of turning product backlog items into the product increment is the goal of sprint planning, I've seen some teams get sucked into trying to figure out *everything* they'll need to do.

The key is to strike a balance. The development team should talk enough about each user story to identify day-long subtasks, but know that it's OK to defer all the nitty-gritty details until they start the sprint.

For example, Sofia, one of the developers, might say, "Hey Lucas, do you think we'll use the new authentication framework here?"

Lucas replies, "Yeah, I think we can do that. Anna would you mind adding a technical note to the user story?" Anna, the product owner, writes a note for the team's reference.

"What unit tests do you think we'll need for that," asks Ben, another developer.

At this point, the conversation devolves into an extremely detailed discussion down to the individual function level within the code, and the QA engineer's eyes start to get a little glassy as she stares off into space, not following the conversation.

Seeing this, the ScrumMaster Ellen realizes they're getting too far into the details. She asks, "Can we add a subtask for you guys to do some brainstorming around this? We need to keep moving along."

Sofia, Lucas, and Ben all nod, and a subtask is added to the sprint task board with an associated hour estimate: "Brainstorm unit testing strategy and which classes need to be updated for new authentication."

This is where an agenda—with a specific a timebox for planning each user story—can come in handy. See the sample agenda in Section 24.5 for ideas.

Don't Skip the "Planning" Part of Sprint Planning

As I talked about in the introduction to this chapter, some Scrum teams think, "This sprint planning thing takes way too much time. Let's just pull some stories in and get started."

Is it possible to get away with this approach and successfully start the sprint? Sure. But there are problems that are introduced.

The first problem is they'll miss out on what I call *pre-visualizing* the work of the sprint—what scholars call *implementation intentions*: the when, where, and how of reaching a specific goal. (Webb & Sheeran, 2007) When under pressure to get the work done *right now*, there will be little time spent sitting back and calmly thinking through what needs to be done next.

The problem is that short-changing the planning process doesn't *eliminate* the need to plan, it just defers it to the worst possible time: when the team is trying to *do the work*.

There's nothing worse than a developer with their head down encountering a roadblock and stopping dead in their tracks. Without a plan, they'll be flying blind and making it up as they go. And because they will inevitably run into questions for the product owner, they've created a crisis. "I need the product owner *right now*, or I can't continue."

Take a deep breath and know that the time the team spends in sprint planning is *part of doing the work*. The planning process is critical to ensuring the team can move as quickly as possible, with everyone putting their heads down and moving in lockstep against a strategy that allowed them to get aligned before charging ahead with the work of the sprint.

The Sprint Goal

The sprint goal provides a high-level understanding for everyone involved that explains, "What are we doing this sprint?" Examples might include, *Get a basic spell checker working* or *Add gift card payment to the checkout process*.

Having a sprint goal helps in two ways:

- *It keeps everyone focused on a cohesive target.* It's easy for the development team to get stuck in the weeds of their daily work. Having a sprint goal allows them to keep aligned with the big-picture outcome they're driving towards.

- *It provides a framework for negotiation.* If one user story turns out to be more difficult than everyone thought, the development team can negotiate with the product owner in a way that can still meet the spirit of the sprint goal, even if the total functionality delivered is less than originally anticipated.

There are two ways the team can create the sprint goal. The product owner could tell the development team, "This is what I'd like for a goal." Then the development team selects as many user stories as possible to meet that goal.

If this technique is used, the development team needs to be careful to not over-commit because they think that's what the product owner wants. Remember that *only the development team can decide how many product backlog items are added to the sprint.*

The other approach is to complete the planning process, identify the theme of the product backlog items selected by the development team, and write the sprint goal to capture that theme.

Either approach is fine; experiment with each and see what works for you.

25.4 Decomposing a Task or Bug into Subtasks

I've talked a lot about creating a plan to code and test user stories, and Section 21.3 includes some examples. But what about the other two types of product backlog items: tasks and bugs?

As a reminder, there are three types of product backlog items. *User stories* represent business value to be delivered to an end user in the form of new or improved functionality. *Bugs*, as you might expect, represent defects—things that aren't working as they should. I use the term *tasks* to represent anything else the Scrum team would like to do that doesn't deliver value directly to business stakeholders.

Tasks can be used to represent technical research—often called a *spike* in agile terminology—required to gain more knowledge about how to complete a user story or fix a bug.

Tasks can also include what some call *chores*, which are other things the development team might want to do to improve their ability to deliver user stories. For example, they may ask the product owner to add a task to the product backlog called *Upgrade developer workstations to latest version of QuickCode*, because they feel the features introduced in the new version will help them write code faster.

Creating a Plan for Tasks

Tasks are so varied that there is no set structure for the subtasks you'll need. However, there is still value in thinking through what's required and making a plan.

For example, for the *Upgrade developer workstations to latest version of QuickCode* task, the subtask breakdown might look something like the following:

Subtask	Hours
Get manager to purchase upgrade with credit card	0.5
Install upgrade on Nathan's computer	0.5
Upgrade source code repository to new solution file format	0.5
Install upgrade on Anna's computer	0.5
Install upgrade on Ben's computer	0.5
Install upgrade on Jack's computer	0.5
Install upgrade on David's computer	0.5
Install upgrade on Ellen's computer	0.5
Insurance for any unexpected problems	2
Total	**6 hrs**

Example of a subtask breakdown for completing a task.

In this case, the subtasks are much less than one day each, but it's helpful to have them as a way to ensure everyone's computer gets upgraded. They act as a checklist, ensuring nothing slips through the cracks.

This is a good illustration of how taking a few minutes to think through the plan and document it via a list of subtasks adds clarity. Now everyone can see a picture of exactly what needs to happen.

During the sprint, the team will always understand the status of completing this task by seeing which subtasks are not yet started, in progress, and done.

Creating a Plan for Bugs

Unlike tasks, most bugs follow the same format: reproduce it, fix it, re-test it to make sure it's fixed. A code review is often also included for good measure.

The subtasks for a typical bug may be fairly straightforward:

Subtask	Hours
Create feature branch for bug fix	0.25
Reproduce bug and identify root cause	2
Writing failing unit test that would have detected bug	0.5
Fix bug	0.5
Manually re-test bug	0.5
Peer code review, edits, and merge bug feature branch	0.5
Total	**4.25 hrs**

Example of a subtask breakdown for fixing and re-testing a bug.

Without thinking through a plan, many of us might have thought, "Fix the bug? Seems pretty easy. Twenty minutes." But once we evaluate how to fix the bug properly and make sure it never comes back, we realize there's a lot more involved.

This is another good illustration of how thinking through the plan ensures you're doing the right thing to *completely* address the bug, which was quite a bit more than the off-the-cuff 20-minute guess.

25.5 How Much of the Team's Capacity Should Be Planned?

To the greatest extent possible, the outcome of sprint planning is not a *guess* as to what the development team will accomplish but a *prediction*. The plan should be attainable.

Teams new to Scrum have a tendency to bite off more than they can chew. They tend to underestimate how much time it will take to get everything done, and miss certain subtasks they'll later discover are required.

This can lead to a feeling of dismay when it becomes obvious half-way through the sprint that there's no possible way they'll get done, and at the end they may feel like, "We failed."

In extreme cases, this can lead to the team throwing up their hands with a, "Scrum doesn't work" attitude, and the naysayers might then descend, telling management, "See, I told you this was a bad idea."

Leave Some Wiggle Room

To combat this, I suggest new teams plan subtasks to fill only a portion of the hours they calculated as their net capacity for the sprint. For brand-new teams, I suggest they plan to 50%

of the available hours, knowing that the rest of the time will likely be filled with continued learning about the Scrum process, subtasks that take longer than estimated, and new subtasks discovered during the sprint.

As the team gains more experience, they'll get better at planning, and they can fill more of their capacity. However, they should always leave *some* wiggle room for the unanticipated.

Below is a table with general guidance. Scrum teams should experiment over time to find the percentage that works best for them.

Sprints Completed	Net Capacity to Consume
0 to 1	50%
2	60%
3	70%
4 or more	80%

I suggest new teams plan to just 50% of their net capacity hours for the sprint. As they gain experience, they can consume more.

I've found it's almost always better to be just on the pessimistic side—pulling in less than the net capacity. Adding work into the sprint if things get wrapped up early is fairly straightforward. Plus, it gives the team a nice "win" to be able to say at sprint review, "We completed what we committed to *and* got a head start on the next sprint."

In contrast, if the team over-commits, they'll be scrambling in the last few days to get everything done. That usually results in rushing to get user stories finished, which increases stress to an unacceptable level, and can lead to mistakes and low-quality work. It can also be tough on the team to explain at their first sprint review that, "They didn't get everything done."

Not getting everything done is *not* a problem with Scrum. If the team *always* meets their commitment once they get up to speed with the process, they're probably not pushing themselves enough. But for the first sprint or two, it's nice to say, "We did it!"

Experiment with various capacities and select a rule of thumb that works for you. If your team gets good at identifying all the subtasks and putting accurate hour estimates on them, perhaps they can get to a point where they plan to 75% to 80% of their capacity. Other teams may find they should stick closer to a more conservative 60% to 70%.

You're at the sweet spot when the team usually gets their commitment done, but sometimes it takes some extra effort toward the end of the sprint, and occasionally they don't complete everything.

If they *always* seem to get everything done and have a bunch of time left over, they risk getting a little complacent and running into Parkinson's Law in future sprints: "Work expands so as to fill the time available for its completion." (Parkinson, 1955)

If they *never* get everything done, stakeholders will start to wonder what's so great about this Scrum thing, and the team may become dejected.

Use Velocity as a Cross-Check

Once the team has a few sprints under their belt, they can use velocity to rationalize the amount of work they're taking on for the sprint.

If their velocity is an average of 20, and they take on 10 story points in a sprint, they should think about why that is. Perhaps there are a lot of bugs that came up and they need to deal with them during the sprint. Or perhaps there is some technical research they'll need to tackle.

They should also talk about what's going on if they take on 40 points. Have they really gotten that much faster? Or are they missing something?

I wouldn't *solely* use velocity as a way to determine how many stories to take on, at the expense of capacity-based planning, but it can be a good tool to help the team cross-check their commitment.

25.6 What If There Isn't Enough Time to Finish the Plan?

The sprint planning ceremony is timeboxed, for example to four hours for a two-week sprint. What happens if the team reaches the end of the timebox, but they're not done with planning all the product backlog items?

If they can't plan the entire sprint, the second-best option is to have a solid outline of the work for at least the first few days of the sprint. That way the team can get started, and add details as time permits, perhaps spending an extra 30 minutes after the first couple of daily scrums in the sprint to finish it off.

This isn't ideal, but it's better than allowing a four-hour sprint planning session to stretch to eight hours. Next time the team can do better about sticking to the agenda and getting through everything.

You Might Need to Use a Placeholder to Make Your Burndown Look Correct

Some agile management tools, such as Jira, will generate the sprint burndown chart based on the total hours from all the subtasks at the moment the sprint is started. If the team didn't complete their planning process and this is the case with your tool, I suggest adding a placeholder subtask with the total unplanned hours remaining.

For example, if the team determines the net capacity for the sprint is 300 hours and they are planning to 50% of that capacity, the target is 150 hours. If they only had time to plan 100 hours of subtasks, they can add a placeholder subtask with a total of an additional 50 hours. They can just call it something like, "Placeholder for additional subtasks."

This will make the burndown chart look correct and they can replace that placeholder with 50 hours of new subtasks as they complete the planning process over the first day or two of the sprint.

The burndown chart is a critical tool to help monitor progress during the sprint, so it's important to ensure it's not going to be thrown off if the team adds 50 *more* hours once the sprint begins.

Don't Be Afraid of Finishing Early

Once the team gets used to the sprint planning process, they may not need the entire timebox to complete their planning. They don't need to artificially inflate the amount of time spent on each user story in order to fill the timebox—they should wrap things up, get the heck out of there, and get moving!

My warning remains, however: *don't skimp on planning*. A solid plan is your best forecast for success during the sprint.

25.7 Scheduling Scrum Ceremonies for the Sprint

One of the rules of Scrum is only the Scrum team can determine when ceremonies occur during each sprint. At the end of sprint planning is a great time to get everyone to agree on when they want them to happen.

Once the team completes a few sprints, they'll likely settle on a set schedule for their ceremonies, but even in this case it's important to review them to ensure everyone is still in agreement.

Once the sprint planning session wraps up, the ScrumMaster or another volunteer on the team should send meeting invites to get the ceremonies on everyone's calendar.

Daily Scrum

Setting a time for the daily scrum with everyone's input is important, because you want to have the entire Scrum team attend whenever possible. Scheduling it as a group ensures that all members have a say as to the best time.

Each person should check their calendar to see if they have any conflicts over the course of the sprint and the group should collectively pick a time that works best for everyone. If you have team members in different time zones, this may be a little tricky, but the team should do their best. Having a verbal daily scrum is much more powerful than attempting to have it via email or instant messaging.

It's likely you'll want to experiment with using a *parking lot*—an additional 15-minute timeboxed discussion period after the 15-minute daily scrum—so be sure to block off 30 minutes for your daily scrums, at least for your first sprint or two.

See Section 6.5 for more about the parking lot.

Backlog Refinement (Optional)

To ensure the next sprint planning ceremony is as efficient as possible, most teams schedule one or two backlog refinement sessions during their sprint. Although this is not an "official" Scrum ceremony, the product owner is responsible for ensuring the backlog is always properly groomed. It's usually helpful to set aside a specific time for the Scrum team to participate.

Although it's not mandatory that the entire Scrum team attends, it's often helpful to get everyone together. The team can review the stories at the top of the product backlog, help the product owner with questions about splitting stories that are too large, and play a short round of Planning Poker to assign story point estimates to any newly-split or newly-added user stories.

I've found that one or two sessions of two hours each is about right for a two-week sprint.

Schedule the final backlog refinement session no fewer than three to four days before the end of the sprint to avoid getting in the way of driving the sprint to done, and to allow the product owner enough time to get any questions or issues addressed before the next sprint planning ceremony.

Backlog Estimating (Optional)

If a good portion of the development team can't make it to at least one backlog refinement ceremony, you may need to schedule additional time to get story point estimates assigned to user stories.

My personal preference is to try to get most, if not all, the development team members to backlog refinement, and skip a separate meeting just for estimating.

If you do find you need to do some estimating, I would just stretch out a daily scrum or two and do some quick Planning Poker to get the story points figured out.

This is sometimes necessary even if you do get the estimating completed during backlog refinement. For example, the product owner may need to add a new user story in the last few days of the sprint based on changing business conditions.

Backlog Prioritization (Optional)

Many product owners have an established system to solicit input from the appropriate business stakeholders, to guide their decisions about the force-ranked priority of the product backlog. In other cases, product owners struggle with this.

If the product owner is having difficulty getting the required input, they can schedule a backlog prioritization meeting with key stakeholders. This is usually attended by the product owner, ScrumMaster, and any relevant stakeholders who influence the product owner's decisions about priorities.

Ideally, this meeting should happen prior to backlog refinement, so the top of the product backlog represents the right priorities.

This is an area where the ScrumMaster can help, especially with new product owners. They can coach the product owner and help facilitate discussions with the appropriate stakeholders.

Sprint Review

Getting the sprint review scheduled typically revolves around the availability of the stakeholders. For your first sprint review, I suggest coming up with a proposed time that works for the Scrum team but then I'd confirm it works for stakeholders. You may need to be flexible, adjusting the start time if they're not available then.

Once you start having sprint reviews, I suggest scheduling the *next* sprint review before everyone leaves. You'll have a captive audience and the stakeholders can all check their calendars to verify it works.

Ideally, you'll have the sprint review at the same time on the last day of each sprint, to get a better feeling of a regular cadence, but sometimes you might need to adjust, depending upon what everyone has going on.

The entire Scrum team should attend the sprint review whenever possible. It's critical to have the team hear feedback directly from stakeholders.

It's encouraging to hear positive feedback, and if there is any negative feedback, it's important for the entire team to hear it. This is a continuation of "programming the team's collective subconscious," ensuring they all understand the motivations behind what they're doing.

If some team members are in different time zones, this may constrain the available times. For example, if some of the team is seven hours ahead, it may require the sprint review to be no later than 10 or 11 a.m.

It's not the best, but if some team members can't make it because stakeholders can't meet until 4 p.m., then you'll have to just go with it, and work to figure out if there's a way to get the sprint review earlier in the future to get the entire Scrum team there.

Retrospective

I like to have teams schedule the retrospective immediately following the sprint review. Everything will be fresh in team member's heads, and they will be able to incorporate any feedback they heard from the stakeholders during sprint review.

It's also a nice way to wrap up the sprint, and immediately forget all about it once everyone walks out the door.

This is an important part of starting the recharge process before they have to do it all over again, starting at the beginning of the next sprint planning ceremony.

The Next Sprint Planning Ceremony

I used to wait until during the sprint to schedule the next sprint planning ceremony, only to discover other things got booked on the team's calendars. To avoid this, I started setting aside the time for the *next* sprint planning before wrapping up the current sprint planning ceremony.

This provides the ability to get that time blocked out and identify any conflicts well in advance.

Be Cautious of Recurring Meeting Appointments

Many teams block out their "standard" times for ceremonies using recurring meeting appointments in their electronic calendar. I like the concept of this idea, especially for your daily scrum, but I encourage you to be careful about using this technique for other ceremonies.

I've found that sometimes when you need to reschedule a recurring meeting, it may not be updated properly for some attendees, especially if they use a mix of different calendar tools. The last thing you want is key stakeholders showing up one hour late to a sprint review, just as it's concluding.

Because of these issues, I encourage you to send meeting invites just for the current sprint plus the next sprint planning ceremony, as non-recurring appointments.

25.8 Finish Sprint Planning by Transitioning to Immediate Action

Since the goal of sprint planning is to outline a plan and then *get going*, it's important to end the sprint planning ceremony by spending a few minutes talking about what everyone will work on between that point and the first daily scrum of the sprint. This forms a bridge between *planning* and *doing*.

Each member of the development team should volunteer for a subtask or two. Since you are already half-way through the day—assuming a four-hour sprint planning ceremony—they may not have time to drive the work to done by the next day's daily scrum, but they can get started.

I don't recommend volunteering for more than one subtask unless at least one can be driven to "done" before the first daily scrum. Keeping subtasks unclaimed gives the team the most flexibility to tackle them based on who's available at the time they come up next in the list.

Don't Forget About Impediments

Although it would be nice to start every sprint without any impediments, sometimes it happens. For example, you might need some help from someone outside the Scrum team. Be sure each team member identifies any immediate impediments so the ScrumMaster can help resolve them as quickly as possible.

Key Takeaways

- Use the detailed guidance in Section 21.3 to calculate the development team's net capacity for the sprint. Team members should look at their calendars and ensure they omit any time they can't spend focused on the work of the sprint task board. Personal time off, company holidays, and all-hands meetings should be subtracted from the time available.

- Creating a plan for the work of the sprint addresses two questions. It allows the development team to determine what will fit into the sprint and spells out a high-level strategy for how they'll turn the product backlog items into a shippable product increment.

- Because the product owner is involved with sprint planning, they can identify when the time required to complete a user story is out of line with the value that story would deliver. They can work with the development team to scale back the scope of the user story to align it more closely with its value.

- Avoid trying to figure out *everything* during sprint planning. A high-level plan that evolves during the course of the sprint is better than not getting to half of the stories because the team talked about too many details for the first story or two.

- A sprint goal helps to focus the team on driving toward a cohesive target. It also provides a framework for negotiation with the product owner if the development team runs into trouble. Adjustments can be made to scale things back while still driving toward the sprint goal.

- Be sure to spend time creating a plan for driving tasks and bugs that are pulled into the sprint to "done." Tasks represent technical research or other work the development team needs to do that doesn't deliver direct value to the product owner and stakeholders. Bugs represent something that's not working quite right. Both will likely take longer than you think, so avoid short-changing planning of these types of product backlog items.

- If you run out of time before planning everything, it's not the end of the world. The most important outcome of sprint planning is a plan for the first few days of the sprint. The team can then add more details as the sprint gets going for the rest of the scope.

- Be sure to schedule the various Scrum ceremonies before ending sprint planning, to confirm that the times work for everyone on the team. If possible, get input prior to sprint planning as to the best time for the sprint review to ensure the key stakeholders will be able to attend. Once you start sprint reviews, you can talk to stakeholders before the end of the review to get the *next* sprint review on their calendars.

- The last thing to do before wrapping up is to create a plan for immediate action. Each development team member should volunteer for a subtask or two. They may not be able to finish between the end of the sprint planning ceremony and the next day's scrum, but they can get started.

- Be sure to identify any impediments that need to be resolved right away. The ScrumMaster can then help drive them to done as quickly as possible so the team doesn't get held up.

Chapter 26

Orchestrating the Daily Work of the Sprint

The great secret is that an orchestra can actually play without a conductor at all. Of course, a great conductor will have a concept and will help them play together and unify them.

- **Joshua Bell**, *American Grammy award-winning violinist and conductor.*

An ancient Japanese proverb reads, "Vision without action is a daydream. Action without vision is a nightmare." (Kriger, 2002)

This is a great summary of the challenge the team faces as they walk out of the sprint planning room. They have a vision—the sprint backlog—and now they need a way to orchestrate the required action to get the work done.

If you adopt my recommended sprint length of two weeks, time is short. Much of the first day is spent planning, and now nine business days remain.

The secret to successfully executing a sprint is clarity and communication. Everyone needs to understand what's left to be done and their overall progress toward completing the sprint goal. Team members need to work together to "inspect and adapt" throughout the sprint—constantly evaluating the plan and adjusting as necessary to deliver results.

There are three keys to driving daily action:

- The *daily scrum*—also called the *daily standup*—provides a way for the team to sync up and create a plan for the next 24 hours, with everyone knowing what each other is working on. This is also a time where impediments to progress can be discussed. This ensures roadblocks are surfaced and removed as quickly as possible.

- The *sprint task board* summarizes the sprint backlog created during sprint planning. By keeping the board up to date, everyone on the team understands exactly where they stand with respect to the plan for completing the sprint.

- The *sprint burndown chart* provides a visual way to let the team understand whether they are on track, ahead, or behind, based on the total hours of work that still need to be done compared to the available time left in the sprint.

To help the Scrum team make as much progress as possible, the ScrumMaster acts as the facilitator and ensures all three of these tools are used consistently, and aggressively keeps track of any impediments to ensure they get dealt with quickly.

Although not "in charge," the ScrumMaster is very much like the conductor of an orchestra, keeping the team in sync to deliver the best results. He can frequently ask them, "What can I do today to help you and the rest of the team be more effective?" (Rubin, 2013)

26.1 Using the Daily Scrum to Stay in Sync

Although we'd love to believe the Scrum team will "just figure out" how to stay in sync, the simple truth is…they won't. Everyone will put on their headphones or close the door, get in the zone, and focus intently on their work of the day. Communication often takes a back seat.

The *daily scrum*—or *daily standup*—provides a 15-minute timeboxed check-in for the team. Held at the same time every day, with attendance required by everyone on the development team, the daily scrum helps the team self-organize to drive progress.

The daily scrum facilitates communication, identifies and resolves impediments, promotes quick decision-making, and improves transparency—all in support of the team self-organizing. (Cho, 2008)

Self-organizing is the key point here. This is not each team member providing a quick progress report and then getting back to whatever they were working on individually. It's to talk as a group to coordinate their work, identify issues, and solve them together.

Alex may say, "I'm having a problem with the search controller," and Anna replies, "I can help you with that. How about we get together after?"

The ScrumMaster pays attention to the interaction—Alex encountered an impediment—and makes a note to follow up to make sure they were able to work it out. This is part of the orchestration job of the ScrumMaster—to pay attention to impediments and ensure they are resolved quickly.

The most important outcome of the daily scrum is a feeling of energy, teamwork, and working together. (Sutherland & Sutherland, 2014)

Team members should leave the ceremony with a feeling of, "We're going to kick some serious ass today."

Use the Sprint Task Board as a Backdrop

Because the sprint task board represents the current plan to achieve the sprint goal, it's often helpful to have it displayed on someone's computer—if meeting in the team's work area—or up on the wall using a TV or projector in the conference room.

When team members talk about working on subtasks, everyone can look at the board to see where each fits into the overall plan.

Stand up If the Team is Co-Located

One of the reasons the daily scrum is also called a daily standup is the attendees are encouraged to *stand up* during the ceremony.

Standing up accomplishes a few things:

- *It makes it easier to keep the meeting short.* No one wants to stand up longer than they have to. (Dahl, 2014)

- *It makes it more difficult to use a laptop.* Have you ever been in a meeting where it seems everyone is looking at their laptop and not paying any attention to each other? Me too. Standing up prevents this.

- *It makes it easier to be engaged.* When standing up, your body is more active than sitting, and everyone's energy levels seem to increase a couple of notches.

The ScrumMaster typically sits since it's difficult to manage the sprint task board from a standing position. However, unless they are also a member of the development team, they won't be providing an update anyway.

Something else to keep in mind is respecting any physical limitations of your team members. If someone has a disability or other condition that makes it difficult or impossible for them to stand, I suggest abandoning the idea of having the team stand up. The ScrumMaster will ensure the team stays on track to keep the ceremony as short as possible.

Consider an Electronics Ban

It's inevitable that during a daily scrum, someone will look down at their laptop or pop their phone out of their pocket. If your development team has a hard time resisting the urge, consider an electronics ban where everyone needs to leave their device at their desk.

For distributed teams, this obviously doesn't work since everyone needs to be on a device to connect to the ceremony. In this case, focus on keeping it as short as possible to avoid tempting team members to multi-task which makes it difficult, if not impossible, to pay attention.

Avoid Discussion

The daily scrum is designed to be very fast and efficient, since any time the entire Scrum team is together, time is being burned at a very rapid rate. A team of 8 people in a room for 15 minutes, for example, is the equivalent of 2 person-hours of time.

Each person should succinctly discuss the three summary items. As a rule of thumb, each team member update should take no longer than 30 to 60 seconds.

If there are any questions or discussion required, or if there is an impediment, the ScrumMaster can make a note to address it during the *parking lot*, which I'll talk about below.

Review the Burndown Chart at the End of Everyone's Update

Once the last development team member finishes their update, the ScrumMaster should show the sprint burndown chart so everyone can see how things are tracking. The sprint burndown chart shows whether the team is ahead, behind, or on track with completing all the work on the sprint task board.

If things are on track or ahead, that's great news. The development team members should keep their heads down and keep cranking along. You never know when something might blow up in their faces and cause a slowdown.

If the team is behind, that's cause for *immediate* concern and there should be discussion about how to course-correct. In Section 26.3, I'll talk about what do to if the burndown chart is off-track.

Leverage a Parking Lot for Quick Problem-Solving

The *parking lot*, which I talked about in Section 6.5, is a way to address quick discussion items and solve problems that surfaced during each team member's update. Timeboxed to no more than an additional 15 minutes, the team goes down the list of items that came up during the daily scrum and a plan of action is determined for each.

Before diving into the discussion, the ScrumMaster should first ask, "Who needs to be here for this?" The answer will often be, "The whole team," but when only a subset of the team is required, this is a way to ensure they aren't wasting time sitting in a meeting where they're not needed.

26.2 Tracking Progress Against the Plan with the Sprint Task Board

All daily work of the team revolves around the sprint task board. It contains the sprint backlog—the product backlog items selected for the sprint and subtasks to complete them—representing the plan created by the team during their sprint planning ceremony.

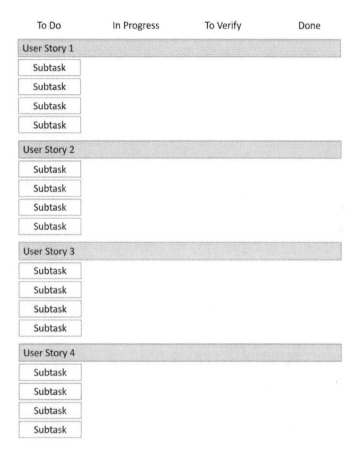

The sprint task board contains the sprint backlog—the items selected for the sprint and the subtasks representing the plan to complete them.

Work from the Top Down

One point I want to make first is it's important to work from the top down, as opposed to jumping all around the sprint task board.

The product backlog items listed first are those the product owner decided are most important. Jumping down to the fourth product backlog item because it seems more interesting flies in the face of what the development team is trying to do—deliver value in order of priority.

If you take this approach, the team will move subtasks from the top left toward the bottom right.

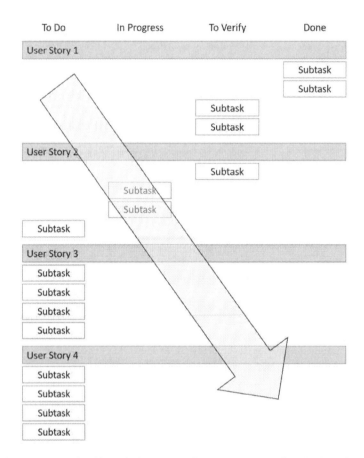

The development team should work from top to bottom, moving subtasks from left to right to complete product backlog items in the priority order specified by the product owner.

To the greatest extent possible, the development team should focus all their effort on the first product backlog item, "swarming" it to drive it to done as quickly as possible.

Depending upon the size of the team, it may not be possible for everyone to work on just one product backlog item. You could run into the "too many cooks in the kitchen" problem, where team members end up stepping on each other's toes.

In this case, some team members can move down to the next product backlog item, but only after determining there's no way they can help with the first product backlog item.

What you want to avoid is the team starting work on *all* the product backlog items at once. This will tend to reduce their ability to "do a little bit of everything all the time," and also risks all the product backlog items being in progress but none getting driven entirely to "done."

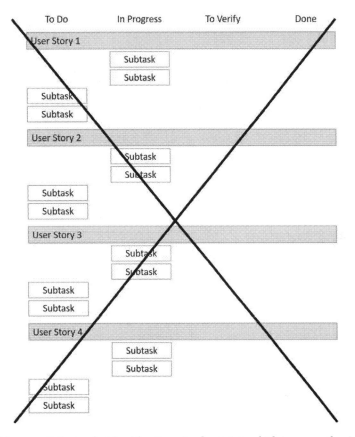

Avoid working on all the product backlog items in the sprint, which increases the risk of getting 80% of all of them done but driving none of them to completion.

It's much better for the team to deliver three out of four 100% complete product backlog items to the product owner than to deliver *none* because they didn't work in priority order.

Keep Track of Who Owns Each Subtask

Because the sprint task board is a communication tool, it's important to keep track of who is working on what. This drives accountability and clarity. There's nothing worse than a team member spending half a day working on a subtask, only to discover that someone else was doing the same thing.

Each team member should "claim" a subtask they are going to focus on, by putting their name on it. This clearly says, "I've got this one," and avoids the problem of another team member doing redundant work.

If the team member is no longer working on a subtask—for example if it's ready for verification by someone else on the team—they should take their name off it. Other than those in the Done column, any subtask that has no name on it says, "This is available for someone to work on."

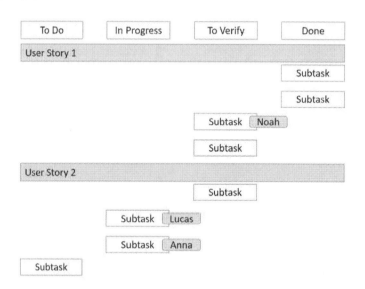

Team members should "claim" the subtask they're working on.
A subtask with no name means anyone on the team can claim it.

One thing to keep in mind is team members *don't need to wait for the next daily scrum* to claim a subtask. If they volunteered for a subtask at the last daily scrum and they got it done, they should find another one near the top of the task board that they can drive forward.

If they're not sure what would be best to work on next, they can talk with their team members to get some ideas. This is a perfect example of what *self-organizing* means: everyone works together throughout every day to drive the work of the sprint forward.

Put Your Name on Only Those Subtasks You'll Work on in the Next Day

I've seen some development teams put names on every single subtask during sprint planning. They had good intentions—they wanted to solidify their plan of attack. The problem is they severely restricted their flexibility.

There are some problems you may run into by trying to guess at the beginning of the sprint who will work on every subtask:

- *The subtask might take longer than anticipated.* The nature of planning is that estimates are just that—a guess as to how long a subtask will take. If the owner of the subtask takes a little longer, they will feel an increasing amount of pressure. In the back of their mind they're thinking about all the *other* work they signed up for.

- *Someone might get sick or pulled away.* If Maria is out sick for two days or gets pulled into helping solve some crisis that's come up, her subtasks will fall behind and may hold up others on the team who are waiting for "her stuff" to get done.

- *It introduces artificial dependencies and critical paths.* If Lucas signs up for all the early work for the first few stories, the team may end up waiting around because they can't do "their subtasks" yet. Any time you have someone "sitting around and waiting," you're losing throughput.

- *It undermines the team becoming more cross-functional.* Anna is the front-end expert, so she signed up for all the front-end coding during sprint planning. In a sprint that's heavy on that type of work, Anna will tend to be overloaded. Anna may be the *best* person to do the front-end work, but if she is the *only* person who can touch that code, the team is going to be severely limited.

- *It undermines the team approach.* If the entire team leaves the office and Adam is there until late at night because his subtasks are falling behind, that's neither fair nor sustainable. Adam is likely to be less productive over time as he gets burned out.

Avoiding this problem is simple: leave names off all subtasks during sprint planning. At the end of sprint planning, team members volunteer for *only* those subtasks they will work on from that point until the next daily scrum.

During each daily scrum, they'll repeat the process, with each team member volunteering for another subtask or two.

This approach keeps the team as agile as possible. If a subtask takes longer than anticipated, whoever owns it can keep their head down. Meanwhile, another team member who is available can take on whatever is next in the list. They might not be as fast as the person who's tied up on that time-consuming subtask, but they can keep things moving.

This is a cross-functional team in action. Anyone who can move a subtask forward *at any speed other than zero* can take it on. I'm all for playing favorites, especially if someone can move work forward at ten times the speed of someone else. If that miracle worker isn't available, however, I'd much rather have *some* progress.

26.3 Keeping the Sprint Task Board up to Date Every Day

The sprint task board is a type of *information radiator*. It allows everyone to understand progress against the plan in close to real time.

If the information on the board is stale by even a day or two, its usefulness declines dramatically. Therefore, it's important to update it every day. (Cervone, 2011)

With just a small amount of care and feeding, each team member can contribute to ensuring information is current.

Move Subtasks from Column to Column

Because the sprint task board helps the team keep in sync, it's important to move subtasks from column to column as their state changes.

There are three key events that trigger a column change:

Work begins. When work starts on a subtask, it should be moved from the To Do column to the In Progress column. If *any* work gets done on a subtask, it should never go back into the To Do column, even if a developer gets stuck or gets pulled away from the subtask for some reason.

If a partially-complete subtask moves back to the To Do column, it's going to be confusing when the next team member comes along and thinks she's starting from scratch, instead of finding out what's already been done and picking up from there.

Work has been completed. Once work has been completed on a subtask, there are two choices: move it to the To Verify column or move it to the Done column.

I like to tell team members, "Everything you do should be peer reviewed. You need to 'have each other's back' to ensure everything is done correctly." Because of this, the default assumption is *every* subtask goes to the To Verify column when the work is done.

There is an exception: if the work of the subtask will be verified by one or more *other* subtasks. An example of this is a coding subtask getting verified by two other types of subtasks: one for testing the user story and another for performing a code review. In this case, the team can decide on a convention of moving coding tasks directly from In Progress to Done.

Work has been reviewed. If the team member reviewing a subtask that's in the To Verify column finds that everything is correct, they move it to the Done column, so everyone knows the work has been completed and peer reviewed.

If they find one or more issues, they should move it back to the In Progress column, adding a note to the subtask describing the issues they found. They should then remove their name so it's "fair game" for someone else on the team to take on.

Some teams decide that when a subtask in the To Verify column gets moved back to In Progress, it should be assigned to the team member who originally did the work. It is usually most efficient for the person who did the work to fix any issues, but just be careful to make sure everyone is on board with this idea. Also, be on the lookout for a subtask that gets stuck because that team member is out of the office for the next two days.

The normal progression of a subtask looks like this:

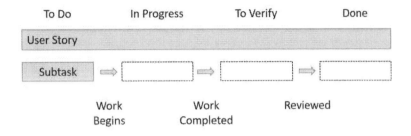

Subtasks are moved from column to column to communicate their current state. In this case the reviewer didn't find any issues and moved the subtask to the Done column from the To Verify column.

If the reviewer finds an issue, the progression looks like this:

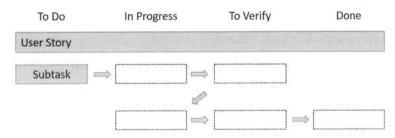

If an issue is found by the reviewer, the subtask goes back to the In Progress column for resolution. Then it moves back to the To Verify column for re-review, then finally to Done.

Update the Sprint Task Board at Least Twice Per Day and Before Each Daily Scrum

Although the Agile Manifesto tells us that *individuals and interactions* are more important than *processes and tools*, it's helpful if the sprint task board always represents the current state of the sprint backlog. If the tool slowly goes out of date, it's going to be difficult to understand what's done versus what's left to do and will hurt the team's ability to visualize and orchestrate their work.

When to Update the Sprint Task Board

The sprint task board doesn't need to be accurate up to the minute. But if it's updated at minimum a couple of times per day, it's going to help everyone keep up with where everything stands.

It's *really* important that all subtasks are up to date prior to the daily scrum, to help facilitate the coordination of work during that ceremony. Everyone on the team should ensure they take a minute or two to review and update any subtasks with their name on it before they go to the scrum to make sure they're up to date.

Here are some ideas of triggers for each team member to update the sprint task board:

- Going to lunch.

- Changing context, for example moving from working on the product to working on email.

- Going into a Scrum ceremony.

- Going into a meeting unrelated to the Scrum team.

- Leaving for the day. This one is *especially* important if the team member is out of the office the next day.

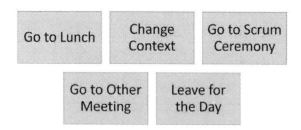

Triggers for development team members to update the sprint task board.

Keep the Remaining Time up to Date on Subtasks

The sprint burndown chart—which I described in Section 8.4 and will discuss further in the next section in this chapter—gives the team a way to determine if they're on track to finish everything by the end of the sprint.

Some teams drive the sprint burndown chart based on completed story points, but I feel that approach is too "chunky," because the burndown chart will only be updated once each user story is driven to done. With only three or four stories per sprint, this may not provide enough information to allow the team to know if they're on track.

Tracking the number of hours remaining on all the subtasks on the sprint backlog will give you a more fine-grained indication of how the team is moving toward completion, because it allows you to track progress of work on incomplete user stories.

If no one keeps the remaining time up to date on the subtasks, this method will be useless. Garbage in, garbage out. To avoid this, each team member should ensure they adjust the remaining hours when they update their subtasks.

Because a product backlog item may take two to four days to complete, this technique also allows everyone to understand how much effort remains to drive it to done.

Update Remaining Time When Moving a Subtask to the To Verify Column

When moving the subtask to the To Verify column, the remaining time should be updated to a reasonable amount of time needed to do the review. Be careful to avoid setting the time to zero hours.

Teams often talk about how much time will be required to verify the subtask during sprint planning. If the team member is unsure how much time to leave for the review, they can just ask the person who is likely to do the review how much time they think they'll need.

Don't Be Afraid of *Increasing* the Remaining Time

Just because the estimate for a subtask is three hours, doesn't mean it will *definitely* take three hours. Sometimes it will take less, which is great. Other times, the subtask was underestimated and will take longer.

One thing to be careful about is not blindly reducing the remaining time by the hours that have been spent. For example, if two hours are spent working on the three-hour subtask, the tendency will be to change the time remaining to one hour. The problem is it might take longer than an hour to wrap it up.

Team members should always make sure the remaining time represents what they *really* think is left to get it done. If they've spent some time working on a subtask that was estimated as four hours, and think there are *still* four hours left, they should set the time remaining to four hours.

Only Track Time Spent Working on Each Subtask if You'll Use the Data

I'm often asked, "Do we need to track the time we spent on the subtask? Isn't that important to help improve our estimates?"

I'm a fan of capturing data *only if it's going to be used*. If team members dutifully track their time but no one ever looks at that data, it's wasted effort.

In my experience, teams seldom take the time to go back and carefully analyze historical information in order to increase their estimating accuracy, so in most cases I don't believe it's valuable to track time spent working on subtasks.

Some teams need to track their time for accounting purposes, often because the hours are needed to properly capitalize the cost of software development in their organization. In this case, keeping track of time spent is a requirement.

Regardless of what you choose, remember that the most important number to help keep the sprint on track is the *remaining* time for each subtask, since it drives the sprint burndown chart.

Add Comments to Each Subtask to Track Progress

We know that individuals and interactions are more important than processes and tools, but that doesn't mean we should *abandon* the use of tools where it makes sense.

One technique I've found works well is keeping track of your progress by adding notes to the subtask you're working on. Where I've found this most helpful is when I'm leaving that subtask for some span of time, for example going to lunch or into a meeting, or leaving for the day.

I like to leave a quick reminder for myself along the lines of, "Finished the basics, need to wrap up the exceptional scenarios" or "Found root cause of bug in the Verify() method in CustomerRepository—the if/then block isn't quite right." This can get me right back on track so I can pick up where I left off.

There's another huge benefit, which addresses what I call the "hit by a bus" problem. If something happens to me—I get sick, I get pulled into a customer emergency, or for some reason I'm unavailable—the team has a fallback. They can read my notes and someone else can take over what I was working on.

This is especially important if it's near the end of a sprint. The last thing the team needs is to have me disappear and have *no idea* what was in my head.

Consider it a contingency plan—a backup for when the *individuals and interactions* concept from the Agile Manifesto isn't adequate.

Flag Subtasks That Are Impeded

Some agile software tools, such as Jira, support the ability to add a flag to a subtask, which typically provides a visual indication on the sprint task board.

If the team discovers a subtask has an impediment—something that prevents it from being moved forward—it's often helpful to flag it and add a comment describing the impediment. It can be discussed at the next scrum or, if the team member is dead in the water, they can immediately talk to others on the team and/or the ScrumMaster for help in removing the impediment.

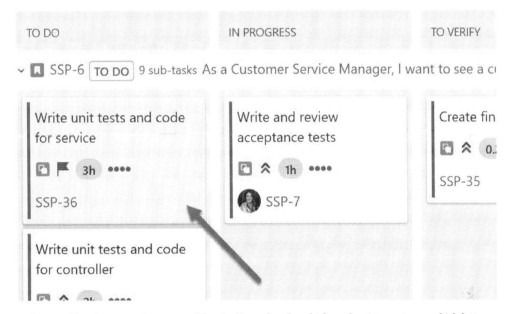

Some agile software tools support "flagging" a subtask, which makes it easy to see which have impediments. In this case, a developer realized some questions need to be addressed before she can code the service (subtask SSP-36).

Add Subtasks as New Work Is Discovered

It's important to remember that the sprint task board should always represent the current, up to date plan for completing the product backlog items in the sprint. It's often the case that there are required steps that are missed during sprint planning.

As soon as it's discovered that something else needs to be done, a new subtask should be added to the product backlog item.

Anyone on the Development Team Can Add a New Subtask

Anyone on the development team can create a new subtask. It doesn't need to wait for the next scrum. If new work to drive a product backlog item to done is discovered, a new subtask should be added, and an hour estimate should be assigned to it.

To keep everyone up to date, the team member who added the subtask can mention it during the next scrum, or they can post a message to the team chat room if it's helpful for everyone to know immediately.

You Don't Need the Product Owner's Approval

It's true that the product owner owns the ROI of the Scrum team. But does that mean team members need to ask for her approval before adding new subtasks?

The answer is, "No."

The sprint backlog—the product backlog items and the subtasks to complete them—belong to the *development team*, not the product owner. Therefore, anyone on the development team can and should add new subtasks as they are discovered.

There is a caveat. The new subtasks should represent additional work to deliver the product backlog item, *not* additional scope that's arbitrarily invented by a member of the team.

For example, if the team is working on a user story named *As a social media user, I want to delete one of my posts, so I can remove an unwanted post*, the team needs to be focused on delivering the vision of the product owner.

Adding a new subtask named *Add confirmation popup* might make sense if it was missed during sprint planning. However, *Add the ability to delete multiple posts* is likely out of scope. Even if it's easy for a developer to add this capability, the product owner probably doesn't care about it right now.

Remember that a key benefit of Scrum is maximizing the work *not* done. If something "neat" or "cool"—what I call four-letter words—is added, it also adds testing time and possible additional time to fix bugs.

This is another example of why it's so important to have the product owner embedded within the Scrum team. They can quickly help course-correct and ensure the development team isn't adding extra scope.

In this case, if they like the idea of adding multiple-deletion functionality, they can add a user story to the product backlog for future consideration. This helps eliminate scope creep, which can threaten the ability for the team to drive the sprint goal to done.

Delete Subtasks That No Longer Apply

Similar to adding a new subtask when an additional step is required, deleting an unnecessary subtask is equally important. As soon as it's obvious that work won't be needed, any team member can delete the extra subtask.

If team members are confused when subtasks disappear from the sprint task board, an alternative is to add something like "DELETED" to the beginning of the subtask name, set its remaining time to zero, and move it to the Done column. If it adds clarity, the team member deleting the subtask can add a comment explaining why it's not needed.

I would only add this extra step if there is a history of confusion. If deleting a subtask—with a subsequent mention at the next daily scrum or in the team chat room—seems to be just fine, stick with the simplest thing that could possibly work and continue that practice.

Don't Do Work That's Not on the Board

There are times where the development team will come together for a daily scrum and someone will provide an update and…it's work that doesn't exist anywhere on the sprint task board.

This has two risks:

- *Communication suffers.* If a team member spends time on something that's not tracked by a subtask on the board, it's difficult for the rest of the team to understand how that work fits into the big picture.

- *The work is unrelated to the current sprint.* This is a worst-case scenario. The product owner has clearly outlined priorities, and what's in the current sprint is the most important. If a team member drifts off and works on something that's ten items down the product backlog, they're not investing time in the most effective area.

The solution is easy. If the work is done, there's no need to add a subtask. It's water under the bridge. You only really care about the subtasks that are not yet done; having a history of completed work is unimportant in the grand scheme of things.

If the work is appropriate and continuing, create a new subtask and record the estimated time remaining to complete it.

If the work is not appropriate because it's unrelated to what's in the scope for the current sprint, the team member should stop working on it and save their energy for when the associated product backlog item makes its way to the top of the sprint.

If the team member did some valuable work on the future product backlog item, I suggest adding a note to that item. For example, "John did some work on this. See the ABC feature branch for the code he wrote."

This highlights another benefit of the daily scrum. If someone is confused and is charging off in the wrong direction on unimportant or unrelated work, they can be reined in with a course correction within 24 hours, as opposed to learning about it 4 days later. This helps support transparency, one of the pillars of Scrum.

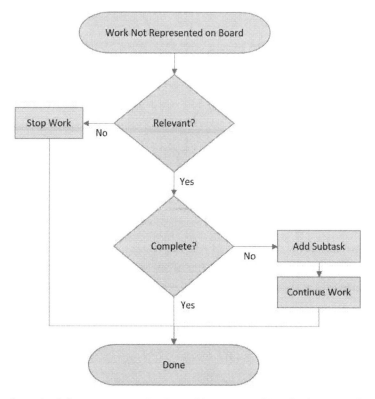

When it's determined that a team member is working on something that's not on the sprint task board, there are a few choices.

26.4 Using the Sprint Burndown Chart to Stay on Track

The sprint burndown chart is the measuring stick used by the team to determine whether they are on track with finishing everything by the end of the sprint. It is a tool they can use to *predict the future.*

The sprint burndown chart provides an immediate indication of the health of the sprint:

- If the line is *above* the guideline, the team is *behind*.

- If the line is *below* the guideline, they are *ahead*.

- If the line is *touching* the guideline, they're *on track*.

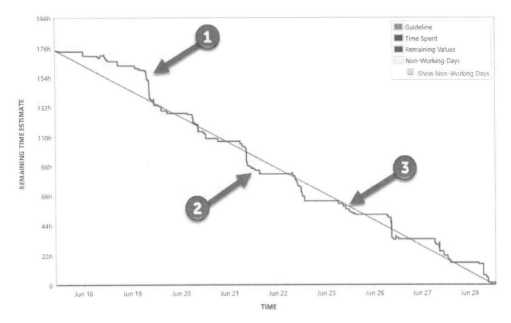

The sprint burndown chart shows if the team is behind (1), ahead (2), or on-track (3).

If the Burndown Is Off-Track at the Midpoint of the Sprint, the Team Is in Trouble

As I've used the sprint burndown chart over the years, I've discovered a recurring theme: if the sprint burndown chart is off track half way through the sprint, the sprint is in trouble.

I've never seen a situation where a burndown that's off track magically fixes itself. Without deliberate effort to course-correct, the development team won't complete everything in the sprint.

I've ignored this to my peril. I've tried to *wish* the sprint back on track—instead of making any changes—and it's never worked out. There was always a user story or two that didn't get done and I thought, "If only I had paid attention to that burndown chart."

If the team chooses to ignore an off-track burndown chart early in the sprint, I strongly suggest they start paying closer attention as the sprint reaches its midpoint and apply a course correction using some ideas I'll outline.

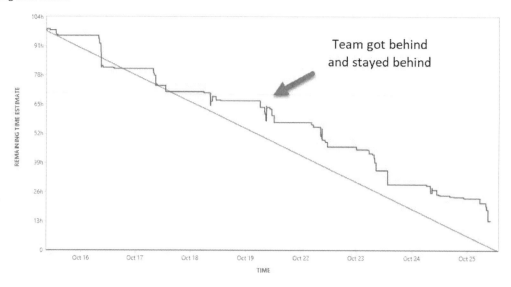

If there isn't a course-correction, the team will never get back on track and won't complete the work in the sprint.

I'm going to repeat that just to make sure it's firmly implanted in your brain. **If the burndown is off-track half-way through the sprint and the team doesn't make a change, they *won't* get everything done.**

Options to Address an Off-Track Burndown Chart

If the team is off-track—that is, the jagged track line is above the straight target line—they have a few options.

Ignore it. If it's very early in the sprint, perhaps the first day or two, the team may still be getting up to speed and gaining momentum. They can keep an eye on things but not make any change to their approach. As I talk about below, however, if the team is off-track half-way through the sprint, it's time to act.

Work smarter. Is everyone being utilized effectively? Or is the development team falling back into waterfall habits and there is too much of a focus on one "specialist" working on one focused area? Are team members spending quiet, focused time working on subtasks? Or are they being interrupted three times a day with unimportant meetings?

Working smarter, with everyone on the development team as fully-utilized as possible, is a way to make a significant improvement to throughput. The ScrumMaster can help identify and address any low-hanging fruit—easy changes that can be made to improve effectiveness.

Work harder. If the team is working smart, sometimes they might want to roll up their sleeves and work a little harder. I'm not saying that every sprint needs to be a death march—that should be impossible since the development team decides how much work to take on. However, progress sometimes requires some extra time and effort. Maybe a few team members can get a pizza and stay an extra hour or two to wrap some things up. Perhaps someone is willing to come in early or pitch in for an hour or two on the weekend.

Putting in extra time on a repeating basis is a symptom of the development team taking on too much work during their sprints and should be addressed for future sprints. But few successful software products were built only during banker's hours—sometimes it's going to require going the extra mile.

Working harder at times is, candidly, what I would expect from a professional development team. However, not at the expense of the Scrum principle of sustainability. The development team can't be burned out on sprint 5 and useless for sprint 6.

Reduce scope. Sometimes the development team bites off more than they can chew, and it becomes obvious that there's no way they'll be able to get everything done and drive the product to a shippable level of quality. In this case, I *don't* recommend the whole team starts working 14 hours per day to get everything done. That will just burn them out and kill their productivity next sprint.

Instead, the product owner should talk to the team and consider dropping the least-important user story from the sprint. An alternative is to split a story that's in the sprint, keeping the portion that the team thinks they can drive to "done," and creating a new story on the product backlog for the rest.

Don't Forget to Look at the Big Picture

Some teams stay on track with the sprint burndown chart through the early stages of the sprint, but still fail to get all their user stories done. If the subtasks are on track, and stories are getting *close* to being done, be careful not to fall into the trap of having all the user stories an hour from completion at the end of the sprint.

Ensuring everything is on track requires both a micro view—looking at the sprint burndown chart to see how the hours from subtasks are being reduced—and a macro "big picture" view.

An easy way to evaluate the big picture is seeing how many product backlog items are done. If the team is half way through a sprint, and they took on four user stories, two of those should be either done or pretty close. If *no* stories are done, the team should take a hard look at what's left and figure out what they need to do to wrap them up.

Sometimes the team has jumped down the sprint task board, abandoning early stories too soon. Perhaps there's a lingering bug that needs to be fixed or the product owner still needs to review it. Whatever the cause, the team should rationalize how they'll get every story done in the time that's left.

This is a perfect time for the ScrumMaster to help facilitate the process. "Hey everyone, these stories are stalled out and we're half way through the sprint. It looks like there are a couple of things left. What's the plan?"

Principal Coding Should Be Done Two Days Prior to the End of the Sprint

As I've experienced the last-minute scramble at the end of more sprints than I'd care to admit, I've tried to come up with a rule of thumb to help ensure everything gets driven to done. What I've found is if principal coding is completed by end of day, two days before the sprint ends, it's going to make it much more likely that everything will get done.

What I mean by *principal coding* is writing the code for new functionality and the associated unit tests. The only remaining coding work should be any bug fixes required once the story is tested, and any minor adjustments the product owner would like to see as a result of their review.

For example, if your sprint ends on Friday, all coding should be done before everyone leaves for the day on Wednesday.

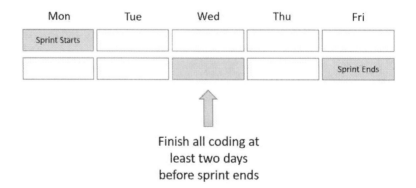

Finish all coding at
least two days
before sprint ends

I've discovered that having all coding completed two days prior to the sprint ending makes it much more likely to get everything done.

One more thing: the team shouldn't be wrapping up coding *all* the stories at that point. Ideally, they'll be finishing just the last story. In a *worst*-case scenario, they'll be wrapping up two stories.

If the development team just finished coding *every* story in the sprint, it's going to be very difficult to do all the required testing, bug fixing, and product owner acceptance in the two days that remain.

The Sprint Burndown Chart Is Not for the Management Team

One thing that's important to keep in mind is that the sprint burndown chart is *not* a tool for managers to look at to "keep an eye on the team." It is *solely* for the use of the Scrum team to identify that they're off track early enough to do something about it.

If you find that management is looking at the burndown chart and peppering the team with questions, or trying to "help," that's a good time for the ScrumMaster to get involved and protect them. It's critical that nothing causes an impediment to the team's self-organization. (James & Walter, 2010)

26.5 Summary of Best Practices

Here is a summary of all the best practices outlined in this chapter.

Sprint Task Board

- ✓ Work from the top down.
- ✓ Keep track of who owns each subtask.
- ✓ Only put your name on subtasks for what you'll work on in the next day.
- ✓ Move subtasks from column to column.
- ✓ Update the sprint task board at least twice per day.
- ✓ Keep the remaining hours up to date on subtasks.
- ✓ Leave time to review when moving a subtask to the To Verify column.
- ✓ Don't be afraid of increasing the remaining time on subtasks as more information is known.
- ✓ Add comments to subtasks to track progress.
- ✓ Flag subtasks that are impeded.

✓ Add subtasks as new work is discovered.

✓ Delete subtasks that no longer apply.

Daily Scrum Ceremony

✓ Use the sprint task board as a backdrop during the daily scrum.

✓ Stand up if the team is co-located, if everyone is physically capable.

✓ Avoid discussion during the daily scrum—save it for the parking lot.

✓ Consider an electronics ban.

✓ Review the burndown chart after everyone's update.

✓ Leverage a parking lot for quick problem solving, but dismiss team members who aren't needed.

Sprint Burndown Chart

✓ If the burndown chart is off-track, you can ignore it, work smarter, work harder, or reduce scope.

✓ If the burndown chart is off-track at the sprint midpoint, a course-correction is necessary in order to get everything done.

✓ Don't forget to consider the big picture—half the user stories should be done or very close to done at the midpoint of the sprint.

✓ Principal coding should be complete two days prior to the end of the sprint.

Key Takeaways

• It's up to the development team to direct their own day-to-day work. Three tools can help them be more effective: the sprint task board, the daily scrum, and the sprint burndown chart.

• Although the ScrumMaster isn't "the boss," they are responsible for ensuring the development team knows how to use these tools effectively. They help orchestrate the Scrum process, so the team can get the best results.

• The sprint task board allows the Scrum team to visualize the plan to get the work done, and the current status of each subtask required to complete product backlog items.

- The team should work the sprint task board from the top down, focusing on the highest-priority product backlog items first.

- To ensure the task board is current, team members should update it at least twice per day, especially before the daily scrum. Subtasks that have been "claimed" should have a name on them, the remaining hours should be up to date, and they should be in the appropriate column.

- Subtasks should be added or deleted as more information is learned by the team during the sprint and they understand more about what it will take to get the product backlog items done.

- The daily scrum is a key way for the team to get in sync and avoid unnecessary meetings. The sprint task board should be used as a backdrop, to provide a framework for the discussion of the team about what they've completed and what they'll tackle next.

- The sprint burndown chart should be reviewed once everyone provides their update during the daily scrum.

- A parking lot can be used to resolve issues immediately following the conclusion of the daily scrum. Anyone who is not required for the discussion should leave so they can get back to work.

- The burndown chart is a tool to predict the future and close attention should be paid to what it's telling the team.

- If the burndown is off track at the midpoint of the sprint, the team needs to take immediate action to make a change, or it's likely they won't get everything done.

- If the burndown chart is off track, options include ignoring it—though I wouldn't recommend this except perhaps the first day or two while the team is gaining momentum—working smarter, working harder, and reducing scope.

- A good rule of thumb is to ensure the coding of all stories is complete two days before the end of the sprint, to leave time for testing, fixing bugs, and the product owner's review. Ideally, only one or two user stories need to be wrapped up in the final days of the sprint.

Chapter 27
A "Zero Defects" Approach to Dealing with Bugs

Don't fix bugs later; fix them now.

- **Steve Maguire**, *Writing Solid Code*

As told by Stack Overflow co-founder and CEO Joel Spolsky, the development of the first version of Microsoft Word for Windows was considered a "death march" project. The schedule kept slipping, the entire team was working ridiculous hours, and the stress was off the charts.

After finally shipping the product, Microsoft sent the whole team off to a tropical island for a vacation and thought long and hard about what happened. (Spolsky, 2000)

What they realized was project managers put so much pressure on the team to adhere to the schedule that the programmers rushed through the coding process, paying little attention to whether the code actually *worked.*

Because bug fixing was not included as part of the schedule, there was no effort to keep the number of bugs to a minimum. The common practice at Microsoft at the time was to postpone all bug fixes to the end of the project. (Maguire, 1993)

As they talked through what went wrong during their post-mortem, they realized that they had created an *infinite defects methodology.* Because there was no focus on addressing bugs right away, the bug count grew without bounds.

To address this, Microsoft adopted what they called a *zero defects methodology.*

27.1 Fix Bugs Before Writing New Code

Zero defects? That may sound like a pipe dream—the idea of never having any bugs in the product. Is that really possible?

What the Microsoft team meant by this philosophy was to eliminate all known bugs before writing any new code.

Benefits of This Approach

There are a few important reasons for this approach:

It makes bugs cheaper to fix. The longer you wait to fix a bug, the more it will cost. When the code is still fresh in the programmer's mind, it's easy to address a bug. If a few days have gone by, the programmer will have to spend a little more time to remember what they were thinking when they wrote the code.

If a few months go by, it will take even longer. And if the bug fix is delayed until after the product ships, the cost to fix it will dramatically increase, since now support engineers are involved and the bug needs to be escalated to the development team. (McConnell, 2004)

It improves coding quality. Bugs are a form of negative feedback that keeps fast but sloppy development teams in check—but only if they're forced to fix them immediately. If the team doesn't work on new user stories until they've fixed all their bugs, they don't risk spreading half-done features throughout the product—they're too busy fixing bugs. If the development team ignores their bugs, they lose that regulation.

It also forces the team to learn from their mistakes and address any shortcomings with their software construction techniques. Fixing bugs as you go provides damage control because the earlier the team learns from their mistakes, the less likely they are to repeat those mistakes. (Maguire, 1993)

It makes your schedule more reliable. When the development team is asked to estimate how long it will take to code and test a new feature, they're usually pretty accurate, particularly by using the story point estimating approach I described earlier in this book.

When asked to estimate how long it will take to fix a bug, however, they're much less successful. Bugs are notoriously difficult to estimate.

If the search feature doesn't display results correctly on an iPhone, the developer needs to first figure out *why*. Only then can they fix it. Sometimes the root cause of a bug will be obvious and will take ten minutes to fix. Other times it will take *days*. No one knows until someone digs in.

If the product backlog is full of bugs in addition to user stories, it's extremely unlikely that the schedule forecast will be close to reality. There's too much unknown time required to fix all of those bugs.

If instead the backlog consists solely of user stories with story point estimates, the schedule will be much more accurate—as much as plus or minus 10%, as I described in Section 21.4.

It gives you more power and flexibility. I've talked a lot in this book about the concept of producing a shippable product increment at the end of each sprint. This supports the principle that the product owner can say "go" at any time, and the next sprint will be dedicated to getting the product out the door.

If there's 12 user stories left and 150 bugs, the product owner doesn't have that power. Worse, because no one knows how long it will take to fix all those bugs, when the product owner asks, "So when *can* we ship," all he'll get in return is blank stares and a few uncomfortable looks.

If there are *zero* bugs, he can ship the product at any time he chooses.

Is This Optional?

Adopting a zero-defect approach for your team is not only a good idea—in my opinion it's required.

Otherwise the entire process falls apart. You'll never be able to predict when the product will be done, and you won't be able to respond to changing business conditions because it will never be in a shippable state.

You might as well write, "I don't know" across your forehead, for all the times someone will ask you, "When can we ship?"

27.2 How to Create a Zero-Defects Culture

The good news is there are only a few simple things the Scrum team needs to do in order to adopt a zero-defects philosophy and build a related culture around this approach:

- The development team presents fully-tested and bug-free user stories to the product owner.

- The product owner rejects any user stories that contain known bugs.

- The product owner places any bugs discovered in previously-accepted user stories at the top of the product backlog.

By the product owner rejecting user stories that contain bugs, the development team is forced to self-correct, because they're not allowed to call the story "done" until it's bug-free.

The beauty of this approach is it's self-correcting. If the development team does a terrible job of testing, they'll end up with stories that have a bunch of bugs.

Their velocity will suffer because they can't "get credit" for the user story until the product owner accepts it.

The development team will have no choice but to improve because of this negative feedback loop. If the team struggles with how to improve, this is a great place for servant leaders to help, as I described in Section 15.3.

To figure out what they need to do to improve, the development team will have to take a hard look in the mirror at the subsequent sprint retrospective and talk about what they need to do differently to avoid bugs making it to the product owner or beyond.

27.3 Using a Standard Bug Format to Effectively Document Defects

Before I walk you through how to deal with bugs, I'd like to talk about how to document them.

This may seem like a trivial topic. You may think, "I know how to write a description of a bug, what's the big deal?"

The big deal is the inordinate amount of wasted time I've seen team members introduce due to bugs that weren't properly documented. If developers don't have enough details, they might not be equipped to fix the bug effectively.

For example, Ellen runs into Adam in the hall and asks, "Hey, did you get that bug fixed? I see it's closed."

Adam thinks for a minute and says, "Oh yeah. I looked at that yesterday afternoon. I couldn't reproduce it, so I just closed it."

Ellen, looking a little perplexed, says, "That was a pretty important bug. Why didn't you ask me about it?"

"I spent about an hour and couldn't get the bug to occur, and I didn't want to bother you," replies Adam.

I've seen this happen time and time again. Programmers tend to throw up their hands and give up if they don't have enough information about a bug.

The Scrum approach of focusing on personal interaction *should* make this problem go away, but I've found it's a big help if the bug is properly documented at the time it's discovered.

I suggest a simple format, which fully explains the steps the tester took to cause the bug, what happened, and what they *expected* to happen.

This is the format I've used successfully with my teams for the last 20+ years:

Tax incorrect in the shopping cart if the customer is in Alameda, CA

Steps to reproduce:
1. Add the Toy Carousel sample product to the shopping cart.
2. Start the checkout process and select John Jones, a customer in Alameda, CA.
3. Continue to the payment page.

Result: Total tax is $1.87

Expected result: Total tax is $2.38

Notes: Total tax should be $2.38 because the tax rate in Alameda, CA is 9.25%. It looks like we're using the statewide California tax rate of 7.25%.

The format I recommend for documenting bugs.

A Good Title Saves Time

Succinctly summarizing the bug makes it easier for the product owner to determine how severe it is and helps the entire Scrum team remember what it is they need to fix.

Checkout isn't working right sounds pretty ominous. However, if that bug is re-written as *Complete Purchase button isn't aligned on last page of checkout*, then it's obvious there's no reason to panic, and the product owner understands how to treat the bug.

Using a consistent format for the title of each bug keeps the level of clarity high. I suggest the following:

[result] when/on [action or location] if [condition]

Where:

- *Result* is the behavior the tester saw that made them think, "This looks like a bug."

- *Action or location* is a short description of the action taken to get the bug to happen ("when"), or the screen/page where the bug appeared ("on").

- *Condition* is an optional portion that is used when the bug only appears under certain circumstances. It's helpful to the developers if you can isolate the specific conditions that make the bug happen and include that in the bug title. It can also help the product owner understand how serious the bug is. If it only occurs on a 5-year-old browser version, that's helpful information.

Examples include:

No warning shown when I delete a user if they are inactive

Vertical lines appear on the shipping page if I use Microsoft Edge

"Invalid use of null" error when I edit and save an existing customer

Notice in the last example the specific error message, *Invalid use of null*, shown in quotes. I've found over the years that including the text of an error message displayed to the user—or at least the first few words of the message—helps everyone understand a little more about the bug.

This can be especially helpful if the same error message is shown in different areas of the application, which may indicate a widespread defect with the same root cause. This might not be as evident if the error message is omitted.

If a Bug Can't be Reproduced, It Will Be Difficult to Fix and Re-Test

Finding the root cause of a bug is usually the riskiest part of fixing it, and that task is made dramatically easier if the programmer can reproduce it to see what's happening behind the scenes.

Ideally, whoever discovers the bug spends a little time to reproduce it, and carefully documents the steps they used to get it to occur. This provides value to the programmer as well as the team member who will re-test it once fixed to make sure it was, in fact, resolved.

It's important to capture the steps right when the bug is discovered, because whoever is reporting the bug may not remember later what they did to get it to happen.

It's Important to Understand Why It's a Bug

Another issue I've seen is when the bug is supposedly fixed but when it's re-tested, it's discovered that although the behavior is different, it's still not quite right.

It's important to describe both the current, incorrect behavior of the product, as well as what the reporter of the bug *expected* to happen. To capture this information, I recommend including two sections in addition to the title and steps to reproduce: *result* and *expected result*.

A benefit of including both pieces of information is to make sure the bug wasn't a *requirements bug*.

A requirements bug is when the behavior is exactly what the original user story spelled out, but when the tester used the feature, they thought the behavior was wrong.

If this happens, team members can have a discussion with the product owner to determine the correct desired behavior.

Sometimes the bug can just be deleted because the product owner confirms the current behavior is in fact correct. Then they can talk about what caused the tester to think it was a bug and work to clarify that sort of problem in the future.

Adding Some Color Commentary Can Also Be Helpful

At first glance, I may not know why the reporter of the bug thinks the total should be $2.38. If there's a chance for confusion or someone asking, "Why," I recommend adding some additional detail, in the form of a *notes* section.

My example at the beginning of this section is a particularly subtle bug due to the wide variation in tax rates in California. The note clarifies what the tester thinks is happening under the covers: *Total tax should be $2.38 because the tax rate in Alameda, CA is 9.25%. It looks like we're using the statewide California tax rate of 7.25%.*

Testers often have an "aha!" moment when they discover a bug because that's what most of them enjoy—figuring out subtle combinations of circumstances that lead to a bug. Adding notes to the bug lets them capture this insight.

Including this type of note will often save the programmer who's fixing the bug a lot of time because they can skip the detective process of thinking about what might be causing the variation between the result and the expected result.

Does This Violate the Agile Manifesto Principle of "Working Software over Comprehensive Documentation?"

I'm all for keeping documentation lightweight and sticking with the simplest thing that can possibly work. In this case, decades of experience tell me that this level of documentation *is* the simplest thing that can possibly work.

The key is this information helps *everyone* who's involved: It helps the product owner understand the nature of the bug. It helps the programmer fix the bug quickly and apply the *correct* fix. And it helps whoever is re-testing the bug to ensure it's been properly addressed.

It would be great if everyone could keep these fine-grained details in their heads, but in my experience, that doesn't work in practice. Capturing this information serves as a reminder to everyone—the original reporter of the bug included—of the nature of the defect.

This is an area where I wouldn't skimp on writing this information down, "Because we're not supposed to do a bunch of documentation now that we're agile."

27.4 How Nasty Is It? Using Priority and Severity to Classify Bugs

Many times, the nature of a bug is self-evident. If the support team comes and tells the Scrum team a customer is "dead in the water," it's probably pretty severe.

On the other hand, if it's a minor layout issue on one screen that no one except a visual designer would notice, it's mild.

However, there are shades of gray in between, so some teams find it's helpful to assign a priority and/or severity to each bug to help everyone understand its nature.

Priority relates to how important it is to get the bug fixed quickly, whereas *severity* speaks to the level of impact on the usability of the product.

Priority tends to be business-focused, whereas severity is more technical in nature. For example, a bug may not cause a major impact to the usability of the product (low severity) but may have a significant business impact (high priority).

Priority	Severity
• Business-focused • How important it is to fix the bug quickly	• More technical • Measure of impact on usability

Priority and severity are two attributes that can be added to bugs to help understand its effect on users.

An example is if the main dashboard page—the first page shown when every user logs in—has a significant visual issue that's obviously a mistake. Users might think, "These guys don't even care enough to make the dashboard look good. Is the rest of the product crappy, too?"

This bug doesn't interfere at all with the ability to use the product, but the effect on the customer is unacceptable. This bug would have a low severity but high priority.

Examples of Priority and Severity Combinations

Most of the time, high-severity bugs will also have a high priority, but not always. Here are some examples of how priority and severity can interact: (Ghahrai, n.d.)

Bug	Severity	Priority
500 error message shown when any user attempts to complete their purchase	High	High
Search results always empty if using Internet Explorer 6 on Windows XP	High	Low
Our company logo is half cut off on every page if using a mobile browser	Low	High
Privacy Policy page takes three seconds to load	Low	Low

Most of the time high-severity bugs will also have a high priority, but not always.

How Priority and Severity Can Be Useful

Since bugs in previously-accepted stories are always placed at the top of the product backlog, priority and severity aren't typically needed for deciding whether bugs are included in the list. However, they can help the product owner understand how to treat each bug and how much time to dedicate to fixing them.

Here are some ways priority and severity can be helpful:

The customer support team can use priority to communicate their feelings about the bug. The support team usually has a pretty good pulse on the customer base. When they interact with an end user about a bug, they can get a feel for the impact it's having on that user and assign a priority level before sending it along to the development team.

Priority can be used to drive business rules. The Scrum team might decide that the support team must always supply steps to reproduce before sending any but the highest-priority, "customer is dead in the water," bugs to the team. A critical-priority bug might mean that the current sprint needs to get interrupted until the customer is up and running.

During the release process, low-priority bugs could be deferred. As I'll talk about in a future chapter, lower-priority bugs that are discovered during the final release process might be added to a Release Notes document and "punted" to the next version as a way to balance the risk of touching the code—and possibly breaking something else—with the risk of those bugs being present.

Sample Priorities

Having a standard definition of each priority and severity is important, to keep everyone on the same page. (Michel, 2016)

You may already have a definition of bug priorities in your organization. If you don't, below is a sample set of definitions you can use. Adjust them as necessary to best fit your company and product:

Priority	Meaning
1: Blocker	Customer cannot use the product. Drop everything and fix immediately.
2: Critical	High impact to customer's ability to use the product or their perception of quality. Fix as quickly as possible, expending whatever effort is necessary.
3: Major	Moderate impact to customer's ability to use the product or their perception of quality. Fix quickly but monitor the level of effort required.
4: Minor	Low impact to customer's ability to use the product. Fix if it's quick and easy.
5: Trivial	Customer may never notice the bug. Do not fix.

Sample bug priorities based on business impact and desired timeframe to fix.

Sample Severities

Like priority, you may already have a severity classification system. If not, a sample is below, based primarily on the impact to usability and whether a workaround exists: (Sabourin, 2006)

Severity	Meaning
1: Critical	Critical functionality or the entire product is unusable. Includes crashes in critical areas of the product, destroyed data, critical performance issues, or incorrect numerical calculations.
2: Major	Feature is unusable, and no work around exists.
3: Minor	Feature is unusable, but a work around exists.
4: Trivial	Cosmetic issue that doesn't affect the use of the product.

Sample bug severities based on impact to usability and whether a workaround exists.

Should We Use Both Priority and Severity?

Using both priority and severity provides the most amount of insight, especially for bugs that come from the customer support team. This approach gives the product owner as much information as possible.

If you pick just one, priority is likely more valuable, since what matters most is the business impact of the bug, regardless of its severity.

27.5 Handling Bugs Introduced during the Sprint

If any bugs are discovered in a user story in the current sprint, it's not "done." I suggest a really simple way to deal with this type of bug. Using the format I described in Section 27.3, create a new subtask within the story.

The summary of the subtask will be the title of the bug, and the description will contain the steps to reproduce, result, expected result, and notes.

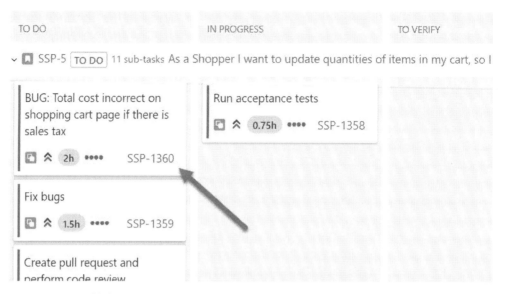

A subtask added to a user story in the current sprint, describing a bug found during testing.

Some teams find adding "BUG" to the beginning of the subtask summary makes it more obvious that this is not part of the original plan to get the user story done.

Once the subtask is created, the team should assign an hour estimate to troubleshoot, fix, and re-test the bug. This can be discussed among team members when the bug is initially discovered, or during the next daily scrum.

The sprint task board can then be used to manage the progress of the bug fix:

- *To Do.* Work to fix the bug is not yet started.

- *In Progress.* Troubleshooting and fixing is underway.

- *To Verify.* The bug has been fixed and is ready for another team member to test. If it's still not working, it goes back to the In Progress column. Adding a comment to the subtask is often helpful to remember why it's still not fixed.

- *Done.* The bug has been fixed and re-tested, and has been eliminated.

Don't Forget a Failing Unit Test

Sometimes developers are quick to fix a bug without adding a unit test. The problem with this approach is it doesn't prevent the bug from being detected if it returns. I like to say that once a bug is fixed, it should *never* come back.

I recommend the developer writes a unit test *before fixing the bug* and making sure it fails. If a unit test is written after the bug is fixed, there's no way to verify that it will, in fact, fail if the bug is present. Writing a failing unit test first ensures the bug will be detected. (Osherove, 2014)

Sometimes a bug can't be covered by a unit test. For example, if a button is misaligned by five pixels, or the background is the wrong shade of green, it's difficult to write a unit test that would detect these kinds of issues. However, visual bugs like these are usually a) not something that will cause a customer to not be able to use the product and b) easy to identify.

In contrast to a minor visual bug, think about my example about the incorrect tax calculation. That type of bug will be very difficult to detect unless someone happens to perform that specific scenario.

This is the application of a unit test—let the computer do the work of testing all possible tax calculations, which is too tedious and time consuming to do manually.

See Chapter 13 for more details about automated unit testing.

Sometimes a Bug is Not a Bug

If you've been in software development for any length of time, you've likely experienced a situation where a stakeholder looks at what's been coded and says, "I was thinking of something different," and therefore considers the code to have a bug.

If this happens when the product owner is reviewing a user story that the development team just spent a few days coding, testing, and getting just right, it may cause a serious interruption to the sprint.

This is one of the reasons it's so helpful having the product owner intimately involved in the day-to-day operation of the team; it's less likely that the team will get way out of sync with what is in his head.

That said, it sometimes happens. The product owner should think about a few questions.

How critical is it to make a change at this point? Is there a real threat to the usability of the product? Or is the new idea different, but not necessarily better?

It may be better to wait until real users get their hands on it before being too quick to make a change, or at minimum have some other people in the company try the feature and see what their reaction is.

If it turns out that a change is important, the product owner has three choices:

- *Change it now.* The product owner rejects the user story as not acceptable, and the development team makes the changes. The product owner should think long and hard about this choice, since it will likely threaten the ability for the team to complete all the other user stories in the sprint.

- *Descope the user story.* The product owner might say, "I hate to say it, but this just doesn't feel like the right behavior. I'm going to pull the story out of the sprint and think about it some more and maybe talk to some stakeholders and customers." This stops the story dead in its tracks and allows the product owner to regroup. This is a nice option because it lets the team continue on with the balance of the product backlog items in the current sprint.

- *Add a new user story to revise the functionality.* If the product owner thinks the story is acceptable, but could be better, they can add a new user story to the product backlog to enhance it. This is a good approach because it allows the story to be completed and gets it into the hands of users, so feedback can be collected. It might be that the new user story is never implemented because they think the behavior is just fine.

This is an area where the ScrumMaster can help coach the product owner, to help them understand their options as well as ensure the team is protected. The ScrumMaster can also make sure this problem is raised during the retrospective to figure out how to enhance communication between the product owner and the development team to avoid this type of issue in the future.

27.6 Newly-Discovered Bugs That Existed at the Start of the Sprint

Sometimes when the team is working on new user stories, a bug is discovered in a previously-completed user story. Nobody's perfect, so sometimes bugs will slip through the cracks, even though the development team is religiously writing unit tests and manually testing to make sure everything is right.

It's important to prevent the development team from getting distracted, so I suggest adding a bug to the top of the product backlog instead of the development team fixing it immediately.

The benefit of this approach is it avoids the development team getting sucked into fixing bugs that existed before they started the sprint, and therefore are out of scope. They volunteered to complete a set of product backlog items that *didn't* include those preexisting bugs.

Checking to See if the Bug Existed at the Start of the Sprint

Sometimes the team isn't sure if the bug was introduced in the current sprint. Whenever there's a question, the tester should go back to the shippable increment from the prior sprint and see if they can duplicate the bug there.

The easiest way to do this is by using the product owner environment if no new user stories have been added to it. Or they can use a *demo* environment, to which the product is deployed after the end of each sprint.

If the bug *did* exist, it means it *wasn't* introduced during this sprint. This is an important distinction, because I suggest treating bugs differently based on whether they were introduced in the current sprint, or they existed at the start of the sprint:

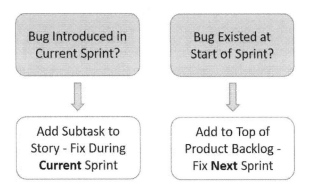

It's important to determine when a newly-discovered bug was introduced, so it can be treated accordingly.

- *Introduced in current sprint.* If a bug was introduced in the current sprint, it needs to be fixed as part of driving the related user story to "done," so a subtask for the bug should be added to the story. See Section 27.5 for details.

- *Existed at start of sprint.* If a bug existed at the start of the sprint, that means it's out of scope and should be added to the product backlog as a new bug.

I strongly suggest those new bugs on the backlog are fixed at the beginning of the next sprint, before writing any new code. This supports the zero-defects culture I described in Section 27.2.

27.7 Dealing with a Customer Issue Caused by a Critical Bug

Sometimes pushing off a preexisting bug to the next sprint doesn't work. As much as we'd like to say, "Wait until next sprint" when an existing defect is discovered, sometimes a "drop everything" bug comes up.

The customer support team may reach out and say, "ACME, Inc. is dead in the water. We've done all we can, but we can't get it working. We need to escalate this to your team and get it fixed *now*."

If this happens there isn't much of a choice—the team needs to deal with it.

I suggest the following tips to help minimize the interruption to the team's work on the scope of the sprint:

Contain the effort. It's not usually necessary for the *entire* development team to become involved in getting the customer up and running. Two team members can volunteer to take the lead, and they can tap into other team members if necessary. I like two team members as opposed to one, so they can feed off each other as they work through the problem. This will typically result in a faster resolution.

I'm a fan of an "all-hands-on-deck" approach to help a customer that's dead in the water, but not if two people are working and five are watching them and not adding anything to the effort. Using only a portion of the team keeps at least some momentum on the work of the sprint.

Get the customer up and running now and fix the root cause in the next sprint. Sometimes it's possible to patch the customer and get them up and running and defer the bug fix to the next sprint, minimizing the interruption to the team's work.

For example, a bug caused some bad data to be written to the database. It may be possible to create a script to fix up the database, which will get the customer up and running. Then the bug that created the bad data can be fixed in the next sprint.

Another option is to find some sort of work-around that will let the customer accomplish their goal while waiting for the real solution in the form of a bug fix.

A benefit of this approach is it's usually faster to apply a short-term patch or workaround than to fully troubleshoot, test, and deploy the bug fix. This gets the customer happier more quickly and reduces the unplanned interruption for the team.

Add a task to the sprint and bug to the product backlog. If it's possible to get the customer running and fix the bug next sprint, as I described in the previous bullet, I recommend adding a task to the top of the sprint backlog of the current sprint. Subtasks that outline the plan to get the workaround applied can be added to the task. A bug is also added to the top of the product backlog to get the root cause addressed next sprint.

If no patch or workaround is possible, then a bug should be added to the top of the sprint backlog, with appropriate subtasks to fix, test, and deploy the bug fix.

Use a hotfix branch for the bug fix. When fixing the critical bug, the team has two choices. They can fix the bug in the current codebase they're working on, or they can make what I call a *surgical* fix to the code that's currently in production. If they choose the former, the problem is they'll be saddled with testing new, unshipped code, or finding a way to turn it off. In either case, that will take more time and delay the deployment of the bug fix.

I recommend the second option—the surgical approach. By using a *hotfix branch*, the team can make a "virtual copy" of the current production code, apply the specific bug fix, and retest just those changes. They can then deploy that new code—with just the surgical fix—to production.

See *Hotfix Branches* in Section 12.5 for more details.

The product owner should be ready to descope some work. The product owner must realize that when faced with this kind of situation, they need to negotiate with the development team because they need to modify the scope of the sprint. In a true crisis situation, the development team should be on board with taking on the work to get the customer running, but they should also expect the product owner to remove an equivalent amount of scope once the dust settles.

Typically, this is in the form of removing the lowest-priority user story or two. I recommend doing this only after the customer is up and running, to avoid the distraction and to get the problem solved as quickly as possible.

Another benefit is everyone will know how much time it took to solve the issue, so they'll understand how much scope needs to be removed.

Process to address a critical customer issue caused by a bug.

Using these tips will ensure the customer gets the attention they need while doing everything possible to keep the sprint moving along.

27.8 Timeboxing the Bug-Fixing Effort

The problem with any but the most trivial bugs is they're difficult to accurately estimate. (Weiss, et al., 2007) As I discussed in Section 27.1, any open bugs introduce schedule risk and is one of the main reasons you want to fix bugs before writing new code.

Because some bugs can take a long time to fix, there's a risk that a developer latches on to a particularly thorny bug and, responding to the challenge, chases it for hours on end.

It's been more than once that I've thought, "You spent *how much* time on this? Holy smokes! This bug was really only worth fixing if you could address it in an hour!"

That was after learning a developer had spent an *entire day* trying to figure it out.

Sometimes It's Not Worth It

Sit down because I'm going to tell you something that disturbs a lot of people: sometimes it's not worth fixing a bug.

How can I say this when I just got done telling you to make sure the developers fix all the bugs before writing new code? It's because, as one of my business colleagues likes to say, "The juice isn't worth the squeeze."

If the team discovers a bug that results in a minor visual issue on the screen, but it only happens in a five-year-old version of Internet Explorer running on Windows XP, and only on Saturday mornings during a leap year and…well, you get the picture. It's probably not worth a lot of time to fix this kind of bug. It may not be worth *any* time.

On the other hand, if any time a user attempts to edit their shopping cart the items in the cart are deleted, it doesn't matter *how* long it takes. The team needs to fix the bug, even if two developers spend two days on it.

Just to be clear, I'm not saying, "Don't fix any annoying bugs." What I'm saying is, "Think carefully about whether the business value derived from fixing this bug with anything more than a couple hours of effort outweighs the risk of leaving the bug in the product."

Here are some reasons a bug might not be worth more than an hour or two to fix:

It has very low impact on the product's usability. A very minor visual glitch that only the user experience designer on the team notices is a good example of a low-impact bug.

I like to ask the question, "Will this bug make a customer question their purchase, or leave them with a bad enough impression that they'll tell someone that our product isn't that good?" If the answer is, "I highly doubt it," that may be a situation where you want to limit the amount of time for the bug fix.

It doesn't impact a sizeable portion of your user base. As distasteful it may be to the customer encountering the bug, if they are one of 5,000 other customers—none of whom are experiencing the issue—it may not be worth a lot of time. On the other hand, if a bug is affecting 4,000 out of your 5,000 customers, that's a different story. A much larger investment will be necessary to get it fixed.

That said, if the one customer encountering the bug is your most important, this argument goes out the window. You need to keep them happy.

If it's a critical bug that results in not being able to use the system, that's a different story as well. There's really no choice in that case; the product needs to *fundamentally work*.

It's rare. If the bug is caused by a very specific set of steps or occurs due to a rare combination of environmental factors—such as my Windows XP example above—it's likely only worth a small effort to fix.

What's It Worth to You?

This kind of situation is where the product owner role really shines. They're the only person who is in a position to decide how much time should be spent on the bug fix. Only they have visibility both into the business side of the equation and what the development team faces with respect to fixing the bug.

For any bug that's not a simple fix, I recommend the product owner specifies a "not to exceed" timebox.

For example, if the development team says, "That's really easy. I think I can fix that in about 5 minutes," I wouldn't worry too much about a timebox.

However, if the reaction is more along the lines of, "Huh. Yeah, I have *no freakin' clue* what would be causing that. I'll have to dig in." Any time a product owner hears, "I don't know," or "I have no clue," that's an immediate indication that the effort could spin off into infinity.

This is a critical moment for the product owner. He should assume that if the developers don't know, it will take *days* to fix the bug.

I'm not saying a black hole is likely for every bug. However, if the product owner doesn't put a box around the effort, developers have a tendency to spend an unimaginable amount of time working the problem. Like a bloodhound that gets a scent, they'll get sucked in and suddenly three-quarters of a day has gone by and they forgot to eat lunch.

The product owner can say something like, "How about you timebox this to four hours? That's an important bug to fix, but not if it's going to take days on end."

This keeps control over the amount of time—and money—spent to fix each bug firmly in the hands of the product owner. Since they own the ROI of the team's efforts, this is what you want.

Work Bugs One Hour at a Time

Many times, fixing bugs is not entirely cut and dry. There may not be a binary choice between "fixed" and "not fixed." Once a developer gets into the code, they may find that they don't know how to *completely* fix the bug. However, they can likely make it better.

For example, there may be a visual issue when displaying a web page on some browsers. Although the developer didn't completely get rid of the problem, they can improve the appearance.

If left to their own devices, the developer may spend another four hours in an attempt to make it *perfect*. However, the product owner might look at the results after an hour's worth of work and say, "That's good enough."

For this reason, our development teams have adopted a rule that says, "Spend no more than one hour at a time fixing a bug without updating the product owner on your progress."

By keeping the product owner in the loop, they can continually weigh the cost of the time spent so far against the current state of the bug. "Good enough" can save a heck of a lot of time and money. This guards against diminishing returns if the developer kept their head down without checking in.

Remember, to paraphrase Voltaire, *Perfect is the enemy of the good.*

27.9 What to Do with Bugs That You Won't Fix

If it turns out that developers spend the time dictated by the timebox, and they still haven't fixed the bug, it may be time to throw in the towel. The decision-making process is simple: the product owner just says, "It's not worth spending any more time on this."

Once the product owner decides to spend no more time on the bug, the bug should be closed and removed from the product backlog. It's often helpful to add some notes to the bug explaining why the decision was made not to fix it.

The Six-Month Rule

One thing to be careful about is saying, "Let's fix this later." If "later" is at some point between now and the product shipping, then I encourage you to *stop*, and fix the bug now.

I use a very unscientific rule for this:

- If you can live with this bug six months or longer, don't fix it. Just close it.

- If you can't live with it for six or more months, fix it now.

This prevents the team from finishing all the user stories for a specific release and being faced with a long list of bugs. At that point, they're not much better off than if they used waterfall. They have no idea how long it will take to ship because they don't know how long it will take to fix all the bugs.

Don't allow bugs to linger on the product backlog. They should either be fixed *now* or *never*.

But...Is This a Responsible Thing to Do?

You may be reading this and you're now aghast. "What the...? Is he saying that we should ship the product with *bugs in it*?"

That's exactly what I'm saying.

No product has *absolutely zero defects*. (Goodliffe, 2007) And yours likely doesn't need to be perfect, either.

Some products may need to be closer to bug-free than others. Avionics software for a passenger jet or the firmware for a medical device needs to be driven to a much higher level of quality than the MVP of a web application for a startup.

I'm not saying there should be any *glaring* bugs in the startup's product, but while they're driving it to absolute perfection, they'll be out of business because they haven't generated any revenue.

You must decide on your own what, "Can I ignore this bug for six months or longer" actually means for your product.

A product owner for a life sciences software product will likely say, "No" a lot more often than the entrepreneur in her basement who is just trying to survive long enough to get the product into the hands of paying customers.

What If the Product Owner Was Wrong?

Sometimes the product owner will make the wrong judgment call. As soon as the next release goes out the door, Murphy's Law kicks in and customers start calling about that bug the product owner decided to punt.

That's fine. Now they know, and the bug can be resurrected, placed back on the product backlog and fixed.

If it's a non-critical bug, I'd argue that it's much better to avoid a *known* cost of an extra day or two of a developer's time banging their head than the *possibility* that the bug may be more of an issue than was originally thought.

I encourage product owners to stick to their guns. Have the developers take a "do whatever it takes" attitude to the truly nasty bugs and cut them off when necessary on the less-risky bugs and move on. That decision can easily be rolled back if necessary.

27.10 Handling Bugs That Can't Be Reproduced

It's a fact of life of software development: it's a heck of a lot easier to fix a bug that can be reproduced with a series of steps. If a bug is difficult to reproduce—for example it seems to handle at random times with no set pattern—the challenge faced by a developer trying to fix it rises accordingly.

There are times when, no matter what series of steps are performed, the developer can't reproduce the bug.

Options for Unreproducible Bugs

Here are a few options to consider for bugs that can't be reproduced:

Examine the log file. If your product has an application log file, sometimes combing through it will help a developer uncover what's going on and permit fixing the bug.

Test more creatively. Using clues from the customer about what they were doing when the bug occurred, someone on the development team can try a bunch of different variations of actions within the application to see if they can get the bug to occur.

Some organizations leverage their customer support team to help with this kind of effort. They often have a unique perspective because they've talked to customers about the variety of issues they encounter and might have some ideas of how to get the bug to happen.

Add more logging and/or telemetry. In order to determine what's happening, developers can add additional logging or telemetry, which monitors the behavior of the user as they navigate their way through the system. This might capture the steps the user performed to get the bug to occur.

If the application is crashing, a cloud exception reporting tool can be used to capture information about the user and their environment when the crash occurs.

A tool such as Microsoft's Application Insights supports all of these options. Other similar tools are also available that the development team might find useful.

Increase the logging level temporarily. If a customer is having a particularly tough time, it might be possible to turn up the logging level for their usage of the application and see if the user can get the bug to occur. This adds much more detail to the application log as compared to the normal setting.

Turning up the volume of logging might make the application slightly slower, depending upon the logging technique used, but it may provide the necessary details for the development team to discover what's going on. This option may or may not be supported by your technology. For example, if you have a multi-tenant cloud application, your ability to increase logging just for one customer may be more limited than a stand-alone application or mobile app.

If you use this option, don't forget to reduce the logging level back to normal once you have the data you need!

Ignore it. If the bug doesn't have a high impact on the ability for users to get value from the product, the product owner could consider closing the bug with some comments from the developer added to it, describing what troubleshooting steps they performed. If the bug comes back over and over, or if someone discovers the steps to reproduce it, the bug can be resurrected and worked on again.

Unfortunately, this may not be an option if customers are complaining about the bug several times a day and support reps are giving developers the evil eye in the lunchroom.

Remember to Keep the Product Owner Informed

Like I discussed in Section 27.7, the product owner needs to be kept informed about the development team's efforts as they apply these ideas, so they can keep a constant eye on the amount of time being invested to ensure it's a worthwhile use of time given the circumstances surrounding the bug.

27.11 What to Do with a Legacy Bug List Inherited by the Team

If the team is starting in on a from-scratch clean-sheet effort, they are in the driver's seat. They just need to follow the guidance in this chapter to aggressively address any bugs that come up and keep the list at zero.

But what if your team has an existing bug list to deal with? It could be their own list that has been slowly growing over time, if they're adopting Scrum for their current product. Or they may have inherited a product from another team, delivered complete with 300 known defects.

How do you go from a list of hundreds of bugs to zero?

Let me point out that the team *must* come up with a plan to address the bug list. As I've said several times, they'll never have an accurate schedule if they are carrying around a list of open bugs. The team can't say, "Well, this is an exception, because we started with this list."

It needs to be driven to zero.

To do this, they have two choices:

- Fix them first.

- Address them over a fixed timeframe.

Fix Them First

The first option, and the one I prefer for reasons I'll talk about below, is to tackle the bug list head-on, not working on any user stories until the bug list is at zero.

I suggest the following process:

Triage the bug list. The product owner should go through the complete list with a fine-toothed comb and close any bugs that are duplicates, no longer apply because that area of the product has changed, or are small, nitpicky things that can be closed until, and unless, they come up again.

The product owner may not have enough context to do this process on their own, so they may need to ask a developer or two for some help on any bugs where they have questions. They may also need to talk to the customer support team to determine how customers are being affected by some of the bugs.

Reproduce each bug. Perhaps by asking for help from the customer support team, reproduce each bug that remains on the list. This serves two purposes. First, it ensures the bug still exists. Second, it ensures that it can be reproduced. Consider closing any non-reproducible bugs if they have a low impact on the ability to use the product. They'll come up again if they're being encountered often.

Force-rank the bugs. Order bugs based on priority to ensure the development team focuses first on the most important bugs.

Timebox each bug. Going through the list, decide on a maximum amount of time to be spent on fixing each bug. I suggest selecting one hour, two hours, or four hours.

If a bug has been sitting on a big list for a while, it's likely not a critical, "Drop everything and fix it, regardless of what it takes" type of defect. If you discover any critical bugs, move them to the top of the list and consider using a larger timebox, for example eight hours or even multiple days.

Work through the list. Using the sprint planning process I outlined in Chapter 25, the development team takes on as many bugs they feel comfortable with each sprint, and they work through the list until no more remain.

Process to address an existing bug list before working on new user stories.

As you probably already figured out, because bugs don't get story point estimates, the team's velocity will be zero until they get through the bug list.

They are *not* producing new business value; they're realizing business value the organization thought it already had—after all, everyone *thought* they were selling a high-quality product—by paying off the technical debt they inherited.

Address Them over Several Sprints

Another option is to take on a certain number of bugs each sprint until the list is at zero.

I would recommend splitting up the list in a way that allows all bugs to be addressed in three to five sprints if possible. Remember that you can't have an accurate schedule until the bug list is at zero, so you don't want to wait any longer than necessary.

Should We Assign Story Point Estimates to Fixing a Batch of Bugs?

Some teams will write user stories to address the bugs, for example, "As a shopper, I want 15 bugs fixed, so the product is more stable." In this case story points *would* get assigned and a velocity would be generated. (Cohn, 2010c)

I'm not a huge fan of this approach, for two reasons. First, as I mentioned before, it's difficult to estimate bugs. Attempting to assign a story point estimate to a "fix a bunch of bugs" user story runs the risk of the team saying, "We need to spend time digging into these to see how hard they will be to fix." That defeats the purpose of rapid estimation using story points.

Second, it confuses the meaning of a user story. Does a user story to fix a bunch of bugs deliver *new, incremental value* to stakeholders? I guess you could argue a more stable product delivers more value, but it's not *new*. As I pointed out earlier, fixing bugs is completing an earlier promise of functionality that supposedly works, not delivering *new* value.

Risks of Spreading Bug Fixing Over Time

There are two risks to think about before spreading the bug fixing out over time, as opposed to fixing all the important bugs first:

- *It may make user stories difficult to estimate.* When the development team starts working on a user story, they may find one or more old bugs from the list impact the story's functionality. Because user stories aren't considered "done" until its related functionality is bug-free, the team may be forced to fix old bugs, which may make it more difficult to plan the work for the user story during sprint planning.

- *Fixing a bug may break newly-added functionality.* If the development team completes ten new user stories over the course of the first few sprints as they continue to fix bugs, the bug fixes they're applying may break one or more of those stories, increasing the amount of work they have on their plate.

This is why I prefer the "clean slate" approach of aggressively triaging the list and fixing them all, before tackling any new user stories.

Key Takeaways

- Unless your bug count is always at zero, the product is not shippable and your schedule is inaccurate due to the unpredictable nature of how much time it takes to fix each bug. I recommend a "fix bugs first" approach; if there are any known bugs, they need to be fixed at the beginning of each sprint, before working on new user stories.

- To keep the bug list at zero, all bugs in any new user story must be fixed before it's accepted by the product owner. If any bugs are discovered in previously-accepted user stories, they must be at the top of the product backlog and fixed at the start of the next sprint.

- When a bug is discovered in a user story in the current sprint, add a subtask to the story. I like to add "BUG" to the beginning of the subtask name and use the standard bug format to document the bug. This subtask needs to be completed—meaning the bug is fixed and re-tested—before the user story is considered "done."

- If a bug is discovered that existed at the start of the sprint, document it using the standard format by adding a bug to the product backlog. This prevents the development team from getting distracted from their current sprint commitment. The exception is if the presence of the preexisting bug affects a user story in the current sprint. In that case, the bug will need to be fixed in the current sprint to drive the user story to "done."

- Effectively documenting bugs is critical to ensure proper communication as well as facilitating re-testing the bug to ensure it's been fixed. Use a standard format for the title, and include steps to reproduce, the result, expected result, and any notes.

- The standard format for the title of the bug helps everyone—especially the product owner—understand it. I've found this format particularly useful: [result] when/on [action or location] if [condition].

- Priority and severity can be helpful to classify bugs. Priority relates to the business impact of the bug—how important it is to get it fixed quickly. Severity speaks to the level of impact on usability of the product due to the bug.

- If a critical customer issue comes up during the current sprint that just can't wait, I recommend getting the customer up and running—for example with a script to fix some bad data in their database or a workaround—then fix the root cause of the bug during the next sprint. This will keep the interruption to the work of the current sprint to a minimum while getting the customer un-stuck and up and running.

- *Timeboxing* is a technique that can be applied to the bug-fixing effort. The product owner decides how many hours is "worth it" to them to fix the bug and limits the effort to that amount of time. Some bugs may be worth fixing if it takes an hour or two, but not if it takes five days.

- Working bugs one hour at a time and checking in with the product owner throughout the day, avoids driving to a perfect solution when a "good enough" solution will suffice. Sometimes a developer can spend one hour on a bug to get it working to a level that's acceptable to the product owner, as opposed to three days for a *perfect* solution.

- Be careful to avoid, "We'll just fix it later." If the product owner can't live with the bug for six months or longer, fix it at the start of the next sprint. If the product owner decides to not fix a bug, close it; don't leave it gathering dust on the product backlog.

- Sometimes bugs can't be reproduced. In this case additional testing can be done to try isolating the steps to reproduce it, logs can be examined, and additional instrumentation can be added to gain more insight if it happens again.

- If the team inherits a legacy bug list, they have two choices: fix them all now or fix them over time. I recommend fixing the bugs now, after carefully triaging them to get rid of any that are outdated or aren't worth spending time on. Do *not* allow legacy bugs to hang around longer than a few sprints, as the product won't be shippable and your schedule will be useless.

Chapter 28
Providing Transparency and Getting Feedback with the Sprint Review

It's really hard to design products by focus groups. A lot of times, people don't know what they want until you show it to them.

- **Steve Jobs**

Trust is a fragile commodity.

Most business leaders, stakeholders, and users want to place unconditional faith in the development team, assuming they will build the product they want. They assume they have accurately and completely transferred their wants, needs, and desires, and can sit back while the team toils away for months and creates the anticipated masterpiece.

This is a poor assumption.

There's actually a *second* bad assumption. Stakeholders also assume they *know* what they want. What we find in reality is they don't *really* know until they sit down and use the product. (Gócza, n.d.)

Many development teams have experienced the heartbreak of working for months or even years on a product, building exactly what customers asked for, then showing it to them and hearing, "That's not what I wanted." There's nothing that will kill trust faster than business leaders investing hundreds of thousands if not millions of dollars into a development effort, only to be faced with a complete "do-over" when it doesn't meet user needs.

You shouldn't stop asking customers and other business stakeholders what they want—unless you're the next Steve Jobs, you likely can't get away with that—but you should *check in with them regularly* to make sure you're on the right track and *let them use the product as it's being built*.

Scrum has an elegant way to address all the issues I outlined above: the sprint review.

Held religiously at the end of each iteration, this ceremony provides transparency for everyone to inspect the product increment, see exactly what progress has been made via a demonstration of new, shippable functionality, and have an opportunity to collaborate with the development team to help guide work moving forward. (Rubin, 2013)

Once the sprint review concludes, the product increment can be deployed to a demo environment so stakeholders can use it.

28.1 Who Should Be Invited to the Sprint Review?

The first thing to think about when planning the sprint review is who should be on the invite list.

First on the list is the entire Scrum team. It's important for the whole team to hear feedback directly from stakeholders. This helps avoid a series of follow-up conversations that start something like, "During sprint review, we heard…"

It's much more efficient for the team to hear feedback firsthand than to rely on secondhand accounts.

Deciding about inviting other attendees is up to the product owner. At minimum, key stakeholders should attend. (Schwaber & Sutherland, 2017)

Who's a stakeholder? According to the Project Management Institute, "A stakeholder is an individual, group, or organization who may affect, be affected by, or perceive itself to be affected by a decision, activity, or outcome of a project." (Project Management Institute, 2013)

My unscientific rule of thumb? A stakeholder is anyone who will be pissed off if they see the product in three months and it's not what they expected, and they wonder why they weren't involved sooner.

Invite the World

Many teams find that inviting others to the sprint review can pay dividends to keep people up to date with their progress. This helps avoid "status meetings" with the sole purpose to answer the question, "How's it coming along?"

As a rule, "invite the world." Those who are interested will show up. (Rubin, 2013)

You might consider inviting the following:

Members of other development teams. In many companies, the work of one team will impact the work of other teams. Inviting other teams is a good way to keep them up to speed with what's going on. Even if there isn't a lot of overlap with their work, it's often nice for them to know what others in the company are working on.

Customer support reps. Most support team members like to know what's coming in future releases of the product. They also typically have a pulse on the user base and can be a source of great intel about what customers are thinking.

Implementers and trainers. Your front-line team members who implement the product and train users also have a wealth of knowledge and insight into the needs of customers. Keeping them up to date with what's coming and getting feedback along the way can be immensely valuable.

Sales and marketing. The sales and marketing team is always excited to see progress on the product. Common complaints I've heard when they don't have this kind of visibility are: "The development team isn't doing much," or, "The developers aren't working on the most important stuff." Usually this is just because they don't have any visibility into what's going on.

They also *love* that the product is usable at the end of each sprint and can often use the demo environment to leverage completed features in their sales process, especially if a prospect or customer is waiting for a specific feature. Because the product is at a shippable level of quality, gone are the days of them showing half-baked features that are months away from being done.

Management. Involving management is critical. Without visible progress, it's easy for managers to either assume the product is coming along more quickly than it is or assume the opposite—that it's not coming along quickly at all. By attending sprint reviews, they know exactly what's going on.

They can also gain more insight about issues the team is facing. They may have already heard about their challenges but attending the sprint review and learning firsthand how the team is being slowed down can drive the point home more forcefully, resulting in a faster resolution.

It's Not for the Product Owner

I've heard some teams say, "The sprint review is for the product owner, so we just need the Scrum team to attend."

Usually when I hear this, it's a symptom of a lack of understanding of the sprint review. The review is for those *outside* the Scrum team. The product owner should be involved throughout the entire sprint, reviewing and accepting or rejecting product backlog items as they're completed.

The opposite is the development team working for the entire sprint and showing the product owner the results at the end. This can cause a major problem if the work the development team completed isn't at the right level of quality or doesn't match what the product owner wanted.

In this situation, usually one of two things happens:

The product owner lowers their standards. Few product owners want to learn at the *very end* of the sprint that things aren't quite right. All too often, the product owner feels pressure to lower their standards and say, "It's good enough."

They *could* reject the work, but then the team will have nothing to show for their sprint's worth of effort. Their velocity will be zero.

There's a move toward Scrummerfall. If the product owner *doesn't* accept the work, and the development team addresses the issues during the next sprint, they've just introduced "Scrummerfall"—a combination of Scrum and waterfall. They're completing work in one sprint and making it right in the next, as opposed to creating a potentially shippable product increment *every* sprint.

28.2 Selecting the Best Sprint Review Duration, Day, and Time

The Scrum Guide provides a guideline of a four-hour maximum duration for a one-month sprint. (Schwaber & Sutherland, 2017) Extrapolating that guidance for a two-week sprint means a two-hour sprint review. I personally feel that's a little long.

One of the principles of a good sprint review is it shouldn't cause a major interruption to the sprint. Instead it should be a natural result of the iteration—part of "wrapping things up." (Cohn, 2004) Two hours feels to me like it flies in the face of this concept.

I recommend a one-hour sprint review for a two-week sprint. This keeps things moving along and—combating a challenge faced by many teams—it makes it much easier to schedule. This is especially helpful for getting busy members of the management team to attend regularly.

Late on the Last Day of the Sprint Is Ideal

As much as the team will try to avoid it, human nature often takes its toll and they're scrambling at the end of the sprint to get everything done. This can cause problems if the sprint review is early on the last day of the sprint.

The other problem with an early start is the rest of the day is often lost. Few teams effectively do a sprint review in the morning and recover enough mental energy to do several hours of sprint planning in the afternoon. For example, if the sprint review is scheduled for 9 a.m., the team will lose more than half the day.

9:00 a.m. Sprint Review	10:00 a.m. Retrospective	11:00 a.m. "Lost" Time for the Rest of the Day

Early sprint reviews often result in lost time.

I'm a big fan of giving the team a break after sprint review, but when most of the last day is outside the structure of a sprint, time-wasting activities tend to creep in.

Having a sprint review early in the afternoon, followed by a retrospective, is a great way to wrap things up and drive a feeling of being "done" with the sprint. I like to encourage the Scrum team to take the rest of the day off and recharge their batteries.

Some teams go out together and do some bonding, whether it's grabbing a couple of beers or going bowling. Other teams like to do their own thing.

Some may want to spend time with family or go out with friends. Others might stay at the office and work on a personal programming project.

9:00 a.m. Wrapping Up Sprint Work	1:00 p.m. Sprint Review	2:00 p.m. Retrospective	3:00 p.m. Team Time Off for the Rest of the Day

I like sprint reviews in the early afternoon, so the team can wrap up and take the rest of the day off and rest up for the start of the next sprint.

A side note for non-technical readers: Many developers like to spend their spare time coding *for fun*—typically on a pet project using a new technology—so don't try to force them off their computer if they're not working on the product. They're probably excited to have the opportunity to spend some focused time without anyone bothering them.

Accommodate Multiple Time Zones If You Can

Many Scrum teams have one or more team members in a different time zone—sometimes offset by several hours. It's often easy to omit those team members from sprint reviews, but if they can never attend, they lose the insight they'd gain by hearing feedback directly from stakeholders.

I'd do your best to schedule sprint reviews at a time when offshore team members can attend. For team members in time zones ahead of you, that may mean the sprint review is earlier in the day—perhaps even earlier than I recommend. If it's a choice between an afternoon sprint review without the entire team, and an earlier sprint review that everyone could attend, I'd choose the latter.

This is another reason to keep the time zone differential as small as possible among members of the same team. As I talked about in Section 17.9, I recommend doing everything you can to ensure at least four to six hours of overlap in daily working hours. That should give you the ability to schedule a sprint review near the middle of the day, which will still provide a few hours of wrap-up the morning of the sprint review.

Rescheduling the Sprint Review

A product owner or ScrumMaster sometimes gets a last-minute message along the lines of, "Hey, Ellen. I'm afraid something has come up. I won't be able to make it to the sprint review. Can we reschedule it?"

To the greatest extent possible, stick with the scheduled time for the sprint review, even if some people can't make it. Everyone on the team is building to a known end of the sprint, and the start of the sprint review is a final "pencils down" time. Everything is either done at the start of the sprint review, or not.

If a critical stakeholder can't attend, the product owner or ScrumMaster could offer to follow up with them separately and talk through what the team accomplished.

Sometimes a sprint review does need to be rescheduled. For example, if you are building a custom product for a client and the key decision-maker can't attend, it might make sense to reschedule the review in that case. (Cohn, 2016a)

Don't Extend the Sprint

If the sprint review does get rescheduled, it's easy to assume that the sprint should be extended as well.

Don't do it.

It's critical to keep a consistent rhythm and cadence to each sprint, since the key metric of a Scrum team is velocity. If the duration of each sprint varies, that metric becomes less meaningful. (Billings, 2017)

It's also helpful for the team to have a constant rhythm. If the sprint length varies, team members are often a little unsure of the schedule. "Remind me, when does this sprint end?" (Cohn, 2017b)

Even if the sprint review gets rescheduled—which should be very infrequent—keep the end day and time of the sprint intact.

28.3 Preparing for the Sprint Review

Getting ready for the sprint review shouldn't be a major production. The review should be a natural conclusion to the sprint, as opposed to a day-long interruption causing the entire Scrum team to stop working so they can prepare.

If the team is spending more time thinking about the mechanics of the sprint review than finishing as much as they can during the last day of the sprint, it may be time to scale back the prep work.

Two Hours Max Prep Time

Sprint reviews should require no more than two hours of preparation. (Cohn, 2014d) For a two-week sprint, it's oftentimes less.

Typical prep work includes reviewing completed user stories and thinking through how to demonstrate them. Doing a practice run through the demo steps is usually a good idea, to ensure everything is working correctly and to avoid stumbles during the review.

Another common task is to reset the demo database back to its "virgin" state, avoiding the presence of any distracting data that was entered during testing.

No Slides

Sometimes Scrum teams get distracted by spending a lot of time creating PowerPoint slides for the sprint review. I suggest avoiding any kind of slides, which consume time to prepare and edit, as opposed working on wrapping up work on the product. (Cohn, 2014d)

Let the demo speak for itself.

Keep It Informal

The sprint review is supposed to be a *discussion*, not a *presentation*. To encourage collaboration between the Scrum team and stakeholders, the sprint review should be kept light and informal. This is not the time to stand behind a podium making a speech to a darkened room.

Attendees should feel free to ask questions at any time, and the Scrum team should speak openly and honestly about how things went and any challenges they faced during the sprint.

Who Should Do the Talking?

Some Scrum teams select one member to act as the spokesperson for the group. Other teams rotate the responsibility among the members, with a different team member doing most of the talking at each sprint review. Yet other teams rotate during the sprint review, for example with a different developer presenting each new completed user story during the demo.

My personal preference is to have the product owner act as the spokesperson for the group, since they typically have had the most interaction with stakeholders to date. They can tie the work of the development team back to conversations they've had. "Alice, see this here? This is how we handled that suggestion you had a couple of weeks ago."

The product owner shouldn't feel like they are the *only* one who can talk, however. If a question comes up that a team member is better suited to answer, the product owner should redirect. This is especially true if the question is technical. Also, having one of the developers demonstrate a user story that they spent a lot of time on can be a nice way to build a sense of pride and ownership.

If the product owner is the *only* person to *ever* do any talking during the sprint review, it may hurt the team's ability to feel pride of ownership, as well as the perception by stakeholders of the team.

Pencils Down Time

Sometimes there can be issues if the development team is making changes right up to the moment the sprint review starts. For example, if the team deploys a code update to the environment being used for the demo during the review, something might break. There's nothing worse than the product owner walking into the sprint review confident about their planned demo, and the product behaving differently than when they practiced it.

Many teams implement what I call *pencils down time*—channeling memories of a teacher's deadline for grade-school quizzes. This is the time after which no changes should be made to the environment that will be used during the sprint review. Most of our Ascendle teams have a deadline of either one or two hours prior to the start of the review.

This doesn't mean the rule can't be bent or broken. If the team is minutes away from squashing the last bug in the last user story and it's 30 minutes before the start of the sprint review, the product owner might take a leap and say, "Let's do it. Deploy the fix once it's ready."

Many times it works out fine, and in those instances where it blows up in the team's face, they can explain what they were trying to do to the stakeholders and ask for forgiveness.

28.4 Discussing What the Team Completed and the Sprint Goal

A great way to start the sprint review is to describe the sprint goal and provide a recap of what the development team took on for product backlog items to achieve that goal. This sets up the rest of the review by providing a high-level overview.

"The goal selected by the team this sprint was to get a basic implementation of sales tax working, focusing on state-level tax. City and county taxes will come along in a future sprint."

The spokesperson can then go on to review the product backlog items, briefly explaining the nature of each, and reminding the attendees that they'll see a demonstration of completed user stories in a few minutes.

"The development team took on five product backlog items this sprint. The first one was a visual bug on the search results page. It was an alignment issue on Microsoft Edge. That's been fixed. The team also took on four user stories…"

This sets up the attendees to have a frame of reference as they watch the demo, to see how the completed stories fit into attaining the sprint goal.

Use the Sprint Backlog as a Backdrop

I find that showing the sprint backlog—with just the product items visible and no subtasks shown—is a nice way to step attendees through the scope of the sprint. Depending upon the agile tool, the team might show a "live" view of the appropriate screen, or they could take a screen shot and show that instead.

If you use Jira, I find that taking a screen shot of the product backlog items that were in scope for the sprint is the best approach, since once you mark the sprint as completed, the summarized view of the sprint is no longer available.

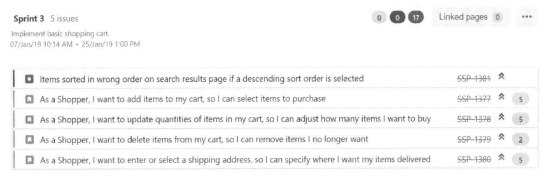

A screen shot from Jira summarizing the product backlog items that were in the sprint.

Our teams have tried using Jira's Sprint Report but—at least as of the time I'm writing this in early 2019—that report doesn't show the product backlog items in the same order they appeared in the sprint.

Recap the Story Points

Part of the benefit of the sprint review is providing visibility for stakeholders into the agile process. If your company is new to agile, this is also a great time to educate them about the fundamentals.

An important part of that education is helping stakeholders learn about story points and velocity. I encourage the team to talk about how many points the development team took on, and how many were done. This ties into what I'll talk about further in Section 28.6, when the team discusses the projected schedule.

What If the Team Didn't Get Everything Done?

There will be times when the product backlog items taken on by the development team don't all get completed. In fact, if the team *always* gets everything done, they probably aren't pushing themselves enough.

The team should get everything they pulled from the product backlog done about 80% of the time. (Cohn, 2014c) That demonstrates that they are being aggressive with what they're taking on but not so aggressive that they're seldom feeling like they were completely successful.

What's more important is the team attaining the sprint goal. By focusing on the sprint goal, the development team and product owner can work together to renegotiate the specific commitment as the sprint evolves. (Overeem, 2016)

For example, if a user story turns out to be much more difficult to implement, the team and product owner can negotiate pulling some of the acceptance criteria out of the sprint and putting it into a new story on the product backlog. Or the entire user story can be descoped, to avoid distracting the team.

There's nothing wrong with the team sometimes not completing all the product backlog items.

That said, they should certainly make an effort. If business stakeholders hear that not everything got done, but the entire team took a couple of afternoons off to go to the beach, they may be wondering about the team's level of commitment to the product.

Finally, if the team is *never* getting everything done, that likely points to a planning problem or lack of clarity around product backlog items. The ScrumMaster should encourage frank discussion during the sprint retrospective about the root cause of not getting to "done," and what to do about it. (Levison, 2009; Cohn, 2014e)

28.5 Demonstrating New Functionality in the Product Increment

The "demo" is typically the most anticipated part of each sprint review. Nothing is more exciting to stakeholders than seeing the product come to life.

There are two approaches I recommend for running through the demo:

One story at a time. Whoever is acting as the spokesperson describes a user story, then the demonstration is performed by them or another team member. They return to the list of product backlog items for the sprint and describe the next one, then the demo, and so on.

This is a nice approach if the stories are somewhat isolated from one another. What's also nice about this approach is it puts each portion of the demo into context, and acts as a checklist of sorts to help the team remember the sequence of user stories.

All stories with a recap at the end. Another approach is to do one demo that includes all the stories, with a recap at the end of which stories attendees just saw. Running through the list of stories after the demo helps ensure none of them were missed and helps reinforce what was completed during the sprint.

I encourage teams to try both styles and see what works best for them. They may even decide to mix and match styles, depending upon the nature of the stories in the sprint. If they are somewhat isolated, they might choose the first option. If they are all intertwined, they could use the second.

Can Stakeholders Ask Questions?

Some stakeholders might feel like the sprint review is a presentation, and they hesitate asking questions. The Scrum team should do everything they can to make it clear that the sprint review is a *discussion* not a *presentation*. Sometimes I tell stakeholders, "This is *your* meeting. Make sure you ask any and all questions so we can have a discussion. We don't want to talk *at* you. We want to talk *with* you."

Stakeholders should feel free to ask questions at any time. "Why did you decide to do it that way?" or "What kinds of problems did you run into?" are great ways for stakeholders to get more insight into what the team was thinking as they built the product increment.

It also helps build trust, since stakeholders will quickly realize the team has their act together. They're not just blindly following a spec—they're thinking deeply about the work they're doing and how to best turn the backlog into a shippable, valuable product.

Which Environment to Use for the Demo?

Some teams use one of the developer's workstations for the demo, but I think that's dangerous. As I talked about in Section 11.2, the product might work on the developer's computer, but not in a "clean" environment.

Instead, one of the test environments should be used for the sprint review demo. My personal preference is using the product owner environment, described in Section 11.3.

This is the environment the product owner uses for their own testing and acceptance of user stories during the sprint. What's nice about this approach is the product owner knows the product is working correctly in that environment.

Also, the environment won't include any incomplete user stories which could cause issues during the demo. The team never wants to say, "Oh, don't look at that. That's not done yet." That flies in the face of the concept of a "potentially shippable" increment being shown to stakeholders.

Only Demonstrate Stories That Are Done

Back when I used waterfall, we would often build the user interface for a new feature first, then fill in the behind-the-scenes code that made it all work. We'd discuss our progress to stakeholders every week or two, showing them the new screens. We wanted to get feedback from them on where we were headed.

I was walking through the office a few days after one of these discussions, when I overheard a sales guy on the phone. "Yep. It's done. I just saw it last week. It will be in the release next week."

I stopped mid-stride in shock when I realized he was *talking about an incomplete feature.* I remember making it *very* clear that "this is not done" during the progress update, and here he was telling a customer it was ready! When he hung up the phone, I talked to him and clarified that it would be several more weeks until the feature was *really* done. He wasn't very impressed when he had to call the prospective customer back.

What I realized back then is there's some part of our brain that doesn't understand, "It's not done yet." If someone sees the user interface—especially those who aren't highly technical—their mind says, "It's done," regardless of your claims to the contrary.

This is why the rule about demonstrating only user stories that are *done done*—meaning they are, in fact, ready to put into a user's hands—is so critical. Because usable functionality is the only measuring stick used to measure progress on a Scrum project, it's critical that you demonstrate only what's truly ready to go.

Don't Lower Your Standards

No one wants to feel like a failure. But that's sometimes what happens when the product owner stands in front of stakeholders and says, "This user story didn't get done."

After this happens a couple of times, the product owner may feel like bending the rules. "I know there's an open issue with this new story, but I think it's usable as is. I'm going to put the bug on the product backlog and we'll just fix it at the start of the next sprint."

This is very dangerous territory and another road to Scrummerfall—calling a user story "done" in one sprint and making it *actually* work in the next.

I like to invoke the *six-month rule* I talked about in Section 27.9 in this case. The product owner should ask themselves, "Can I live with this bug for six months or more?"

If the bug is minor and unlikely to be encountered, the product owner might say "Yes," and can ignore the defect for now. If users later find it to be a problem, they can add a bug to the product backlog and get it fixed.

However, if the answer is "No," I encourage product owners to consider the user story incomplete and avoid the urge to "punt" a bug to the next sprint.

Bugs should only be added to the backlog for defects that *existed at the start of the sprint*—as I described in Section 27.6—but *not* for defects in a newly-completed user story.

As the product owner, don't let your desire to always have the team complete every product backlog item get the best of you. Hold the line on your standards and keep the bar high.

Can We Ever Demonstrate Incomplete Stories?

On a *rare* occasion, there may be a reason to show stakeholders something that's not done yet. This may be because it's super critical to get their feedback before it's complete. For example, the team may want to get input on the user interface wireframes for a new feature.

I encourage you to tread carefully. Remember that "it's not done yet" tends to not be heard.

Here are some tips to help avoid stakeholder confusion:

- *Show something that doesn't look at all usable.* Instead of showing pixel-perfect comps, consider showing stakeholders low-fidelity wireframes, either hand-drawn or created with a tool such as Balsamiq or even PowerPoint. You can use a higher-fidelity tool such as UXPin or InVision, but remember the more "real" it looks, the more risk you have that stakeholders assume what they're looking at is ready to ship.

- *Don't talk about it during sprint review.* Do your best to treat any functionality demonstrated during sprint review as "sacred." Repeat yourself often, telling stakeholders, "Everything I'm going to show you is at a shippable level of quality. I won't show you anything that is not ready for prime time." Any time you want to get feedback on something that's incomplete, do it outside of the context of sprint review.

Stick to the rule of "only demonstrate shippable functionality" as often as possible, but don't hold back from soliciting stakeholder input when it's required.

Just be careful to avoid any confusion.

28.6 Talking About What's Next on the Product Backlog

One of the biggest advantages of Scrum is the ability for the business to turn the ship—i.e. adjust priorities—at any time, and have those new priorities steer the Scrum team in a different direction.

Although the product owner should keep in touch with stakeholders often enough to understand the business landscape, the sprint review provides an opportunity for them to speak up if something seems out of order.

This is usually a great way to utilize your agile tool. The product owner can just bring the product backlog up on the screen and talk about the next five to ten user stories—or whatever might end up fitting into roughly the next two sprints.

The product owner briefly discusses each user story and adds any additional commentary that would be helpful. "We're doing this one next because it's a really important part of the feature the team will be working on, and I want to get my hands on it early so I can use it myself, and show it to a few people to get their feedback."

If stakeholders see critically important user stories they feel are too low in the product backlog, they should speak up and discuss it with the Scrum team then and there. If an extended discussion is necessary, the product owner may want to set aside some time after the sprint review—but before the next sprint planning ceremony—to clarify and get the top of the product backlog ready for planning.

28.7 Discussing Average Velocity and the Projected Schedule

Once the team has completed user stories, it's important to start talking to stakeholders about velocity.

Since this is the key measurable to provide visibility into how fast the team is moving, early sprint reviews should include some light discussion about story points and velocity for any stakeholders new to Scrum. This is a good topic for the ScrumMaster to discuss.

Once three sprints have been completed, a release burndown report is helpful to illustrate how the team's been completing story points over time and to see the projected number of remaining sprints.

A version report is useful when 10% of the story points for the next release have been completed, at which point it will project a completion date, plus optimistic and pessimistic dates.

See Section 3.5 and Section 3.6 for more about release burndown and version reports.

28.8 Tips for a Successful Sprint Review

Sprint reviews can sometimes be stressful. For many Scrum teams new to the process, they've never had as much attention paid to them by the "higher ups." They don't want to disappoint or "look stupid."

If you're the product owner or other team member who will act as the "spokesperson," and you're feeling like this, take a deep breath. I think you'll find the stakeholders who show up for the sprint review are excited and want to see you succeed. They know you're new to the process—as they are—and you'll work together to figure it out as you go.

Remember That It's a Conversation Not a Defense

One thing to keep in mind is the sprint review is a collaborative interaction between the Scrum team and stakeholders. It's a conversation among individuals that are collectively driving toward one result: satisfying the needs of the business as effectively as possible.

The sprint review isn't intended to be a situation where one team member is standing in front of the room and being grilled by everyone else. Sure, you'll face some tough questions if things didn't go so well but remember that everyone's goal is the same—to have the team be successful.

But Also Remember That You Need to Instill Confidence

Although the sprint review is designed to be informal, it *is* the time where the Scrum team is "on stage" in front of stakeholders, so it's important to make sure they feel confident that the product is in good hands.

Here are a few things to consider:

Be organized. Having stakeholders sit around watching you attempt to get the projector working or figure out where you put your notes is not a great way to get off on the right foot. Show up early, make sure everything is working, and consider doing a dry run if you're particularly nervous.

Be confident. Stakeholders want to know they have nothing to worry about. It's important to convey a sense of absolute knowledge and ownership over the product. Answer questions confidently and truthfully. That includes saying, "I don't know…but I'll find out," if asked a question to which you don't know the answer.

Own it. Sometimes things didn't go as well as everyone hoped. Especially when delivering bad news, be sure to own it. Discuss what the team did to try to combat the problem—for example working more creatively, going to others for help and advice, or even putting in a few extra hours. Talk about what you and the team could have done better or differently and *never* blame others.

Leave stakeholders with a feeling of, "OK, they ran into some trouble. But they did their best to deal with it. They learned some lessons. And I'm confident they'll do their best to never let that happen again."

I think you'll find that regardless of how well the sprint went, stakeholders will gain confidence and trust in the team when they experience clear, transparent communication during every sprint review.

Use Realistic-Looking Data

My teams sometimes roll their eyes at me when they ask me to take a look at what they're planning to show at their sprint review and I look closely at the new functionality they built, but even more closely at the sample data they are showing.

"Why do you have a customer called 'Test Customer' and why is 'Tom Jones' missing an 's' at the end?" might be some typical feedback.

This is the result of something I've discovered over the years: stakeholders seem to understand new functionality much more easily if the data they see is as realistic as possible.

What I've found is realistic data provides *context*. It's easier for stakeholders to put themselves in the shoes of an end user if the data makes sense. If I demonstrate a new geographic search feature using our home office zip code, and local towns come up, it's much easier for everyone to understand what's happening.

If instead I type in "00000" as the zip code and see "Test town 1," "Test town 2," and "Test town 3" appear, it's really difficult to "get it."

Do your best to create realistic data to show to stakeholders and make sure you delete any dummy data you used for quick and dirty testing. Seeing "asdfasdfadf" or "Another [expletive] product" can be very distracting to those attending the sprint review and does little to reinforce your level of attention to detail and professionalism.

Don't Treat It as a Product Owner Acceptance Meeting

One trap teams sometimes fall into is assuming the sprint review is for the product owner. You should *never* be in a situation where the product owner is seeing anything for the first time during the sprint review.

The product owner should be reviewing user stories throughout the sprint and accepting or rejecting them. The demonstration during sprint review should only be comprised of user stories the product owner accepted *before* the start of the meeting.

Don't Treat It as a Stakeholder Acceptance Meeting

Another trap some teams run into is the perception that the sprint review is an acceptance meeting for stakeholders. The product owner is the *only* person empowered to accept or reject the work of the development team, acting as the embedded stakeholder representative.

Stakeholder input is important, and if they see something that's not quite right, the product owner should take it into consideration. But be careful not to allow stakeholders to feel like they have ultimate decision-making power as to whether user stories are acceptable. That rests solely on the shoulders of the product owner.

There is, of course, an assumption that the product owner is doing a great job soliciting input from all relevant stakeholders to ensure the right product is getting built. If there is a huge amount of pushback from stakeholders during sprint review, that may indicate the product owner needs to improve in getting their feedback.

Talk to Negative Stakeholders Before the Sprint Review

Sometimes it seems like some stakeholders show up to sprint review just to heckle the product owner and the rest of the Scrum team. They find the most negative things to say at the worst possible time, and can leave the team feeling deflated.

This may be a sign that the stakeholder isn't feeling heard. Maybe they used to feel like they were "in charge" prior to moving to agile and now they feel powerless, and they're lashing out as a result.

If faced with this situation, it may be worthwhile for the product owner to spend some time with this person *before* the sprint review, talking to them a few times during the sprint about what's going on and what they should expect to see at the end. If they feel a little more integrated into the process, they may tone down the negative feedback.

Just be careful to ensure they don't misinterpret the extra attention as being granted control over the process. If they have input, the product owner should listen intently, make some notes, and say, "Thanks, that's great feedback. Let me see how that fits into the plan." No promise is being made, but the stakeholder feels like they're being heard.

Always Start and End on Time

It's important to start all Scrum ceremonies on time, and for the sprint review, it's also important to end on time. Business stakeholders often have packed schedules and if you have a habit of running over the allocated time, they will miss the end of the discussion. Ensure the sprint review starts and ends precisely on time.

28.9 A Sample Sprint Review Agenda

As I've outlined in this chapter, there are four major phases of the sprint review: providing an overview, performing the demo, reviewing next priorities, and discussing the velocity and schedule.

I recommend four major phases during the sprint review.

Here is a more detailed agenda for a one-hour sprint review, which I find about the right length for a two-week sprint.

Description	Duration
Welcome, review sprint goal and product backlog items included in sprint	10 min
Demonstration of completed user stories	30 min
Review of what's coming up next on the product backlog	10 min
Discussion of velocity and projected schedule	10 min
Total	**1 hour**

Sample agenda for a sprint review for a two-week sprint.

Feel free to adjust this agenda as you see fit. If you have many stakeholders attending your sprint review, you might find you need to extend the duration closer to the two-hour maximum for a two-week sprint.

Key Takeaways

- The sprint review is the key event that provides visibility to stakeholders, and takes place at the end of each sprint. It provides a feeling of comfort to those outside the team because they can monitor progress by the only metric that matters: working, fully-tested, potentially shippable functionality.

- The most important attendees to invite to the sprint review are key stakeholders. Many teams find inviting others within the company is helpful. This might include other development teams; implementation, training, and support reps; and sales and marketing team members.

- The maximum duration for the sprint review for a two-week sprint is two hours. However, keeping the sprint review to an hour will make it easier to fit it into stakeholder schedules.

- Early afternoon on the last day of the sprint is often best, since it provides the morning for the team to wrap up any last-minute items. It also gives the team a break in the late afternoon to catch their breath and build up some energy for the start of the next sprint.

- To avoid getting distracted, no more than two hours should be spent preparing for the sprint review and no PowerPoint slides should be created. The sprint review is intended to be an informal, collaborative discussion, as opposed to a structured and stuffy presentation.

- Anyone on the Scrum team can talk during the sprint review. I find that having the product owner be the "spokesperson" for the team works well, since they typically have had the most interaction with the stakeholders who are attending. However, any other team members who would like to participate—for example to demonstrate a user story they worked on—should be encouraged to do so.

- A *pencils down time*, after which no more changes can be made to the environment that will be used for the demo during the sprint review, can often be helpful to avoid last-minute surprises.

- The first part of the sprint review is discussing what the team took on for product backlog items and how much they got done.

- The next part is demonstrating completed user stories. It's important that only *really* done user stories are demonstrated, to ensure stakeholders get a true understanding of the progress of the product.

- There *are* times when incomplete user stories can be discussed, for example if it's critical to get stakeholder feedback about them. But this should be the exception and it should be made abundantly clear to everyone that, "This one doesn't count because it's not quite done." Ideally this type of discussion takes place outside of the sprint review.

- After the demo, what's coming up next on the product backlog should be reviewed, so stakeholders have an opportunity to provide insight about any changing business conditions that may adjust priorities.

- The sprint review wraps up by discussing velocity and a schedule projection, if enough sprints have been completed to generate meaningful data. For the first few sprints, the ScrumMaster should be careful to explain the concepts of story points and velocity and how they're used to estimate the schedule to any stakeholders new to the Scrum process.

- The release burndown report and version report can be used to show the team's progress and estimated schedule. See Section 3.5 and Section 3.6 for more details about these reports.

Chapter 29

Driving Continuous Improvement with the Sprint Retrospective

Give me six hours to chop down a tree and I will spend the first four sharpening the axe.

- **Abraham Lincoln**

It would be wonderful if a new team could learn the fundamentals of Scrum, start executing the process, and produce great results right away.

But nothing in life comes quite that easily.

Because Scrum is—by design—incomplete, it's up to each team to determine how to fill in the missing pieces. The framework doesn't say, "This is exactly how to do it," because each combination of business problem, technology, and team is different, and requires a unique variation of the process to produce the best results.

Instead of trying to guess what will work, teams instead just start using the fundamentals of the Scrum framework and see what happens. Then they set aside time to talk about how things went and how to improve.

The next sprint, they experiment with the adjustments they identified and see if those changes made things better, worse, or had no effect.

This scientific process—of experimenting and reviewing the results—is at the heart of the empirical theory upon which Scrum was founded, with a focus on transparency, inspection, and adaptation. (Schwaber & Sutherland, 2017)

Although this inspect-adapt progression happens throughout the Scrum process, there is one ceremony set aside for the team to look in the mirror and think through ways to improve: the sprint retrospective.

29.1 Is This Really a Valuable Use of Time?

Before I talk about the details, it's probably a good idea for me to address a frequent objection: "Shouldn't we be working on the product instead of *talking about* working on the product?"

Sprints can be stressful, particularly the first few sprints a team executes. Often the last thing they want to do once the sprint review is over is sit around and talk about what happened during the last two weeks. This is especially true if the sprint didn't go very well.

But this is *precisely* what they need to do. Otherwise, every sprint will be just as painful because they won't be consistently improving. (Derby & Larsen, 2006)

The End Is Too Late

The differences between a traditional postmortem and Scrum retrospective boils down to a difference of perspective and mindset. Retrospectives are about changing how work is being done *now*, versus a traditional end-of-project postmortem which *might* assist the next team, but happens too late to help the current team.

Many teams have experienced a postmortem held at the very end of the project. A retrospective is different in three specific areas: action, permission, and ownership. (Cagley, 2013)

Action. A traditional postmortem happens at the very end of the project. By then it's too late—it's over! In contrast, agile retrospectives happen at the point of highest usefulness. Lessons learned can be applied *now*, improving the process when it matters most—when it can improve the effectiveness of the team for the longest amount of time.

Permission. A postmortem is intended to address the needs of a standard process, whereas the retrospective is about meeting the needs of the Scrum team. The retrospective is about discovering changes that will help the team deliver more value than the last sprint. They don't need to ask permission to make adjustments.

In contrast, since the traditional postmortem is focused on the standard process, the team can only make recommendations. The focus is on the standard process because at the end of the project the team is often disbanded and reformed, so discoveries relating to individuals and how they work together don't make sense.

Ownership. The retrospective is a team tool, whereas the classic postmortem is done for the organization, for example for the project management office (PMO) or management. Postmortems can include anyone involved in the project or supporting the process. In contrast, only the Scrum team attends sprint retrospectives.

The deliverable of a postmortem is typically a formal report that may never be looked at again. The only deliverable from a retrospective is a few notes and reminders about actions the team would like to take. Any documentation is for the benefit of the team and not intended for consumption elsewhere. That said, teams frequently share their notes with other teams in the organization to help spread new ideas, discoveries, and learnings.

29.2 The Art of Self-Reflection: A Variety of Retrospective Formats

Many developers aren't—how shall I say this politely—talkative. Sometimes it takes an act of Congress to get them to speak their minds.

To avoid team members spending their retrospectives sitting around looking at each other and saying nothing, a variety of leading questions are often used to get the conversation going. I find that once the ice is broken, team members engage—even the quiet ones—and will provide input.

Questions vary, but they are typically asked in groups of three or four. The purpose of the questions—in addition to getting the team to talk—is to uncover three types of information:

- *What's working?* What is the team doing that is making the process go well? This is important because a constant celebration of success imparts energy to the team, driving them to experiment further. (Kua, 2013)

- *What's not working?* How is the team getting held back from reaching their potential? Inspecting what didn't go so well is a key to understanding how to improve.

- *What should we do differently?* Deciding on specific actions to take or changes to make to the process is the most important outcome of the retrospective, since it is the engine of improvement.

Some teams have members answer questions verbally. Co-located teams sometimes use sticky notes for rapid-fire brainstorming. The ScrumMaster reads the sticky notes and the team discusses each idea, then they collaboratively decide what actions to take and changes to try.

In the balance of this section, I'll outline some different sets of questions you can use with your team. (Morales, 2017; Gonçalves & Linders, 2014) I've included a few sample answers for each question to illustrate what your team might say in response.

Although I've included only a handful of examples for each question, teams shouldn't limit themselves. They should talk about everything they can think of and drive toward applying what they learned to the next sprint.

Try a few different sets of questions over time and see what works best for your group!

Start/Stop/Continue

What should we **start** doing?	What should we **stop** doing?	What should we **continue** doing?

Start/stop/continue questions are action-focused.

What should we *start* doing? This question helps the team think about new actions or practices they can adopt.

- "What if we started having all developers do code reviews, instead of just the senior developer?"

- "What if the ScrumMaster helps with testing toward the end of the sprint?"

- "What if we start adding an 'insurance' subtask to each story to help account for things we forget during sprint planning?"

What should we *stop* doing? Time-consuming but low-value activities can slow the team down. This question helps identify things the team is doing now, but probably won't miss if they stop.

- "The weekly 'Completed Features' report really isn't necessary any longer because stakeholders can just come to the sprint review. How about we work with them to eliminate it?"

- "Putting names on all the subtasks during sprint planning is limiting our flexibility. What if we stop doing that, and instead just put names on what we'll work on in the first day or two?"

- "Creating high-fidelity mockups for every screen is really time-consuming, and we're often waiting for them to be completed. We've reached a point where all the UI patterns are established. What if we just draw a whiteboard diagram for each user story giving us the general idea, and we see if we can produce the same result without the mockups?"

What should we continue doing? When the team finds things that work, it's important to reinforce how valuable they are. This helps ensure the team keeps their most successful practices in place. It can also be a way for the team to acknowledge that an idea from earlier retrospectives turned out to be a winner.

- "Starting testing before the entire user story is done is working well. We are able to discover things that the programmers might have missed earlier than we used to."

- "Taking the time to set up continuous deployment to deploy a user story whenever new code is committed is saving a *huge* amount of time."

- "The new team chat room is making communication much easier for our distributed team, especially when we have a quick question for the product owner."

Did Well/Could Have Done Better/Ideas/Actions

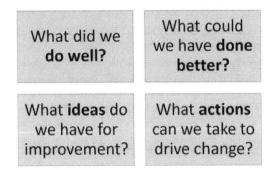

This set of questions forces teams to take a hard look in the mirror and decide on specific changes to make.

What did we do well? This question starts the team off on the right foot, focusing on their positive accomplishments during the sprint.

- "We got all the stories done that we committed to!"

- "We remembered to try our experiment ideas from the last retrospective."

- "Alex did some pair programming with Noah when he got stuck."

What could we have done better? This puts the team in a self-critical mode, so they can identify ways to improve.

- "We're still not sticking within the 15-minute timebox for daily scrums."

- "We could have started testing story 208 earlier in the sprint to avoid the scramble at the end."

- "When Anna (the product owner) is going to be out on a personal day, we should get any questions to her before she leaves."

What ideas do we have for improvement? This question allows the team to focus on the experiments they want to run in the upcoming sprint. These often, but not always, relate directly to the, "What could we have done better" answers.

- "Have the daily scrum a little later since some of us run into traffic on the way in."

- "Pair program more often when someone gets stuck."

- "Get all coding completed by the end of the day, two days before the end of the sprint."

What actions can we take to drive change? These are specific to-do items that need to be accomplished. Each of them should have a name associated with it, indicating who is responsible for driving it forward. This is often the ScrumMaster, but can be anyone on the team.

- "Ask Bob in sales to stop coming down and distracting the team so often. (Emma)"

- "Remind us during sprint planning to schedule the daily scrum 30 minutes later. (Emma)"

- "See if there's a new version of our code analysis tool that supports new language features. (Ben)"

The Sailboat

Some teams draw a picture of a sailboat on the whiteboard in conjunction with this exercise. Included are some islands in the distance, rocks up ahead, an anchor dangling in the water, and clouds and wind blowing the sails.

Islands represent the team's goals and vision. **Rocks** represent risks they may encounter along the way. The **anchor** is everything that slows them down on their journey. The **clouds and wind** represent everything that helps them reach their goal. (Gonçalves & Linders, 2014)

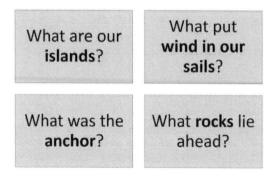

A whimsical twist on classic retrospective questions.

What are our islands? This prompts the team to think about their big-picture vision and goals.

- "I'd like to adopt test-driven development."

- "I want to get a round of applause at just *one* sprint review like I've heard other teams have experienced."

- "I want to finish a sprint without *any* late nights or last-minute stress."

What put wind in our sails? This question helps the team think about what helped their productivity during the sprint.

- "The customer support team helped coordinate the hotfix to address a critical customer bug."

- "Alex and Jack stayed late on Wednesday night to get our last story coded."

- "We've gotten a lot better at keeping the daily scrum to less than 15 minutes and using the parking lot."

What was the anchor? Anything that gets in the way of the team making progress and slowing them down—or stopping them dead in the water—can be discussed as a response to this question.

- "We had to deal with a critical customer bug, which meant we had to descope one story and it caused a big distraction."

- "Belinda was out sick one day and no one knew what she had worked on because the board wasn't up to date, and she wasn't reachable."

- "We forgot unit tests on the second story and had to scramble to get them added."

What rocks lie ahead? There may be things the team sees lying ahead that they might "crash into" and cause a slowdown.

- "If we don't start writing unit tests as we're writing code, we may run into more issues with forgetting to add them."

- "There's a three-day all-company offsite meeting for the entire product team the second week of next sprint—Anna (the product owner) will be out, so we need to make sure we get the info we need from her before then."

- "If we don't get our backlog grooming done this sprint, the schedule won't be right because there are stories with no story point estimates."

The Four L's

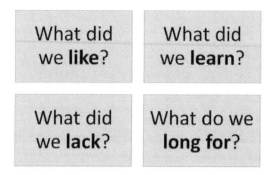

This set of questions encourages the team to think broadly about their sprint.

What did we like? Starting off on a positive note is usually the best way to get a retrospective going. This question focuses on the high points of the sprint.

- "We really worked together well when the burndown was off-track. Everyone volunteered to help however they could, and we got caught up."

- "We got a round of applause at sprint review!"

- "Ellen (the ScrumMaster) is a superhero. She helped keep everyone communicating, especially when things got tough in the middle of the sprint. And she got pizzas for us when we decided to stay late one night."

What did we learn? Every sprint is an opportunity to learn. Here the team can highlight what they discovered this sprint.

- "If we wait too long to do a code review, we slow down the process."

- "We over-committed. We should consume less of our total capacity during sprint planning."

- "If the burndown is off-track half-way through the sprint, it will never get back on track unless we take action."

What did we lack? Teams, especially at the beginning, may find that they are missing something, and that's causing them to slow down.

- "We keep running into problems with unit testing asynchronous code. I'm not sure if we have the right knowledge about how to do this right."

- "We only have one team test environment. We really need two so we can test multiple stories at the same time."

- "We ran into a bottleneck with front-end coding. Some of our back-end guys need to learn more about front-end coding so they can help when we run into this problem."

What do we long for? Another way to think about this question is having team members complete the phrase, "Wouldn't it be great if…"

- "We could use some more training on how to properly run a sprint planning session."

- "We need a technical resource we can go to with questions about tricky unit tests."

- "We need more support from DevOps to let us spin up our own environments."

Glad/Sad/Mad

What made us **glad**?	What made us **sad**?	What made us **mad**?

This final set of questions focuses on the emotions of the team during the last sprint as a way to improve.

What made us glad? This question starts the team off on a positive note, discussing what got them excited and proud, and put a smile on their face.

- "All the key stakeholders showed up for sprint review."

- "Adam in sales didn't come down and bug us three times a day like he had been doing."

- "We got everything done more quickly than we thought and pulled in and squashed three bugs."

What made us sad? Here the team talks about things that they were a little bummed out about. This is usually focused on things they could have done better.

- "We were confused about some stories during sprint planning, so we weren't as efficient as we usually are."

- "There were a lot of bugs in the gift card story."

- "Our experiment of shortening the sprint planning meeting blew up in our face."

What made us mad? Any frustration the team felt surfaces in response to this question. Answers to this question are often focused on outside influences or team dynamics that aren't what they should be.

- "The component that team 'Betta Fish' provided for us didn't work as they promised. It looks like they didn't test it properly."

- "We got the discount code story done and the product owner said it wasn't what she wanted."

- "Alice from accounting attended the sprint review and was very critical. We're not sure if she understands the Scrum process."

29.3 Leading Questions to Ask During the Retrospective

Most teams find good things to say about the sprint, but some teams struggle with finding things to criticize, especially during their first few retrospectives.

Here is a list of leading questions the ScrumMaster or others on the team can ask to help get the conversation going:

- Is everyone keeping busy with valuable work throughout the sprint?

- Are we communicating effectively?

- Is everyone holding up their end of the bargain—i.e. doing their part?

- Was anyone frustrated at all during the sprint?

- Did our sprint planning session create a solid plan?

- How many bugs did we find in each user story?

- Are we finding fewer bugs than we used to?

- Did we miss any acceptance criteria when the stories were implemented?

- Was anyone confused about any of the user stories?

- Are we writing effective unit tests?

- Are unit tests getting written before writing new code?

- Is the right code being covered by unit tests?

The list of questions could go on and on, but this should provide a good starting point for you.

Be Careful about "Metrics"

Focusing on any metric other than velocity is a mistake in my opinion, because I believe it distracts teams from the only thing that matters: how fast they're producing valuable, usable software that meets a high standard of quality.

For example, if a team is measured by how many problems they find during a code review, they're likely to magically stop finding any more issues, regardless of the quality of the code. This achieves the short-term goal of satisfying the metric, but some poor sap down the road is going to inherit a bunch of crappy, difficult-to-maintain code.

As another example, if teams are measured on an arbitrary code coverage percentage, they'll tend to write unit tests that exercise the code—but never fail. I saw that first-hand a couple of years ago at a large company. The development team had added thousands of tests. The problem? None of them included code to check whether the test passed or failed.

But their code coverage number was *fantastic*!

Metrics can be very dangerous due to risk of distracting a team from what matters most: building the product *quickly* and building it *right*. Tread carefully.

29.4 Leave Egos, Titles, and Experience at the Door

I attended a keynote speech last year presented by John Foley, a former pilot for the Blue Angels, the United States Navy's flight demonstration squadron.

He talked a lot about leadership and discipline, but what I was especially interested in was the debrief process the team conducts after every flight—their version of a "retrospective."

He explained that when you're flying over 600 miles per hour as close as *18 inches* from another fighter jet, mistakes can be *very* costly, and the only way to ensure the best performance and the highest degree of safety is to take a hard look in the mirror and carefully criticize everything that could have gone better.

He showed a video of one of their debriefs. It's a little dated, since it was from back when he was a member of the flying team, but it's very informing.

In the video, the commanding officer first explains how the process works. "Rank doesn't come into play. Experience levels—those are good, but you have to set those aside when the criticism starts to come, because that's the only way you're going to learn the maneuver, and that's the only way you're going to get to where the maneuver looks good and it's safe."

This is an important point you can bring to your own retrospectives. The team should focus on having a *candid, critical discussion*. It doesn't matter if one team member has been at the company ten years and another ten months. Everyone should feel free to open up about what they're thinking.

The other thing I noticed is that every team member focuses on what *they* could have done better. You don't see finger-pointing and blaming others. In addition to focusing on their mistakes, they *take ownership of fixing them*, ensuring they never happen again.

This is one of the most-accomplished teams in the world, and if you've ever seen one of their shows, you wouldn't think they make mistakes. But they do, and they talk carefully about them, and they take ownership over making sure the mistakes are never repeated.

These are some valuable lessons you can take to your own team.

You can watch the debrief portion of the video on YouTube by following this link:

http://bit.ly/blueangelsdebrief

29.5 Don't Be Too Nice

"We don't seem to be making much progress," Alice says, her eyes drifting down to the floor. "We have lots of little problems, but I can't seem to get the team to acknowledge them, let alone address them."

Alice, the ScrumMaster on one of our teams, had come to talk to me about their retrospectives, which she didn't feel were going well. When I asked why, she explained, "We keep having issues come up during the sprint, and some of the team members aren't getting along, but I couldn't get them to talk about any of it. They all said they thought things were going along just fine, but I don't see it that way. I know we can do better."

"How about I attend the next retrospective?" I offered. "Maybe I can help nudge things in the right direction."

"That would be great."

I spent the next week talking to a few different team members, gently inquiring about how things were going. I picked up on a few issues the team was facing. I looked forward to seeing how they talked about them during the sprint retrospective.

A few days later, after a great sprint review, it was time for the retro. The team had a good 20-minute discussion, talking about what they did well, what they thought they could do better, and they even came up with a new idea to experiment with during the next sprint.

But they didn't talk about any of the issues that might cause conflict during the meeting. When I had chatted with team members during the week, I heard a few. Noah was frequently late to daily scrums, and Maria had on several occasions committed to driving subtasks to done toward the end of the sprint but left the office early and was frequently running personal errands at critical times when the team needed her.

Once they finished, I asked, "Do you mind if I ask some questions?" Once they gave me the thumbs up, I said, "One of the most difficult things about this process is talking about things that make people uncomfortable.

"This is a time to talk about your accomplishments, and that's super important. But more important, it's a time to take a hard look in the mirror and air any dirty laundry about what went wrong. That's one of the reasons I suggest that no one is allowed to attend this ceremony except the Scrum team. You all need to be comfortable that you are in a 'safe place' to have a frank discussion.

"My key piece of advice is: *just say it*. If you have something on your mind, just say it out loud. It may be uncomfortable at first, but over time if everyone just says it, you'll build trust within the team and start working as a more cohesive unit."

I went on to facilitate a more in-depth discussion and—without violating any confidences—teased out the uncomfortable feedback I had heard privately. Although the initial reaction to hearing criticism from their teammates was a little negative, team members were very respectful and explained why they were concerned about some of their behavior.

Over the next couple of sprints, the team completely eliminated the issues they talked about and—although they occasionally encountered other snags—they increased their velocity. They started delivering on their sprint commitment time and time again, to the delight of stakeholders.

Most important they started having more *fun*.

Do yourself and your teammates a favor—don't hold back when you need to address the elephant in the room and have an uncomfortable conversation.

29.6 How to Make Sure Change Happens

Sometimes teams have a productive discussion during their retrospective and…nothing happens. They come up with some great ideas on how to adjust their process, but they seem to forget all about them once they leave the retrospective room.

Here are a few ideas to help ensure changes happen:

- *Create an "experiments list."* At the end of each retrospective, the team can create an "experiments list," where they list the process changes they plan on trying. I like using the word "experiment" because it reinforces two things: First, the team is not saying,

"This is cast in stone." Second, it underscores the nature of the change. It says, "We expect this change to produce a positive result."

- *Review past experiments.* One way to ensure experiments don't get forgotten is to review them at each sprint retrospective. The team discusses each experiment they tried and makes a binary decision: keep doing it, because it produced a positive result, or stop doing it, because it didn't make any difference or produced a negative result.

- *Have the ScrumMaster take ownership.* As part of their role of "owner of the process," the ScrumMaster can take ownership of the experiments identified during the retrospective, ensuring they are employed in the next sprint. The ScrumMaster can also make some notes about what they see—positive or negative—as the outcome from the experiments, to help the team make a decision at the next retrospective.

It's great for a team to sit around and talk about how to make things better. But talk is cheap. *Action* is the most important outcome of the sprint retrospective. Be sure to focus on how ideas turn into implemented changes to drive the process to a higher level.

29.7 Common Problems and How to Address Them

Retrospectives can be hard. Leaving your title, seniority, and ego at the door is a tricky thing to do, but it's critical to ensuring the team improves.

Below are a few different challenges you might face in retrospectives. I'll briefly describe each and give you some ideas about how you might address them.

Criticism Turns into Finger-Pointing

There's a very fine line between providing constructive feedback and harshly criticizing a fellow team member to the point that it's demeaning. If your retrospectives are starting to turn into a yelling match about who is to blame for a recent failure, here's a few things to try:

- *It's about the team.* Remind everyone that the goal is to get the *team* to be better. No one is here to "fix each other."

- *Leave your ego at the door.* Another reminder for everyone is to leave the ego at the door. Everyone should be open-minded and ready to acknowledge criticism and think about how to improve, for the good of the team.

- *Self-criticism only.* An experiment you can try is for the duration of one retrospective, the only criticism that can be discussed by a team member is about themselves.

Remember, the goal isn't to walk out of the room feeling like everyone screwed up. Improvement only comes by recognizing what mistakes were made. That's why just saying what's on your mind is so important. It will identify the problems as well as drive a higher level of trust within the team.

Team Members Don't Want to Talk

Sometimes, despite a valiant effort by the ScrumMaster, team members simply don't…want…to…talk.

An experiment you can use is to write the retrospective questions up on the whiteboard, then have everyone write their answers on sticky notes and stick them in the appropriate column on the wall. If you're *still* having trouble getting participation, require that everyone on the team comes up with at least one answer to each question.

Once the questions are written, the ScrumMaster reads through each of them, and attempts to get discussion going. At best, the ideas will jump-start a discussion and the team will get talking. At worst, the ideas have been extracted from the team and improvements can be made.

For virtual teams, you can use the same technique, but use the team chat room instead of sticky notes.

Management Uses our Retrospective Notes Against the Team

Many teams store their retrospective notes in a team wiki such as Confluence. In some less-than-healthy organizations, management sifts through the team's notes and looks for reasons things might not be going well.

In this worst-case scenario, instead of applauding the team's transparency and honesty as a road to improvement, management repurposes the information as a way to point out the team's flaws and penalize them.

Some Options

This is a terrible situation, and teams faced with this scenario may feel like they have no way out. Here are a few ideas:

Educate management. In this situation, managers may simply not understand the purpose of the retrospective and the harm they're causing by interfering with the process. The ScrumMaster can work with them to teach them more about the process and why it's in *their* best interest for the team to be candid amongst themselves in a safe environment. This is a critical success factor for the type of cultural change the company is undergoing. (Project Management Institute, 2017)

Enlist the help of an external agile trainer or coach. Many times, companies hire an external agile trainer or coach because it's easier for someone "from the outside" to talk candidly without fear of fallout. If the team is working with an outside coach, they can leverage them to go to bat on their behalf with management to help them course correct.

Enlist the help of the team's managers. If the ScrumMaster can't make any headway directly with the managers who are interfering with the process, team members might need to go to their own managers for help. Usually whenever any leader hears, "There's someone getting in the way of us producing the best results as quickly as possible," they'll work to get to the bottom of it and help to straighten things out.

Go up the org chart. This isn't a great option, but if a team is in a situation where *all* their managers are not responding to repeated requests to let them run the process, and there is no external trainer or coach to turn to, the ScrumMaster may need to get more aggressive. Skipping up one level in the chain of command is usually tricky, but if there's a sympathetic ear at a higher level of management, it might be time to carefully provide some information that things aren't going well, and the managers are getting in the way. Senior executives will often stop by to chat with the team and pulling them aside afterwards might be something that's workable without causing a problem.

I realize there are many dynamics and politics often come into play, especially in larger companies, so you'll have to be the judge as to what the best option is for your particular environment.

Less-Than-Ideal Options

If none of the ideas above seem to be working, below are some less-than ideal options.

These don't address the root cause—a lack of understanding that transparency is *in everyone's best interest*—but it may give the team a little more privacy. This can help them continue with what they should be doing, which is continuing to have candid, no-holds-barred retrospectives in the interest of continuous improvement.

- *Make the notes accessible only to the team.* By using the security features in the wiki tool, the team can lock down access so managers can't review the retrospective notes. This may only be a temporary solution but could cause the issue to be driven to a resolution if all other attempts have failed.

- *Only write down experiments to try.* The teams hold their retrospectives as usual, but don't write down any of the criticism. They write down their ideas for experiments—so they can review their ideas and see how well they worked—but nothing else.

- *Don't write anything down.* The "nuclear option" is to simply not write anything down. The team has their candid conversations, but they don't make any notes in any centrally-accessible storage system.

If you get to the point where these ideas are the only options you have, things are *very* broken. But if it's a choice between the two extremes—stopping retrospectives entirely or sticking with the process—it's imperative that the team continues with their retrospective. There's no greater argument to be made than real, measurable progress, in the form of the team improving their throughput. That only comes from the inspect and adapt process at the heart of Scrum.

This is another reason that it's so critical that the team has support from above. If their managers can't help negotiate these types of problems, the team will have a very difficult time succeeding, as they'll often feel cast adrift with no power to make real change.

Team Members Don't Respond to Feedback

It's been three retrospectives in a row where the team has—as politely as they can—told David that he's letting the team down. He's just not engaged like the rest of the team, and they feel like they're carrying extra weight because he's not doing his part.

Here are a few ideas to try:

- *A private conversation.* The ScrumMaster or another team member can pull David aside and have a talk with him personally. Maybe he felt attacked in the group setting and a one-on-one conversation can help.

- *Escalation to a manager.* If the team isn't getting anywhere, asking for help from a manager can be a great next step, to give David some coaching and mentoring to help him improve.

- *Removal from the team.* The last resort, if all else fails, is to get David off the team. This is typically something handled by the team's managers and human resources.

It's very difficult to get someone to change if they don't take ownership themselves of what the team is seeing as the problem. If they *do* own it, usually the problem goes away. But if not, it's up to the team to make sure the problem gets properly addressed.

It's Always Good News

I'm an optimist, and to a degree that sometimes annoys my team members, I almost always look on the bright side of things. When I participate in a retrospective, it's not as easy for me to come up with a list of things we could have done better.

It's great starting with good news. There's nothing better than to celebrate the "wins" of a particularly good sprint. But the team needs to realize there is always something they can do better.

It's easy at the beginning. The team will likely be messing up all kinds of things. But as time goes by, it will become more difficult to come up with ideas for improvements.

The different question formats I outlined in Section 29.2 can help, as well as the leading questions in Section 29.3. They ensure the team is forced to think critically about their sprint, which will help fight the tendency to gloss over bad news.

Here again is an opportunity for the ScrumMaster. By facilitating the retrospective, they can pull ideas out of reluctant team members to help drive positive change.

Key Takeaways

- Every team has a unique combination of business problem to solve, technology, and individuals. This is why Scrum—by design—is incomplete; it's up to each team to determine how to customize the process to work best for *them*.

- The best way for teams to figure out how to produce the best results is by starting the agile process, seeing how things work, and driving constant improvement. This supports the Scrum concepts of transparency, inspection, and adaptation.

- Teams inspect and adapt throughout each sprint. The sprint retrospective is specifically set aside for inspecting how the sprint went and adapting the process to introduce innovations to increase momentum while improving the level of quality.

- Traditional postmortems held at the end of the project come too late. In contrast, the insight gained through a retrospective can be applied immediately to the next sprint.

- Most teams find asking a series of questions during the retrospective helps everyone think about how the sprint went and come up with ideas to improve. The format varies, but the questions are typically aimed at addressing three things: what's working, what's not working, and what should the team do differently to improve.

- When entering the retrospective, team members need to leave egos, titles, and experience at the door. This is the only way to talk plainly about what needs to change without feelings getting hurt. The team should remember that it's about *the team* and not them as individuals. However, individual criticism may be required to get the team where it needs to be.

- Many teams are a little too nice during their retrospectives, afraid of hurting feelings. Team members should *just say it*, without fear of the uncomfortable conversations that sometimes follow. That's the only way teams will uncover the root cause of issues and build the much-needed trust they need to succeed.

- To ensure changes happen, many teams enlist the help of the ScrumMaster to ensure new ideas and experiments are tried in the sprint following the retrospective. Teams should also review any experiments in the next retrospective and keep or abandon them.

- Retrospectives are hard—no one likes to talk about the parts of the sprint that didn't go so well. But it's critical to the team's continuous improvement that they unpack their issues and address them head-on.

Chapter 30
Confidently Releasing Your Product into Production

The only purpose of starting is to finish, and while the projects we do are never really finished, they must ship.

- **Seth Godin**, *American author and former dot com business executive.*

I was having lunch with one of our clients a few months ago and he was expressing frustration with one of his teams. "They've created this great product," he began. "I mean, it's *really* good. Revolutionary, even. They cranked it out in about ten months, which is four months faster than a similar product we built a few years ago."

"That doesn't sound so bad," I replied. "What's the problem?"

With a thin smile he said, "It's on a QA server, but it's been sitting there for months. It's not in production. I have this great product, but I can't get any credit for it. None of our customers can use it." With a more serious expression, he finished by saying, "The team just can't seem to ship."

Sadly, this happens all too often in the software world. There's usually a strong focus on getting the product built, but during development little attention is paid to what will be required to get it all the way into production.

I think in some cases there is a subconscious resistance to thinking about the release process. Many of us who have experienced waterfall projects worked our butts off to drive the product to what we thought was "done," only to walk into the office the next day to the phones ringing off the hook and the support ticketing system blowing up because no one can complete their order in the shopping cart. No wonder we don't want to think about production; it scares the hell out of us.

If you've never had this kind of experience, I applaud you. I've lived this nightmare. More times than I care to admit.

The good news is after almost four decades of experimentation, I think I've nailed it. We've been using the process in this chapter for the last six years and I'm happy to report that it works. I can't think of any time we were unable to release on schedule and there's never been more than a small handful of bugs that made it into production.

30.1 A Tried-And-True Release Process

By keeping the product in a potentially shippable state at all times, the team should be able to deploy to production within the timespan of *one sprint* from when the product owner says, "Go." This is commonly referred to as a *release sprint*.

Technically, there is no special sprint type in Scrum called a "release sprint," so this is simply another iteration. It just happens to have a sprint goal of, "Deploy the product into production." (Schwaber & Sutherland, 2017)

In Section 23.11 I talked about what you can do early on to lay the groundwork, to avoid getting delayed by external factors such as provisioning timelines, security audits, and compliance sign-offs. Assuming you followed the steps in that section, and you've used the techniques I described throughout this book to keep the product in a potentially shippable state, using the strategy in this chapter should be fairly painless.

Over the years I've distilled the release process into five steps, including what I call "certifying" the release in three separate environments: Staging, Pre-Release, and Production. These steps all take place during the release sprint. To be clear, this means if you're using two-week sprints, everything I'm going to talk about in this chapter needs to be completed within two weeks.

Our teams typically require an entire two-week release sprint for their first deployment of a new product, to deal with inevitable hiccups during the process. However, once they get to their second or third release, the entire process typically only takes a few days. They then use the balance of the release sprint to make early progress on the *next* release.

The process looks like this:

1. *Isolate source code for the release.* Creating a separate branch of the source code—called a *release branch*—provides the team with a "virtual code freeze," permitting final testing and fixing last-minute bugs, while giving the team flexibility to start moving ahead with work on the next release. This is important because there are many times when there are team members who can't help with the release process due to "too many cooks in the kitchen." In this case, they can start working on a user story for the next release while other team members wrap up the current release.

2. *"Certify" the release branch in the Staging environment.* Using an environment that closely matches the Production environment, the team performs final end-to-end testing on the product and fixes high-priority bugs. I like the word "certify" because it implies the Scrum team has put their stamp of approval on the release and deemed it ready for prime time.

3. *Update the production codebase.* Once the development team and product owner are happy with the release branch, it's merged into the Master branch. As a reminder, the Master branch always contains the current production code. See Section 12.5 for details on how I suggest managing source code with the Git Flow process.

4. *Certify the Master branch in the Pre-Release environment.* Before taking the leap into deploying the code into production, I like to do a final check in what I call the *Pre-Release* environment. This matches the Production environment *exactly* and is connected to a copy of the production database. However, this environment is not exposed to end users.

5. *Deploy the Master branch to Production and perform final certification steps.* This last step involves making the code live and doing a few final checks to ensure everything looks like it's working correctly. This avoids the "fire and forget" trap that teams sometimes fall into, where they deploy tested code to production but fail to verify the product works as expected.

I'll talk in more detail about each of these steps throughout this chapter.

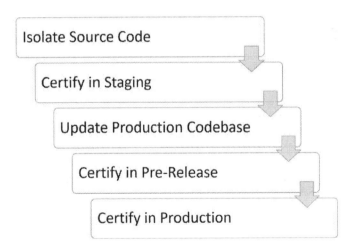

I've found this five-step process helps teams reliably get their product into production during a release sprint.

30.2 Test Environments Required to "Certify" the Release

Before I talk more about the step-by-step details, I'd like to discuss each of the environments I've found helpful to support the release process. You may already have a similar strategy of using multiple environments to perform final testing, though you might use different names to describe each environment.

The three environments involved in the release process are what I call the *Staging environment*, *Pre-Release environment*, and *Production environment*.

These environments are in addition to the other environments I described in Chapter 11.

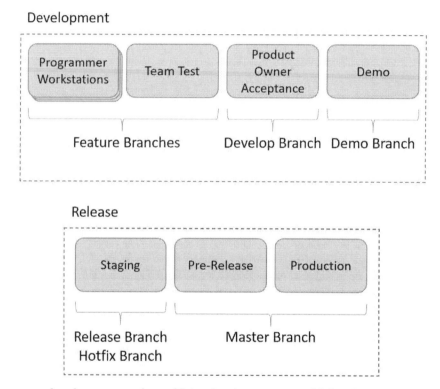

To support the release process, three additional environments are added to the team environments I described in Chapter 11.

The Staging Environment

Some companies call this the "QA" environment, but I like to avoid that name because this environment is used only when preparing a new release for deployment to production. I don't like the implication that quality assurance only happens once in a while, since it should be happening continuously during each sprint through the use of the team test environments.

Computing Horsepower and Multiple Instances

The Staging environment should closely match the configuration of the Production environment. (Goldfuss, 2017) However, it doesn't need to be fully configured in exactly the same way. For example, if Production has a massive amount of computing power and typically has 15 instances running, you likely don't need all of that for Staging.

However, you do need to have Staging configured in a similar fashion when it comes to multiple computing instances. For example, if your product is designed to leverage scale-out technology to run several parallel instances, Staging should have at least two. If your product uses a microservices architecture and Production is configured with a Kubernetes-managed cluster of Docker instances, Staging should be configured in the same way.

Again, you don't need the same scale—computing power or number of instances—as Production. You just need to ensure any configuration that may cause issues with your application once it gets to Production is replicated in Staging.

External Services

If your application communicates with external services such as a payment-processing system or SaaS subscription-management service, the Staging environment should be connected to a sandbox version of the external service or use a testing API key.

At this stage you want as much flexibility as possible, so you don't want to be constrained by tying into "real" external services and feeling like you need to tiptoe around your testing.

Database

Every environment I describe in this book should connect to its own separate database. No two environments should share one database if at all possible. Staging is no exception.

I'm talking about special environments in this chapter used for the release process, so the treatment of the database is slightly different than team environments. Developer workstations, team test environments, and the product owner environment typically use a database generated from creation scripts within the branch being tested. For example, a feature branch for developer workstations and team test environments, and the Develop branch for the product owner acceptance environment.

For the Staging, Pre-Release, and Production environments, I recommend a slightly different strategy, which varies based on whether this is the *first* release or a *subsequent* release.

For the first release, the database simply needs to be generated, including any "system data" the product requires to operate. For example, database tables with lookup values the product will assume exist. For subsequent releases, if there are any schema changes, the database needs to be *updated in place*, without losing any data and gracefully adding any new system data required by new features.

First Release

Assuming you utilize source code version control to manage your database creation scripts, for the first release the database can be created directly from the database scripts in the release branch. If the scripts include creating a set of test or "demo" data, I like to *turn off that part of the script*. This results in a "blank" database that contains only the system data required for the application to run.

I like taking this approach because sometimes the team goes twelve sprints without ever testing the application with an empty database. This strategy of using an empty database ensures the tires will get kicked and any bugs caused by there being no data will be discovered at this point.

Subsequent Release

If this is *not* the first release of the application, you have a major exposure: ensuring the structure of the production database will be updated properly. If the team added a new feature that relies on a new column being present in the database, that feature will likely crash hard if the column doesn't exist. You want to discover that as quickly as possible.

My goal for the Staging environment is to look for bugs caused by *database structure issues*, not data issues. Testing for data issues will come at the next stage, in the Pre-Release environment.

For a subsequent release, I like to generate a "clean" database—with no test or demo data—from the Master branch. Then I like to deploy the release branch to the Staging environment, and have it update that database. This simulates the database schema upgrade that will happen when you apply the code in the release branch to the production database.

Remember, the Master branch at this stage of the game has the code for the release that's currently in Production. Your release branch has the code that is being certified to go into Production. So, a database generated from the Master branch will create, say, your Version 1.3 database. Then you apply your Version 1.4 code from the release branch and have its scripts update the database.

Again here, the goal is to detect bugs caused by a structural issue—often due to a bug in the database update script—and not data-specific bugs.

But We Have a NoSQL Database. Do We Need to Deal with This?

Some products use a NoSQL database such as MongoDB or Azure Cosmos DB. These databases are typically called "schemaless" or "schema-agnostic" because they store data in a very flexible fashion, where the structure can evolve over time as things change. (MongoDB, 2009; Shukla, 2017)

Schemaless doesn't mean unstructured, however. Depending upon the programming language and the types of changes from one version to the next, your development team *may* still need to deal with migrating the schema for a new release. (MongoDB, n.d.)

Even if a schema migration is not required because your NoSQL database will gracefully handle updates to existing features, you should still be careful. Attention needs to be paid to the behavior of the product when a new version "touches" the prior version's database structure, to ensure it's as graceful as you think.

The Pre-Release Environment

The Pre-Release environment is where "things start getting real." I like to use an *exact* match of the Production environment if possible, even if I have to scale it back or shut it down when it's not being used to save money.

The reason is I really, *really* don't want to find any issues once the application gets into Production.

Once it's in Production, problems become a big hassle because your users are impacted. If you discover some nasty bug and it will take a half day to address it, you now need to figure out what to do. Do you roll back the release and say "just kidding" to your users? Do you tell your customers things are a little broken right now, but you'll have it fixed soon? Or do you not say anything and pray no customers notice?

In short, if you let an issue get all the way to Production, you have a gun to your head. If you can accelerate the discovery of any issues into earlier steps in the process, you have *control*. You can take the time to fix it right, make *sure* it's fixed, and *then* deploy to Production.

Computing Horsepower and Multiple Instances

Like I said above, I suggest the Pre-Release environment is an exact match for the Production environment. Some technology supports this quite easily. For example, in Microsoft Azure there's a feature for web applications called "deployment slots." This allows you to deploy code into a parallel slot that lives alongside your Production slot. When everything looks good, you "swap it in" to Production. In a worst-case scenario, you can click a button and swap it back. The introduction of this technology was my original inspiration for introducing the Pre-

Release environment into the process, because it provides so much flexibility. (Karanfilovska, 2018)

If you don't have this luxury, you'll need to create and maintain two environments that have the same configuration.

As far as computing horsepower, this likely depends upon your specific situation. If it's simply not possible to exactly mirror the Production environment's computing horsepower—because of technology, cost, or some other reason—do your best to match it as closely as you can.

Remember your goal is to find any and all issues *before* deploying to Production. Use your best judgment as to what it means to "match Production exactly." Don't get tied up in knots if you can't get approval to create a second $150,000 environment that's a perfect duplicate.

This reminds me of a meme I saw recently, which had a picture of the guy from the Mexican beer commercials which said, "I don't test often. But when I do, I test in Production."

Don't be *that* guy.

External Services

At this stage, because you're trying to mimic Production exactly, the application should be tied into live services and using live API keys. This is obviously going to restrict the types of testing you'll be able to do, but I'll address that later in this chapter as I step you through the test approach I recommend in the Pre-Release environment.

Database

Like the Staging environment, the database strategy for the Pre-Release environment varies depending upon whether it's the first release of the product or a subsequent release.

First Release

For the first product release, I suggest using the database creation script in the Master branch, which contains the product code you're about to release. Like you did for Staging, ensure you turn off any code or scripts that create test or demo data, so you have the database in a clean state.

Subsequent Release

If this is not the first release of the product, I suggest making a copy of the live, production database, and connecting that to the Pre-Release environment. Then deploy the Master branch, so the database update code for the new release can be executed against the production database.

This will let you detect two types of bugs:

- Those caused by *structural issues* in the database. Although you've already tested the upgrade from a "virgin" database created by the scripts for the prior release in the Staging environment, this will be the first time you're updating the actual production database. Sometimes this will uncover unpleasant surprises you didn't see earlier.

- Those caused by *data* in the database. There's no way to properly test the product in the context of real customer data until it's connected to the copy of the production database, so this is important. I've never ceased to be amazed over the years by bugs that only occur when the product sees customer-created data.

The Production Database and Privacy Concerns

Many companies have restrictions around access to the production database, often due to privacy or compliance rules. It may be that no one on the Scrum team has the ability to see under the covers into the raw data. This may make it difficult to troubleshoot any issues discovered during testing in the Pre-Release environment against a copy of the production database.

This may mean you need to get creative about testing at this stage in the process.

One option is getting someone on the Scrum team approved to see production data. That person can then be the one who digs in under the covers to see what's going on if there's a data-related issue.

Another option is to *mask* the data in the database. This could be done with something like Azure's "dynamic database masking" feature, which hides the contents of certain database columns based on the rights of the user but leaves the underlying data intact.

If your technology platform doesn't support a feature like this, you may need to use a tool or create your own database script to mask, scramble, or encrypt specific columns in the Pre-Release database after it's been copied from Production.

If you do create your own script, be careful to ensure the product will still function properly with the adjusted data.

The Production Environment

The Production environment—which some shorten to just "Prod"—is the live, customer-facing environment that hosts your product day to day. It's the "real deal."

The exact configuration of the Production environment differs widely based on technology, the size of your customer base, the type of product, and more. I won't try to tell you what your Production environment should look like.

There are a few characteristics that Production environments share. Some may be obvious, some not. I'll include a brief summary in the interest of completeness.

Computing Horsepower and Multiple Instances

For Production, the computing horsepower is whatever is required to support the typical number of simultaneous users accessing your product without performance degrading below whatever standards you have set. The same goes for the number of multiple instances—it will depend upon the demand of your customers.

Today's cloud frameworks include *auto-scaling* options, which automatically ramp up computing horsepower and/or the number of instances running your product. Once configured, the platform will automatically add more capacity when needed, and ramp it back down when it's not, which saves money.

Database

The Production environment should have its own database, and given it contains extremely valuable and irreplaceable information, a solid backup strategy must be implemented to ensure you never lose any customer data. It's beyond the scope of this book to talk about techniques to handle this, but this is another area where cloud platforms such as Azure and AWS come into play. They have multiple features for securely backing up your data, including options to back up your data in a *geo-distributed* fashion, storing copies in different physical locations around the world.

First Release

For the first release, I recommend having the database scripts in the Master branch build the initial database. This will ensure its structure matches what's been used throughout development.

Subsequent Release

For any release beyond the first one, the database should be updated in-place, again using the scripts in the Master branch. The big benefit you get from this approach is replicating the update process that's been tested on earlier environments.

Leveraging Continuous Deployment

In Section 23.10, I talked about continuous deployment, which automates the process of taking the product code from a branch in the source code repository and configuring it on a specific environment.

I've found the use of continuous deployment very helpful during the release process as well. Here's how I recommend configuring it:

Staging. Once the release branch is created, connect the Staging environment directly to it. This will make the process go more quickly because whenever a bug fix or other adjustment is made in the release branch, the code will automatically re-deploy, and the environment will have the latest changes in a few minutes. This makes testing faster and easier.

Pre-Release. I suggest connecting this environment directly to the Master branch. That way, once the Master branch is updated by merging in the release branch, it will be automatically updated. If a hotfix is required during the process of certifying the product in Pre-Release, the environment will be automatically updated when the hotfix branch is merged into the Master branch.

Production. I do not recommend configuring continuous deployment for the Production environment. A few years ago, I thought I'd be fancy by connecting Production directly to the Master branch. Then someone inadvertently updated Master with some code that wasn't fully tested, and Production was updated automatically. It was a mad scramble to roll things back once we discovered the mistake.

Today we use Azure deployment slots to swap Pre-Release and Production when we're ready, allowing us to control deployment via a manual "we know exactly when it's going to happen" process.

Environments Summary

Below is a summary of the environments I talked about in this section.

	Staging	**Pre-Release**	**Production**
Computing Horsepower	Moderate to High	Same as Production	As Necessary
Multiple Instances	Similar to Production	Same as Production	As Necessary
External Services	Development/Sandbox	Live	Live
Source Code Branch	Release or Hotfix	Master	Master
Database (Initial Release)	Generated from release branch (No test/demo data)	Generated from Master branch (No test/demo data)	Generated from Master branch (No test/demo data)
Database (Subsequent Releases)	Generated from Master, updated from release branch	Copy of production database, updated from Master branch	Production database, updated from Master branch

A summary of environments used during the release process.

30.3 The Five-Step Release Process in Detail

I'll detail the process step-by-step in this section. Here's what it looks like start to finish:

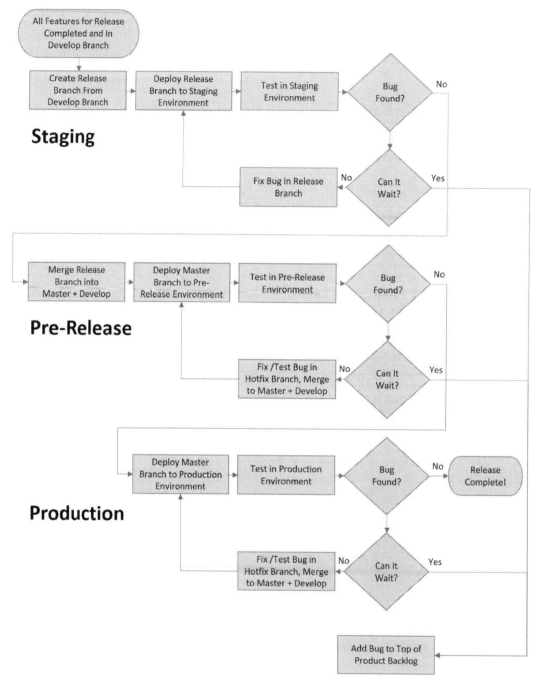

The complete release process.

Step 1: Isolate Source Code for the Release

Years ago, we didn't have today's sophisticated version control technology. Because it was a pain to isolate the code for the release, we would instead "freeze" the code. No one was allowed to make changes, since new code in one area of the product would often break something in another.

This was extremely inefficient because although everyone on the team tried to help, inevitably there were some team members who couldn't contribute. We ended up losing efficiency as we searched for something for them to do.

Today we're blessed with technology such as Git, which makes it super easy to branch the code—effectively creating a virtual copy. By creating a *release branch*, the code can be *virtually* frozen, by isolating it. This allows the team to focus on final testing and fixing critical bugs. (Driessen, 2010)

With this in mind, the first step in the five-stage release process is to create a release branch.

See *Release Branches* in Section 12.5 for more details. If your team decides not to use Git Flow, I'd still encourage creating a separate release branch to isolate the code.

Step 2: Certify the Release Branch in the Staging Environment

With Scrum, testing is accelerated much earlier in the process as compared to traditional waterfall-based software development. You might be familiar with using a Production-like environment for testing, but you likely aren't used to the type of testing you'll perform in this environment in a Scrum world.

It's *dramatically* more lightweight than what you might be used to. Why? Because quality has been *accelerated* into each sprint.

Remember—the Scrum team has said at the end of each sprint, "We believe the product is at a level of quality that it can go into Production today, *without any further testing*."

I'm not saying you *shouldn't* do any further testing, but the team has said, "This is good to go!"

What to Look For

Making the assumption for a moment that the team has followed all my advice so far in this book about how to accelerate quality and ensure the product is potentially shippable, that means the only testing that's left is of the "kick the tires" variety.

There are specific situations the team is looking at now that's a little different than what they may have tested day in and day out during each sprint.

These include:

Environmental concerns. If you use scaling technology in Production, verifying the product works correctly when being run in a cluster of multiple computing instances is a really good idea.

An empty database. Testing with an empty database is important and might not be something the team has done on a consistent basis. This is especially critical for the first release but is also important in a multi-tenant product. When a new customer signs up, from their perspective they'll effectively be using an empty database.

An upgraded database. For any release other than the first one, ensuring the database will be properly upgraded is critical. Although the team has simulated a database upgrade each time they update the product owner acceptance environment, taking a step back and doing a full upgrade from the current database schema being used in Production is not something they've likely done.

How to Test

In Section 14.5 I talked about creating an automated *smoke test*, focused on hitting all the key business workflows in the application and ensuring everything is working. This is a critical tool to use during the release process.

Even if the team hasn't automated the smoke test, it's still an important tool, as it will ensure there is a structured approach to making sure the product actually works.

If the smoke test is created properly, leveraging a key subset of the acceptance tests that have been written for the product, it will exercise all the key areas.

There is a big point here: you will *not* be testing the whole product. There's not enough time. You're kicking the tires, albeit in a structured and deliberate fashion, and then "calling it good."

This underscores how critically important it is for the rest of your quality strategy to be sound. If you don't have automated unit tests that are all written properly and passing, this won't work. If the team hasn't written and executed acceptance test plans, this won't work. If the team hasn't fixed bugs along the way and kept the product in a potentially shippable state, this won't work.

In short, the *only* way you can release in one sprint is if the amount of testing and related bug fixing is minimized to an amazing degree. This is only the case if the product is already 99% where it needs to be.

What About All the Other Testing We Need to Do?

You may be reading this and thinking, "*Kick the tires?* That's not going to work. Our company requires security audits, compliance review, penetration testing, performance testing, and the list goes on. When do we do all of that?"

The short version is you don't have time for all that stuff during a release sprint. Have you ever been able to request, get completed, and address any issues from a penetration test within a day or two? If not, you won't have time to wait until the release sprint.

Am I saying that you shouldn't do that testing? No. But all that needs to be accelerated to occur prior to the release sprint, alongside all the other testing that makes the product increment potentially shippable at the end of each sprint.

Security, compliance, and performance are all what I call *cross-cutting concerns*. That is, they apply across the product as a whole. You can't wait until the release sprint to address these types of things *and* get the product reviewed to ensure you've met any required standards.

See both *Cross-Cutting Concerns* and *Performance* in Section 22.2 for more about how to leverage user stories to address these kinds of requirements.

The Process Step by Step

Below are the typical steps for certifying a web application in the Staging environment. Your steps will likely vary, but this should give you a general understanding of how the process works.

1. *Generate a database to be upgraded.* First, the Master branch—representing the current release in Production—is deployed and the product is accessed to force the generation of a blank database using the scripts in that branch. (This step is skipped if it's the very first release of the product.)

2. *Deploy the release branch.* Using continuous integration tools, the release branch is deployed to the Staging environment. Once the product is accessed, the database upgrade script will automatically be executed against the blank database created in the previous step, for every release except the first one.

3. *Test.* The automated smoke test is executed. If for some reason the team chose not to automate the smoke test, they run it manually. Because the team was careful to ensure the smoke test covers the core business workflows in the application, this should be the only testing they need to do during the release sprint. Some teams will enhance the smoke test at this stage in the process if they discover holes in their strategy.

4. *Fix bugs.* Bugs are fixed in the release branch, the code is automatically re-deployed as changes are made, and each bug is re-tested in the Staging environment to ensure it's been fixed. Minor bugs are timeboxed to ensure continued momentum toward certifying the release. Bugs that can wait until the next release are added to the top of the product backlog. I'll talk more about triaging bugs during the release sprint later in this chapter.

5. *Certify the release.* Once the team is satisfied the product has been appropriately tested, all bugs have been fixed, and the product owner gives the stamp of approval, the release is considered "certified" in the Staging environment.

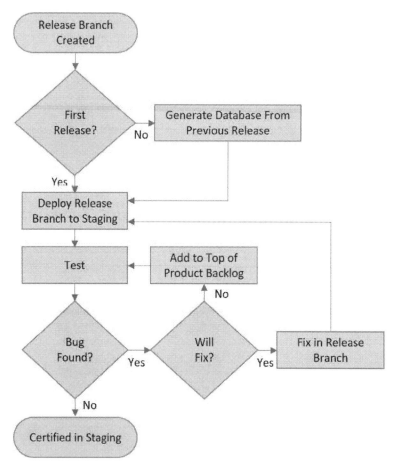

The process to certify the product in the Staging environment.

Step 3: Merge the Release Branch into the Master Branch

Once the release branch has its stamp of approval, the code is merged from the release branch into the Master branch.

The release branch is *also* merged back into the Develop branch. This is important because you want to make sure you carry any bug fixes and other adjustments that have been made directly to the release branch back into the Develop branch. Otherwise, they won't make it into the *next* release. Some desktop-based Git tools—such as Sourcetree—do this for you, by letting you "finish" the release, which merges the release branch both to Master and Develop. (Sourcetree, 2012)

Most teams delete the release branch at this point, since Git supports tagging a specific point in the history of code changes, making it easy to get back to a certain release if necessary.

Some teams—particularly those who must support multiple deployed versions of an application such as a desktop or mobile app—might choose to keep the release branch. This makes it easier to go back and test a specific version at some point in the future by deploying that release branch to a team test environment. For example, the team might need to reproduce a bug discovered by a customer using an older version.

Step 4: Certify the Master Branch in the Pre-Release Environment

At this stage in the process, the team should be pretty satisfied that the product is ready for prime time. The primary use of the Pre-Release environment is to do a dry run of putting the product into an environment that's very close to Production, including being tied to a copy of the production database, to detect problems.

Some teams skip this step, going directly from Staging to Production. I used to be one of them. But I found inserting this step avoids the unpleasantness and pit in your stomach when you realize the product has a bug that could have been detected if you had tested in this environment.

What to Look For

At this point the team is looking for issues caused by situations that are different from earlier environments, typically because of a) using a copy of the production database and b) tying into real, "live" external systems.

Specific things to pay attention to are:

Bugs caused by the data in the production database. It always amazes me that there are certain combinations of data that sneak into the database and cause a bug, even though it's never been seen before during all the other testing with sample data the team has done over time.

For example, a user might have performed a specific series of steps that caused bad data to be introduced into the database, and that data is incompatible with a feature in the new release.

Performance issues caused by the volume of data in the production database. Although the team should have done performance testing prior to the release sprint, sometimes there's a certain table under the covers that has a lot of data which causes a performance issue with a new feature. The team should keep a lookout for this type of problem.

Issues caused by tying into live systems. Although at this point the product should have been thoroughly tested with sandbox or development versions of external systems such as payment processing, sometimes things don't work when it's "for real."

Needless to say, if your customer can't make an in-app purchase because the product doesn't work when talking to the live payment service, that would be a nasty problem.

Data loss caused by a database schema change. One of my biggest fears whenever upgrading a deployed version of our products was somehow destroying data when the database was upgraded. Any database schema changes should be carefully tested to make sure the upgrade scripts didn't wreak havoc with production data.

How to Test

Like the Staging environment, the smoke test can be leveraged in the Pre-Release environment to detect issues. However, there are some things to keep in mind:

- *Adjustments might be needed for touchpoints with external systems.* If the smoke test makes a $200 purchase using a fake credit card number, this likely won't be supported with the live payment processing service. You'll want to adjust that part of the smoke test for use in this environment, for example creating a $1 product and using a real credit card.

- *Additional testing might be required.* The smoke test might not include performance testing. This is an area that you may want to beef up during testing in the Pre-Release environment. At least some basic performance testing may be needed to ensure you detect issues specific to the data that's in the production database. The team will also likely want to pay careful attention to any areas of the database impacted by a schema change.

Because of the team's level of confidence by this stage in the process, the amount of testing in the Pre-Release environment should be dramatically less than the Staging environment.

The Process Step by Step

This is the process to certify the product in the Pre-Release environment:

1. *Make a copy of the production database.* The copy is made and named pre-release. The Pre-Release environment is configured to connect to this database.

2. *Mask production data if necessary.* If there are restrictions around development team members seeing production data, the data is masked. The key here is the development team needs to be able to access the copy of the production database so they can troubleshoot any issues they discover. See The Production Database and Privacy Concerns earlier in this section for more details.

3. *Deploy the Master branch.* The Master branch is deployed to the Pre-Release environment. If the Pre-Release environment is directly connected to the Master branch via continuous deployment tools, this will happen automatically once the release branch is merged into the Master branch. In this case, the team needs to ensure the production database has been copied and the environment is attached to it before the product is accessed so any database upgrade scripts will be executed.

4. *Test.* Like the process for the Staging environment, the team now tests the product, focused on scenarios specific to being connected to the production database and live external services.

5. *Fix bugs.* The hope is by this point, there are no bugs to be discovered. If any issues are found, the product owner will triage them and decide whether it's worth the risk to fix them, as I'll talk about in the next section. We have a very specific rule that no changes are allowed to be made directly to the Master branch, so if a bug needs to be fixed, it's done using the hotfix process I described in Hotfix Branches in Section 12.5. The Staging environment can be used to test the hotfix branch before it's merged back into Master, which will re-deploy it to the Pre-Release environment.

6. *Certify the release.* Once the team and product owner are happy, they "certify" the release in the Pre-Release environment.

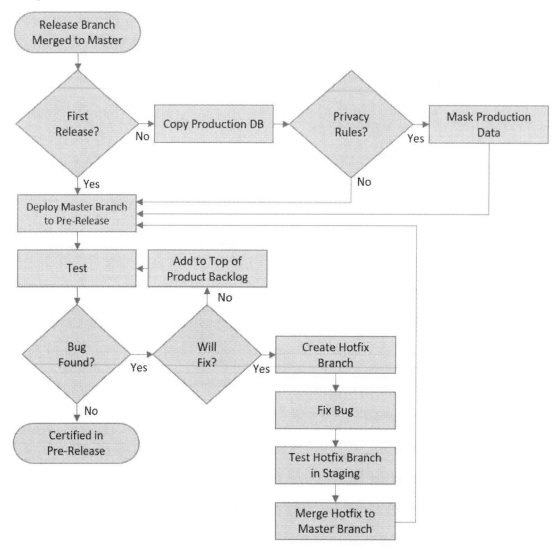

The certification process in the Pre-Release environment.

Step 5: Certify the Master Branch in Production

As much as it would be nice to push a button to deploy code to Production and go home for the day, I suggest being a little more paranoid than that. Sometimes things don't go as expected.

What to Look For

At this stage you're looking to do a basic sanity test. The things I typically would verify are:

- *Did it deploy correctly?* Taking a quick look at the product to verify the new version did in fact deploy is a good first step. It's easy to do—just check to see if a new feature or adjusted functionality is present in the product.

- *Does it basically work?* The worst-case scenario is deploying a new product and something fundamental no longer works for some reason. For example, users of an e-commerce product can no longer make a purchase.

Beyond these two fundamentals, you're trusting the rest of the testing process up to this point was thorough enough to ensure the product is working correctly.

If you find that you either aren't comfortable with this light amount of testing, or there are all kinds of bugs making it through to production, it's again time to take a hard look at all the quality-driven steps in the process leading up to this point.

Something is broken if you aren't *very* confident in the level of quality at this point.

How to Test

I like to see teams create what I call an *abbreviated smoke test* for use at this stage of the game. This is a smaller subset of the smoke test, focused on only core, highly critical workflows. If the smoke test is focused on the 20% of the product used 80% of the time, the abbreviated smoke test might be focused on the 3% of the product that's going to cause 97% of the headaches if something isn't working correctly.

There's another difference between this plan and the regular smoke test: it's tuned to the production environment. Since the team is now in the "real" product, they need to be careful about what data is modified, and they'll need to clean up after themselves.

For example, to test the checkout process they may decide to create a fake product. Once they make the purchase, they'll have to ensure they roll it back so the shipping department doesn't get confused if they try to fulfill the order. Removing the fake product from the catalog would be a good idea too.

Another example is if the team creates a new customer signup in a SaaS product. They'll want to delete that trial subscription once they create it to avoid confusing the onboarding team.

The Process Step by Step

This is the process for certifying the product in Production:

1. *Verify backup of Production database.* Before deploying the code to the new release, the first step is to verify whatever backup process you have in place is actually working. There's nothing more stressful than a production deployment that goes wrong and causes an issue with your data.

2. *Swap Pre-Release and Production.* Using the deployment slots feature in Azure, our teams click a button to "swap" the Pre-Release code into the Production environment. Depending upon the technology in your product, the team may be able to do the same thing using a feature of your deployment platform. Or, they may need to deploy the new Master branch to the Production environment if "swapping" is not supported.

3. *Test.* The team performs limited testing as I described earlier in this section. They'll be careful to follow the steps in the abbreviated smoke test to clean up after themselves, so no test data remains in the product.

4. *Fix bugs.* The goal of all the quality-focused work leading up to this point is to discover any bugs before you reach production. However, if an issue is found, a hotfix process needs to be kicked off to address it. The Staging environment can be used to test the hotfix branch before it's merged back into Master, then the Pre-Release environment can be used to re-test the Master branch code before updating the Production environment with the fix.

5. *Certify the release.* Assuming everything looks good, the product owner blesses the release and says, "We're done!"

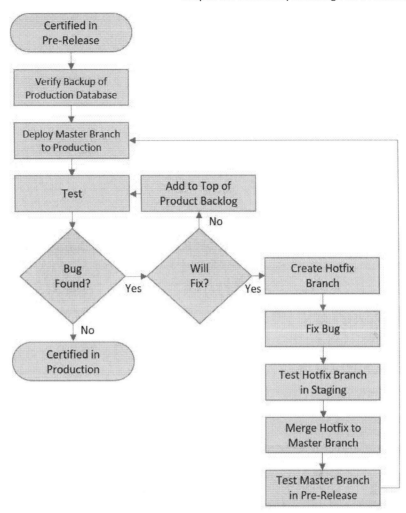

The final step: certifying the release in the Production environment.

30.4 Triaging Bugs Discovered During the Release Sprint

In Chapter 27 I talked about timeboxing the bug-fixing effort to ensure the team avoids getting sucked into a black hole—spending hours or days fixing a low-impact bug. During the release sprint, carefully considering bug-fixing trade-offs takes on a higher level of importance.

There are two reasons to think carefully about whether to fix bugs during the release sprint:

- *You might not have enough time.* Reproducing a bug, writing a failing unit test, fixing it, and re-testing it takes time. But time during a release sprint is limited. If the team gets sucked into spending a lot of time on bugs that don't materially impact the usability of the product, they might not ship within the timeframe of the release sprint.

467

- *Something else might get broken.* Unfortunately, the law of unintended consequences is in full effect any time you touch the code. Fixing a minor bug *may* create a nastier bug.

During the release sprint I encourage teams to be a little more selective about fixing bugs. Addressing a fundamental problem with the checkout process is a no-brainer. Dealing with a label on the screen that's one pixel too low might be something that can wait.

Leveraging Bug Priority and Severity

The triaging process can be made less subjective by using priority and severity ratings such as what I described in Section 27.4, driving a strategy to use with your team to guide decision-making at each step in the process.

The product owner can then use the rules to decide whether a bug discovered during the release sprint will be fixed or "punted" to the next release. I'll talk more about how to deal with punted bugs later in this section.

To keep things simple, instead of using both priority and severity, the team could create a strategy based solely on priority, which is a measure of the business impact of a bug.

For example, they might create a set of rules such as the following:

- *Normal sprints.* Fix bugs with any priority, checking in with the product owner after every hour of effort so they can monitor progress and decide whether to abandon the bug-fixing effort.

- *Release sprint (Staging).* Fix Major, Critical, or Blocker bugs. Punt Minor and Trivial.

- *Release sprint (Pre-Release).* Fix Critical or Blocker bugs. Punt Major, Minor, and Trivial.

- *Release sprint (Production).* Fix Critical or Blocker bugs. Punt Major, Minor, and Trivial.

Here's a summary of this strategy:

	Blocker	Critical	Major	Minor	Trivial
Normal Sprints	Fix	Fix	Fix	Fix	Fix
Staging	Fix	Fix	Fix	Punt	Punt
Pre-Release	Fix	Fix	Punt	Punt	Punt
Production	Fix	Fix	Punt	Punt	Punt

A sample triaging strategy based on bug priority.

You may find it's better to use a combination of priority and severity. Regardless of the strategy you choose, it's helpful to have a set of rules in place so everyone knows the plan for how bugs are dealt with during the release process.

What to Do with "Punted" Bugs

Bugs that are "punted" don't get brushed aside and thrown under the rug. They should be placed at the top of the product backlog and documented using a standard bug format such as what I described in Section 27.3.

If the team finds themselves with extra time during the release sprint, they could consider bringing a bug into the sprint and fixing it in a feature branch. If they finish the bug, that branch can be merged into the Develop branch for inclusion in the *next* release. It *shouldn't* be merged into the release branch because the product owner decided not to fix it for the release being certified for deployment.

If it turns out the bug was super-simple to address, and the code change was very localized and unlikely to affect other functionality, the product owner *could* decide to apply that fix to the release branch. This should be done only after careful consideration of the risk/reward equation by asking the question, "Is it worth the risk of something else potentially getting broken by introducing this fix?"

Bugs Discovered Immediately after Deploying to Production

No one wants to hear the day after the product was deployed to production that a customer found a bug. After all the work the team did to make sure nothing snuck past them, it can be depressing to get this kind of news.

There are a few choices to handle this situation:

Ignore it. In this case, a bug is added to the top of the product backlog and it's fixed in the next release. Customers will have to live with the bug until then. This is likely only a viable option if the bug has a low impact to the usability of the product and/or affects only a small number of users.

Apply a hotfix. Using the hotfix process I described in *Step 5: Certify the Master Branch in Production* in Section 30.3, the team can make a surgical fix, test it, and apply it to the production code to resolve the problem.

Roll back the release. If the bug is really bad and would require major surgery and a lot of time to fix, the team could decide to roll back the deployment, swapping in the previous release. How easy this is to do likely depends upon your technology platform.

For example, with Azure deployment slots, this may be easy, if the database is backwards-compatible with the prior release. Otherwise, its schema might need to be rolled back as well. This "do-over" option is likely the riskiest.

30.5 Orchestrating the Work of the Release Sprint

Just like any other sprint, the work of the release sprint needs to be orchestrated through the use of the Scrum process, and that means one or more product backlog items.

Leveraging the Product Backlog

I have experimented with both tasks and user stories on the product backlog to represent the release process. I've decided that user stories are better than tasks for this purpose.

Deploying a release into production certainly provides benefit to business stakeholders, and that means a user story is more appropriate. Plus, there's real effort involved, so assigning a story point estimate to the release story can be beneficial.

The user story can be as simple as something like the following, written with a generic "User" role, *As a User, I want Version 2.6 deployed, so I can use its features.*

The development team can estimate the story point value for this story just like any other, and they can also split the user story as the release sprint draws near. For example, they might create split user stories along the lines of:

- As a User, I want Version 2.6 certified in Staging, so I know it's ready for my use

- As a User, I want Version 2.6 certified in Pre-Release, so I know it's ready for my use

- As a User, I want Version 2.6 certified in Production, so I can use its features

Splitting the stories like this makes it easier for the team to separate the individual steps—represented by subtasks within each story—as they move their way through the release process.

As the team gets more proficient they might experiment with using two stories, or even one story when they get *really* good.

Communicating about the Release

One thing to remember when getting close to release is to ask the question, "Who else needs to know about this?" Other departments likely need to be kept apprised of the status of the release. Some may need to know weeks or months in advance. Others might not need to know until the release is out the door.

Stakeholders May Already Have Enough Information

If the right stakeholders are showing up to every sprint review, or even every other sprint review, appropriate areas of the business should know well beforehand details about the timing of the release, since during each sprint review the team will review the projected schedule. However, you might not have this situation in your company. In this case, you need to think about who needs to be informed.

Keeping Track of Communication Requirements

Like everything else done by the team, the product backlog can be used to track the necessary communication with other parts of the company. This could be as simple as adding a user story along the lines of, *As a Company Stakeholder, I want to be kept informed about the Version 2.6 release, so I can coordinate my department's work.*

Another option is to use multiple stories, such as:

- As a Client Services Stakeholder, I want to be kept informed about the Version 2.6 release, so I can keep customers informed

- As a Sales Stakeholder, I want to be kept informed about the Version 2.6 release, so I can keep prospects informed

- As a Marketing Stakeholder, I want to be kept informed about the Version 2.6 release, so I can adjust my marketing campaigns

Some of these user stories might need to be brought into sprints prior to the release sprint. Others might be able to be deferred until the release sprint.

30.6 But It's Not This Easy at My Company

At this point you might be rolling your eyes and thinking, "Dave is oversimplifying this," or, "Dave is out of touch with reality—he must be living in a dream world. It won't be this easy at my company."

Look, I know that every company is different, and you might not be able to make things as simple as I've outlined. But assuming for a minute you have two weeks to complete the release process, your process simply *can't* be too much more sophisticated than what I've outlined. You won't have enough time.

The bottom line is your company *needs* to ship as fast as possible. It's a key way for businesses to remain competitive. Customers no longer will be happy waiting six to twelve months for you to update your product. The world is moving too quickly for that. (Lomas, 2018)

You Can Do It

I encourage you to apply what you can from this chapter, but *don't lower your standards*. If your sprint length is two weeks but it takes you five weeks to ship, don't throw up your hands and say, "It's different for us. We need more than two weeks to ship."

Take a hard look at what happened during those five weeks and ask yourself some questions based on the problems you encountered that stood in the way of getting everything done in two weeks:

- *There was too much work.* Why couldn't we have done more of that work during earlier sprints? Is everyone working as efficiently as possible? Is any of this work unnecessary, perhaps being a holdover from our waterfall days?

- *Too many bugs were discovered.* Why were there so many bugs? What does that indicate about holes in our quality strategy? Can we examine the bugs and identify and address the root cause of them not being detected during earlier sprints? Did we truly create a *potentially shippable* product increment at the end of each sprint? If not, what needs to change to make that a reality?

- *Testing took too much time.* Are we spending too much time testing because we didn't employ a solid unit testing strategy? Are we testing more than the 20% of the product that is used 80% of the time? Can we add automation to make time-consuming manual testing more efficient?

- *The oversight process was too slow.* What steps could have been done earlier to address things such as security audits and penetration testing? For any processes that *must* be done during the release sprint, what could we have done to better schedule the necessary resources or get them the information they needed earlier?

Remember that Amazon releases on average every 11.7 *seconds*. Two weeks is an *eternity* compared to that. (Null, 2015)

Instead of thinking, "There's no way we can do this in one release sprint," I'd like to suggest you instead ask, "What needs to change so we *can* do this in one sprint?"

I realize this requires a shift in thinking compared to those who are used to waterfall projects. Keep the big picture in mind and stay optimistic. It will come together with some work. (SmartBear Software, n.d.)

Remember the Key Principles

Everyone's release process will be different. Regardless of the individual steps, remember these key success factors:

- *Accelerate quality.* Ensure you are truly producing a *potentially shippable* product increment at the end of each sprint. If quality is too low at the start of the release sprint, you'll never ship fast enough. Figure out how to drive quality higher earlier in the process, which will boost efficiency. (Li, et al., 2010)

- *Test in multiple environments.* Use additional environments beyond the team testing environments I described earlier in this book, each focused on a specific purpose and each being a little closer to matching the Production environment.

- *Focus on database upgrades.* If your product uses a database, ensure that upgrading the production database schema will work and won't cause any bugs.

- *Don't let bugs get to production.* Although it always seems like *something* makes its way into Production, treat this situation as a failure somewhere in the process. Figure out what to do to avoid any bugs making it that far the next time around.

The release process is an area where I've lost years of my life in the past, but today things are different. I *never* worry about the ability of our teams to ship.

They work the process and the results speak for themselves. I can't think of any time when a team was unable to release in one sprint, and once the product is in production, our clients and their customers struggle to find any bugs.

30.7 Life After the Release Sprint

Years ago, my development teams' quality process was nowhere near as sophisticated as it is today. We didn't have automated unit tests. We had automated integration tests, but they were fragile and unreliable. We spent an enormous amount of time focused on manual testing before each new release went out the door, but it was difficult to test everything properly.

Back then there wasn't much of a mystery as to what we'd be doing after the release. We'd be fixing bugs for about six months. Today it's different. When we get a new release out the door, there are *very* few bugs, perhaps three to five for a release that involved three months of development.

This leads to a question. If the team won't be spending six months fixing bugs, what the heck *will* they be doing after the release sprint?

The First Product Release Is the Starting Line

If you've been in the software business for a while, you know the very first release of a new product isn't the end—it's the beginning. Even if you had some early adopters using pre-release versions, they likely didn't truly put it through all the paces. Once the "real" release is out the door they typically take things more seriously as they start to put the product into daily use.

At this point you'll learn what the product *actually* needs to do. This is why agile focuses on building a small product quickly and getting it into users' hands.

What this means is most teams will continue working as they have been. They'll wrap up the release sprint and move directly into planning their next sprint. After all, the release sprint is just another iteration. It just happens to include the process of getting the product into production.

Pushing the Pause Button

Some companies will decide to release the product and "push the pause button." That is, they'll have the team halt development until some time goes by, allowing users to experience the product as-is and provide feedback to guide the next round of development.

This could range from a few weeks to a few months. It all depends upon the business conditions and the goals of the organization.

During this time, the team might stay together and chip away at things on the product backlog the product owner really wanted to get into the product but then ran out of time. Or they could take time to do some technical work, such as refactoring some areas of the product the team thinks could be a bit better. In this case they'll have to sell the product owner on why that work is valuable so they're not changing things for the sake of change.

There will likely be bugs discovered by customers, so the team can tackle those as necessary. Critical bugs might require a hotfix, which they can focus on to get the customer back up and running, as I described in Section 27.7. Other bugs can be fixed and included in the next release.

In some cases, team members might be reassigned temporarily to help other teams. They'll then regroup and start sprinting again once feedback comes in from users and the product owner has had enough time to adjust the backlog based on what was learned.

Note that I recommend if the team continues doing *any* work, they keep leveraging the Scrum process. It's easy to believe a scaled-back amount of work can be managed by "winging it," but in my experience things fall completely apart as soon as the safety net of a sprint is removed.

Scaling Things Back

Sometimes an organization will "throw bodies" at a product development effort so they can get it out the door faster. They might have a large Scrum team or even have multiple teams pushing to get the first release done.

Once the product ships, the company may decide they can scale back the development effort. They may disband two of the three teams working on the product. Or they may reduce the Scrum development team from nine people to five.

The scaled-back team will continue to work on the product, adding enhancements and fixing bugs as they come up.

But Our Projects Have a Start and an End

When moving to agile we like to abandon thinking about *projects* with a discrete start and end, and instead think about *products* with a long lifetime. However, sometimes the project concept still applies.

This might be due to applying an agile approach to projects that aren't software-related. For example, moving the corporate office across town. Scrum could be a great fit for this type of project. There's a to-do list which likely should be ordered by business priority. There are probably several team members involved, and they need to effectively coordinate their work. And it's probably important to have one person in charge of making decisions about what success looks like and ensuring everything is being done to an acceptable standard.

If there is a discrete deliverable or outcome that doesn't require ongoing care and feeding, there's no reason to keep a team in place. In this example, the office move happened, the dust has settled, and we're done. The team can move on to other things.

Key Takeaways

- I've had great success with a five-step release process: 1) Isolate source code for the release, for example by using a release branch. 2) "Certify" the release branch in a Staging environment. 3) Update the production codebase by merging the release branch into the Master branch. 4) Certify the production code in a Pre-Release environment. 5) Certify the production code in the Production environment.

- The Staging environment is similar to the Production environment, but likely doesn't have the same amount of horsepower and strict security configuration. It ties into development or sandbox versions of external systems, and database upgrade scripts are tested against the database version from the prior release. If this is the first release of the product, the database is generated from the release branch code.

- Key things to examine in the Staging environment are environmental concerns, for example ensuring the product is working in a multiple-instance, clustered environment similar to what will be encountered in production. It's also important to test with an empty database and an upgraded database if this is not the first release.

- The Pre-Release environment should be a close duplicate of the Production environment, if not an exact duplicate. It ties into "real," live versions of external systems and uses a copy of the production database.

- Depending upon your company's compliance requirements, the copy of the production database used in the Pre-Release environment might need to have some data masked for privacy reasons. It's important to complete this step so the development team can view the data if there's a problem with testing in this environment.

- In the Pre-Release environment, it's important to check for bugs caused by the product working against the production data. Included might be performance issues due to large volumes of "real" data. Also important is to look for any issues due to connecting to live external systems as well as ensuring no data is lost when the database structure is updated.

- The Production environment is "the real deal." It's what's used daily by end users, so it needs to be configured to support the required workload and security requirements.

- Two key things to check in the Production environment is that the new version of the product deployed correctly and that its core functionality works.

- The amount and depth of testing diminishes as the release makes its way through each environment. This is because most of the testing should have been performed—and quality "baked in"—during each sprint leading up to the release sprint. If intensive testing is necessary or a lot of bugs are found during the release sprint, the team needs to evaluate what they can do to accelerate quality earlier in the process.

- Bugs should be triaged more aggressively during the release process as compared to during a normal sprint. Bug priority and severity can be used for this purpose. A simple way to approach this is to experiment by using just priority to govern which bugs are fixed versus punted to the next release.

- Work of the release sprint needs to be orchestrated just like any other sprint. One or more user stories can be used—along with their associated subtasks—to coordinate the work of the team.

- You may have additional challenges at your company that makes it difficult to release during just one sprint. If you are having trouble, I encourage you to believe it can be done and challenge assumptions. Look closely at what is delaying the process and work to accelerate those things into earlier sprints.

- For software products, the release sprint isn't the end; it's the beginning. Once users have a "real" version they'll typically use the product more often and more thoroughly. This is when you'll start to get feedback about their experience and learn what the product really needs to do, which then guides the team's work moving forward.

- Some companies "push the pause button" after a release to allow feedback to come in and guide additional work of the team. During this time they might work on product backlog items that didn't make it into the release and fix bugs that are on the product backlog.

- Scaling back the size of the team might make sense for some companies, especially if there was a big push to get the first version of the product out the door and they staffed up to get things moving faster.

- If the team produced a discrete deliverable or outcome that doesn't require care and feeding, it might make sense to treat that as a *project* as opposed to a *product*. A project starts and ends, whereas a product has a continuing need for maintenance over time. In the case of a project, the team can likely be disbanded after the release process if there is no follow-on work.

References

Abrahamsson, P., Babar, M. A. & Kruchten, P., 2010. Agility and Architecture: Can They Coexist?. *IEEE Software*, March/April, pp. 16-22.

Agile Alliance, n.d. *Acceptance Testing*. [Online]
Available at: https://www.agilealliance.org/glossary/acceptance/

Agile Alliance, n.d. *Sustainable Pace*. [Online]
Available at: https://www.agilealliance.org/glossary/sustainable

Alnuaimi, O. A., Robert, L. P. J. & Maruping, L. M., 2010. Team Size, Dispersion, and Social Loafing in Technology-Supported Teams: A Perspective on the Theory of Moral Disengagement. *Journal of Management Information Systems,* 27(1), pp. 203-230.

Alzoubi, Y. I., Gill, A. Q. & Al-Ani, A., 2015. Distributed Agile Development Communication: An Agile Architecture Driven Framework. *JSW,* 10(6), pp. 681-694.

Andreessen, M., 2011. *Why Software Is Eating the World*. [Online]
Available at: https://a16z.com/2016/08/20/why-software-is-eating-the-world/

Atlassian, n.d. *Gitflow Workflow*. [Online]
Available at: https://www.atlassian.com/git/tutorials/comparing-workflows/gitflow-workflow

Atwood, J., 2006. *The Last Responsible Moment*. [Online]
Available at: https://blog.codinghorror.com/the-last-responsible-moment/

Bavota, G. & Russo, B., 2015. Four Eyes Are Better Than Two: On the Impact of Code Reviews on Software Quality. *Proceedings of the 31st International Conference on Software Maintenance and Evolution (ICSME),* pp. 81-90.

Beck, K., 2003. *Test-Driven Development: By Example*. Boston, MA: Addison-Wesley.

Beck, K. et al., 2001a. *Manifesto for Agile Software Development*. [Online]
Available at: http://agilemanifesto.org/

Beck, K. et al., 2001b. *Principles behind the Agile Manifesto*. [Online]
Available at: https://agilemanifesto.org/principles.html

Berndt, D., Jones, J. & Finch, D., 2006. Milestone markets: Software cost estimation through market trading. *Proceedings of the 39th Annual Hawaii International Conference on System Sciences,* Volume 9, p. 230a.

Berryman, S., 1991. Designing Effective Learning Environments: Cognitive Apprenticeship Models. *IEE Brief.*

Billings, S., 2017. *Why Not to Extend a Sprint.* [Online]
Available at:
https://www.scrumalliance.org/community/articles/2017/september/why-not-to-extend-a-sprint

Bleiberg, J. & West, D. M., 2015. *A look back at technical issues with Healthcare.gov.* [Online]
Available at: https://www.brookings.edu/blog/techtank/2015/04/09/a-look-back-at-technical-issues-with-healthcare-gov/

Boehm, B., 1984. Software Engineering Economics. *IEEE transactions on Software Engineering,* pp. 4-21.

Brede Moe, N., Dingsøyr, T. & Dybå, T., 2008. Understanding Self-organizing Teams in Agile Software Development. *IEEE 19th Australian Conference on Software Engineering,* pp. 76-85.

Brooks, F., 1995. *The.* Anniversary ed. Boston, MA: Addison-Wesley.

Cagley, T., 2013. *Retrospectives: Retrospectives vs. Classic Postmortem, a Difference in Mindset.* [Online]
Available at: https://tcagley.wordpress.com/2013/08/20/retrospectives-retrospectives-versus-a-classic-post-mortem-mindset-differences-daily-process-thoughts-august-20-2013/

Cervone, H. F., 2011. Understanding agile project management methods using Scrum. *OCLC Systems & Services: International digital library perspectives,* 27(1), pp. 18-22.

Chacon, S. & Straub, B., 2014. *Pro Git.* 2nd ed. New York, NY: Apress.

Chapman, A., n.d. *Conscious Competence Learning Model.* [Online]
Available at: https://www.businessballs.com/self-awareness/conscious-competence-learning-model-63

Cho, J., 2008. Issues and Challenes of Agile Software Development With Scrum. *Issues in Information Systems,* 9(2), pp. 188-195.

Classic FM, n.d. *Leonard Bernstein Quotes.* [Online]
Available at: https://www.classicfm.com/composers/bernstein-l/guides/leonard-bernstein-quotes/great-things/

Cockburn, A., 1996. *Walking Skeleton.* [Online]
Available at: http://alistair.cockburn.us/Walking+skeleton

Cohn, M., 2004. *User Stories Applied.* Boston, MA: Pearson Education, Inc..

Cohn, M., 2006a. *Agile Estimating and Planning.* Upper Saddle River, NJ: Prentice Hall.

Cohn, M., 2006b. *Selecting the Right Iteration Length.* [Online]
Available at: https://www.mountaingoatsoftware.com/articles/selecting-the-right-iteration-length

Cohn, M., 2010a. *Choosing to Start Small or Go All In when Adopting Agile.* [Online]
Available at: https://www.mountaingoatsoftware.com/articles/choosing-to-start-small-or-go-all-in-when-adopting-agile

Cohn, M., 2010b. *Succeeding with Agile: Software Development Using Scrum.* Upper Saddle River, NJ: Addison-Wesley.

Cohn, M., 2010c. *Should Story Points Be Assigned to a Bug Fixing Story?.* [Online]
Available at: https://www.mountaingoatsoftware.com/blog/should-story-points-be-assigned-to-a-bug-fixing-story

Cohn, M., 2013. *Sprint Zero: A Good Idea or Not?.* [Online]
Available at: https://www.mountaingoatsoftware.com/blog/sprint-zero-a-good-idea-or-not

Cohn, M., 2014a. *ScrumMasters Should Not Also Be Product Owners.* [Online]
Available at: https://www.mountaingoatsoftware.com/blog/scrummasters-should-not-also-be-product-owners

Cohn, M., 2014b. *Story Points Are Still About Effort.* [Online]
Available at: https://www.mountaingoatsoftware.com/blog/story-points-are-still-about-effort

Cohn, M., 2014c. *Capacity-Driven Sprint Planning.* [Online]
Available at: https://www.mountaingoatsoftware.com/blog/capacity-driven-sprint-planning

Cohn, M., 2014d. *Reusable Scrum Presentation.* [Online]
Available at: https://www.mountaingoatsoftware.com/agile/scrum/resources/a-reusable-scrum-presentation

Cohn, M., 2014e. *Unfinished Work at the End of a Sprint is Not Evil.* [Online]
Available at: https://www.mountaingoatsoftware.com/blog/unfinished-work-at-the-end-of-a-sprint-is-not-evil

Cohn, M., 2015a. *Estimates on Split Stories Do Not Need to Equal the Original.* [Online]
Available at: https://www.mountaingoatsoftware.com/blog/estimates-on-split-stories-do-not-need-to-equal-the-original

Cohn, M., 2015b. *Should You Use Zero-Point Estimates on Your Product Backlog?.* [Online]
Available at: https://www.mountaingoatsoftware.com/blog/should-you-use-zero-point-estimates-on-your-product-backlog

Cohn, M., 2016a. *Don't Defer a Meeting Because One Person Can't Attend.* [Online]
Available at: https://www.mountaingoatsoftware.com/blog/dont-defer-a-meeting-because-one-person-cant-attend

Cohn, M., 2016b. *Incentives and Deterrents for Starting Daily Scrums On Time.* [Online]
Available at: https://www.mountaingoatsoftware.com/blog/incentives-and-deterrents-for-starting-daily-scrums-on-time

Cohn, M., 2017a. *Five Simple but Powerful Ways to Split User Stories.* [Online]
Available at: https://www.mountaingoatsoftware.com/blog/five-simple-but-powerful-ways-to-split-user-stories

Cohn, M., 2017b. *The Four Reasons to Have a Consistent Sprint Length.* [Online]
Available at: https://www.mountaingoatsoftware.com/blog/the-four-reasons-to-have-a-consistent-sprint-length

Cohn, M., n.d. *User Stories.* [Online]
Available at: https://www.mountaingoatsoftware.com/agile/user-stories

Collins, A., Brown, J. & Newman, S., 1989. Cognitive apprenticeship: Teaching the crafts of reading, writing, and mathematics.. *Knowing, learning, and instruction: Essays in honor of Robert Glaser,* Volume 18, pp. 32-42.

Coplien, J. & Bjørnvig, G., 2010. *Lean Architecture for Agile Software Development.* West Sussex, UK: John Wiley and Sons, Ltd..

Dahl, M., 2014. *Work Smarter: Meetings Are 34 Percent Shorter If You're Standing Up.* [Online]
Available at: https://www.thecut.com/2014/05/work-smarter-for-shorter-meetings-stand-up.html

DeMarco, T. & Lister, T., 2013. *Peopleware: Productive Projects and Teams.* 3rd ed. Upper Saddle River, NJ: Addison-Wesley.

Derby, E. & Larsen, D., 2006. *Agile Retrospectives: Making Good Teams Great.* Raleigh, NC: The Pragmatic Bookshelf.

Dorman, S., 2007. *Why Coding Standards Are Important.* [Online]
Available at: https://scottdorman.github.io/2007/06/29/Why-Coding-Standards-Are-Important/

Driessen, V., 2010. *A successful Git branching model.* [Online]
Available at: https://nvie.com/posts/a-successful-git-branching-model/

Duvall, P. M., Matyas, S. & Glover, A., 2007. *Continuous Integration: Improving Software Quality and Reducing Risk.* Upper Saddle River, NJ: Addison-Wesley.

Eckert, P., 2006. Communities of practice. In: *Encyclopedia of language and linguistics.* s.l.:s.n., pp. 683-685.

Florentine, S., 2016. *More than half of IT projects still failing.* [Online]
Available at: https://www.cio.com/article/3068502/project-management/more-than-half-of-it-projects-still-failing.html

Fowler, M., 1999. *Refactoring: Improving the Design of Existing Code.* Reading, MA: Addison-Wesley.

Fowler, M., 2013. *GivenWhenThen.* [Online]
Available at: https://martinfowler.com/bliki/GivenWhenThen.html

Freeman, S. et al., 2014. Freeman, S., Eddy, S.L., McDonough, M., Smith, M.K., Okoroafor, N., Jordt, H. and Wenderoth, M.P.. *Proceedings of the National Academy of Sciences,* 111(23), pp. 8410-8415.

Fry, C. & Greene, S., 2007. Large Scale Agile Transformation in an On-Demand World. *Proceedings of the AGILE Conference 2007,* pp. 136-142.

Furuhjelm, J., Segertoft, J., Justice, J. & Sutherland, J., 2017. *Owning the Sky with Agile: Building a Jet Fighter Faster, Cheaper, Better with Scrum.* [Online]
Available at: https://www.scruminc.com/wp-content/uploads/2017/02/Release-version_Owning-the-Sky-with-Agile.pdf

Gafni, R. & Geri, N., 2010. Time Management: Procrastination Tendency in Individual and Collaborative Tasks. *Interdisciplinary Journal of Information, Knowledge, and Management,* Volume 5, pp. 115-125.

Gao, J., Bai, X. & Tsai, W.-T., 2011. Cloud Testing- Issues, Challenges, Needs and Practice. *Software Engineering : An International Journal (SEIJ),* 1(1), pp. 9-23.

Ghahrai, A., n.d. *Severity and Priority – What is the Difference?.* [Online]
Available at: https://www.testingexcellence.com/severity-and-priority-difference/

Gócza, Z., n.d. *Myth #21: People can tell you what they want.* [Online]
Available at: https://uxmyths.com/post/746610684/myth-21-people-can-tell-you-what-they-want

Gonçalves, L. & Linders, B., 2014. *Getting Value out of Agile Retrospectives: A Toolbox of Retrospective Exercises.* s.l.:Leanpub.

Goodliffe, P., 2007. *Code Craft: The Practice of Writing Excellent Code.* San Francisco, CA: No Starch Press, Inc..

Gorlick, A., 2009. *Media multitaskers pay mental price, Stanford study shows.* [Online]
Available at: https://news.stanford.edu/news/2009/august24/multitask-research-study-082409.html

Gottesdiener, E., 2013. *Cure Your Agile Planning and Analysis Blues: The Top 9 Pain Points.* [Online]
Available at: https://www.ebgconsulting.com/blog/cure-your-agile-planning-and-analysis-blues-the-top-9-pain-points/

Green, P., 2011. Measuring the Impact of Scrum on Product Development at Adobe Systems. *Proceedings of the 44th Hawaii International Conference on System Sciences,* pp. 1-10.

Grenning, J., 2002. Planning poker or how to avoid analysis paralysis while release planning. *Hawthorn Woods: Renaissance Software Consulting,* pp. 22-23.

Grenning, J., 2011. Launching Extreme Programming at a Process-Intensive Company. *IEEE Software,* November/December, pp. 3-9.

Hargrove, M. B., Becker, W. S. & Hargrove, D. F., 2015. The HRD Eustress Model: Generating Positive Stress With Challenging Work. *Human Resource Development Review,* 14(3), pp. 279-298.

James, M. & Walter, L., 2010. *Scrum Reference Card.* [Online]
Available at:
https://www.collab.net/sites/default/files/uploads/CollabNet_scrumreferencecard.pdf

Janzen, D. S. & Saiedian, H., 2008. Does Test-Driven Develompent Really Improve Software Design Quality?. *IEEE Software,* Issue March/April, pp. 77-84.

Johnson, M., 2013. *What Is A Pull Request?.* [Online]
Available at: http://oss-watch.ac.uk/resources/pullrequest

Johnson, S. a. K. B., 1983. The C Language and Models for Systems Programming. *Byte,* August, pp. 48-60.

Jørgensen, M., 2004. A review of studies on expert estimation of software development effort. *Journal of Systems and Software,* 70(1-2), pp. 37-60.

Kajko-Mattsson, M., Azizyan, G. & Magarian, M. K., 2010. Classes of Distributed Agile Development Problems. *Agile Conference,* pp. 51-58.

Knuth, D., 1971. An empirical study of FORTRAN programs. *Software: Practice and experience,* April, pp. 105-133.

Knuth, D. E., 1974. Structured Programming with go to Statements. *Computing Surveys,* December, pp. 261-301.

Kriger, R. A., 2002. *Civilation's Quotations: Life's Ideal.* New York, NY: Algora Publishing.

Kua, P., 2013. *The Retrospective Handbook: A guide for agile teams.* s.l.:Leanpub.

Lacey, M., 2012. *The Scrum Field Guide: Practical Advice for Your First Year.* Upper Saddle River, NJ: Addison-Wesley.

Lampson, B. W., 1983. Hints for Computer System Design. *Operating Systems Review,* October, pp. 33-48.

Latane, B., Williams, K. & Harkins, S., 1979. Many Hands Make Light the Work: The Causes and Consequences of Social Loafing. *Journal of Personality and Social Psychology,* 37(6), pp. 822-832.

LaToza, T. D., Venolia, G. & DeLine, R., 2006. Maintaining Mental Models: A Study of Developer Work Habits. *ICSE,* pp. 492-501.

Lattenkamp, K., 2017. *SPIDR – FIVE SIMPLE TECHNIQUES FOR A PERFECTLY SPLIT USER STORY.* [Online]
Available at: https://blogs.itemis.com/en/spidr-five-simple-techniques-for-a-perfectly-split-user-story

LeBolt, D. W., 2015. *Ten reasons you shouldn't coach your own kid, and what to do if you absolutely must.* [Online]
Available at: https://www.soccerwire.com/blog-posts/ten-reasons-you-should-never-coach-your-own-kid-and-what-to-do-when-you-absolutely-must/

Lenfle, S. & Loch, C., 2010. Lost Roots: How Project Management Came to Emphasize Control Over Flexibility and Novelty. *California Management Review,* 53(1), pp. 32-55.

Levison, M., 2009. *When to Extend an Iteration/Sprint.* [Online]
Available at: https://www.infoq.com/news/2009/10/extend-iteration

Levison, M., 2013. *Choosing A Sprint Length – Shorter Trumps Longer.* [Online]
Available at: https://agilepainrelief.com/notesfromatooluser/2013/07/choosing-sprint-length-shorter-trumps-longer.html#.XBpOZ1xKiHs

Li, J., Moe, N. B. & Dybå, T., 2010. Transition from a Plan-Driven Process to Scrum – A Longitudinal Case Study on Software Quality. *Proceedings of the 2010 ACM-IEEE International Symposium on Empirical Software Engineering and Measurement,* pp. 1-13.

Liu, Z., 2018. *Automated Integration Testing.* [Online]
Available at: https://medium.com/jettech/automated-integration-testing-a295d21e513a

Lomas, A., 2018. *Why Do Great Product Companies Release Software To Production Multiple Times A Day.* [Online]
Available at: https://www.netsolutions.com/insights/why-do-great-product-companies-release-software-to-production-multiple-times-a-day/

Mackinnon, T., Freeman, S. & Craig, P., 2000. Endo-Testing: Unit Testing with Mock Objects. *Proceedings of the International Conference on eXtreme Programming and Flexible Processes in Software Engineering (XP),* pp. 287-301.

Madison, J., 2010. Agile-Architecture Interactions. *IEEE Software,* March/April, pp. 41-48.

Maguire, S., 1993. *Writing Solid Code : Microsoft's Techniques for Developing Bug-free C Programs.* Redmond, WA: Microsoft.

Maguire, S., 1994. *Debugging the Development Process.* Redmond, WA: Microsoft Press.

Mahnic, V., 2011. A Case Study on Agile Estimating and Planning Using Scrum. *Elektronika ir Elektrotechnika,* 111(5), pp. 123-128.

Mahnic, V. & Zabkar, N., 2012. Measuring Progress of Scrum-based Software Projects. *ELEKTRONIKA IR ELEKTROTECHNIKA,* 18(8), pp. 73-76.

Maximilien, E. M. & Williams, L., 2003. Assessing Test-Driven Development at IBM. *Proceedings of the 25th International Conference on Software Engineering (ICSE),* pp. 564-569.

McConnell, S., 1996. *Rapid Development.* Redmond, WA: Microsoft Press.

McConnell, S., 1998. *Software Project Survival Guide.* Redmond, WA: Microsoft Press.

McConnell, S., 2004. *Code Complete.* 2nd ed. Redmond, WA: Microsoft Press.

McConnell, S., 2006. *Software Estimation*. Redmond, WA: Microsoft Press.

McConnell, S., 2008. *Productivity Variations Among Software Developers and Teams: The Origin of 10x*. [Online]
Available at:
http://www.construx.com/10x_Software_Development/Productivity_Variations_Among_Software_Developers_and_Teams__The_Origin_of_10x/

McIntosh, S., Kamei, Y., Adams, B. & Hassan, A. E., 2014. The Impact of Code Review Coverage and Code Review Participation on Software Quality. *Proceedings of the 11th Working Conference on Mining Software Repositories (MSR)*, pp. 192-201.

Melnik, G. & Maurer, F., 2004. Direct Verbal Communication as a Catalyst of Agile Knowledge Sharing. *Agile Development Conference, 2004*, pp. 21-31.

Meyer, A. N., Fritz, T., Murphy, G. C. & Zimmermann, T., 2014. Software Developers' Perceptions of Productivity. *Proceedings of the 22nd ACM SIGSOFT International Symposium on Foundations of Software Engineering*, pp. 19-29.

Meyer, R., 2013. *No Old Maps Actually Say 'Here Be Dragons'*. [Online]
Available at: https://www.theatlantic.com/technology/archive/2013/12/no-old-maps-actually-say-here-be-dragons/282267/

Michel, B., 2016. *Bugs & Priority*. [Online]
Available at: https://hackernoon.com/bugs-priority-3b5cf5f6aadd

Miller, G. A., 1956. The Magical Number Seven, Plus or Minus Two: Some Limits on our Capacity for Processing Information. *The Psychological Review*, 63(2), pp. 81-97.

Miranda, E., 2001. Improving subjective estimates using paired comparisons. *IEEE Software*, January, pp. 87-91.

Miranda, J., 2014. *How Etsy Deploys More Than 50 Times a Day*. [Online]
Available at: https://www.infoq.com/news/2014/03/etsy-deploy-50-times-a-day

Morales, K., 2017. *5 Fun Sprint Retrospective Ideas with Templates*. [Online]
Available at: https://www.atlassian.com/blog/jira-software/5-fun-sprint-retrospective-ideas-templates

Morales, R., McIntosh, S. & Khomh, F., 2015. Do Code Review Practices Impact Design Quality? A Cast Study of the Qt, VTK and ITK Projects. *Proceedings of the 22nd International Conference on Software Analysis, Evolution, and Reengineering (SANER)*, pp. 171-180.

Muldoon, N., 2014. *Building an Ideal Agile Team Workspace*. [Online]
Available at: http://www.velocitycounts.com/2014/01/building-best-agile-team-workspace/

North, D., 2007. *What's in a Story?*. [Online]
Available at: https://dannorth.net/whats-in-a-story/

Null, C., 2015. *10 companies killing it at DevOps.* [Online]
Available at: https://techbeacon.com/10-companies-killing-it-devops

Osherove, R., 2014. *The Art of Unit Testing.* 2nd ed. Shelter Island, NY: Manning Publications Co.

Overeem, B., 2016. *The 11 Advantages of Using a Sprint Goal.* [Online]
Available at: https://www.scrum.org/resources/blog/11-advantages-using-sprint-goal

Parkinson, C. N., 1955. Parkinson's Law. *The Economist,* November.

Pietri, W., 2009. *10 rules for great development spaces.* [Online]
Available at: http://agilefocus.com/2009/04/20/10-rules-for-great-development-spaces/

Poppendieck, M. & Poppendieck, T., 2003. *Lean Software Development: An Agile Toolkit.* Boston, MA: Addison-Wesley.

Pries-Heje, L. & Pries-Heje, J., 2011. Why Scrum works: A case study from an agile distributed project in Denmark and India. *IEEE 2011 Agile Conference,* pp. 20-28.

Project Management Institute, 2013. *A Guide to the Project Management Body of Knowledge.* 5th ed. Newtown Square, PA: Project Management Institute.

Project Management Institute, 2017. *Agile Practice Guide.* Newtown Square, PA: Project Management Institute.

Project Management Learning, 2010. *What Is Student Syndrome in Project Management?.* [Online]
Available at: https://www.projectmanagementlearning.com/what-is-student-syndrome-in-project-management.html

Reuters, 2018. *U.S. CMS says 75,000 individuals' files accessed in data breach.* [Online]
Available at: https://uk.reuters.com/article/us-cms-breach/u-s-cms-says-75000-individuals-files-accessed-in-data-breach-idUKKCN1MT2WT

Ries, E., 2011. *The Lean Startup.* New York, NY: Crown Business.

Rogers, E. M., 1995. *Diffusion of Innovations, 4th Edition.* New York, NY: The Free Press.

Royce, D. W. W., 1970. Managing the Development of Large Software Systems. *Proceedings, IEEE WESCON,* Issue August, pp. 1-9.

Rubin, K. S., 2013. *Essential Scrum: A Practical Guide to teh Most Popular Agile Process.* Upper Saddle River, NJ: Addison-Wesley.

Sabourin, R., 2006. Go With the Bug Flow. *BCS SIGIST The Tester,* Issue 15, pp. 14-19.

Schuurman, R., 2017. *10 Tips for Product Owners on (Business) Value.* [Online]
Available at: https://www.scrum.org/resources/blog/10-tips-product-owners-business-value

Schwaber, K. & Beedle, M., 2001. *Agile Software Development With Scrum.* Upper Saddle River, NJ: Prentice Hall PTR.

Schwaber, K. & Sutherland, J., 2017. *The Scrum Guide.* [Online]
Available at: https://www.scrumguides.org/scrum-guide.html

SmartBear Software, n.d. *Automated Testing in Agile Environments.* [Online]
Available at: https://smartbear.com/learn/automated-testing/testing-in-agile-environments/

Sourcetree, 2012. *Smart branching with SourceTree and Git-flow.* [Online]
Available at: https://blog.sourcetreeapp.com/2012/08/01/smart-branching-with-sourcetree-and-git-flow/

Spolsky, J., 2000. *The Joel Test: 12 Steps to Better Code.* [Online]
Available at: https://www.joelonsoftware.com/2000/08/09/the-joel-test-12-steps-to-better-code/

Spolsky, J., 2007. *Evidence Based Scheduling.* [Online]
Available at: https://www.joelonsoftware.com/2007/10/26/evidence-based-scheduling/

Staats, M., Gay, G., Whalen, M. & Heimdahl, M., 2012. On the Danger of Coverage Directed Test Case Generation. *15th International Conference on Fundamental Approaches to Software Engineering (FASE),* pp. 409-424.

Stack Overflow, 2018. *Stack Overflow Developer Survey Results 2018.* [Online]
Available at: https://insights.stackoverflow.com/survey/2018/

Stockton, N., 2014. *What's Up With That: Why It's So Hard to Catch Your Own Typos.* [Online]
Available at: https://www.wired.com/2014/08/wuwt-typos/

Sutherland, J. & Sutherland, J., 2014. *Scrum: The Art of Doing Twice the Work in Half the Time.* New York, NY: Crown Business.

Tanner, M. & von Willingh, U., 2014. Factors Leading to the Success and Failure of Agile Projects Implemented in Traditionally Waterfall Environments. *International Conference of Human Capital Without Borders,* pp. 693-701.

U.S. Government Accountability Office, 2014. *HEALTHCARE.GOV: Ineffective Planning and Oversight Practices Underscore the Need for Improved Contract Management,* s.l.: s.n.

VersionOne, 2018. *12th Annual State of Agile Report.* [Online]
Available at: https://explore.versionone.com/state-of-agile/versionone-12th-annual-state-of-agile-report

Vincent, M., 2016. *Emergent Architeture - Just Enough Just in Time.* [Online]
Available at: https://www.agilealliance.org/resources/sessions/emergent-architecture-just-enough-just-in-time/

Wake, B., 2003. *INVEST in Good Stories, and SMART Tasks.* [Online]
Available at: https://xp123.com/articles/invest-in-good-stories-and-smart-tasks/

Walker, D., 2004. *Enhancing Problem Solving Diposition, Motivation and Skills through Cognitive Apprenticeship.* [Online]
Available at: https://repository.lib.ncsu.edu/bitstream/handle/1840.16/3273/etd.pdf

Waterman, M., Noble, J. & Allan, G., 2015. How Much Up-Front? A Grounded Theory of Agile Architecture. *Proceedings - International Conference on Software Engineering,* pp. 347-357.

Webb, T. L. & Sheeran, P., 2007. How do implementation intentions promote goal attainment? A test of component processes. *Journal of Experimental Social Psychology,* 43(2), pp. 295-302.

Weiss, C., Premraj, R., Zimmermann, T. & Zeller, A., 2007. How long will it take to fix this bug?. *Fourth International Workshop on Mining Software Repositories (MSR'07:ICSE Workshops 2007),* pp. 1-8.

Yourdon, E., 1997. *Death March: The Complete Software Developer's Guide to Surviving "Mission Impossible" Projects.* Upper Saddle River, NJ: Prentice Hall PTR.

Index

A

abbreviated smoke test, 465
acceptance criteria
  defined, 31
  examples, 31, 36, 243
  product owner's checklist, 31
  purpose of, 32
  when to write them, 243
acceptance tests
  benefits, 152, 154
  defined, 151
  example, 153
  format, 154
  given/when/then format, 154
  product owner review, 157
  scope changes, 156
  smoke test, as a basis of, 158
  timing of writing, 156
agile
  approach, 87, 88, 90
  benefits, 88, 163
agile adoption
  evolution of project manager role, 190
  impact on organization, 184
  impact on product management, 184
  impact on project management, 186
  impact on software development, 187
  impact on upper leadership, 187
  key success factors, 189
  new roles for project managers, 190
  pilot team vs big bang, 192
  pilot team, selecting, 200
  reasons for failure, 183
  role of PMO, 191
  sample timeline, 196
  separating product owner and ScrumMaster
    role, 207
  success factors, 193, 196
  support from the top, 196, 203, 222
  suspending disbelief, 196
  timeframe, 195

agile architecture
  avoiding YAGNI, 168
  benefits of, 162
  coding standards, 178
  communities of practice, 178
  defined, 162, 168
  emergent, 162
  fundamental strategy, 164
  implementation strategy, 176
  invention, limiting, 166
  limiting risk, 166
  one hand rule, 178
  refactoring, 170
  static code analysis, 178
  team ownership, 171
  technical design, 176
  template, 165
  up-front decisions, 163
  walking skeleton, 163
agile certifications, 230
agile estimating
  absolute size,problems with, 250
  absolute vs relative size, 249
  adjusting date range, 280
  Cohn Scale, 251
  cone of uncertainty, 278
  creating subtasks, 274
  gross capacity, 271
  initial schedule forecast, 269
  initial vs backlog refinement, 265
  net capacity, 272
  Planning Poker, 253, *See also* Planning Poker
  predicting velocity, 270
  relative size, 248, 249
  relative size, examples of, 250
  taking too long, 266
agile estimating techniques
  anchor stories, 259
  Planning Poker, 34
  story points, 34
  t-shirt sizes, 33
Agile Manifesto, 17, 31, 49

agile software construction
   acceptance tests, 151, 157
   automated smoke test, 159
   automated unit tests, 138
   cloud-hosted testing environments, 114
   code coverage, 145
   code reviews, 123
   concepts, 103
   continuous deployment, 113, 116, 125
   continuous integration, 141
   defined, 102
   develop branch, 126
   distributed version control system, 122
   failing unit test, 146
   feature branch, 127
   hotfix branch, 130
   IaaS, 114
   integration tests, 136, 147
   isolating dependencies, 142
   master branch, 125
   product owner environment, 110
   programmer workstations, 108
   release branch, 128
   team test environments, 107, 109, 112, 128
   test-driven development, 144
   tools, 114, 116
   traditional version control, 120
Amazon Web Services (AWS), 114
Angular, 164
ASP.NET, 164
automated unit testing
   addressing a failure, 141
   benefits of, 136, 141
   code coverage, 145
   common problems, 140, 151
   continuous integration, 140
   defined, 135, 138
   example of, 139
   failing unit test, 147
   integration testing, 147
   isolating dependencies, 142
   red-green-refactor, 144
   test-driven development, 144
auto-scaling, 454
AWS. *See* Amazon Web Services
AWS CodeDeploy, 117
Azure. *See* Microsoft Azure
Azure Continuous Deployment, 117
Azure Cosmos DB, 451

Azure DevOps, 122, 310

B

backlog estimating ceremony, 62
   agenda, 63
   attendees, 62
   desired outcome, 63
   scheduling, 345
   timebox, 62
   timing of, 62
backlog prioritization meeting, 63
   agenda, 63
   attendees, 63
   desired outcome, 63
   scheduling, 346
   timebox, 63
   timing of, 63
backlog refinement ceremony, 60
   agenda, 61
   attendees, 61
   desired outcome, 24, 62, 170
   scheduling, 345
   timebox, 61
   timing of, 61
Bamboo, 116
behavior-driven development (BDD), 154
best practices
   daily scrum ceremony, 374
   sprint, 373
   sprint burndown chart, 374
   sprint task board, 373
Bitbucket, 117, 122, 310
bugs
   critical customer issue, 392
   dealing with, 377
   defined, 21
   during release process, 386
   example of, 22
   existed at start of sprint, 390
   feature branch, 127
   fixing before writing new code, 377
   hotfix branch, 130
   introduced during sprint, 387
   legacy bug list, 400
   not fixing, 394, 397
   notes, 383
   one hour at a time, 396
   priority and severity, 384

priority, examples, 386
product owner deciding how much time to
    spend fixing, 395
requirements bugs, 389
result and expected result, 383
severity, examples, 387
six-month rule, 397
standard format, 380
steps to reproduce, 383
subtasks for, 340
timeboxing, 394
title, 382
unit test, writing failing, 159, 388
unreproducible, 398
zero defects culture, 377
zero defects culture, creating, 379
burndown. *See* release burndown chart *or* sprint
    burndown chart
business value
    defined, 240

C

certifications, agile, 230
certifying a release. *See* release process
chores. *See* tasks
code coverage
    analysis of, 146
    defined, 145
code inspections. *See* code reviews
code reviews, 123, 227
    benefits, 123
    bottlenecks, avoiding, 133
    coding standards and, 133
    pull request, 123
coding standards, 178, 308
    one hand rule and, 178
cognitive apprenticeship model, 221
Cohn Scale, 251
communication, 49, 152
    team chat room, 214
    verbal, 214
    written, 214
communities of practice, 178, 191
cone of uncertainty, 278
conscious competence model, 220
continuous deployment, 312, 454

continuous integration, 311
    benefits of, 141
    defined, 140
Cosmos DB. *See* Azure Cosmos DB
cross-cutting concerns, 288, 459

D

daily scrum ceremony, 54, 351
    agenda, 15, 55
    avoiding discussion, 354
    best practices, 374
    desired outcome, 56, 65
    electronics ban, 353
    format, 54, 55
    parking lot, 354
    purpose of, 14
    scheduling, 345
    sprint burndown chart, off track, 369
    sprint burndown chart, reviewing, 354, 368
    sprint task board, 353
    sprint task board, using, 355
    standing up during, 353
    timebox, 14, 55
    timing of, 14
daily standup. *See* daily scrum ceremony
death march projects, 39
    no more, 322
definition of done, 91, 307
    benefits, 93
    defined, 91
    example, 92
    sprint review, which stories to demonstrate,
        93
definition of ready, 307
demo
    during sprint review ceremony, 415
    incomplete stories, 417
    outside of sprint review ceremony, 418
demo environment, 163, 391, 406, 407
dependency isolation
    benefits, 142
    defined, 142
    example, 143
developer workstations
    configuring, 309
development team
    characteristics, 75
    common problems, 3

defined, 73
members, 14
responsibilities, 41, 52, 77
size of, 74
distributed teams, 213, 326
Planning Poker and, 257
sprint review ceremony, 409
distributed version control systems
benefits of, 122
continuous deployment, 125
defined, 122
Git, 124
Git Flow, 124, *See also* Git Flow
tools, 122
Docker, 116

E

environments
auto-scaling, 454
benefits of, 107
cloud-hosted testing, 114
demo, 163, 391, 406, 407
during release process, 448
pre-release, 448, 451
product owner, 110, 126
production, 448, 453
programmer workstations, 108
staging, 448, 449
team test, 107, 109, 128
types of, 108
eustress, 40, 42
extending the sprint, 410

F

feature branch, 127
features
brainstorming for each user role, 236
converting to user stories, 237
flagging subtasks, 365
frameworks
Angular, 164
ASP.NET, 164
Node.js, 164
React, 164

G

Git, 120, 122

Git Flow, 124
develop branch, 126
diagram, 131
feature branch, 127
hotfix branch, 130
master branch, 125, 461
release branch, 128, 457
GitHub, 122, 310
given/when/then acceptance test format, 154

H

hotfix, 130
hotfix branch, 130

I

impediments, 348
implementation strategy, 176
initial code framework, 310
integration testing
common problems, 135, 137
defined, 135
when to use, 148
invention, limiting, 166
INVEST, 296
isolating dependencies. *See* dependency isolation
iteration. *See* sprint

J

Jenkins, 116
Jira, 307
release burndown chart, 26
sprint burndown chart, 81
sprint task board, 80
velocity, 26
version report, 27
job titles
avoiding, 13

M

merge conflicts, 132
merge hell, 132
metrics, 435
Microsoft Azure, 114
minimum viable product, 94
MongoDB, 451
MoSCoW model, 239

MVP. *See* minimum viable product

N

Node js, 164
NoSQL databases, 451

O

one hand rule, 178

P

parking lot, 59, 354
    agenda, 60
    attendees, 60
    desired outcome, 60
    timebox, 59, 60
    timing of, 59, 60
pencils down time, 412
pilot Scrum team
    characteristics, 200, 202
    distributed, 213
    forming the development team, 209
    product selection, 201
    selecting, 200
    selecting product owner, 202
    selecting ScrumMaster, 205
    time zones, multiple, 213, 214
Planning Poker, 34, 253
    anchor stories, 259
    benefits of, 254
    cards, 256
    coffee cup card, 259
    common mistakes, 263
    distributed teams, facilitating with, 257
    duration of, 264
    infinity card, 258
    mobile apps for, 256
    process, 261
    question mark card, 258
    rounding up estimates, 264
    sand timer, 267
    which stories to estimate, 263
    zero point card, 258
pre-release environment, 448, 451
product
    defined, 88
    definition of done, 91
    MVP, 94
    purpose of, 16
    reducing scope, 91
    shippable vs ship, 94
product backlog
    benefits of force-ranking, 242
    bugs, 21
    business value, defined, 240
    completion date range, 27
    creation process, 233
    defined, 25
    estimating, 62
    existing specs, 244
    force-ranking, 240
    ideal size, 236
    items, 20
    prioritization buckets, 238
    prioritization of, 19, 21, 63, 68
    prioritizing by business value, 240
    product owner, management of, 68
    projected timeframe, 26
    purpose of, 16, 19, 20
    refinement, 24, 60
    release, 25
    release burndown chart, 25
    tasks, 21
    user roles or personas, 235
    user roles, generic, 235
    user stories, 20
    velocity, 25, 26
    version report, 26
product increment
    defined, 87, 94, 101
    develop branch, 126
product owner
    acceptance criteria, 31
    accepting work of the development team, 31
    defined, 17, 22
    product backlog, ownership of, 68
    product backlog, prioritization of, 68
    reporting structure, 209
    responsibilities, 13, 69
    ROI responsible for, 68
    separating from ScrumMaster role, 207
    sources within organization, 204
    testing, 110
    traits of, 203
    understanding business drivers, 23
    vacation, 327

production
    deploying to, 312
production environment, 448, 453
programming language
    C#, 164
    Java, 164
    JavaScript, 164
pull request, 123, 227

R

React, 164
red-green-refactor, 144
relative size, 248
release
    defined, 25
release branch, 128
release burndown chart
    defined, 25, 27
    example of, 26
    story points, 25
    velocity, 25
release process, 446
    abbreviated smoke test, 465
    after the release sprint, 473
    auto-scaling, 454
    bugs during, 467
    certifying in pre-release environment, 461
    certifying in production environment, 464
    certifying in staging environment, 457
    challenges, 471
    continuous deployment, 454
    environments for, 448
    environments summary, 455
    isolating source code, 457
    key principles, 473
    master branch, 461
    merging release branch to master, 461
    NoSQL databases, 451
    orchestrating the release sprint, 470
    pre-release environment, 448, 451
    production environment, 448, 453
    release branch, creating, 457
    staging environment, 448, 449
release sprint, 446, *See also* release process
retrospective. *See* sprint retrospective ceremony
revision control. *See* version control

S

Scrum, 4, 5
    antipatterns of, 101
    applicability based on project characteristics, 6
    applications of, 10
    artifacts, 16
    benefits of, 9, 45, *90*
    ceremonies, 14
    characteristics of, 5
    defined, 17, 99
    guideposts, 13
    lightweight and incomplete, 13
    roles, 13
    rules, 41
    status reports, 83
    vs waterfall, 43
Scrum artifacts, 16
Scrum ceremonies, 14
    backlog estimating, 62, 345
    backlog prioritization, 63, 346
    backlog refinement, 60, 345
    characteristics of, 14
    daily scrum, 14, 345
    on-time incentives and penalties, 307
    optional, 59
    parking lot, 59
    recurring meeting appointments, 347
    schedule, typical, 64
    scheduling, 344
    sending meeting invites, 326
    sprint planning, 14
    sprint retrospective, 15, 347
    sprint review, 15, 346
Scrum roles, 13, 67
    benefits of, 67
    defined, 67
    development team, 73
    product owner, 68
    ScrumMaster, 70
Scrum team
    dedicated vs part-time team members, 202, 207
    seating arrangement, 211
Scrum training
    agile coaches, 229
    cognitive apprenticeship model, 221
    development team topics, 226

learning stages, 220

managers and upper leadership topics, 224

methods of training, 223

required topics, 224

role of certifications, 230

Scrum team topics, 225

who needs training, 223

Scrum values, 334

ScrumMaster

defined, 70

reporting structure, 209

responsibilities, 13, 55, 71, 83

separating from product owner role, 207

sources within organization, 207

traits of, 206

servant leadership, 171

shippable vs something you would ship, 94

six-month rule, 397

smoke test, abbreviated, 465

software construction, 100

source code management. *See* version control

source control. *See* version control

Sourcetree, 461

SPIDR user story splitting model, 291

spikes, 292

splitting user stories, 283

can't split, 295

combining splitting strategies, 290

cross-cutting concerns, 288

CRUD operations, 287

data, 294

data boundaries, 286

interfaces, 294

INVEST model, 296

new stories adding up to original estimate, 300

operational boundaries, 286

paths, 293

performance, 289

priorities, 290

rules, 294

six-way model, 284

SPIDR, 291

spikes, 292

team members to involve, 299

too many small stories, 300

which stories to split, 284

sprint, 39

activities during, 42

avoiding gap between, 325

benefits of, 40, 44, 46

best day of week to start, 321

best practices, 373

bugs introduced during, 387

bugs that existed at start of sprint, 390

definition of done, 91, 307

definition of ready, 307

duration, 40, 319

extending, 410

keys to driving daily action, 351

one-week duration, 321

outcome of, 42

preparing for first, 304

purpose of, 87

recommended duration, 320

release, 446

schedule forecast, 46

scheduling around stakeholder availability, 325

scope changes, 41, 156

status reports, 83

UX design, 305

what to do if off track, 369

when to finish coding, 372

sprint backlog, 52

defined, 77

during sprint review, 413

format, 79

Jira, 80

other documentation, 84

purpose of, 16

sprint burndown chart, 81

sprint task board, 78, 80

time estimate, 81

tracking progress, 81

sprint burndown chart, 368

benefits of, 82

best practices, 374

defined, 81

Jira, 81

management team and, 373

midpoint of sprint, 369

purpose of, 83

what to do if off track, 369

sprint goal, 338
  defined, 25
  negotiating within, 52
  purpose of, 52
sprint planning ceremony, 51, 333
  activities during, 14, 77
  agenda, 53
  attendees, 53, 327
  benefits of, 50
  benefits of planning, 335
  capacity percentage based on sprints
    completed, 342
  desired outcome, 14, 50, 54, 64
  estimating team capacity, 334
  format, 53
  gross capacity, 51, 335
  how much capacity to consume, 341
  how much work to take on, 335
  meeting space, 328
  micro-planning, 51
  multiple time zones, 326
  net capacity, 51, 335
  not enough time, 343
  preparing for, 328
  preparing team for, 334
  product owner unavailable, 327
  sample agenda, 330
  scheduling, 326, 347
  scheduling Scrum ceremonies, 344
  setting sprint goal, 338
  starting sprint, 348
  time of day, 326
  timebox, 14, 53
  timing of, 14, 50, 53
  velocity as a way to check commitment, 343
sprint retrospective ceremony, 58, 425
  agenda, 59
  attendees, 58
  common problems, avoiding, 438
  desired outcome, 59
  did-well/could have done
    better/ideas/actions format, 429
  don't be too nice, 436
  ensuring change happens, 437
  formats, 427
  four L's format, 432
  glad/sad/mad format, 433
  leading questions to ask, 434

  leaving egos, titles, and experience at the
    door, 435
  metrics and, 435
  purpose of, 15, 65
  sailboat format, 430
  scheduling, 347
  start/stop/continue format, 428
  timebox, 15, 59
  timing of, 58
  value of, 426
  versus postmortems, 426
sprint review ceremony, 56, 405
  activities during, 15, 56
  agenda, 57
  attendees, 56, 57, 406
  definition of done, 93
  demo, 415
  demonstrating only done stories, 416
  demonstration environment, 416
  desired outcome, 58
  discussing the sprint goal, 413
  discussing what the team completed, 413
  distributed teams, 409
  duration of, 408
  extending sprint, 410
  incomplete stories, 417
  invite the world, 406
  multiple time zones, 409
  no slides rule, 411
  pencils down time, 412
  preparing for, 411
  product backlog, discussing, 418
  purpose of, 15, 56, 65
  rescheduling, 410
  sample agenda, 422
  schedule, discussing, 419
  scheduling, 346
  sprint backlog, using as backdrop, 413
  stakeholder questions, 415
  story points, 414
  team didn't get everything done, 414
  time of day, 408
  timebox, 15, 57
  timing of, 15, 56, 57
  tips, 419
  two-hour max prep time rule, 411
  who should talk, 412

sprint task board, 353, 355
adding comments to subtasks, 364
adding new subtasks during sprint, 365
best practices, 373
deleting subtasks, 367
example, 79
flagging subtasks, 365
format, 79
increasing remaining time on subtasks, 363
Jira, 80
purpose of, 78
subtasks, moving from column to column, 360
subtasks, owner of, 357
subtasks, which to put names on, 358
top down, working from, 355
tracking elapsed time, 364
updating, 360
updating remaining time, 362
when to finish coding, 372
when to update, 361
work that's not on the board, 367
sprint zero, 314
staging environment, 448, 449
standup. *See* daily scrum ceremony
static code analysis, 178
story points, 251
anchor stories, 259
benefits of, 252
defined, 34
during sprint review, 414
Planning Poker, 34
versus time, 260
subtasks
adding comments, 364
adding to item in sprint, 365
deleting, 367
flagging, 365
increasing remaining time, 363
owner of, 357
tracking elapsed time, 364
trigger list, 275
updating remaining time, 362

T

task board. *See* sprint task board

tasks
defined, 21
example of, 22
subtasks for, 339
team. *See* development team *and* Scrum team
Team Foundation Server, 122, 310
Team Foundation Version Control, 120
team test environments, 311
technical design, 176
test-driven development (TDD)
benefits of, 144
defined, 144
red-green-refactor, 144
time zones, multiple, 214, 326, 409
timeboxing bugs, 394
tools
Amazon Web Services (AWS), 114
AWS CodeDeploy, 117
Azure Continuous Deployment, 117
Azure DevOps, 122, 310
Bamboo, 116
Bitbucket, 122, 124, 310
deploying, 306
Docker, 116
Git, 120, 122
Git Flow, 128
GitHub, 122, 310
Jenkins, 116
Microsoft Azure, 114
Sourcetree, 461
Subversion, 120
team chat room, 214
Team Foundation Server, 122, 310
Team Foundation Version Control, 120
Tools
Azure Cosmos DB, 451
MongoDB, 451
topic branch. *See* feature branch

U

unit testing. *See* automated unit testing
user experience (UX) design, 305
user roles
brainstorming features for, 236
converting features to user stories, 237
for other systems, 235

user stories
    acceptance criteria, 31
    additional details, 34
    api, 235
    creating from brainstormed features, 237
    defined, 20, 31
    definition of done, 91, 307
    definition of ready, 307
    estimating size of, 33, 36
    example of, 30, 36
    format of, 30
    INVEST model, 296
    notes on, 31, 35
    product owner, 31
    purpose of, 29
    roles, generic, 235
    splitting, 283, *See also* splitting user stories
    story points, 34
    subtasks for, 274
    supporting materials, 37, 38
    telling a story about, 241
    traditional specifications, 36
    traveling, 284

V

velocity
    defined, 25
    example of, 25
    predicting before project start, 270
verbal communication, 214
version control, 119
    benefits of, 120
    branching, 120
    code reviews, 123
    configuring, 310
    develop branch, 126
    distributed version control. *See* distributed
        version control systems
    feature branch, 127
    Git Flow, 124, *See also* Git Flow
    hotfix branch, 130
    master branch, 125, 127, 461
    pull request, 123
    release branch, 128, 457
    Sourcetree, 461
    systems for, 120
    traditional version control systems, 122
version report
    defined, 26, 27
    example of, 27

W

walking skeleton, 163, 310
waterfall
    100 percent schedule and/or cost overrun,
        106
    approach, 89
    characteristics of, 43, 88
    common problems, 19
    compared to Scrum, 9, 90
    cost overruns, and, 106
    disconnection between team and business
        needs, and, 68
    evolving requirements, and, 24
    lack of urgency, 39
    layer-by-layer approach, 87
    phased approach, 8, 39
    shippable only at the end, 40
    top-down management, 67
    unpredictability, and, 43
written communication, 214

Y

YAGNI, 168

Z

zero defects culture, 377
    creating, 379

Made in the USA
Lexington, KY
07 December 2019